THE VITAL DEAD

THE VITAL DEAD

Making Meaning, Identity,
and Community through Cemeteries

Alison Bell

THE UNIVERSITY OF TENNESSEE PRESS / *Knoxville*

Library of Congress Cataloging-in-Publication Data
Names: Bell, Alison (Alison, Kay), author.
Title: The vital dead : making meaning, identity, and community through
    cemeteries / Alison Bell.
Description: First edition. | Knoxville : The University of Tennessee Press, 2022.
    | Includes bibliographical references and index. | Summary: "This book
    builds on recent anthropological work to explore the social and cultural
    dynamics of cemetery practice and its transformation over generations in
    Virginia's Shenandoah Valley. Anthropologist Alison Bell finds that people
    are using material culture—images and epitaphs on grave markers, as well
    as objects they leave on graves—to assert and maintain relationships and
    fight against alienation. She draws on fieldwork, interviews, archival sources,
    and disciplinary insights to show how cemeteries both reveal and participate
    in the grassroots cultural work of crafting social connections, assessing the
    transcendental durability of the deceased person, and asserting particular
    cultural values. The book's chapters range across cemetery types, focusing
    on African American burials, grave sites of institutionalized individuals, and
    modern community memorials"— Provided by publisher.
Identifiers: LCCN 2022033652 (print) | LCCN 2022033653 (ebook) |
    ISBN 9781621906964 (hardcover) | ISBN 9781621906971 (pdf)
Subjects: LCSH: Cemeteries—Social aspects—Shenandoah River Valley Region (Va.
    and W. Va.) | Sepulchral monuments—Shenandoah River Valley Region (Va. and
    W. Va.) | Shenandoah River Valley (Va. and W. Va.)—Social life and customs.
Classification: LCC GT3210.V6 B45 2022 (print) | LCC GT3210.V6 (ebook) |
    DDC 363.7/5097559—dc23/eng/20220909
LC record available at https://lccn.loc.gov/2022033652
LC ebook record available at https://lccn.loc.gov/2022033653

To Nell and John McDaniel,
whose generosity launched many an anthropological journey,
and in grateful memory of Jim Deetz,
who paved the way for seeing the profound in the quotidian.

CONTENTS

Acknowledgments xiii

CHAPTER 1 "Green Sod Above, Lie Light, Lie Light":
Meeting the Valley Dead 1

CHAPTER 2 "Give This Man His Wings":
Imagining Lives and the Afterlife 29

CHAPTER 3 "The Wrong Kind of Creature for This World":
Asylum Cemeteries 53

CHAPTER 4 "The Colored Dead":
African American Burying Grounds 83

CHAPTER 5 "The Bivouac of the Dead":
Military Conflicts and Cemeteries 109

CHAPTER 6 "Don't Forget about Daddy and Me":
Reunions of the Quick and the Dead 141

CHAPTER 7 "She Had an Affinity for Snowmen and Roosters":
Relational Identities 163

CHAPTER 8 "The Grasshopper Not the Ant":
The Ludic, Populist Cemetery 195

Epilogue: "The Smallest Sprout" 217

Appendix: List of Cemeteries 225

Notes 231

Works Cited 245

Index 261

ILLUSTRATIONS

FIGURE 1.1. Thornrose Cemetery, Staunton — 2

FIGURE 1.2A AND B. Gravestone with Figurines and a Portrait, Thornrose Cemetery, Staunton — 3

FIGURE 1.3. Engraved Pig Headstone, Thornrose Cemetery, Staunton — 4

FIGURE 1.4. Location of the Valley of Virginia — 6

FIGURE 1.5. Woodland Union Church Cemetery, Millboro, Bath County — 6

FIGURE 1.6. Blue Grass Cemetery, Highland County — 7

FIGURE 1.7. Superman Headstone in Sunset Memorial Park, Beckley, West Virginia — 15

FIGURE 1.8A. Locations of Cemeteries Visited in the Northern End of the Valley of Virginia — 23

FIGURE 1.8B. Locations of Cemeteries Visited in the Central Part of the Valley of Virginia — 23

FIGURE 1.8C. Locations of Cemeteries Visited in the Southern End of the Valley of Virginia — 24

FIGURE 2.1. Memorial Items on a Fence, Dayton Cemetery, Rockingham County — 32

FIGURE 2.2. Butterfly Dreamcatcher, Riverview Cemetery, Waynesboro — 32

FIGURE 2.3. The Meadow Natural Burial Ground, Lexington — 33

FIGURE 2.4. Unknown Soldier Headstones, National Cemetery, Staunton — 35

FIGURE 2.5. Headstone in Sunset Memorial Park, Beckley, West Virginia — 38

FIGURE 2.6. Greenwood Ames Cemetery, Bridgewater — 39

FIGURE 2.7. Sunset View Memorial Gardens, Shenandoah County — 47

FIGURE 2.8. Glebe Burying Ground, Augusta County   50

FIGURE 2.9. Mount Hebron Cemetery, Winchester   51

FIGURE 3.1. Western State Hospital Cemetery (oldest part), Staunton   54

FIGURE 3.2. Western State Hospital Cemetery (largest part), Staunton   55

FIGURE 3.3A AND B. Western State Hospital Cemetery, Staunton   56

FIGURE 3.4. Pleasure Grounds at Western State Hospital, c. 1871   61

FIGURE 3.5. Building 21, Central Virginia Training Center   69

FIGURE 3.6. Western State Hospital Cemetery, Staunton   73

FIGURE 3.7. Later Marker, Western State Hospital
Cemetery, Staunton   79

FIGURE 3.8. Author's son, Alone Community Cemetery,
Rockbridge County   80

FIGURE 4.1. Traveller's Grave, University Chapel and Lee Mausoleum   84

FIGURE 4.2. Fishersville United Methodist Church, Augusta County   85

FIGURE 4.3. Ebenezer Methodist Church Cemetery, Augusta County   86

FIGURE 4.4. Falling Spring Presbyterian Church Cemetery,
Rockbridge County   87

FIGURE 4.5. George W. Cleek Cemetery, Bath County   90

FIGURE 4.6. Evergreen Cemetery, Lexington   95

FIGURE 4.7. Deacon J. A. Pettigrew, First Baptist Church, Lexington   97

FIGURE 4.8. Evergreen Cemetery, Lexington   100

FIGURE 4.9. Looking toward Original Burial Place,
Corner of South Randolph and Nelson Streets, Lexington   102

FIGURE 4.10. Remains of the Anonymous Woman Found during
Construction, Randolph Street United Methodist Church, Lexington   104

FIGURE 4.11. Orrix Creek Percherons and Carriage Service   104

FIGURE 4.12. Locally Grown Flowers on the Coffin of Anonymous
African American Woman. Evergreen Cemetery, Lexington   105

FIGURE 5.1. National Cemetery, Winchester   110

FIGURE 5.2. Falling Spring Presbyterian Church Cemetery,
Rockbridge County   113

FIGURE 5.3A AND B. Calvary United Methodist Church,
Augusta County   118

FIGURE 5.4. Morning Star, Temple Hill Cemetery, Bland County   121

FIGURE 5.5. Temple Emanuel Cemetery, Roanoke   123

FIGURE 5.6. Adjacent to Weavers Mennonite Church Cemetery,
Harrisonburg   125

FIGURE 5.7. Calvary United Methodist Church, Augusta County   127

FIGURE 5.8. Stonewall Section of Mount Hebron Cemetery,
Winchester   129

FIGURE 5.9. Tinkling Spring Presbyterian Church Cemetery,
Augusta County   132

FIGURE 5.10. Union Soldiers, National Cemetery, Winchester 133

FIGURE 5.11. Godwin Cemetery, Fincastle 135

FIGURE 6.1. Sharon Union Baptist Church, Alleghany County 146

FIGURE 6.2. Prospect Hill Cemetery, Front Royal 147

FIGURE 6.3A AND B. Augusta Memorial Gardens, Augusta County 148

FIGURE 6.4. Elk Run Cemetery, Elkton 148

FIGURE 6.5A AND B. Riverview Cemetery, Waynesboro 151

FIGURE 6.6. Lebanon Presbyterian Church Cemetery,
Rockbridge County 152

FIGURE 6.7. Morning Star, Temple Hill, Bland County 153

FIGURE 6.8A. Augusta Memorial Gardens, Augusta County 155

FIGURE 6.8B. Card Nearly Buried in the Grass, Augusta
Memorial Gardens, Augusta County 155

FIGURE 6.9. Monticello Memorial Park, Albemarle County 158

FIGURE 6.10. Tinkling Spring Presbyterian Church Cemetery,
Augusta County 161

FIGURE 6.11. James Deetz's Headstone, Westernport, Maryland 162

FIGURE 7.1. Thornrose Cemetery, Staunton 164

FIGURE 7.2A AND B. Monticello Memorial Park,
Albemarle County 170

FIGURE 7.3. Sunset Memorial Park, Beckley, West Virginia 172

FIGURE 7.4. Mt. Hermon Cemetery, Augusta County 173

FIGURE 7.5. Mt. Hermon Cemetery, Augusta County 174

FIGURE 7.6. Elk Run Cemetery, Elkton 175

FIGURE 7.7A AND B. Riverview Cemetery, Waynesboro 176

FIGURE 7.8. Westview Cemetery, Blacksburg 178

FIGURE 7.9A AND B. Rock Creek Cemetery, Washington, DC 181

FIGURE 7.10. Mount Hebron Cemetery, Winchester 184

FIGURE 7.11. Sunset Memorial Park, Beckley, West Virginia 186

FIGURE 7.12. Morning Star Temple Hill Cemetery, Bland County 187

FIGURE 7.13. Calvary United Methodist Church, Augusta County 189

FIGURE 7.14. Mount Crawford Cemetery, Rockingham County 190

FIGURE 8.1. Thornrose Cemetery, Staunton 196

FIGURE 8.2. East End Cemetery, Wytheville 197

FIGURE 8.3. Green Hill Cemetery, Buena Vista, Rockbridge County 198

FIGURE 8.4. Green Hill Cemetery, Buena Vista, Rockbridge County 199

FIGURE 8.5. Mt. Carmel Presbyterian Church Cemetery,
Augusta County 199

FIGURE 8.6. Glebe Burying Ground, Augusta County,
September 30, 2017 204

FIGURE 8.7. Southwest Virginia Veterans' Cemetery, Pulaski County 207

FIGURE 8.8. Lone Star Cemetery, Alleghany County 209

FIGURE 8.9A AND B. Holly Memorial Gardens, Albemarle County 211

FIGURE 8.10. Douglas Turner Day, Musicians Against the Klan,
Charlottesville   214

FIGURE 8.11. Downtown Pedestrian Mall, Charlottesville   214

FIGURE 8.12. Honorary Heather Heyer Way, Charlottesville   215

FIGURE E.1. "The Ruins," Liberty Hall Academy, Ancestor
of Washington and Lee University   221

FIGURE E.2. Elizabeth McGee '24 and Jamie Winslett '21,
Washington and Lee University, Fall 2020   222

ACKNOWLEDGMENTS

Not everyone, it would seem, loves the dead like I do. Suffering through awkward silences at obligatory cocktail parties, I've come to understand that not everybody is hopelessly smitten with graveyards, obituaries, death records, and headstones.

As sociologist Pierre Bourdieu observed, "Taste is what brings together things and people that go together." (A theme of this book, in fact.) Venturing into archaeological sites, burying grounds, old houses, courthouses, archives and microfilm reels, I have found my people. I'm grateful for the camaraderie of these compatriots, fellow travelers pursuing routes into the past. I'm also thankful for those who might not totally "get it," but nonetheless out of kindness, affection, or – in the case of students finding themselves in my courses beyond the drop deadline – necessity, have gamely supported my amazed attention to domains of the dead.

I hope I'll be forgiven for "lumping" most of my thanks into one paragraph. I tinkered with registering my debts by social category, but I can't really tell where students end and mentors start, as I'm lucky to have learned from both. Former students and mentors have also become friends, as have peers, colleagues, and neighbors. Thank you all for letting me be in your band.

Debbie Alden, Marylin Evans Alexander, Colleen Baber, Arthur Bartenstein, Victoria Britton, Mikki Brock, Virginia Busby, Tom Camden, Lynny Chin, Stephanie Chung, Keith Clark, Tom Contos, Liz Crowell, Anjana Cruz, Eric Deetz, Kelley Fanto Deetz, Bryan D'Ostroph and his grandmother, Anne DePoy, Clint DePoy, Louisa Dixon, Joseph Edgette, Jon Eastwood, Byron Faidley, Nat Faulkner, Josh Fox, Katie Gardner, Henry Glassie, Sascha Goluboff, Seth McCormick Goodhart, Kristen Green, Dick Grefe, Jeff Hantman, Don Hasfurther, Coye Heard, Lisa Hochhauser, Philip Hyre, Chase Isbell, Krzysztof Jasiewicz, Lorie Lichtenwalner, Dale Lyle, Karen Lyle, Kristina Killgrove, Julia

King, Jeremy Ledbetter, Hank Lutton, Chris Mann, Harvey Markowitz, Turk McCleskey, Lisa McCown, Alex Meilech, John Metz, Lulu Miller, Sarah Milov, Judy Moody, Elizabeth Moore, Paul Mullins, Carole Nash, David Novack, Lesley Novack, Maggie O'Berry, Carol Dannelly O'Kelley, Merry Abbitt Outlaw, Jeannie Palin, Marc Perdue, Martin Perdue, Marcos Perez, Dana Perkins, Sara Prysi, Lynn Rainville, Suzanne Rice, Ron Robinson, Tonia Deetz Rock, Kurt Russ, Richard Sauers, Erin Schwartz, Elizabeth Scott, Kassie Scott, Kristin Sharman, Jeanne Nicholson Siler, Julia Skeen, Lorna Smith, Glenn Stone, Amy Tillerson-Brown, Tim Truxell, Beverly Tucker, Richard Veit, Patricia Wattenmaker, Camille Wells, Thomas Wells, Eric Wilson, and Chris Wise.

I apologize for omissions. I hope they'll be rightly recognized as a function of my absentmindedness rather than a deficit in appreciation or affection.

Students in my classes at Washington and Lee University – including but not only courses on Domains of the Dead, the Anthropology of American History, the Anthropology of Death, Introduction to Anthropology – have enriched my thinking. I'm thankful for their excellent engagement and questions.

I've benefitted too from attendees' comments at presentations I've made to meetings of the Archaeological Society of Virginia, the Mid-Atlantic Popular and American Culture Association, the Society for Historical Archaeology, the University of Virginia's Department of Anthropology, the Virginia Forum, Virginia Humanities, W&L's Sociology/Anthropology cohort, and Wofford College.

I'm appreciative to Washington and Lee University for supporting my research through Lenfest Summer Grants (2016-2018) and through a sabbatical leave (academic year 2017-2018). I'm thankful, too, to have benefitted from the collaboration of W&L students whose research was sponsored by the Leyburn Scholars Fund in Anthropology, a source of support founded by John and Nell McDaniel. Their commitment and vision continue empowering W&L students to hone their analytical, interpretive, and communicative skills.

I'm also extremely grateful for the residential fellowship that Virginia Humanities extended to me (2017-2018). The time, space, and collegiality that opportunity afforded me were indispensable for the creation of this book. I thank the fundraisers, staff, and donors.

Heartfelt appreciation to Don Gaylord: walking Google, archaeologist extraordinaire, maker of strong coffee, patient caregiver to all the creatures – two-legged and four – that cross our threshold. I'm truly fortunate to have a partner who's so brilliant, knowledgeable, and kind. This book is largely a result of our collaboration at the kitchen table: thinking and talking and supposing.

My deep and joyful thanks to my twins, Schuyler and James, who've spent much of their young lives tolerating (if barely) my inability to pass a cemetery without stopping. James and I had some lovely long road trips in remoter reaches of the Valley with booming music and open windows. Schuyler beautifully negotiated the teen years despite her mother's eccentricity and obsession with all things dead. You two are the light of my life. I'm inexpressibly grateful for and proud of you both.

During the course of this research, some bright spots in my life went dark. I miss being in touch with Jennifer Ashworth, Douglas Turner Day IV, Barbara Deetz, Ted DeLaney, Hannah Robinson Gaylord, Barrett "Bear" Wharton, Arlene White, and Ken White. Godspeed, my friends. My last surviving ancestor was my grandmother, Ethel Hamilton Smith (1916-2015). She was six years old in 1922, when her family moved from southwestern Virginia to North Carolina. She lived more than ninety years in North Carolina, but when anyone asked where she was from she always answered, "Virginia."

CHAPTER 1

"Green Sod Above, Lie Light, Lie Light"
Meeting the Valley Dead

A DAY IN THE DOMAIN OF THE DEAD

Walk over the hills in Thornrose Cemetery, on the west end of Staunton, Virginia (Figure 1.1). The morning dew wets your shoes as your shadow slides along the stones. At midday, the sun offers little oblique light to distinguish marble or granite surfaces from words and images etched on them. Linger as the shadows lengthen again and you'll see sedans sidling along the winding pathways.

A woman emerges from one. Dark hair streaked with gray, maybe she's in nurses' scrubs. Or perhaps she wears navy coveralls, the uniform of a local chocolate plant's employees. Perhaps it's pumps and pearls, making a stop between her job at the credit union and her teenagers at home. The woman steps carefully to a grave site, bag in hand. She stoops, pulls fading fabric flowers out of a vase and replaces them with bright, seasonal ones. She might also tuck an envelope into the new bouquet, or leave a seashell, pebble, or matchbox car on the gravestone. Perhaps she's brought a paper towel or whisk broom to clear away cobwebs and dried grass. She rises to view the little memoryscape she's made. She has done what she could for the person interred here—a husband or a sister, a son or a grandmother. She drives home to dinner with loved ones

FIGURE 1.1. Thornrose Cemetery, Staunton.

who still live, as others arrive in the cemetery on the same quiet, compassionate errand. As the sun sinks behind the Allegheny Mountains, the hillsides begin to glow with hundreds of solar-powered lights that the living left to brighten the spaces of the dead.

Some days at Thornrose, you see a widower park his pickup truck, lift (with a bit of difficulty) a mower out of the back, and cut the grass of a single grave; he wants his wife's resting place to stay perfectly groomed. Down the hill, a young man and a pair of toddlers climb out of a Honda Civic. He ties a bouquet of Mylar balloons to a gravestone and coaches his little ones on wishing their mother a happy birthday in Heaven. On Father's Day you notice a teen with tattoos and Carhartt shorts sitting silent on a grave, head bowed and a card ("To Dad") in hand.

On the crest of Thornrose's tallest hill looms a soaring memorial to the nearly two thousand soldiers, the "Confederate Dead." Most are known, but "around this shaft are gathered also the remains of about 700 Confederate soldiers, not recorded by name, from fields of Alleghany, McDowell, Cross Keys, Port Republic, Piedmont, &c. Virginia forgets not any who died in her defence." Staunton, like most of the Valley of Virginia, was wholly embroiled in the Civil War. Its presence persists.

Farther on is a recent burial, a rectangle of sod carefully placed over the remains of a little girl who died of cancer. When you first see her grave site, it's marked just with an aluminum plate that the funeral home supplied, a small,

FIGURE 1.2A AND B. The grave site of Hayley Elizabeth Kudro (2004–2011) includes a bench and headstone with an enclosed space for photographs and mementoes. Thornrose Cemetery, Staunton.

smooth stone painted like a ladybug, and dried flowers tied with a green ribbon. On a return trip to Thornrose Cemetery, you note that the memorial her family has ordered has arrived (Figure 1.2). Its inscription explains that "God's Garden has a need for little flowers." People who loved her can sit on her bench and leave gifts in a niche on her gravestone: framed photographs of the lost child beside a hopeful porcelain angel figurine.

Nearby, four gravestones in a row have a symbol of knowledge—an Egyptian lamp with smoke ascending—and lines from literary sources. One quotes Roman philosopher Seneca: "This day, which thou fearest as thy last, is the birthday of eternity." Its neighbor bears lines from a poem by Mark Twain: "Warm summer sun, shine kindly here/ Warm southern wind, blow softly here/Green sod above, lie light, lie light/ Good night, dear heart, Good night, good night."

Walking on, you see seemingly countless columns and obelisks, motifs of praying hands, crosses, Bibles, lambs, doves, angels, Masonic symbols, flags, roses, lilies, and dogwood flowers. But then some other images engraved on

FIGURE 1.3. The grave site of Bonnie S. Neil (1953–2014) refers to her as "Maw" and features a pig. The pinwheel behind the stone includes handwritten messages to the deceased. Thornrose Cemetery, Staunton.

recently erected gravestones catch your eye—a dog, a cat, a parakeet, ducks, some dolphins. Cars, trucks, deer, barns. Logos for Atlanta Braves baseball and Washington Redskins football. A bowling ball and pins. A man lifting weights. A smiling pig labeled "Maw" (Figure 1.3).

As you wander and wonder at this explosion of imagery, this quirkiness, this liberality and informality, you arrive at a grave with images of softball players, the Boston Red Sox logo, and the Starship Enterprise from *Star Trek*. If you were to experience an inkling that something different is happening in cemeteries—that you're seeing a marked departure from precedent—you'd be partly right. In some ways, recent changes in cemetery practice mark an extraordinary moment, a unique pivot point, in cultural and civic experience. In other ways, these developments represent something like a swinging of the pendulum back to earlier iterations of social connection and responsibility, if in a selective manner.

This book examines these movements and tensions through anthropologically informed, humanistically intimate glimpses of the lives, deaths, and memorials of hundreds of people—buried in scores of cemeteries—in the Valley of Virginia between the mid-eighteenth century and the present. Residents of the Valley, of Virginia, of the United States and beyond have tussled for centuries over who gets to count as part of their specific community or as a full member of the general human community, and who gets to decide, and how cemeteries trace these claims and counterclaims at work. Public, visible material expressions of social and cultural dynamics, burying grounds are sites of contest. Through epitaphs, images on headstones, and votive gifts, people assert their understandings of whose lives mattered, who should constitute the community (Springate 2015:13), what ideals should be upheld, and where power should reside.

The Vital Dead traces these currents from the mid-eighteenth century to the present through asylum cemeteries, African American burying grounds, Confederate memorials, municipal cemeteries, and resting places affiliated with a wide range of religious denominations in the Valley. One conclusion is that these mortuary landscapes encode and reveal, beginning in the 1980s, simmering sociocultural currents that exploded to global attention with the 2016 US presidential election and persist years later.

VIEWING THE VALLEY

The Valley—or "Great Valley"—of Virginia runs northeast–southwest in the western part of the state (Figure 1.4). The Blue Ridge Mountains bound it to the east, and the Allegheny Mountains to the west. The Valley comprises a series of watersheds, together some 300 miles long, from Frederick County near Washington, DC, south to Washington County near the Tennessee state line. The northern watershed is the Shenandoah Valley, some 180 miles long and, at its widest, 20 miles across (Keller 1997, 106; Simmons 1997, 159). The Shenandoah River flows northeast, joining the Potomac and emptying into the Chesapeake Bay. The Shenandoah Valley is also called the "lower valley," as opposed to the "upper valley" to the southwest, because of differences in elevation. Moving southwest from the Shenandoah Valley are the James River Valley and headwaters of the Roanoke River Valley, both of which flow east through the Piedmont and Coastal Plain to the Chesapeake. Even farther southwest in the Great Valley—on the western side of the Continental Divide—is the New River Valley. Water falling into this catchment moves toward the Gulf of Mexico. In this book I'll refer to the Great Valley of Virginia as "the Valley," understood to encompass parts of the Shenandoah, James, Roanoke, and New River Valleys that are between the Blue Ridge and the Allegheny Plateau.

Vast stretches of the Valley are decidedly rural. In the far western part of the commonwealth, Bath County has a population of about 4,500, an average of eight people per square mile (Figure 1.5). Highland County ("Virginia's

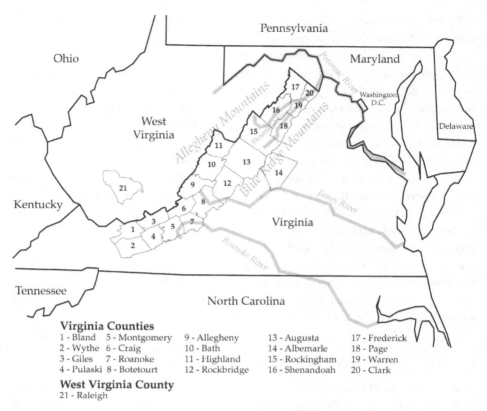

FIGURE 1.4. Location of the Valley of Virginia. Map courtesy of Donald Gaylord.

FIGURE 1.5. Woodland Union Church Cemetery, Millboro, Bath County.

FIGURE 1.6. Blue Grass Cemetery, Highland County.

Little Switzerland") has some 2,200 residents—or five people per square mile (US Census Bureau 2011; Figure 1.6). The Valley contains some cities—Winchester (27,500 residents), Harrisonburg (53,000), Staunton (24,000), Roanoke (100,000), and Blacksburg (45,000), for example.

Native American people have been in the Valley of Virginia for at least 11,500 years, "more than a hundred centuries before the arrival of Europeans" starting in the 1730s (Hofstra 2004, 18). If we estimate a generation as being 28 years, some 10 generations of Europeans have occupied the Valley, compared to more than 400 generations of indigenous people. The earliest people in the Valley were small, mobile bands of gatherers and hunters (Barber and Barfield 1997, 135). By about 10,000 years ago, some groups were more sedentary foragers, collecting nuts, seeds, and berries, for example, along with hunting deer, turkey, fish, and turtle. Starting around 3,000 years ago, some people occupied larger-scale settlements; grew corn, beans, and squash to complement wild resources; and buried their dead in earthen mounds.

Native Americans in the Valley during the seventeenth century likely included the Monacan, Tutelo, and Saponi (Bodie 2011, 12). Disease, dislocation, and conflict decimated native groups; during the eighteenth century, Valley groups moved north and joined the Iroquois Confederacy (Barber and Barfield 1997, 146–47). When Europeans began arriving in the 1730s, they generally encountered remains of tribal settlements—including burial mounds—rather than residents themselves (Hofstra 2004, 18). The indigenous peoples they saw and with whom they interacted tended to be members of the Iroquois Confederacy traveling through and hunting in the area. In a nineteenth-century study—*A History of the Valley of Virginia*—Samuel Kercheval recounted stories of Native American movement in the Valley: "The author has seen and conversed with several aged and respectable individuals, who well recollect seeing numerous . . . parties of the Northern and Southern Indians, passing and repassing through the Valley" (Kercheval [1833] 1902, 34). His interlocutors, descendants of early European settlers, also recalled "numerous sites" formerly occupied by indigenous peoples. Near Luray, he wrote, stand "the remains of a large mound. This like [other mounds in the Valley] is considerably reduced by plowing, but is yet some twelve or fourteen feet high, and is upwards of sixty yards at the base. It is found to be literally filled with human skeletons, and at every fresh plowing a fresh layer of bones [is] brought to the surface" (Kercheval [1833] 1902, 39). Kercheval regretted this destruction, suggesting that "no reflecting man can view so many burying places broken up, their bones torn up with the plow, reduced to dust, and scattered to the winds, without feeling some degree of melancholy regret. . . . Many of them were doubtless the work of ages" (Kercheval [1833] 1902, 40–41). Indeed they were perhaps the work of a thousand years, that millennium being only the latest in which Native Americans hunted, foraged, cooked, built fires, had families—in short, lived and died in the Valley—before migrating from the homelands of their ancestors, bidding for their own survival and that of their descendants.

One of the oldest surviving European American burials in the Valley is rooted in the legacy of continuing indigenous uses of the land, on the one hand, and colonial settler presence and mistrust on the other. In late 1742, "a party of thirty Indians, mostly Oneidas and Onondagas from the Six Nations Iroquois, departed their homelands in New York and turned south along the Susquehanna River. They were headed for the Carolinas to raid long-standing enemies, the Catawbas" (Hofstra 2004, 17). They called the Shenandoah Valley "Jonontore," and their leader was Jonnhaty (17). Passing through Pennsylvania and Virginia, Jonnhaty seems to have called on the expected colonial representatives for authorization of safe passage; nonetheless through the misreading of a movement or motive, a member of Captain John McDowell's militia reportedly fired on Jonnhaty's group. The ensuing conflict resulted in the death of McDowell and others (44–47). His remains are interred in a family cemetery, near Fairfield, under a hand-carved stone with vernacular spelling common in the period: "HEER LYES THE BODY OF JOHN MACK DOWELL" (McDowell Cemetery, Rockbridge County).

McDowell and his family had been among the first wave of Europeans migrating with intent to settle in the Valley of Virginia. His fight "on the Virginia frontier in December 1742 provoked widespread fear of a continental war" because it related to global and colonial machinations. Beginning in the 1730s, Virginia Governor William Gooch had encouraged White, Protestant settlement west of the Blue Ridge as a land claim and buffer against the French (Mitchell 1997, 28). Gooch and other Anglo-Virginians feared an alliance between the French and Native Americans, and they worried that the French were "slowly developing a communication—a stranglehold from the English perspective—between Canadian and Louisiana colonies" (Hofstra 2004, 68). Military force alone was "too weak and too expensive to defend the frontiers," and therefore Protestant settlers, of whatever European derivation, seemed to offer the best buffer to protect British aspirations west of the Blue Ridge (Hofstra 2004, 56). Most people who received land grants were neither "men of substance" nor English, but rather "Persons of a low Degree" from northern Ireland and the Palatinate region of Germany, many of them recent immigrants in Pennsylvania, who seemed likely to be able to "persuade a multitude into a Voluntary Expedition" in the Virginia backcountry (Hofstra 2004, 92). Other settlers were Dutch, French, and Welsh (MacMaster 1997, 89; Keller 1997, 99). Those with "English ancestry were a minority everywhere west of the Blue Ridge" (Hofstra 2004, 21).

If colonial authorities sought Protestant Europeans—of virtually any status or religious inclination—to people the Valley as demographic buffers, settlers for their part were attracted to the area, in the words of one, "by the common fame of the goodness and Cheapness of the Land" (in Hofstra 2004, 133). This confluence of interests meant that dissenters from the Catholic and Anglican churches, particularly families in reformed traditions of German and Scottish cultures, populated the Valley: they had "disavowed the Anglican book of Common Prayer and the social authority it bestowed on an upper class of clerics and aristocrats. They turned to the Scriptures and to each other in the communion of the congregation under ministerial leadership for advice on how to harmonize action and belief" (Hofstra 2004, 119). This arrangement resulted in diverse religious and ethnic bodies in the Valley—with Quakers, Baptists, Presbyterians, Methodists, "Menonists" (Mennonites), "Tunkers" (or Dunkers, now Church of the Brethren; MacMaster 1997, 82–88). Although the Anglican Church and English government remained intertwined arms of colonial authority, the Valley's particular settlement proposition required a spirit of toleration. Quakers built meeting houses unencumbered, and—to cite a gubernatorial order from 1736—a Presbyterian minister was "not to be molested in the exercise of his ministry so long as he behaves himself loially to the King and peaceably towards the Government" (Hofstra 2004, 184–85).

Historian Stephen Longenecker (2000, 185) finds that "no denomination dominated religious life" in the area, making it "a community of minorities, much more similar to Pennsylvania than to eastern Virginia." Indeed, most "settlers came neither directly across the ocean nor across the Blue Ridge. Rather, settlers headed south by southwest out of Pennsylvania, through Maryland, and into Virginia's Shenandoah Valley" (Wallenstein 2007, 52). Although some researchers detect traces of interethnic tension below the surface, by most indications, immigrants of different European backgrounds, languages, and denominations formed connections with each other through civic service (McCleskey 1997), proximity in country neighborhoods, and intermarriage (MacMaster 1997, 84). Architecture, too, suggests "an active, reciprocal exchange of ideas between ethnic groups" by the early nineteenth century (McCleary 2000, 97). Hearts and vines characteristic of German woodwork—as seen on mantels and stairs—decorated English settlers' homes, and similar designs "began to appear even on gravestones of Scots-Irish Presbyterians" (McCleary 2000, 100).

Early European settlers in the Valley cultivated a range of crops—especially wheat and corn—and kept horses, cows, swine, sheep, turkeys, and chickens (Koons and Hofstra 2000, xviii). This agricultural diversity came to characterize the Valley's economy throughout and beyond the colonial era. Unlike eastern Virginia with its dedication to tobacco as a cash crop, Valley residents produced primarily wheat, but also rye, barley, apples, peaches, cattle, linen, iron, distilled liquors, and hemp (Mitchell 2000, 36; Hofstra and Geier 2000, 53; Koons 2000).

Producing varied crops—especially but not only wheat—encouraged the growth of settlements of various sizes. The presence of towns, particularly the northern city of Winchester, distinguished the Valley from the Virginia Tidewater, famous for supporting few urban spaces during the colonial period (Musselwhite 2019). Wheat production required a range of craftspeople—including wagon makers, wheelwrights, millers, blacksmiths, and coopers—in hamlets, villages, and towns (Mitchell 2000). By the mid-nineteenth century, much of the Valley consisted of "open-country neighborhoods"—family farms distributed around hamlets—focused on wheat production; "of grist mills powered by local streams, where wheat was ground into flour and packaged into barrels; and of the tracks, lanes, and roadways upon which wheat was transported by wagon, both from the farms to the mills for processing and, as flour, from the mills to markets outside the region" (Koons and Hofstra 2000, xix). The town of Lexington in Rockbridge County demonstrates the fluidity between "urban" and agricultural spaces, at least into the mid-nineteenth century, as merchants regularly exchanged dry goods, clothing, and other commercial wares for produce such as butter, eggs, lard, turnips, onions, potatoes, tomatoes, corn, strawberries, cherries, and plums—much of it grown on family farms, and likely some in kitchen gardens in town (Horton 2000, 114; Hofstra 2004, 308).

Perhaps it seems idyllic: religious freedom and tolerance, German- and

English-speaking neighbors on their own small farms growing wheat for market and home use, bringing butter and cherries to town in exchange for buttons or bowls. Perhaps in some ways, to some people, living in the eighteenth-century Valley of Virginia was like Heaven on earth. Their peace and plenty, though, came at the expense of others. European Protestant settlers were, after all, in the Valley at the behest of Virginia's colonial government as demographic buffers not only against the French to the north and south, but also against Native American peoples to the west. As the 1742 skirmish that resulted in Captain McDowell's death foreshadowed, the presence of Native Americans—even traveling through the land with permission—was increasingly at odds with European expansion in the Valley. Settlers' plowing through ancient burial mounds, letting bones crumble to dust and scatter to the winds was both claiming the land and erasing native existence from it—past or present. Local history often cites "Indian massacres" in the area (Kercheval 1902), rather than Native Americans' defense of the land that had nurtured their ancestors for 400 generations.

British officials welcomed White Protestant settlers west of the Blue Ridge not only as a stronghold against Native groups farther west, and not only as a wedge between French outposts to the north and south, but also to prevent the mountains from becoming a beacon to enslaved people seeking freedom (Hofstra 2004). Colonial leaders feared that the ridges ringing the Great Valley could become like the Great Dismal Swamp on the Virginia–North Carolina border: a refuge for escaped bondspeople, along with runaway indentured servants and Native Americans seeking safety (Grant 2016). In the Valley, however, relationships between European settlement and African captivity went further than preventing maroon sanctuaries, as the seemingly bucolic landscape of family wheat farms and peaceful religious coexistence was a landscape, too, of human enslavement.

Slaveholding took root gradually but surely in the Valley. The Scots-Irish "eagerly adopted the institution"; their German neighbors did so beginning in the 1760s (Simmons 1997, 164). Although Quakers and Dunkers generally opposed slavery, one of the Valley's largest slaveholders descended from a prominent Dunker family. William Weaver's great-grandfather had founded the faith in Germany ca. 1729; starting in 1749, his grandfather led the Germantown, Pennsylvania, congregation (Dew 1994, 15). In 1781, Weaver was born into this church community; though he grew up with its tenets of asceticism, the universality of Christian brotherhood, and the abject immorality of enslavement, by 1815 he had started on his path to becoming a prominent Valley ironmaster and enslaver with the purchase of "Mary and her two youngest daughters for $700" (Dew 1994, 25). At his death in 1863, Weaver owned 70 human beings: 26 men, 14 women, and 30 children (Dew 1994, 324).

Although the size of Weaver's labor force was unusual in the Valley, the presence of captive people was not. In 1790, one in seven Valley residents had been enslaved, and "in some counties this proportion might reach one in four by century's end" (Hofstra 2004, 337; Simmons and Sorrels 2000, 169). In Rockbridge County, enslaved people comprised 17% of the population in 1810 and 23% by 1860. In the antebellum era, proportions of free Black people were smaller: at most 2.5% of the county's population and 5% in the town of Lexington (after Simmons and Sorrels 2000, 195; McCleskey 2014). Proportions of Africans to Europeans tended to be lower west of the Blue Ridge than east of it, as did the proportion of White settlers who held Black people in captivity (Simmons and Sorrels 2000, 169). In Augusta County and other parts of the Valley during the eighteenth century and antebellum eras, "most households did not own slaves," and "those who did own slaves owned only one slave" (Simmons 1997, 164).

These numbers, however, belie the virtual ubiquity of people of African descent in the Valley—not only because some were free, but also because of the "hiring out" system. Slaveholders frequently hired out the people whom they enslaved to others. Black people were sent from their families and home plantations to plow fields, for example, build roads, wash laundry, chop wood, haul freight, make bricks, and perform any number of other back-breaking tasks for those—close by or many miles away—who had hired them for days, months, or longer. The first of January was often a dreaded, tearful time, as mothers, fathers, spouses, and siblings departed for the year. The labor they performed lined the pockets of the people who hired them out and who legally owned them. These hiring practices "made slavery pervasive" through much of the Valley; it rendered the use of enslaved labor accessible to individuals who did not themselves own slaves, and enabled slaveholders to increase the size of their workforces when needed (Simmons and Sorrels 2000).

The strength, knowledge, and exertion of captive peoples were foundational in creating not only the prosperity of prominent White families but also many of the roads, houses, barns, and other structures still in use today. As archaeologist Mike Parker Pearson observes, "The dead are everywhere, inhabiting our memories and forming our world." We live in the houses they built, "work and play in the places that they created and used" (Parker Pearson 2008, 124). Landscapes of the dead—some burying grounds overgrown and forgotten, others manicured and cherished—reflect not only past inequalities but also ongoing debates about collective identity, cultural values, social belonging, and who is thought to matter.

Virginia has long been central in contests of human valuation. Race-based slavery started at Jamestown almost as early as English colonialism itself. Slavery soon spilled over the Coastal Plain into the Piedmont and then, over the Blue Ridge, into the Valley (McCleskey 2014) —the appropriation of labor from African Americans and of land from Native Americans fueling European expansion and wealth. As following chapters show, formerly enslaved people and their descendants waited long and worked hard, in the face of towering structural inequality, to be able to send their loved ones off to eternity with enduring markers of respect, affection, appreciation, and acknowledgment of their full and equal humanity. Staunton, Virginia—home to Thornrose Cemetery—was also an epicenter of eugenics: the turn-of-the-twentieth-century effort to dramatically narrow the gap through which people passed en route to claiming rights to liberty, to adulthood, to parenthood, to life. The people who lived and died in Staunton's "Western State Lunatic Asylum," a great many of whom are buried in its starkly anonymous cemetery, occupied ground zero in this struggle that extended around the globe. Western State doctors collaborated and compared notes with Nazis in the 1930s, as they shared an interest in weeding out those "unfit" for citizenship, personhood, and (often) existence itself.

The force of the past remains manifest in present-day cemetery landscapes through racialized practices and experiences. With few exceptions, antebellum African Americans' burial places in the Valley of Virginia are difficult to locate; often ephemeral to begin with—marked by wooden posts, for example, or fieldstones—they've been forgotten by many, paved over and built on. Claiming their freedom after the Civil War, many African Americans were able to create churches and adjacent burying grounds of their own (though maintaining a viable population base to support them was often challenging, as explained below). Other cemeteries, both municipal and church-associated, were clearly segregated. A road divides the City of Buena Vista's Green Hill Cemetery, for example: African Americans on the downhill side and Whites on the high ground. It appears that many burials in the former space are now unmarked. In Rockbridge County, the old section of Collierstown Presbyterian Church Cemetery includes an area in what was the farthest corner from the church for interment of African Americans. Bethlehem Lutheran Church Cemetery in Augusta County has a sprawling, historic cemetery behind it. Again, at the furthest remove from the church on the lot is a row of pine trees and a carpet of periwinkle denoting unmarked graves. A brass plaque on a little brick pediment reads, "Erected June, 1979 in remembrance of the Bethlehem 'Colored Brethren' buried here from the early history of the church until 1925. Blessed are the dead who die in the Lord."

The Valley of Virginia serves as the case study for *The Vital Dead* because it's large and diverse enough to offer glimpses into historic and contemporary cultural trends, but it's small enough to be interpretively manageable. It's historically significant as the breadbasket of the Confederacy, for example, and as an epicenter of the eugenics movement. Not insignificantly, the Valley offers a feasible location for my fieldwork, as I live and work here. Though some of the region's historical experiences might be more pitched than those in other parts of Virginia and the nation, it shares with them long-running currents of patriotism, racism, revolution, enslavement, persistence, and negotiation of social identities.

Gravestones testify powerfully to the pathos of past lives in part because they so often combine words and images. They mobilize text and motif to convey aspirations of the dead, for instance, or their worldviews or greatest affections. My fascination with the written and the wrought coalesced when, as an undergraduate double majoring in English and Anthropology/Archaeology, I read the work of James Deetz. His 1977 book *In Small Things Forgotten: The Archaeology of Early American Life* urged readers to not only "read what we've written" but also to "look at what we've done." I'd always been enamored of archaeology thanks to *National Geographic's* glossy pages of digs and jewels and bones. But only by encountering *In Small Things Forgotten* did I come to understand how profoundly objects encode past ways of thinking. Words, extraordinary as they are, don't charter the only path to mind.

Deetz looked at many categories of material culture—especially headstones, houses, and dishes—in New England from the eighteenth and nineteenth centuries, and he read in them the evolution of American cultural thought. Headstones that had been chatty fell silent; earlier markers often exhibited the *memento mori* tradition of the dead advising the living: "Remember me as you pass by. As you are now, so once was I. As I am now, soon you will be. Prepare for death and follow me." Later headstones, Deetz said, closed off communication between the quick and the dead, simply reporting the deceased's name, age, and date of death (see also Sloane 1991:8-22). Houses, too, became less conducive to broad conviviality as central passages and other barriers to entry arose to interpose between residents and visitors. And where colonial diners might have shared a bench or mug, by the nineteenth century many aspired to having one glass and one chair per person. Deetz saw this emergence of isolated individualism through things that people had made and used: material culture. He described the salient emergent ethos as being "a place for everything, and everything in its place." Privatized gravestones, houses, and plates were expressions of a worldview that valorized order and control: the discrete, the distinct, the bounded. Examining historic houses in central Virginia, Henry Glassie (1975) had come to much the same conclusion; he called the trend "the evolution of alienation." Being able to detect cognitive transformation in material culture—floor plans, chimney placement, and roof pitches—opened a new intellectual world to me as an undergraduate.

After graduating from college, I was delighted to begin graduate work in anthropological archaeology with Jim Deetz at the University of California at Berkeley. I took every course he taught, and when he revealed that he was moving to the University of Virginia, two other students and I left Berkeley for Charlottesville. Jim had the idea of "digging around Henry's houses," the folk houses in middle Virginia that Glassie had analyzed. This topic became my dissertation, and it turned out to be the last thesis Jim supervised before his death in 2000.

It was against this background and with this intellectual orientation that I began perceiving that something important was happening in contemporary Virginia cemeteries. I'd long loved the realms of the interred and, for decades, had walked through cemeteries for fun and fascination. The urns can be so beautiful, as can the angels, the weeping willows, the carved bud with broken stem representing the death of a child. The way people used to refer to their spouses as "consorts" and themselves as "relics" on old gravestones, and the tradition of inscribing on stones the number of years, months, and days someone had lived.

And then there's a new gravestone depicting a man, his water truck, and his pet emu. And a marker with Tweety Bird from Looney Tunes. Others with images of pickup trucks, NASCAR logos, and Jesus watching over a horseshoe game. Chihuahuas, cement mixers, and barbed wire. One has a gas station on it. Another has the blue dancing bear associated with the Grateful Dead. And witticisms too: "Stuff It" inscribed on one recent headstone; "Me Mudder" on a memorial.

FIGURE 1.7. Gravestone honoring Todd Aaron Smith (1988–2006), "A Real Super-Man." Sunset Memorial Park, Beckley, West Virginia.

This recent transformation in grave marker expression was at least as profound—perhaps even more profound—than the transformation that Deetz detected in eighteenth-century burying grounds. If the move from community-oriented gravestones ("Remember me as you pass by") to ones that isolated the individual signaled the "evolution of alienation," what does the appearance of Dallas Cowboys' helmets, or Superman's S, the Nike "Swoosh," or an image of the Virginia Beach fishing pier on gravestones portend (Figure 1.7)?

THE CULTURE IN MATERIAL CULTURE

Scholars often talk about "things" as "material culture": the culturally influenced modification of natural materials that turns a tree, for example, into a chair or a stone into a grave marker (Glassie 1999). *Materiality* is a broader term that nods to the point that not every "thing" with which humans interact is the product of the imposition of human will on nature (Fowler 2002; Thomas 2002). We slip in wet clay, for example, or lose breath climbing a steep hill because of their materiality.

The Vital Dead takes an anthropological approach to querying cemeteries, looking toward the material to divulge the cultural. I've taught anthropology since 1996, and my definition of the enterprise is this: Anthropology is the study of humanity from its origins to the current day, focusing on anything that helps us understand culture (what people think) or behavior (what people do). Some anthropologists study human origins or evolution. Others analyze relationships among current language, cultural thought, and social networks. Some anthropologists live with others, observing and participating in their daily rounds to understand their culture and behavior. In the American tradition, archaeology is the analysis of material culture—buried or extant above ground—in ways that generate insight into people's beliefs and actions. It's like looking to a print to understand dynamics of the foot.

In my peregrinations through scores of cemeteries, Jim Deetz's example was always in the back of my mind. He and Glassie had shown how material culture reveals culture. By "culture" Deetz ([1977] 1996) meant (and I mean) ideas: learned ways of thinking, evaluating, assuming. These ideas lead to actions, and actions usually involve materiality—the material world. Looking at things, we can gain inklings of thoughts people had in the remote past, the historic past, or in our contemporary communities (Dawdy 2013; Hicks and Beaudry 2018; Miller 2010; Tilley et al. 2013). Believing that community members were responsible for each other influenced the production of gravestones with *memento mori* formulations. Believing that individuals are autonomous, isolated, and self-contained encouraged the creation of grave markers that distinguish the person from the group.

Scholars in many fields, of course, research the past, often with different methods, conventions, and disciplinary expectations. Architectural historians, geographers, historians, linguists, political scientists, and countless others study the same past communities through different means, questions, and goals (Dawdy 2016; Gordon-Reed 2009; Miller 2020; Wells 2018). My approach—to use the title of a course I often teach—is an Anthropology of American History. I want to understand the thoughts that motivate the placement of an emu, for example, on a headstone; a pouch of chewing tobacco on an otherwise unmarked grave; a letter to a dead daughter in the classified section of a newspaper. Following Glassie's (1982, xiv) example, I "search through forms for meanings." Distinguishing between the natural sciences and humanities, Glassie (1982, 13) observed that "culture is not a problem with a solution." "Studying people," he said, rather than "planets or orchids" involves "refining understanding, not achieving final proof."

"ANTHROPOLOGY THAT BREAKS YOUR HEART"

Anthropologist Alfred L. Kroeber is credited with the often-cited characterization of anthropology as "the most humanistic of the sciences and the most scientific of the humanities." Anthropologist Eric Wolf emphasized this disciplinary identity in his 1964 book, *Anthropology*, and H. Russell Bernard reaffirmed it in a panel at the American Anthropological Association's 2011 annual meeting (Antrosio 2018). In this "big tent" model of anthropology—one with respectful room for the humanistically inclined, the scientifically inclined, and the many varieties in between—my fascination bends toward the humanistic, hoping to understand people's diverse experiences, bridging to the arts, incorporating first-person perspectives, and creating scholarship that's potentially relevant to contemporary social problems (Gleach 2013). The Society for Humanistic Anthropology (n.d.) explains that its practitioners aim to "evoke, represent, or give account of the human subject both visually and in writing. Humanistic anthropology involves the recognition that professional inquiry takes place in a context of human value. The humanistic orientation is particularly concerned with the personal, ethical, and political choices facing humans." This orientation encourages "a haunting and minor practice among anthropologists who study death of folding into academic work accounts of their own terror, anger, sadness, rage, wonder, and enchantment with personal losses" (Engelke 2019, 38). Thus, I look not only to humanistic scholars of past generations but also to several of my own experiences and to the work of contemporary humanistic scholars who are also, in some cases, good friends.

In November 2000, following Jim Deetz's funeral in Williamsburg, Virginia, friends and family gathered for a wake. Henry Glassie was there and stood to recognize Jim's nine children including Kelley Fanto Deetz, the youngest, or as Henry warmly put it, "the beautiful caboose of the family." Kelley and I, close friends then and now, laughed along with the assembly. Sowing humor into mourning carried the company along as we worked to process the depth, shape, and significance of this loss. I wasn't among those who rose to speak at the wake, but I was thinking of the epigraph in the book that Jim had just published with his wife, Patricia Scott Deetz (2000), *The Times of Their Lives: Life, Love, and Death in Plymouth Colony*. The quote was from Governor William Bradford: "As one small candle may light a thousand, so the light here kindled has shown unto many."

Kelley Deetz is among her father's many bright legacies, and her 2017 book—*Bound to the Fire: How Virginia's Enslaved Cooks Helped Invent American Cuisine*—is a prime example of the contemporary humanistic scholarship in which I position my work. Embodied, imaginative analysis is salient in *Bound to the Fire*. Kelley Deetz draws on her former experience as a professional chef and on her intellectual grounding in African Diaspora Studies to understand the extraordinary intellectual, physical, and emotional capacities of enslaved cooks. Writing about visiting Virginia plantation museums, Deetz (2017, 6) recalled, "Occasionally these tours include a brief pass through the kitchen and then continue on, as if nothing or nobody existed in that space. But the smell of old fires, the sight of decaying iron pots, and the thought of hard labor would overcome me every time, leading me to stay behind and try to envision that room in use." Crafting an empathetic inquiry grounded in demonstrable realities of recipes, cooking utensils, and architectural spaces, Deetz (16) helps readers better appreciate that "cooking for a Virginia plantation was a challenging task, one that required culinary talents, nuanced social skills, and physical strength. The labor was intense—lifting huge pots of water, standing for hours by the open fire." In hot, humid Virginia summers, with temperatures often over 90 degrees, "the hearth fire burning at over 1,000 degrees would make the kitchen torturous" and tempt cooks to sleep outside despite "mosquitos, horseflies, spiders and snakes" (46). Frequently, though, "workday bled into the night" without time or space for respite (16). Amid such countless grueling exigencies, enslaved cooks "took ownership of their food and received compliments for their skills" (63). Particularly on larger plantations where sophisticated dishes were expected, they read recipes and employed math: "with baking, perfect measurement is essential, as the recipe is like a chemical equation. These recipes unveil the cooks' ability to count and perform educated tasks" (56). They maintained their own dignity (63) and nourished the wellbeing of others in the enslaved community, not only through victuals but also social concourse: the kitchen was often "a black landscape within a larger white landscape," and "a relatively safe social space for the greater plantation community to gather together" (72).

Whitney Battle-Baptiste's approach to the history and archaeology of enslaved—or as she tends to say, captive—Africans in the United States is similarly grounded in humanistic principles. She wrote *Black Feminist Archaeology* purposefully and unapologetically, "in a personal way. There are both scholarly and narrative elements intertwined throughout the text. I write this book for my colleagues, my peers, my elders and my children" (Battle-Baptiste 2011, 20). She understands herself to be accountable to all these audiences (20–21), bearing responsibility to tell stories "not just about archaeology or artifacts, but about people and places, women and men, leisure and labor, with details that can be relevant to contemporary struggles for social justice and liberation" (31). In considering "women of the African Diaspora," Battle-Baptiste (170) seeks to "recognize the roles within their families, the amount of work they completed in their lives, the effort, the blood, sweat and tears and the contribution to the global community."

To do so, Battle-Baptiste (2011, 102–5) looks thoughtfully to archaeological features and artifacts. She envisions ways, for example, that captive Africans regularly gathered around an in-ground cooking pit that she and her colleagues discovered during excavations at US President Andrew Jackson's Tennessee plantation, the Hermitage. Battle-Baptiste interprets the area of the brick-lined cooking pit "as a social space because of the material relating to food preparation, cooking activities, a harmonica part, several straight pins and buttons, three mouth harps, and fishhooks. This meant that at this location all genders and ages came together to make music, play games, and do other activities like prepare food, make soap, and sew worn clothing."

For "captive Africans, when work was done, that was the time when their bodies became their own again," and this cooking pit became "the intimate gathering place and . . . center of life for the occupants" (Battle-Baptiste 2011, 104). In another example, Battle-Baptiste relays a sense of profound connection that W. E. B. DuBois expressed when holding a pair of tongs from his boyhood home place: "From its long hiding place I brought out an old black pair of tongs. Once my grandfather, and mayhap his, used them in the great fireplace of the house. Long years I have carried them tenderly over all the earth" (quoted in Battle-Baptiste 2011, 169).

In addition to memoir and archaeology, Battle-Baptiste also draws on the arts, including fictional accounts of African American experience like Toni Morrison's 1987 Pulitzer Prize–winning novel, *Beloved*. This "touching and tragic story of Sethe is essentially about a mother's love, a father's inability to protect his family from within the system of slavery, death, and the fragility of freedom," based on the true account of Margaret Garner, a woman who escaped slavery with her daughter (Battle-Baptiste 2011, 43). When captured, Garner killed her daughter rather than see her return to slavery. The fictional *Beloved* offers readers a glimpse of the endless terrors that nonfictional enslaved people endured, often most hauntingly the prospect of losing a child, forever, to the auction block.

MacArthur Fellow Jason De León's 2015 opus—*The Land of Open Graves: Living and Dying on the Migrant Trail*—offers another extraordinary, compelling example of humanistic anthropological traditions. De León opens this ethnographic and archaeological study of contemporary undocumented migration by sharing memories of his first day on the southern US border: "Flies. I mostly remember the goddam flies." They were swarming the "limp body flopped on the dirt. This dude has been dead for less than an hour and yet the flies were already there in full force. They were landing on his milky eyeballs and crawling in and out of his open mouth. . . . Finally some Good Samaritan showed up with a Dallas Cowboys bedsheet and covered him up" (De León 2015, 1–3). De León chooses to write in ways "at times acerbic or in nonstandard English" because he is

> trying to match the frankness, sarcasm, and humor of my interlocutors, as
> well as the grittiness of the difficult worlds they inhabit. It is also because I see
> little public or personal benefit to "toning down" what I have seen, heard, and
> experienced while trying to get an anthropological handle on the routinely
> chaotic, violent, and sometimes tragicomic process of clandestine migration.
> Like many scholars before me, I aim to sully the often sterile anthropological
> discussion. (De León 2015, 14)

De León marshals not only extraordinary prose and images—through his collaborator Michael Wells's photographs—to convey inklings of migrants' experiences, but also empathetic imagination. He asks readers to consider "how desperate must one be to leave . . . children behind and accrue thousands of dollars of debt to undertake a dangerous trip with no guarantees one will survive," or how desperate a parent must be to entrust a son "to the hands of smugglers who will run him through a desert gauntlet where . . . suffering and death are likely outcomes" (De León 2015, 277). It might be easy, De León says, to criticize undocumented migrants "if you have never watched your own children starve."

De León (2015, 153) acknowledges approvingly the famous declaration by anthropologist Ruth Behar about the importance of humanism. "Call it sentimental," Behar (1996, 177) wrote, "but I say that anthropology that doesn't break your heart just isn't worth doing."

Behar was thinking, in part, about death. She had wanted to stay in Florida to "help [her] grandfather die" naturally, peacefully, and surrounded by affection. She was told, however, that "life had to go on" and that she should leave for planned research in Spain, and she heeded this advice (Behar 1996, 85). Years later, Behar regretted the choice and recognized the call to pivot from death toward work as a facet of "the chain of production and consumption that keeps our capitalist cultures running." She observed that "we place the dying in the secret zones of institutions so that they will not interrupt" our labor, as emotion should be eschewed and productivity embraced. The young Behar had acceded, leaving her grandfather's deathbed. The mature Behar resisted, insisting in ways both personal and intellectual on the value of sorrow. She cited the Holocaust documentary *Shoah*, explaining that filmmaker "Claude Lanzmann's aim is not to present gruesome images from the past, but to grapple with the impossibility of telling the story of the Holocaust. His effort is to 'screen loss.' He wants to make 'present in the film the absence of the dead'" (176).

Emotion, no less than intellectual comprehension, is a way of knowing (Rosaldo 2014; Rosaldo 2018). We need both to understand how people grapple with death (Metcalf and Huntington 1991:2-5).

"THE ENTHUSIASM JUST ISN'T THERE": QUALITATIVE RESEARCH

My approach to cemetery material is not only humanistic but also unapologetically qualitative. Qualitative research is an exploratory and analytical disposition conducive to understanding trajectories in human thought. Projects are often, like this one, field based, drawing on observation and conversation to detect cultural currents. Glassie (1982:642) explained, "Come to some strange place, we find people inviolably unique, all in motion, preoccupied beyond us. We watch, and with time discover pattern in the motion." The vast majority of his research—in Northern Ireland, Turkey, Bangladesh, Brazil, and beyond—is qualitative: watching, asking, listening to people giving account of their culture and actions. The same is generally true of the luminous contemporary scholarship mentioned above.

Qualitative research can lay the groundwork for quantitative (numerical, statistical) analysis by formulating theses that can be cast as testable hypotheses. However, qualitative work is also valuable and valid on its own; it's not a second-tier methodology or meek handmaid to mathematics.

Thinking back to November 2016, poll after poll predicted that Hillary Clinton would win the presidential election (Flood 2016). Headlines tell the story. In days leading up to the contest, even on the morning of November 8 itself, the numbers were in her favor. The *New York Times* calculated that Clinton had an 85% chance of winning. Reuters put the number at 90%; ABC News at 95%.

FiveThirtyEight is a website designed to "accumulate and analyze polling and political data in a way that is informed [and] accurate" in order "to give you the best possible objective assessment of the likely outcome of upcoming elections." Its quantitative rigor is founded on a number of factors:

> We assign each poll a weighting based on that pollster's historical track record, the poll's sample size, and the recentness of the poll. More reliable polls are weighted more heavily in our averages. Secondly, we include a regression estimate based on the demographics in each state among our "polls," which helps to account for outlier polls and to keep the polling in its proper context. Thirdly, we use an inferential process to compute a rolling trend line that allows us

to adjust results in states that have not been polled recently and make them "current." Fourthly, we simulate the election 10,000 times for each site update in order to provide a probabilistic assessment of electoral outcomes based on a historical analysis of polling data since 1952. (Silver 2008)

Election morning, FiveThirtyEight concluded that Clinton had a 71.4% chance of winning the election. Quantitative analysis is not infallible. Indeed, one of the people who correctly called the election for Trump used predominantly qualitative observation and analysis.

In July of 2016, filmmaker Michael Moore published "Five Reasons Why Trump Will Win." Moore did include a little math:

> Mitt Romney lost by 64 electoral votes. Add up the electoral votes cast by Michigan, Ohio, Pennsylvania and Wisconsin. It's 64. All Trump needs to do to win is to carry, as he's expected to do, the swath of traditional red states from Idaho to Georgia (states that'll never vote for Hillary Clinton), and then he just needs these four rust belt states. He doesn't need Florida. He doesn't need Colorado or Virginia. Just Michigan, Ohio, Pennsylvania and Wisconsin. And that will put him over the top. This is how it will happen in November.

Moore was right. But how did he know that some states would "never" go for Clinton? It was largely by being on the ground: traveling through the United States, talking to people, and watching their actions at rallies or protests. He came to recognize the significance of the "broken, depressed, struggling, the smokestacks strewn across the countryside with the carcass of what we use[d] to call the Middle Class. Angry, embittered working (and nonworking) people who were lied to by the trickle-down of Reagan and abandoned by Democrats" thought "this is their chance! To stick [it] to ALL of them, all who wrecked their American Dream! And now The Outsider, Donald Trump, has arrived to clean house!" Moreover, many young voters didn't like Clinton: "Not a day goes by that a millennial doesn't tell me they aren't voting for her. No Democrat, and certainly no independent, is waking up on November 8th excited to run out and vote for Hillary the way they did the day Obama became president or when Bernie was on the primary ballot. The enthusiasm just isn't there." Because of these sentiments, and because of "the anger that so many have toward a broken political system, millions are going to vote for Trump" (Moore 2016). Moore cited additional reasons, but most of them, too, came to him through qualitative observation and comprehension of the cultural currents around him.

LACING UP AND LEAVING THE LIBRARY

In the tradition of Moore, for example, and of Glassie, my work is about leaving the office and the library—gathering up maps; lacing up boots; driving through forests, fields, little cities, and country crossroads; walking through

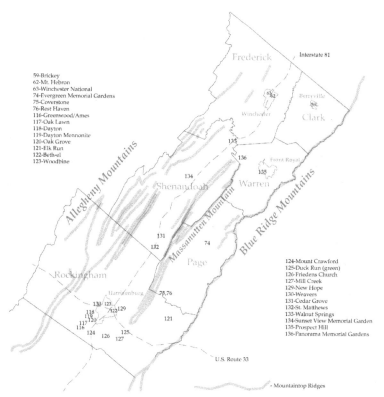

FIGURE 1.8A. Locations of cemeteries visited in the northern end of the Valley of Virginia. Map courtesy of Donald Gaylord.

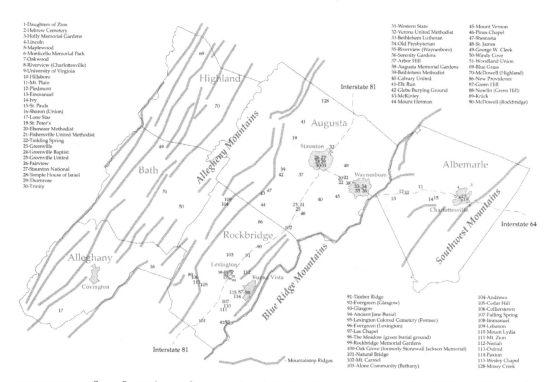

FIGURE 1.8B. Locations of cemeteries visited in the central part of the Valley of Virginia. Map courtesy of Donald Gaylord.

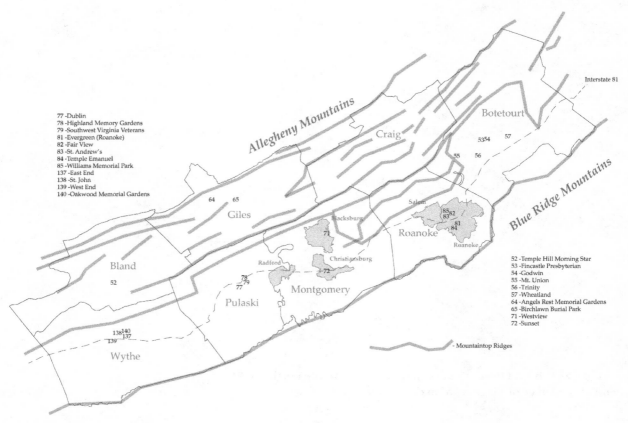

77 -Dublin
78 -Highland Memory Gardens
79 -Southwest Virginia Veterans
81 -Evergreen (Roanoke)
82 -Fair View
83 -St. Andrew's
84 -Temple Emanuel
85 -Williams Memorial Park
137 -East End
138 -St. John
139 -West End
140 -Oakwood Memorial Gardens

52 -Temple Hill Morning Star
53 -Fincastle Presbyterian
54 -Godwin
55 -Mt. Union
56 -Trinity
57 -Wheatland
64 -Angels Rest Memorial Gardens
65 -Birchlawn Burial Park
71 -Westview
72 -Sunset

- Mountaintop Ridges

FIGURE 1.8C. Locations of cemeteries visited in the southern end of the Valley of Virginia. Map courtesy of Donald Gaylord.

cemeteries of all sizes and types; and developing a sense of place. Since 2015, I've visited more than 140 cemeteries in nineteen counties in the Valley, plus independent cities like Winchester, Harrisonburg, Roanoke, and Wytheville (Figure 1.8; Appendix). Culturally, the Valley of Virginia has fuzzy borders, and I've dipped into southern West Virginia, for example, and east over the Blue Ridge to Albemarle County, Charlottesville, and Richmond. Most of the Valley is rural and politically "red," and so casting an eye toward more urban, more blue, left-leaning places like the state capitol in Richmond enabled me to see whether trends extended in those directions.

My methods included making a list of cemeteries in each of the counties in my study area. I'd map them and choose ones to visit based on typological information, so that the analysis would include burying grounds associated with families, communities, and diverse faith traditions and ethnicities. Arriving at a cemetery, I'd conduct an informal survey, walking or driving through it (depending on its size) to get a sense of scale, variation among markers, and their spatial organization. Often the spatial and temporal distribution of burials correspond: the older ones tend to be at the bottom of a hill, for example, and more recent ones higher up. Other cemeteries appear to be more structured by family plots, and still others by variables like price; at some burial places, the most accessible grave sites are among the most expensive.

I did not record all markers. (That enterprise would consume multiple lifetimes.) I photographed few plain stones and few with normative or popular nineteenth- and twentieth-century motifs: "crosses, flowers, praying hands, rays of light, ivy, roses, hearts, birds, scrolls, and Bibles" (Rainville 2014, 30). In choosing markers to photograph, I attended most closely to those that

(a) exhibited creativity, idiosyncrasy, informality, humor, or other departures from formerly normative practice;

(b) hinted toward a narrative with potential humanistic anthropological resonance that I could investigate post–cemetery fieldwork;

(c) positioned the decedent relative to a larger social group, conveying an assumption about the relationship between the individual and community;

(d) represented the resting place of people who had been disabled or disadvantaged;

(e) overtly expressed particular values, beliefs, opinions, or cultural orientations including about authority and autonomy;

(f) were on grave sites that had "gifts," objects such as notes, toys, plantings, or books that people had left there for the dead.

STRUCTURE OF THE BOOK

Chapter 2, "'Give This Man His Wings': Imagining Lives and the Afterlife," provides an overview of the diversity of lived experience and conceptions of death in the Valley of Virginia. Few people in this area are world famous; the vast majority escape history books. Indeed, many are only fleetingly detectable in census returns and lack death records or obituaries. Some have graves only marked with fieldstones, or not at all. Within these constraints, the goal is to catch glimpses of the dead, to pull out of the past information that allows the framing of vignettes. This effort illuminates an immense range of human experience in the Valley as reflected in the diversity of its burying grounds. This chapter concludes by surveying epitaphs that frame particular deaths, per long Western cultural tradition, as "good" or "bad."

Chapter 3, "'The Wrong Kind of Creature for this World': Asylum Cemeteries," considers cemeteries on the grounds of institutions for "lunatics" or the "feebleminded." In the early twentieth century, Virginia was a leader in the global eugenics movement, an effort by governmental, medical, and educational authorities to improve their nations by allowing only the "best" people to have children. The nadir of this practice materialized in Nazi Germany, and some American doctors looked jealously at the Third Reich's "success." Many Virginians who were compulsorily sterilized are buried at institutions originally called the Virginia State Colony for Epileptics and Feebleminded near Lynchburg and Western State Lunatic Asylum in Staunton. This chapter relates the experiences of some inmates who were considered "unfit" or "mad" or "delirious"—the latter term deriving from the Latin word *lira* for "furrow"; people had "gone out of the furrow" or deviated from the straight, officially acceptable path (Foucault [1961] 1999, 99). Doing so was easy during the first decades of the twentieth century because the "furrow" was extraordinarily narrow. Virginians were sterilized for having a lisp, for masturbating, for inhaling tobacco fumes, for "insanity" brought on by "hard study" or "religious excitement," and for countless other behaviors that authorities deemed socially disqualifying.

Chapter 4, "'The Colored Dead': African American Burying Grounds," focuses on another population whose members have had to strive to be accorded full legal and social humanity. Before the Civil War, many African Americans, both free and enslaved, were buried on farms or in the corners of town lots that have since been abandoned or built over. The earliest visible African American burials in the Valley are now anonymous. They likely were originally marked with wood or fieldstones that have since been displaced. A few African Americans during the nineteenth and early twentieth centuries were laid to rest under marble stones that paid homage to their "white friends." This chapter traces cemetery practices from the mid-nineteenth century to the present, showing the determination of Black Virginians, amidst a persistently hostile mainstream context, to assert the full humanity of their deceased loved ones.

Chapter 5, "'The Bivouac of the Dead': Military Conflicts and Cemeteries," focuses on the war dead broadly construed. The Valley of Virginia contains burials of veterans from the "Indian Wars" to the American Revolution, the Civil War, the Great War, World War II, Korea, Vietnam, and the "War on Terror" in Iraq and Afghanistan. Conflict claimed the lives of many buried in the Valley; other veterans survived their time in the service. This chapter includes both, and also considers noncombatants affected by wars, particularly Jewish people who immigrated to Virginia after the Holocaust. Grave markers often frame war—survival, sacrifice, service—as the defining experience of people's lives. Who they "were," their identities expressed on their graves, is often what they "did" for their families, communities, nation, and the world during military contests. Valley cemeteries are not only sites of memory, not only backward looking, not only about the identities of the deceased. Cemeteries are also spaces of current contest in identity formation, particularly over the meaning of the Confederacy, the battle flag, and the rebel dead. Though at first blush, grave markers associated with all wars may seem "the same" in the Valley, as they all pay respect to veterans, in practice Civil War grave sites are functionally different. The shining Southern Crosses and fresh Confederate flags on graves of Confederate States of America veterans suggest that—in distinction to veterans of the Revolutionary War, for example, or World War I—attention to the Lost Cause in cemeteries often goes beyond commemoration to canonization. Some White Virginians are enlisting Confederate memorials in current cultural debates about race and ethnicity, the location of power (local versus national), and Southern and American identity.

Chapter 6, "'Don't Forget about Daddy and Me': Reunions of the Quick and the Dead," continues the pivot to Valley cemetery practices in recent decades and suggests that many people are acting as if social ties survive death. The dead, in some ways, are framed as vital parts of ongoing daily life. Many think of deceased loved ones as being "at home" in the cemetery, cognizant, capable of receiving news and gifts. The sense of enduring social networks expressed on countless contemporary grave markers often extends to society more generally. Much as the medieval and early modern traditions of *memento mori*—remember that you'll die, and live accordingly—allowed the dead to advise the living at large, so now some graves offer advice to any passerby. Formulations on recent grave markers frequently resist social alienation and embrace a sense of responsibility for the community.

The next chapter builds on the theme of contemporary constructions of community by examining ways in which people often express their identities relationally on grave markers. Thus chapter 7, "'She Had an Affinity for Snowmen and Roosters': Relational Identities," shows how many people in the Valley of Virginia in recent decades have, on their headstones, claimed who they "were" through their associations with other people, animals, objects, tasks, work, activities, communities, buildings, and land. This is not the isolated, alienated modern Western individualism that so much scholarship has documented as emerging in the eighteenth century and reigning through the mid-twentieth. On the ground in Virginia, in scores of cemeteries spread over hundreds of miles, a different kind of identity is emerging, one in which the individual is presented as a node in a web of people, places, and things.

Chapter 8, "'The Grasshopper Not the Ant': The Ludic, Populist Cemetery," looks at expressions of informality and humor on recent grave markers. The use of nicknames, the choice of lighthearted epitaphs, and references to pop culture in cemeteries complement expressions of enduring association (chapter 5) and relational identity (chapter 6) in gesturing toward a deep cultural shift. Much current cemetery practice is creative, idiosyncratic, quirky, and playful in ways that anthropologists (e.g., Turner 1982) might recognize as a rejection of the status quo and a form of cultural rebellion. Laughter can be revolutionary, presenting "an element of victory" not only over death but also "the defeat of power, of earthly kings, of the earthly upper classes, or all that opposes and restricts" (Bakhtin [1968] 1984, 88). The veteran whose gravestone remembers him as "The Grasshopper Not the Ant" illustrates this rejection of mainstream expectations of striving and propriety. He's not the ant who worked hard; he was the grasshopper who played through the summer.

Contemporary ludic expressions bring this study of Valley cemeteries full circle, from the "lunatics" who were rejected by authorities to many in the populace rejecting the status quo. Many now don't seek to follow the straight and narrow furrow delineated by elites in the Beltway, the Ivory Tower, or the Vatican. They proudly claim, instead, identities outside of them. In a populist vein, they reject prescriptive norms of propriety for decorum. Theirs is a do-it-your-self authority, a claiming of power on the local level and determination on the personal plane. This sociocultural redefinition is two sided, both liberating and potentially socially corrosive. It can tighten bonds within groups but widen gaps among them. It lays the groundwork for struggles over who will be counted as part of the community, and whose full humanity will be honored.

CHAPTER 2

"Give This Man His Wings"
Imagining Lives and the Afterlife

A world away from the Great Valley of Virginia, Cookhouse is a small village in South Africa. I have not visited Cookhouse, but it's rarely far from my mind because of the poem, "Cookhouse Station," by South African writer Chris Mann. I encountered this poem in a volume honoring Jim Deetz, *The Art and Mystery of Historical Archaeology*, edited by two of his former students—Anne Elizabeth Yentsch and Mary Beaudry (1992)—who themselves became luminaries in the field. In addition to his archaeological projects in Virginia, Massachusetts, California, and South Dakota, Deetz also conducted research in South Africa. Wherever he and his students have sunk shovels into ground, wherever we've elicited memories of local elders or consulted the weighty, leather-bound volumes of county deeds and wills—all tools of the trade in historical archaeology—we've sought to see the "shades of those who once lived there."

COOKHOUSE STATION

If you ever pass through Cookhouse Station
make certain you see what is there.

Not just the long neat platform beneath the escarpment,
and the red buckets,

and the red and white brooms
but the Christmas beetle as well
which zings like a tireless lover
high in the gum-tree all the hot day.

And whether your stay is short
and whether your companions
urge you to turn from the compartment window
does not matter,
only make certain you see
the rags of the beggar-man's coat
before you choose to sit again.

And though there might be no passengers
waiting in little heaps of luggage when you look
make certain you see
the migrant workers with their blankets
as well as the smiling policeman,
the veiled widow as well as the girl
the trainee soldiers whistle at, otherwise
you have not passed that way at all.

And if it is a midday in December
with a light so fierce
all the shapes of things quiver
and mingle, make certain you see
the shades of those who once lived there,
squatting in the cool of the blue-gum tree
at ease in the fellowship of the after-death.

And if you ever pass through Cookhouse Station
make certain you greet those shades well
otherwise you have not passed that way at all.

—Chris Mann (copyright 1979; reprinted with permission)

In this chapter, I do my best to introduce you to the shades of some people who once lived in the Valley of Virginia. Whether or not you've physically been here, encountering them might provide a sense of having passed this way and having gleaned inklings of their variety of experiences, their values, or the varied ways that they understood the good life and the good death.

MARKING AND MEETING THE DEAD

A glimpse, first, of the sheer diversity of mortuary spaces in this part of the Commonwealth—the Valley of Virginia has cemeteries associated with varied ethnic groups, languages, and religious traditions, both historic and contemporary. They include municipal burying places like Evergreen Cemetery maintained by the City of Lexington; privately owned memorial gardens run as profit-generating businesses (e.g., Augusta Memorial Gardens); cemeteries organized as nonprofits such as Thornrose in Staunton; family cemeteries on private land like the Knick burying ground in Rockbridge County; and burying grounds associated with many religions and denominations—Jewish, Mennonite, Brethren, Lutheran, Baptist, Methodist, and Presbyterian. Some cemeteries, Sunset Memorial Park in Beckley, West Virginia, for example, have areas designated for Muslim burials.

Many early markers, whether stone or wood, are no longer visible on the landscape because of decay or overgrowth. A large granite tablet, recently erected, marks the "Alone Cemetery, Established about 1772" in Rockbridge County. A bronze plaque explains that "the first Alone Community settler to die was Andrew Kirkpatrick about 1772. In those days, graves were simply marked with stacks of field stones." Burying places in the Valley, such as Elk Run in Elkton, frequently contain unmodified pieces of limestone as markers of graves for people now unknown.

Some early historic burying grounds include gravestones written in German. At Friedens Church Cemetery in Rockingham County, several weathered sandstone tablets begin with the phrase "Hier Ruhet Dem Leibe," or "Here Lies the Body." Another gravestone, in English, commemorates someone now known only as "German Girl / Born Sept. 23, 1816 / Died Age 10 Yrs, 10 Mon." It's not clear why her age was known so precisely but her name lost to time. Other aged markers incorporate Latin phrases such as "Hic Jacet," meaning "Here Lies," and "Hodie Mihi Cras Tibi," or "Today Me, Tomorrow You." This epitaph is a *memento mori* formulation, the dead reminding the living of life's transience.

More recent Valley grave markers also draw on world languages. "Schlar in himmlischer Ruh!" (Sleep in Heavenly peace!) is a German epitaph from a gravestone memorializing a woman who died in 1996. Another marker incorporates a Latin phrase, "Amaviums Amamus Amabimus." (We have loved. We love. We will love.) There's also Greek, "Sagapo" (I love you) in a veterans' cemetery (d. 2015); and Spanish, "Dios Necesita Un Angel" (God Needed an Angel); and an epitaph in Igbo for a 25-year-old man (d. 1997), "MGBE ANYI GA AHU OZO" (TILL WE MEET AGAIN).

In Jewish cemeteries, in the Valley and countless other places, stone markers appear with the term *Genizah*, meaning sacred books and objects. Per Jewish prescription, any book or paper that includes the name of God should be solemnly buried, not casually discarded. Another Jewish tradition manifest in local cemeteries is the practice of veiling the headstone for at least a month and up to a year after the person's passing. Most common is placing a small rock on a head marker, as a token of having remembered and visited the deceased.

The Catholic faith is visible in Valley cemeteries in many ways, among them images of Jesus hanging on the cross and rosaries etched into

FIGURE 2.1. The grave of Randy Wayne Waggy (1960–2016) is marked with fabric floral displays, photographs, solar-powered lights, and other mementoes affixed to a span of chain link fence. Dayton Cemetery, Rockingham County.

FIGURE 2.2. Butterfly dreamcatcher, Riverview Cemetery, Waynesboro.

gravestones. Protestant denominations are varied and seemingly innumerable, with thousands of burying grounds, vast and diminutive, associated with Baptists, for example, the Brethren, Episcopalians, Lutherans, Mennonites (new and old orders), Methodists, and Presbyterians.

Some graves in the Valley and adjacent areas are commemorated with handmade markers, due often—but not always—to a lack of funds. Even if their pockets are nearly empty, many people are determined to grace the graves of those they loved. They get two pieces of wood, make a cross, and write the name of the deceased on it with Sharpie. They pour cement into a small mold and, as it dries, push marbles into it, or shells, or pieces of tile or glass. One marker incorporates a drawer pull as a decorative flourish. They raise, at the head of a grave, a short span of chain-link fence and cover it with wreaths and photographs (Figure 2.1). The only marker on many graves is the aluminum sign, intended to be temporary, that funeral homes provide. Sometimes those left behind complement these markers with affordable expressions of affection, for example, solar lights, hand-painted signs ("God Is Love"), and plastic flowers (Figure 2.2).

On the other end of the cost spectrum are massive, elaborately carved memorials and mausoleums— and these, too, attest to affection for the lost. Carvers turned marble into realistic replicas of trees cut down or topped and logs stacked, buds with broken stems, and shocks of wheat—all symbols of life cut short. Other expertly rendered, three-dimensional motifs include anchors (symbolizing faith), willows (mourning), and hands; a finger pointing up suggests the deceased has moved to Heaven, and two hands grasping denotes a marital bond suspended by death.

Diversity in social, economic, religious, and cultural aspects of mortuary practice extends to varied ways of treating the dead body. In the late twentieth century, it was not uncommon to see grave markers acknowledging that the deceased's body is not interred on site but was instead "Given to Science." Another

FIGURE 2.3. The Meadow Natural Burial Ground, Lexington.

trend was noting on gravestones that the deceased had been cremated. A 1990 gravestone, for instance, simply includes the name and dates of the deceased and the word, "Cremains." Another from 1994 observes at the top that the departed was "An Inspiration to All Who Knew Her" and says at the bottom, "Ashes."

Lately, too, some people are opting for interment in "green cemeteries," burying grounds that eschew chemical embalming, concrete crypts, and artificial memorials. Duck Run Cemetery in Rockingham County, like The Meadow near Lexington in Rockbridge County, offers unmediated burials—little or nothing between the body and the earth to which it's committed—and unobtrusive markers made of native wood, stone, and flora. These burials lack conventional markers not because of cost, but because of cultural preference. The Meadow has some extraordinary hand-forged steel memorials, their dedications known to their creators but not most visitors (Figure 2.3). It also has benches and picnic tables, inviting the living to spend companionable time with the dead. Duck Run fuses the quick and the dead together through its florescence of wildflowers, friendly resident ducks, picturesque bovines on the other side of a fence, and the Blue Ridge cutting, as a backdrop, across the horizon.

THE BIG NAMES, THE UNKNOWN, AND THE MANY IN BETWEEN

Some of the Valley "shades" who are perhaps "at ease in the fellowship of the after-death" were prominent in life and remembered in burial grounds. Cemeteries here contain interments of US congressional representatives and Virginia governors, military luminaries, founders of universities, and other figures famous on national and international stages. Among the most notable are Confederate Generals Robert E. Lee and Thomas "Stonewall" Jackson, both buried in Lexington. US President Woodrow Wilson's wife, Edith Bolling Wilson (1872–1961), is memorialized at East End Cemetery in her hometown of Wytheville. Her cenotaph explains that "Edith became one of the most significant women of the twentieth century when she acted on behalf of the president after he suffered a stroke in 1919. She is the only first lady buried in the National Cathedral in Washington DC." Renowned country singer Patsy Cline (1947–1963) is buried in Winchester on the opposite, northern end of the Valley. A month before her death, Cline recorded one of her most famous songs, "Sweet Dreams" ("Why can't I forget the past?"). At another Winchester cemetery is Russell Leroy "Rusty" Mason (1922–2012). His gravestone describes him as "the quintessential straight ahead jazz musician" who "was in the delivery room when swing was born." Lew DeWitt (1938–1990) is buried in Waynesboro; he was a tenor for the Statler Brothers and wrote their hit, "Flowers on the Wall" ("Playing solitaire till dawn with a deck of 51"). Leigh Buckner Hanes (1893–1967), interred in Roanoke, was a Poet Laureate of Virginia ("An oak that flaunts a leaf that's dead,/ waving it bravely overhead,/ as if it were a living thing;" Hanes 1930).

Rows of Union soldiers—some named, many "unknown"—rest in a US military graveyard; it's outside of downtown of Staunton and an instance of the nation using its dead to (re)claim territory that had seceded (see Eggener 2010, 22; Figure 2.4). Among the dead are Consider Frost from Ohio, Valentine Klinger from Pennsylvania, and James Simpson from Northern Ireland. George Magary from New Jersey might be among the unknown there. Son of a glassblower, Magary was a student at Oberlin College in Ohio when war broke out. He volunteered and was "killed in action from a gunshot to his head" in 1862 at the Battle of Port Republic "and left on the field." Many Union dead were eventually retrieved and interred in Staunton National Cemetery: "Since the US Government has no record of his burial, he may well be an unknown burial there. This is not unusual since of 994 Union soldiers buried there, 518, or 52% are unknowns."[1]

FIGURE 2.4. American flags honor soldiers, many of them "unknown," on Memorial Day. National Cemetery, Staunton.

The vast majority of people buried in the Valley of Virginia did not leave their mark in national memory or popular culture. The thousands upon thousands of people who were anonymous on the national stage were, nevertheless, part of the social fabric—members of families, congregations, communities—with moments both quotidian and extraordinary. Thinking back to Mann's poem, the richness of human experience requires that we see "the migrant workers with their blankets as well as the smiling policeman, the veiled widow as well as the girl the trainee soldiers whistle at." Life need not be lived in the spotlight to offer poignant testimony to what people have done and tried to do,[2] to what they thought, and to what they believed.

Robert R. Alexander's date of birth was not recorded, but his final words were. His gravestone in Lexington's historically African American cemetery says that he "Died Aug. 25, 1917 Aged about 76 years." Alexander's exact age was not known because he was born before the Civil War, and birth records were spottily kept for the enslaved or free people of color. His gravestone continues with the inscription of "His last words. Hallelujah tis done. I believe in the Son. I am saved by the blood of the crucified one."

The tradition of recording final utterances is an ancient practice. Robert Alexander's last words echo those of Jesus— "It is done." Many are familiar with Julius Caesar's final question ("Et tu, Brute?"). Less well known, if also ironic, are those of renowned artist Leonardo da Vinci ("I have offended God and mankind because my work did not reach the quality it should have"). Perhaps the last words of prophet Nostradamus strike us as more accurate ("Tomorrow, at sunrise, I shall no longer be here"). Queen Elizabeth I's final words poignantly acknowledge death as the great equalizer ("All my possessions for a moment of time"). Or rather less poignant, the last sentiment of whiskey distiller Jack Daniel ("One last drink, please").

Back in the Valley of Virginia, in Page County, Martha Arrington's gravestone says that she died in 1910 "aged 45 yrs. 9 mos. 10 days." Her last words were "I will eat or drink no more in this life." Her epitaph reminded me of Jane Hirshfield's poem (2006), "It Was Like This: You Were Happy." I happened to first read it as I sat in 2012 beside my mother's bed, wondering if it was her deathbed. A hospice nurse told me, "Sometimes they just keep sleeping and don't wake up. Sometimes they pop right up and ask for a hamburger." My mother did not pop right up and ask for a hamburger.

Hirshfield wrote, "It was like this:/ You were happy, then you were sad, / then happy again, then not. / It went on./ . . . Actions were taken, or not./ At times you spoke, at other times you were silent./ . . . Now it is almost over. . . . / Eating . . . is a thing now only for others./ It doesn't matter what they will make of you/ or your days: they will be wrong" (Hirshfield 2006, 92).

Inevitably and inadvertently, I'll get things wrong as I try to narrate some vignettes of the Valley dead. I'm not even sure of my mother's story: I didn't hear her last words because, on what turned out to be her last cognizant night, I'd gone to sleep early, thinking I needed to pace myself for coming weeks of care. I remember though a few days earlier, sitting on my mom's back porch with her and my brother. We asked her if there was anything she wanted to tell us, any regrets? She fixed her dark eyes on me and said, as she had so many times through the years, "You were an ugly baby."

Moments later, she spotted our father. He'd died nine years earlier, but here he was! "He's right there," Mom insisted, incredulous and a little irritated that we were acting like we didn't notice him. "In his Navy whites"—his uniform in their courting days of the 1960s. She seemed pleased, and just a little surprised, that her husband was so young, so healthy, and so clearly striding across the lawn toward her.

"EVERY BRICK HAS A STORY"

Up and down the Great Valley of Virginia—whether socially influential or little known, indigent or wealthy, superannuated or stillborn—people's memorials hint at stories of beauty, striving, heartbreak, and, most of all, love. These cemeteries make, in their own way, much the point of the poet Mann: richness of experience and depth of affection do not scale with social or economic clout.

In Waynesboro, the Serenity Garden provides a place "for people to reflect on the courage, dignity, and hope of those who have overcome this disease [cancer] and those who have fought it so bravely, but lost." It's "supported through the sale of engraved bricks which honor or memorialize friends and/or families who have fought the ravages of cancer" (Waynesboro Parks and Recreation n.d.) At the entryway, one message epitomizes not only the Serenity Garden's philosophy but also a premise of this book: "Every brick has a story to tell." Every grave marker, every person buried in the Valley, has a story. A brick dedicated to Brayden "D" Barr encapsulates this assumption of great stories in small places: "To the world, you are one person. To one person, you are the world."

Expressions of love are extensive and extraordinary in many cemeteries. According to his death certificate, Joseph Eugene "Jody" Henley (1961–1979) died when he was eighteen of multiple injuries as a "passenger in auto that went out of control and turned over."[3] His headstone remembers him as "one of the four of God's most beautiful creations," and an adjacent memorial says, "Wait for me, my darling son. Be patient while I stay to finish up God's will on earth. Then I'll slip away to be beside you forever and a day. Love, Mom."

Lional August Herrald (1932–1999) is remembered in his obituary as having been a West Virginia state trooper, beer commissioner, president of an equipment company, US Air Force veteran in the Korean War, Methodist, husband, father, grandfather, and "avid golfer."[4] But none of this appears on his grave marker. His epitaph is instead a poem he wrote: "Lay me down beside of Rachel.

Lay me down and let me sleep./ Near the ponds and simmering pine trees where the winds of nature sweep./ Lay me down beside of Rachel. Lay me down and let me wait/ Til the blare of Heaven's trumpet signals our eternal fate."

Rachel Elaine McGraw (1988–1997) was Lional Herrald's s granddaughter and is, indeed, buried next to him. Her grave marker depicts silhouettes of characters from A. A. Milne's stories of Winnie-the-Pooh: Eeyore, Tigger, Kanga, Roo, Rabbit, Owl, Piglet, and Pooh (Figure 2.5). The back of the marker features a girl holding her bear's hand as they skip over the grass, away from the viewer and says, "So, they went off together, but wherever they go, and whatever happens to them on the way, in that enchanted place on the top of the forest, a little girl and her bear will always be playing" (adapted from Milne 2009, 177). Rachel was eight years old when she died in an automobile accident, returning home from a medical appointment (Zeger 1997). Rachel had cerebral palsy (Fox 1999) and had benefitted from being able to participate in Brownies,

FIGURE 2.5. The headstone for Rachel Elaine McGraw (1988–1997) depicts silhouettes of characters from A. A. Milne's Winnie-the-Pooh stories. Sunset Memorial Park, Beckley, West Virginia.

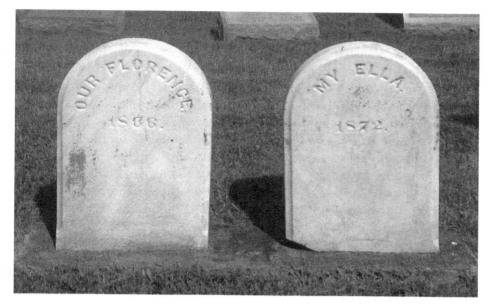

FIGURE 2.6. "Our Florence" died when both of her parents were alive, but Philander Herring's wife died a month before their other daughter passed, leaving him alone to mourn "My Ella." Greenwood Ames Cemetery, Bridgewater.

cheerleading, and horseback riding (Zegeer 1997). Newspaper accounts explain that her parents established programs in her honor to help other children with disabilities participate in meaningful activities.

One can only imagine the affection that Rachel's grandfather had for her, as after his own long life of accomplishment, the sole statement on his grave mourns her loss and asks to be laid down next to her.

Some headstones express affectionate bonds in unadorned terms. Rachel Lula Knick's (1868–1950) says "Daughter of Hugh T. Knick." She never married and was buried in the family plot in Rockbridge County. Her kinsman erected her memorial and created her epitaph: "I love her, Jimmy Entsminger."

Even the simplest stones can, given context, tell a moving story. A pair of small markers say simply "Our Florence 1866" and "My Ella 1872" (Figure 2.6). These are daughters of Philander Herring (1818–1901) and Margaret Back Herring (1827–1872). When their Florence died in 1866, both parents were bereft, but Philander's wife Margaret died of typhoid fever September 25, 1872,[5] and their daughter Ella succumbed to the same disease October 17, 1872.[6] Newly widowed, he alone was left to mourn "My Ella."

Other gravestones gesture toward relationships forged and lost. Some headstones were meant for two, but only one side is inscribed—usually because a surviving spouse remarried and was interred with a subsequent partner. Certainly, most grave markers designed for two were intended for couples—a shared last name at the top, the husband's name on the left and the wife's on the right being most conventional. But some pairs were siblings, apparently having reached the end of their lives without a marital partner. Brothers share a stone in an Augusta County church cemetery. Above one name is the word, "Father," and above the other's is "82nd Airborne." The obituary for the latter mentions stepchildren, but neither his nor his brother's mentions a wife. Thus, it seems that they had families of their own but came to rest together as brothers.

In another church cemetery, a brother (1921–1968) and sister (1926–1994) are buried together. He was a veteran of World War II, married, and an employee of the Waynesboro DuPont plant, producer of acetate yarn. His death certificate indicates that he died at home of "Gunshot wound to head. Was shot in Head by Him Self." A contributing condition was "Depression." His sister was married twice, the first time at age 17 to a 20-year-old steelworker. They divorced a few years later and both remarried; she was later granted a second divorce, this time for "desertion." Thus, she came to be buried next to her older brother who'd died by his own hand a quarter century earlier.[7]

CULTURE SCRIBED IN COPPER AND STONE

Just as every commemorative brick or grave marker has a story to tell, so memorials attest to diverse cultural orientations, values, and beliefs of people who lived and died in the Valley. In some cases, creeds are plainly, overtly stated. In other cases, as we've seen with the work of Jim Deetz, social and historical context facilitates understanding of more subtly communicated values.

Influential cadres of social scientists have embraced the proposition that people can be counted on to put their resources on social view through material displays like grave markers (Parker Pearson 1999; Bell et al. 2019). We might expect investment in memorials to correspond to the deceased's wealth, and while this correlation often holds, exceptions abound. Some markers scale more with the amplitude of grief than of assets, particularly those of fiercely loved children who, even if from economically modest households, may be expensively memorialized. Future years of imagined expenditures dissolve— perhaps a quinceañera, perhaps a car or college, perhaps a wedding— and the only opportunity that remains is for memorialization.

The cost of gravestones can diverge from wealth of the dead in the other direction. Some prominent nineteenth-century men in the Valley, despite their accomplishments and assets, had modest gravestones. Small and plain, they often list just the name of the deceased along with birth and death dates.

For instance, in the 1860 federal census, 42-year-old Philander Herring of Rockingham County had real estate worth $9,000 and personal property worth $4,000, values toward the high end of neighborhood valuations.[8] He enlisted as a private in the Confederate Army in November of 1861, and months later was elected captain.[9] The 1870 census found him with a diminished estate but real property still valued at $5,000 (while near neighbors had values ranging from zero or $200 to $10,000).[10] Herring appears to have been elected in 1881 to the Virginia Legislature and to have been remembered, following his 1901 death, as "one of our oldest and most prominent citizens."[11] Yet Herring's gravestone is just a little tablet with his name and dates.

Similarly, some modestly sized and plainly inscribed memorials in Lexington's Oak Grove (formerly Stonewall Jackson Memorial) Cemetery honor giants of local education, religion, and commerce. The Scots-Irish valuing of thrift doubtless informs many of these commemorative choices.

Gravestones encode cultural values in additional ways, including gender roles and expectations salient in the Valley. Male priority is etched into countless couples' head markers with "him" first and "her" second. Reading from top to bottom or left to right, the viewer encounters the man's name first. Occasionally, wives are anonymous except in relation to their husbands. William R. Speck (1811–1854), for example, in Bridgewater has a beautifully carved stone with willow, urn, and flowers. Next to his stone and appreciably smaller is an undecorated one reading simply "Wife of William R. Speck." In Rockbridge County, the name of a woman (1917–2005) appears in parentheses: "Mrs. Matthew (Inez C.) Fitzgerald."

Values expressed on grave markers often incorporate lines from poems, books, hymns, or other songs. A gravestone at the former Shemariah Presbyterian Church in Augusta County draws from a hymn to memorialize Margaret C. Randolph "who departed this life Sept. 3rd, 1857, Aged 21 Years 3 Months & 19 days. Death rides in every passing breeze and lurks in every flower. Each season has its own disease, its peril every hour." Lexington's Oak Grove Cemetery includes a headstone for Gerald Paul Bunton (1940–2005) with epitaph, "He played the game." This line is the refrain of Robert Service's poem entitled "The Lost Master" and extols the virtue of striving for the sake of righteousness rather than renown. Thinking toward his death, the poem's narrator says, "Ye shall not lay me out in state/ Nor leave laurels at my head/ Nor cause your men of speech orate." Rather than a monument or "column in the Hall of Fame," he asks for a simple line on his gravestone: "He played the game." The poem concludes with the honoring of this wish. When his life or "glorious task was done," his compatriots thought not of his accomplishments, fame, and "battles won," but of "the pride with which he fought," his "zest, his ringing laugh," his "trenchant scorn of praise or blame. And so we graved his epitaph, 'He played the game" (Service 1912).

Consistent with the sentiment of the poem inscribed on his headstone, Gerald P. (Jerry) Bunton's obituary indeed suggests a life of rigor, adventure, and duty:

At age 11, he began working in the rodeo in Cody, Wyoming. He was a bareback, saddle bronc and bull rider on the rodeo circuit through high school. After college he joined the 101st Airborne and then the CIA where he served two tours in Beirut, including one as replacement for Chief of Station William Buckley after he was kidnapped. Mr. Bunton also served in Dahran, Oman, Nairobi and Frankfurt. He retired from the CIA in 1992. He remained on contract with the agency, traveling to Bosnia, Iraq, Afghanistan, Pakistan, Macedonia, Zimbabwe, Germany and the Czech Republic.[12]

Words of Columbian novelist Gabriel García Márquez appear on a 2011 headstone in an Episcopal church cemetery in Albemarle County, bordering the Valley to the east. They convey a cultural orientation of hope, faith, and assurance: "Be calm. God awaits you at the door"(Márquez 1988).

In Bland County, a haiku from seventeenth-century Japanese poet Matsuo Bashō provides the epitaph for a couple. In 2002 the wife predeceased her husband after 42 years of marriage: "Fall Going, And We Part, Clamshells on the Beach." This is a "departure poem"; the "hinged, empty clamshells are actually there, but they are also a metaphor for the feeling of connection and loss" (Hass 1997).

A hand-painted grave marker in a Rockbridge County cemetery draws on another tradition in expressive culture to convey a different sense of bereavement: "What a shame to judge a life you can't change. God please give this man his wings." This epitaph for Samuel Hall (1978–2009) derives from the rock band Shinedown's 2008 song, "What a Shame." The lyrics include these sentiments: "There's a hard life for every silver spoon/. . . And for this working man they say could barely stand/ There's gotta be a better place to land/ Some kind of remedy for a world that wouldn't let him be/ . . . What a shame, what a shame/ To judge a life that you can't change/ The choir sings, the church bells ring/ So, won't you give this man his wings?"

Hall's obituary explains that he died "from gun shots due to a vicious murder and crime over a car in Palm Beach, Florida."[13]

Several recent grave markers in the region are inscribed with the phrase, "Rest High on the Mountain,"[14] the title of a popular 1995 song by country singer-songwriter Vince Gill: "I know your life on earth was troubled/ And only you could know the pain./ You weren't afraid to face the devil./ You were no stranger to the rain./ Go rest high on that mountain, Son./ Your work on earth is done./ Go to heaven a-shoutin' Love for the Father and the Son" (Gill 2009).

This song is one of several that describes a life of difficulty and sin, but with hope for redemption. Another appears on the 2013 gravestone of a young man buried in Mt. Carmel Presbyterian Church Cemetery (Augusta County). His epitaph derives from country singer Eric Church's 2006 hit, "Sinners Like Me." The song explains, "On the day I die I know where I'm gonna go/ Me and Jesus got that part worked out/ I'll wait at the gates til his face I see/ And stand in a long line of sinners like me" (Church 2006).

Other grave sites incorporate more playful themes from pop culture. A woman (1962–2004) in Waynesboro has a marker with Jimmy Buffett lyrics as an epitaph: "I'd rather die while I'm living than live while I'm dead." They're from the song, "Growing Older but Not Up" and celebrate the eternally festive: "I'm growing older but not up./ My metabolic rate is pleasantly stuck./ Let those winds of change blow over my head./ I'd rather die while I'm living than live while I'm dead" (Buffett 1981). Similarly, in Winchester, Robert B. "Boo" Grady (1972–2006) is memorialized with an epitaph taken from a Hank Williams Jr. song, "All My Rowdy Friends." ("And the hangovers hurt more than they used to./ And corn bread and ice tea took the place of pills and 90-proof./ . . . And nobody wants to get high on the town./ And all my rowdy friends have settled down." Williams 1981).

People reach for these sentiments, spread through print or verse, time and again because they strike a cultural chord. Funny or mournful, looking Heavenward or looking back on a life with some regret, or with no regrets at all, sentiments that poets, pop stars, or hymnists penned are, for many, just the right last words.

CULTURAL CONSTRUCTIONS OF DEATH

Understanding culture is central to understanding death. This premise might seem odd at first blush, because death is a biological reality. The end of life is not only a biological fact, however, because humans are not only sinew and organs. We are, everywhere, deeply enmeshed in social networks and in "webs of significance"—ways of thinking—spun by members of families, congregations, and communities (Geertz 1973; Benedict 1934). Human death is a biological, cultural, and social experience.

Social scientists studying death have long pointed out the multiple facets of its impact (Hertz [1906] 1960; Van Gennep 2018). When the biological being dies, the community must come to terms with the loss of a member who played particular roles in it. Effort is mobilized to repair or reknit the social fabric. This necessity appears in the saying, "The King is dead. Long live the King!" One meaning of this assertion is that, although the physical body of one king has died, the social institution of kingship survives and will be buoyed by appointment of a new leader (Tarlow 1999, 95). The community must be salvaged, a project involving the recruitment of others to step into positions vacated by the deceased. Because death "does not confine itself to ending the visible bodily life of an individual" but "also destroys the social being grafted upon the physical individual," the "destruction" of one is "tantamount to a sacrilege" against the social whole (Hertz [1906] 1960, 77). Often the "collective consciousness refuses to consider this loss irrevocable. Because it believes in itself, a healthy society cannot admit that an individual who was part of its own substance, and on whom it has set its mark, can be lost forever. The last word must remain with life: the deceased will rise from the grip of death and will return, in one form or another, to the peace of human association" (Hertz [1906] 1960, 78).

A person's death, therefore, might be conceived of as sleeping, or undertaking a journey, or being behind a door—present if invisible. Death is in this way culturally constructed, its imaginings variable not only over time and space but also within localities. Indeed, one of the great lessons of anthropology is that options often exist; realizing that people conceptually frame death in diverse ways reminds us that we're not bound to think of it through any singular metaphor or paradigm. It can be thought of as a temporary interruption in communication; the dead can be "like friends with no cell phone reception."[15] Death can be a gentle retirement from life, a tragic loss, or a gaping question mark. A variety of lenses color views of death, life, and love.

Social historian Philippe Ariès's book, *The Hour of Our Death* (1981), is a canonical survey of Western imaginings of death. He described "an attitude toward death that remained almost unchanged" beginning in the fifth century and fading during the eighteenth that viewed death as "tame" (Ariès 1981, 29). This cultural lens paired a regret for leaving life as being "hand in hand with a simple acceptance of imminent death. It bespeaks a familiarity with death" (15). Ariès points to Russian literary examples of the tame death. In Tolstoy's 1859 short story "Three Deaths," an "old coachman is breathing his last in the kitchen of an inn, near the big stove" and he understands: "When a peasant woman asks him kindly how he feels, he answers, 'Death is here, that's how it is,' and nobody tries to deceive him" (10). Ariès (16) also cites Solzhenitsyn's 1966 novel *Cancer Ward* as an example of the tradition of the tame death:

> Now, pacing the ward, he recalled how those old people had died in their villages. . . . They did not bluster, fight back or boast that they would never die. They took death calmly. Far from postponing the final reckoning, they got ready, little by little, and in good time decided who was to get the mare and who the foal, who the homespun coat and who the boots, then they passed on peaceably, as if simply moving to another cottage.

Often in medieval Europe, "the encounter between man and Death is not violent. The gesture of Death is almost gentle: 'My hand must fall on you'" (Ariès 1981, 116). Another contemporaneous, frequent imagining was the "Triumph of Death"—not the "personal confrontation between man and death, but the collective power of death. Death, in the form of a mummy or skeleton, stands with his symbolic weapon in his hand, driving a huge, slow chariot drawn by oxen" (118). In later centuries, death was variously understood as "the miraculous communion with the sources of being, the cosmic infinity"; or "simply the transition from an active life to an inactive life"; or a "disgusting" tragedy to be avoided as much as possible (474, 542, 569). As will be seen below, many other metaphors were adopted in Western cultural frames generally and, as evident through cemeteries, in the Valley of Virginia specifically—death as sleeping, as waiting, as undertaking a journey.

A thread running through these paradigms, varied as they are, is the cultural inclination to categorize particular deaths as "good" or "bad." The good death is anticipated and didactic; it provides time for reflection, communication, and planning (Mytum 2004, 158). Elderly people who completed the run of life in comfort and company were generally seen as dying good deaths. Bad deaths are sudden, unanticipated, and tragic. Often befalling the young, bad deaths rob the person and the community of youth, vivacity, and a sense of beneficent rationality in the universe (158).

THE BAD DEATH

At a church cemetery in Waynesboro (Augusta County), Benjamin S. Brown's grave marker says that he "Died from a wound received at 1st Manas [Manassas]. Aug. 15, 1861, aged 26 Yrs. & 15 ds." His half-brother John G. Brown was "Murdered July 1, 1863, aged 46 Yrs. 10 Mo. & 6 ds." These Valley grave markers share a tendency with many others in the Western tradition to mark "bad deaths" such as drownings, accidents, and killings through epitaphs (Tarlow 1999, 63).

Nancy Lee Caul (1949–1955) and Edward Yolanda Caul (1948–1955) are remembered on their shared headstone as "Sweetly Sleeping Fire Victims." A lamb tops their gravestone in Staunton's historically African American cemetery. These five- and six-year-old siblings died, according to their death certificates, of "burning by fire" at home when the "stove exploded setting house afire."[16] In Collierstown (Rockbridge County), James A. Ford's gravestone records that he "Died from Suffocation in His Burning Building at Clifton Forge VA, July 13, 1895 aged 58 years." At Weavers Mennonite Church Cemetery near Harrisonburg, Joseph E. Keister's (1884–1913) gravestone mourns him as having been "Killed in Railroad Wreck." Alfred D. Hartman was a paper hanger and painter who died in an automobile accident. Hartman's stone says he was "Born Apr. 27, 1898, Killed May 16, 1953."

Twelve-year-old Carrie Bernice Kiser was born in 1913 and, as her headstone notes, "Drowned Sept. 1, 1926." The local newspaper, the *Harrisonburg Daily News Record*, wrote,

> Tragedy stalked into this happy community late today and tonight finds Bridgewater in mourning and grief-stricken as it seldom has been before. The drowning of Miss Bernice Kiser . . . while she bathed with a party of Sunday School picnickers at six o'clock this evening, gave Bridgewater one of the biggest shocks of its life. . . . The body was recovered about two hours later. It was found within a few feet of where the girl disappeared in a pool of 15-feet depth at the bend of the river. . . . The body was washed a short distance upstream by the

strong undercurrent in the pool. O. A. Arey, former mayor of Bridgewater, who was the only adult with the party of girl swimmers, made a desperate effort to save Miss Kiser when he saw her disappear below the surface into the hole which was unknown to members of party. Mr. Arey went down twice in his death struggle with the drowning girl, but without assistance [was] unable to pull her out.

Children's deaths are generally understood as the saddest deaths—the most heart-wrenchingly bad deaths—in the community. This grief crosses ethnic and religious boundaries and is especially poignant for children who died during or soon after birth.

One baby's epitaph is "Nov. 19, 1979–Nov. 19. 1979. How very softly you tip-toed into my world. Only a moment you stayed. But what an imprint you have left upon my heart." Another reads, "May 2, 2017 9:42 A.M." At a Mennonite church cemetery "Beautiful Baby Boy/ Jeremiah Ifiok George" was "Born and Passed away on Thursday August 20, 2015. Mummy and Daddy Love You So Much. Until We Meet Again. Matthew 18:10." This Bible verse refers to Jesus's reminder not to look down on any of "these little ones. For I tell you that their angels in Heaven are always in the presence of my Father in Heaven."[17] In a Waynesboro municipal cemetery, Titus Croston Spencer was "Born in Silence May 21, 2007," and at an Episcopal church cemetery in Albemarle County rests "Emmanuel Eaton, Beloved Unborn, Sept. 5, 2008."

In Shenandoah County, two-month-old John David Seekford died the day after Christmas in 1967, or as his grave marker suggests, "Wynken, Blynken, and Nod One Night Sailed Off in a Wooden Shoe" (Figure 2.7). This poem by Eugene Field imagines a child going to sleep, sailing "on a river of crystal light/ into a sea of dew" while "Mother sings/ of wonderful sights that be,/ and you shall see the beautiful things/ as you rock in the misty sea"(Field 1947).

Although sometimes young children are buried near family members, many young parents aren't prepared for the death of an infant; they don't have burial plots or the thousands of dollars on hand to purchase them. For this reason— and also because the thought of deceased children being buried amidst other children might, if even slightly, ameliorate the extraordinary weight of grief— many cemeteries have "baby lands," areas set aside for the interment of infants and toddlers. Plots are usually a third the size of adult burial places, mak-ing them relatively affordable. Some baby lands are largely populated with standardized grave markers, often listing the deceased simply in relation to their parents: "Infant daughter of Mr. and Mrs. Scott Brown." Others are more personalized such as burials in an Augusta County memorial park baby land: "Baby 'Kati-Bug,' Kaitlyn J. Hinson, Aug. 15, 2003–Dec. 28, 2003" and "Play-ing in God's Garden, Our Little Angel Jose Martin Rodriquez-Loya, July 18, 1996–Aug. 11, 1996." Many older cemeteries, however, including those asso-ciated with churches have gravestones inscribed with a single word, "Infant."

FIGURE 2.7. Grave marker for John David Seekford (October 1967–December 1967) with an epitaph excerpted from Eugene Field's poem, "Wynken, Blynken, and Nod." Sunset View Memorial Gardens, Shenandoah County.

Serial child deaths also mark the landscape of Valley cemeteries. Christian and Elizabeth Hartman, for example, had nine children born between 1844 and 1858. Within the space of a month in 1862, five of their children died—probably all of diphtheria. At Mill Creek Church of the Brethren Cemetery in Rockingham County, a single stone remembers them:

Children of Christian and Elizabeth Diehl Hartman
John—Mar. 4, 1849–Sept. 14, 1862
Samuel—Oct. 1, 1850–Sept. 24, 1862
Isaac—Apr. 12, 1852–Sept. 25, 1862
Peter—Jan. 18, 1854–Sept. 28, 1862
Mary A.—Nov. 2, 1858–Oct. 10, 1862

It's likely that the Hartmans, buried in this Brethren cemetery, were members of that denomination; if so, their faith proscribed slave holding and taking up arms. The war came to them, however. According to an historical marker erected by Virginia Civil War Trails (n.d.) this cemetery and church stand "on the site of an antebellum house of worship that, during the Battle of Cross Keys on June 8, 1862, was used as a hospital. Amputated arms and legs were dropped outside from a window and piled up until they finally reached the sill." It's possible that the Hartman children contracted diphtheria in the aftermath of war-related presence of disease in their community in 1862. Diphtheria is a highly contagious bacterial infection; beginning with a sore throat, fever, and cough, the illness can progress to swelling in the throat that blocks the airway. One can only imagine parents Christian and Elizabeth Hartman—opposed to both slavery and war—in the midst of a war largely about slavery, witness their five young children struggle for breath and die. But the death of multiple young daughters and sons is, tragically, not only at a multigenerational remove. In Staunton, three matching gravestones—"In Loving Memory" with a bowed, praying angel—mark resting places of daughters born and lost to a couple: Krystle Lynn (1990–1991), Lindsey Jean (1992–1993), Chloe Marie (2003–2003) Schroers.

Many work toward framing a "bad" death in positive, hopeful terms, often through expressions of faith. Valley gravestones, for example, often describe children who died as now being protected. The marker for a one-year-old buried in a Baptist church cemetery (1926, Greenville) says, "Sheltered and Safe from Sorrow." And at a Lutheran church cemetery (1955, Botetourt County), simply "Sheltered." A fourteen-year-old in Harrisonburg's municipal Woodbine Cemetery (1934) is "Released from the uncertainty of the year and safe from time."

A Methodist church cemetery in Augusta County memorializes an eighteen-year-old boy who died in 1958, and his parents who passed, after long lives, in 2014. Their epitaph reads, "There Will Be No Tears in Heaven," and offers a poignant example of the cultural dialectic of tragedy and affirmation. "Tears in Heaven" is a Grammy Award–winning song cowritten and sung by Rock and Roll Hall of Fame inductee Eric Clapton. In 1991, Clapton's four-year-old son Conor fell to his death from a window on the 53rd floor of a building in New York City. "Tears in Heaven" is a tribute to the boy and asks him," Would you hold my hand/ If I saw you in heaven?/ Would you help me stand/ If I saw you in heaven?/ . . . Beyond the door/ There's peace, I'm sure/ And I know there'll be no more/ Tears in heaven" (Clapton 1992).

A 2013 readers' poll in *Rolling Stone* named "Tears in Heaven" as the "Saddest Song of All Time." But Clapton recognized music as "a healing agent, and lo and behold, it worked. I have got a great deal of happiness and a great deal of healing from music" (ABC News 2006).

GOOD DEATHS

"Good deaths"—those concluding long, satisfying lives—are often acknowledged on Valley grave markers, very frequently with reference to religious faith or the wonder that lies beyond. At Mount Hebron Cemetery in Winchester, an epitaph seems to address the deceased herself (1898–1966): "God saw the road was getting rough, the hills were hard to climb. So He closed your weary eyes and whispered, 'Peace Be Thine.'" Others frame death in positive terms through assurances: "All is well. Safely rest. God is nigh."[18] Or describe the deceased as en route to Heaven: "Getting to go where only the winners get to go."[19] Or entering a new life—at Brickey Cemetery in Craig County, Ronald L. Sarver's gravestone says, "On Earth May 24, 1948. In Heaven April 3, 1999."

Likewise, Grace Irene Albright was "Born on Earth February 14, 1918. Born into Eternity May 27, 2007."[20]

In the Valley of Virginia—and well beyond, throughout the United States and United Kingdom (Tarlow 1999)—people often employ metaphors to affirm the goodness of death. Among the most common are going home, undertaking a journey, sleeping, and resting. Less frequently, life and death experiences are envisioned as transactions between Heaven and Earth: "God Gives Us Love, Something to Love He Lends Us."[21] In this view, the decedent had only been on loan: "God in his wisdom has recalled the boon his love had given, and though the body slumbers here the soul is safe in Heaven."[22] This metaphor applies sometimes to children's epitaphs—"God loaned you to us Dec. 22, 1989. And called you home Nov. 26, 2007,"—and to parents', "God's Greatest Gift, Returned to God – Our Mother" (1997).[23]

Many grave markers describe death as a "homegoing." In this view, death is nothing to avoid or mourn; life is something of an aberration, time spent away from Heaven. A 2016 headstone in Pulaski County explains, "I'm not afraid. This was my temporary home." In a Staunton memorial park, a marker for a couple (d. 2006 and 2017) describes them as being "Home & Happy," and in Waynesboro, one 2004 gravestone reads, "Thank God Moma, I am Home." This formulation was common in earlier decades too. In 1908 in Lexington's historically African American cemetery, a young woman "faltered by the wayside, and the angels took her home." In a nearby county at a traditionally White Presbyterian church cemetery, an older woman's epitaph states, "She has gone to her home."

Sometimes this understanding is phrased as the deceased's having completed their earthly journey. A gravestone remembers "Mother, Sarah Anne Forbes, Born Greening. Lifes Pilgrimage Begun at Gretton Gloucestershire Eng. July 2, 1843. Fulfilled at Greenwood VA June 20, 1921." In other imaginings, death is a kind of traveling. At the McDowell family cemetery in Fairfield (Rockbridge County), a gravestone is sacred to the memory of Andrew Trevey, "Born Oct. the 16th 1790 who departed this life / Jan. the 2nd 1848 Aged 57 years, 2 months / and 17 days." The convention of "departing this life" is especially common in earlier parts of Valley history: "In memory of Elizabeth Argenbright, Consort of George Argenbright Who departed this Life June 8th, 1856 Aged 67 Years."[24]

If many decedents are envisioned as journeying from this world, others are understood to be waiting for the second coming of Jesus. A mid-twentieth-century headstone in a Methodist church cemetery explains that the deceased is "Resting in Hope of a Glorious Resurrection"; an early twentieth-century couple's grave marker in a municipal cemetery reads, "Sweet be thy sleep till He bids thee arise." A late twentieth-century marker in a Mennonite church cemetery says, simply, "Waiting."

Many early Protestant gravestones—such as those at Timber Ridge Presbyterian Church in Rockbridge County—are aligned on an east–west orientation with the dead's head to the west so that, when the Rapture transpires, they will sit up facing east and the coming Christ: "It will happen suddenly, quicker than the blink of an eye. At the sound of the last trumpet the dead will be raised. We will all be changed, so we will never die again" (I Corinthians 15:52). Beginning in the first decades of the nineteenth century, graves were more commonly oriented to roads or church walls.

The metaphor of the dead as resting has long been popular, and its use often but not necessarily implies a belief in subsequent resurrection. Gravestones say that people are "Laid to Rest," or "Having Finished Life's Duty They Now Sweetly Rest," or "Thy Trials Ended, Thy Rest is Won."[25] A number of gravestones in the Valley's Jewish cemeteries include the phrase "May She Rest in Peace," or "May He Rest in Peace."

The related metaphor of death as sleeping is very common in the Valley of Virginia and beyond, from the mid-eighteenth century to the present. Graves themselves are often designed as beds—many having a headstone (headboard), footstone (footboard), and sometimes rails framing the long sides of the plot[26] (Figure 2.8). Epitaphs often claim that the person interred is "Not dead, just sleeping." A small 1936 headstone in a Rockbridge County Presbyterian church

FIGURE 2.8. The grave of Colonel John Wilson (1701–1773) and his wife Martha Wilson (1715–1775) resembles a bed, with an upright footstone, flat ledger stone in the center, and upright headstone. Glebe Burying Ground, Augusta County.

IMAGING LIVES AND THE AFTERLIFE

cemetery observes that a couple's daughter is "Only Sleeping." Some inscriptions quote Jesus: "He is not dead, but sleepeth." In Matthew 9:22–25,[27]

A synagogue leader came and knelt before Jesus and said, "My daughter has just died. But come and put your hand on her, and she will live." Jesus got up and went with him, and so did his disciples. . . . When Jesus entered the synagogue leader's house and saw the noisy crowd and people playing pipes, he said, "Go away. The girl is not dead but asleep." But they laughed at him. After the crowd had been put outside, he went in and took the girl by the hand, and she got up.

Other framings of death as sleep are more secular. The gravestone for a couple in Waynesboro says, "I love you honey. Goodnight babe. I'll see you in the morning."

Finally, given the band's name, it should be unsurprising that images and lyrics from the Grateful Dead also help lay the deceased to rest. The back of Brian K. Kenney's headstone (1980–2006) in Winchester has the Dead's iconic blue bear, dancing or high stepping, with the words "Fare Thee Well Sunshine Day Dreamer"(Figure 2.9). The epitaph gestures toward their song "Sugar Magnolia" ("Sunshine daydream/ Walk you in the sunshine") as well as "Brokedown

FIGURE 2.9. The gravestone memorializing Brian K. Kenney (1980–2006) features a blue dancing bear and lyrics from songs of the Grateful Dead. Mount Hebron Cemetery, Winchester.

Palace." The latter incorporates images of death as sleeping, as leaving, and as going home: "Fare you well, my honey/ Fare you well my only true one / . . . Going to leave this brokedown palace / . . . Make myself a bed in the waterside / . . . River going to take me,/ . . . Sing me sweet and sleepy/ all the way back home" (Grateful Dead 1970).

Here as in centuries past, death can be tame, a gentle courier assisting souls in their homeward movement.

POTHOS

When I met Jim Deetz in Berkeley in 1992, he invited me to a small dinner party. The ceiling of one room in his house was strung with vines—hanging pothos that must have taken years to spread vertically and horizontally across the whole space. I commented on them—such a rich garden descending—and he shrugged. He said he'd begun planning for his upcoming move to Virginia and, because moving the plants seemed unfeasible, he'd stopped watering them. If memory serves, someone staged an intervention and adopted them, but his apparent contentment with the prospect of living beneath browning leaves made me think. For some, perhaps particularly for many of us who study the dead, a good death—a peaceful parting after a long life—may come to seem more familiar than fearsome. A plant dies and becomes fertilizer for another sprout, and a new chapter begins.

CHAPTER 3

"The Wrong Kind of Creature for This World"
Asylum Cemeteries

INTRODUCTION: "IT TAKES YOUR HEART AWAY"

A hill behind some of the most elegant, historic brick buildings in Staunton, Virginia, contains the mortal remains of nearly three thousand people (ca. 1825–1981).

One gravestone with a weeping willow was raised "In Memory of Ann C., wife of John James Flournoy of Prince Edward County Va. Died July 21st, 1854." Ann Carrington Cabell (1788–1854) was born into a prominent Virginia family and married into another. Her father, William Cabell (1759–1822), was a member of the General Assembly (1789–1797, Wythepedia 2017). Census returns reflect her husband John James Flournoy's growing wealth as measured by the number of enslaved people in their household, from 17 in 1810[1] to 48 in 1830.[2] Ann and John had six children of their own, one of whom—Thomas Stanhope Flournoy—became a US representative and colonel in the Virginia Cavalry.[3] He along with several of his brothers and brothers-in-law were attorneys. In 1850, Ann was 65 years old; she and her husband lived with their son—William C. Flournoy, a lawyer with real estate valued at $30,000—as well as his wife and their children.[4] By 1860, Ann's 79-year-old husband was living with a daughter, Ann Wood, and her husband, Henry Wood, Attorney at Law.[5] In the intervening

53

years, Ann Flournoy had been admitted to Western State Lunatic Asylum in Staunton. Her intake record says she suffered from "reverse of fortune" and was "apprehended," meaning apprehensive, fearful, and anxious. Fourteen months later, she died from marasmus—severe malnutrition or "wasting."[6] She was buried on the hill behind the asylum.

Fannie C. Hines (1868–1913) is interred nearby. Fannie's parents, Mary and John Hines, were economically modest farmers.[7] When Fannie was 12 years old, she and her four siblings lived with their widowed mother.[8] Mary later remarried, and the 1900 federal census lists Fannie as a single 32-year-old in their household.[9] Three years later Fannie was admitted to Western State Hospital, as it was then called. She was suffering from a recurrent, hereditary "mania."[10] She lived there for a decade, succumbing in 1913 to pellagra, a disease caused by niacin deficiency in protein-poor diets and characterized by dementia, dermatitis, and gastrointestinal distress. Records note that her father had been "epileptic" and that a factor contributing to Fannie's death was "insanity."[11]

Ann Carrington Cabell Flournoy and Fannie C. Hines were certainly different, born nearly a century apart to families of differing socioeconomic stations.

FIGURE 3.1. Nearly all of the 104 graves in Western State Hospital's "Old Graveyard" (1839–1847) are unmarked. Burial place of Major Hiram Gough, Staunton.

FIGURE 3.2. Section of the second Western State Hospital Cemetery (1847–1980s) where the great majority of grave markers are blank concrete slabs. Staunton.

Ann married and had children; Fannie's death record identifies her as a "Miss" who never married. On the other hand, both were White. In the cemetery that Ann and Fannie share, their most evident commonality is their commemoration. They're in the tiny minority of former inmates whose families raised gravestones in their memory.

The vast majority of the Western State Lunatic Asylum dead are interred in anonymous graves (Figure 3.1). Some, particularly the earliest, are wholly unmarked, appearing as depressions in the earth only visible with oblique rays of light at sunset or with a dusting of snow. Most of the final resting places are furnished with deteriorating slabs of iron and cement (Figure 3.2). The practice was to use iron straps or rebar as the skeleton for poured cement rectangles (Figure 3.3). When dry, they were whitewashed and labeled with the row or terrace and plot of the decedent. Most of the paint is long gone, but some grave labels remain, for example, "G 62" and "2133." These faded codes, these crumbling tablets of cement and rusting rods of iron, are the only visible physical testimony to lives of difficulty that brought people to their ends in the asylum. If they're buried here, it means that family members didn't come

FIGURE 3.3A AND B. Detail of a grave marker with crumbling cement revealing rusted iron innards, and a grave marker that retains its whitewash and plot number, "G 62." Western State Hospital Cemetery, Staunton.

to retrieve their remains. If they're buried here under whitewashed painted cement markers, it means that family members also didn't erect a gravestone in their memory.

Ann Carrington Cabell Flournoy and Fannie C. Hines were exceptions. Someone mustered the funds and initiative to install marble markers with their names and dates of death, and in Ann's case her relations and home county. The mortal remains of the great majority of patients were left in the hands of the state, to be buried under numbered slabs.

Different families doubtless accepted these circumstances for different reasons. Some simply could not afford a gravestone or a trip to Staunton. Some likely felt comfortable with hospital practice and authority, trusting that their burial policies were appropriate. Indeed, some still defend the anonymity of Western State Hospital graves as needed to protect patient confidentiality (although records are available at the Library of Virginia and, in many cases, online). Some other families, perhaps, were embarrassed or for other reasons relieved to be "rid" of members who had been unstable (Wood 2004).

Views of people experiencing disabilities varied not only within communities but also across time. There is no one-to-one correspondence between time period and culturally informed ways of thinking, but in the case of Western State specifically, the divergent approaches of superintendents both reflected and influenced ways that their contemporaries in the public, in the profession, and in the government perceived disability.

This chapter traces contested views of "insanity"—an umbrella phrase during the nineteenth and early twentieth centuries—at Western State Lunatic Asylum (later "Western State Hospital") founded c. 1825 in Staunton and the State Colony for Epileptics in Amherst County, abutting the Valley to the south. The "Colony" as it's often called was chartered in 1910. By 1912 it became the State Colony for Epileptics and Feebleminded (Lombardo 2008), the first in a series of name changes including the last—"Central Virginia Training Center"—before its closure in 2020. Both Western State and the Colony have cemeteries on site: nearly three thousand former inmates are interred at the former and just over a thousand at the latter.

Imagine standing at the foot of the cemetery hill at Western State. It's over three acres, roughly the length of a football field and more than twice the width. The hill is chopped into dozens of narrow terraces, ascending among ancient oaks. Scores of slabs of concrete and rusting iron in varied states of collapse line each terrace.

The sight "takes your heart away," said a former patient interviewed in 2008 when he and others began an effort to improve the cemetery (Santos 2008). Another patient characterized the collapsing, anonymous markers as "very dehumanizing. It's no different than the way everyone was dehumanized at the mental hospital then." This treatment of the dead, they note, mirrors historic treatment of patients during their lives, as well as common contemporary views of people experiencing mental illness or disability. One advocate called on twenty-first-century Virginians to recognize these former patients "as people. We owe the same recognition and dignity to the mentally ill today." A Western State chaplain who had presided over the burial of two dozen patients shared that he was "thankful for this opportunity to acknowledge them and the lives they lived." They, too, he said, "dreamed their dreams, hoped their hopes" and "fought their own battles with love and faith and doubt" (Santos 2008). We'll do our best to meet some of them in following pages.

Most patient names below are pseudonyms. Online—at the Find A Grave website, for example—researchers have uploaded hundreds of historic hospital records that are no longer subject to privacy laws. In a few cases, descendants have removed records from public sites, presumably because they don't want to see information that could be construed as negative or embarrassing about their ancestors. I respect that position. Indeed, the first commandment of anthropology, like medicine, is to try to do no harm. Moreover, a key intent of this book is to underscore the full humanity of everyone in the Valley. For this reason, I want the people under discussion to have names. My response to this pair of needs is to use fictional first names with the same gender and first letter of the real person's name. Thus "Adam" becomes "Alex," and "Evelyn" becomes "Edith." Their stories, though, are factual. Exceptions—with real first and last names below—are when narratives are abstracted from newspapers, or when descendants granted me permission to share their family stories. I gathered information about these patients in a variety of ways: visiting hospital cemeteries, researching original records archived at the Library of Virginia in Richmond, and consulting images of primary sources such as death records, obituaries, marriage records, census returns, and military documents electronically through sites such as Ancestry.com, Fold 3, and Newspapers.com.

The aspiration of this chapter, its conceit really, is to relay humanistic glimpses of individuals who were often dehumanized in life and death. I'd like to offer some memorialization—modest though it is—to supplement the patches of fescue, bits of iron bar, or powdering concrete on Western State graves, and the standardized plaques in line after line at the State Colony. Over the years in which these patients lived and died at the asylums, medical paradigms came and went; some are likely to strike us as benevolent or benign, others draconian. But through it all variability persisted. People who thought or observed differently, or whose emotions ran electrically; who talked differently—too little, not enough, incoherently, or wildly; who moved differently—rocking, running at odd times, flattening themselves against walls or floors—could find themselves confined.

Such variation still persists. My friend's autistic son was 22 years old when he died following difficulties while institutionalized. As I write this, another friend's 18-year-old autistic son is spending his second day in a hospital that used to be an asylum. My son, too, is 18 and autistic. He's at home; in the meantime, his twin sister is starting college.

Experiences of my family and friends, as well as historic case studies from the Valley, raise questions about whether only some kinds of intelligence are culturally approved. What if the cerebral circuitry that fuels creativity—thinking, talking, or moving differently—is deemed inappropriate? Whose differences are celebrated? Whose are closed down or shut away? What are the social and human costs of intolerance for difference? In some ways, answering these questions might be easier by looking to the past, to the people whose stories are finished and whose remains rest behind asylum buildings.

MORAL MEDICINE

> When does a man so urgently require the aid of a rational fellow being to guide his footsteps, as when he wanders thus in mental darkness? Or when does he so much need the knowledge and guidance of others, as when his own mind is a wild chaos agitated by passions that he cannot quell, and haunted by forms of terror which the perverted energy of his nature is perpetually calling into being, but cannot disperse?
>
> —Dr. Francis T. Stribling, 1838 (quoted in Wood 2004, frontispiece)

At Western State, one of the first gravestones bearing a former patient's name is a military marker for Hiram Gough (1779–1840), commissioned as a major in the Randolph County militia. After the War of 1812, Gough served as justice of the peace and was a large cattle dealer. On one trip, according to a newspaper account, Gough

> was attacked by a band of highwaymen near Baltimore and brutally beaten over the head. . . . The beating rendered Gough insane. Completely disoriented, he wandered about Baltimore for several months, nearly starving to death, until someone finally recognized him. His family rode to Baltimore to retrieve him and took him home. But Gough was never rational again, and a special strong-room had to be built for him adjacent to the home. Finally, he was admitted to what was then Western Lunatic Asylum at Staunton on July 19, 1836. He died July 30, 1840. (Culbertson 2014)

Tragedy also befell farmer Peter Hinkle. The 1850 census found Peter and his wife Margaret Jane Hinkle, both age 26, living with two daughters (a toddler and an infant).[12] Hinkle "family tradition tells us that Peter cut himself while grubbing out a tree on his farm in the 1850s. The cut became infected with gangrene and a high fever left him brain damaged."[13] Hinkle was admitted to Western State in 1856 and died in 1858.[14] His grave is marked with a small tablet of white marble behind the asylum.

Margaret McGhee (1811–1871), wife of a prominent farmer,[15] was admitted to Western State in 1851 when she was 40 years old. According to family tradition, "Having spent much of her adult life at this institution, Margaret was buried here at her request."[16] Relatives raised a marble marker over her grave. Mrs. McGhee's choice for burial location may not be surprising as the two decades she spent there (1851–1871) were the salad days of Western State. It was, for many, truly an asylum, a "sanctuary or inviolable place of refuge and protection."[17]

Dr. Francis T. Stribling served as physician and superintendent of Western State from 1836 until 1873 (Allis 2011, 9). Like many of his contemporaries, Stribling was a proponent of "moral medicine." This approach to mental illness championed gentle, humane treatment, seeking to eliminate the use of restraint, coercion, and punishment. It held that removing sources of agitation and providing soothing, positive experiences could empower the patient to return to mental health (Wood 2004).

This perspective informed architecture and landscaping at Western State. In designing many of the buildings and features, Thomas Blackburn, "a Thomas Jefferson protégé who worked at the University of Virginia and who designed many of the hospital's buildings, gardens, porticos, and colonnades" (McNair 2006) worked with Stribling (Wood 2004). Architectural historian Bryan Green observed that Stribling and Blackburn's was "the only known collaboration of physician and architect to construct and implement such a marriage of treatment technique and physical setting." Handsome spaces, they believed, promoted wellbeing (Figure 3.4). Thus, some buildings "had elaborate roof walks to provide mountain views. Inside, details like aligning the iron bars on the windows with the mullions, the installation of a beautiful spiral staircase ascending toward a domed cupola, and the elegant molding and glass work around doors and windows were meant to create an atmosphere of elegance and beauty that would aid in the healing process" (McNair 2006).

Richard, a married 42-year-old merchant plagued with "mental fatigue," was admitted to Western State in 1845.

Emma and Nellie were twins, daughters of a laborer, born in 1809. Both were admitted to Western State in 1853. Nellie suffered "ill health & trouble." Emma suffered from the "derangement of [her] sister." Nellie died within the year; Emma lived a decade longer. Both succumbed to "pulmonary consumption" or tuberculosis.

Herman, admitted in 1857, was a 60-year-old married blacksmith suffering from "loss of sleep etc."

Daniel had experienced "domestic trouble" for some five months. He arrived at the institution in 1854 and died two months later due to "exhaustion from abstinence."

During the mid-nineteenth century, professional psychological wisdom held that

some simple men, who a century earlier, thought only about obtaining daily sustenance, now study subjects that compel their brains to labor with greater

FIGURE 3.4. Pleasure Grounds at Western State Hospital, c. 1871. *Report of the Board of Directors & Medical Superintendent of the Western Lunatic Asylum of Virginia For the Fiscal Years 1871–72 and 1872–73.* Courtesy of the Library of Virginia.

energy and exhausting zeal than those of any former generation. Results are students who grapple with subjects that they cannot master and sink under the burden of perplexity that they could not unravel. . . . [Any subject] can impose great anxiety and mental labors that often resulted in insanity. (Wood 2004)

Prominent thinking maintained that "all customs, habits, occupations, or other agencies whatsoever which exhaust the power of the brain and the nerves, bringing the body into a weakened condition, may . . . become the origin of mental disorder. Such influences are, indeed the ramified root from which insanity springs" (Pliny Earle, quoted in Foucault [1961] 1999, 227–28). The "perpetual agitation of the mind"—particularly when not mitigated by social intercourse and physical activity—"can have the most disastrous effects" (Foucault [1961] 1999, 217). Too much solitary reading or thinking, or too passionate a concern with religious subjects, brought people to a culturally unacceptable extremity.

Agnes, a carpenter's daughter, had suffered from "hard study" for two years before her admission to Western State Lunatic Asylum in February 1850.

Gavin, a 21-year-old single laborer, was subject to both "religious excitement and disappointed love." Admitted to Western State in 1861, he died a year and a half later.

Rose, 27-year-old wife of a laborer, in 1853 was committed for "religious excitement."

Harley, an attorney, arrived at Western State in 1848. He was single and 27 years old, suffering from "hard study." He died in 1864.

In response to Stribling's request, the asylum's directors purchased "four acres of meadowland and 56 acres of upland adjacent to the hospital. They also provided the hospital with a piano, books, newspapers, and horse and carriage" (Wood 2004). Stribling observed that carriage rides calmed many patients, likely through a combination of mountain vistas and sensory motion of the carriage itself. By 1838 he replaced patients' coarse uniforms with clothes similar to those they'd worn before admission and installed warm baths, as he found that they soothed patients and aided in recovery. Later additions included a billiard table, ninepin bowling, chess, and checkers (Wood 2004). Stribling wrote, "the tones of a well-strung piano, the soothing melody of the flute and the enlivening notes of the violin, produced by a skillful performer, tranquilized the furious and animated and cheered those who were sometimes sad or gloomy" (Wood 2004).

Phoebe's troubles stemmed from the "death of her brother &c."

Jonathan, a blacksmith, was 60 years old and had health issues resulting from "loss of property by fraud."

Culbert, a baker from Germany who had moved to Virginia, was single when admitted in 1869 due to "disappointed love." Two years later he was buried at Western State, having suffered from "Melancholia. Death from suicide by hanging."

Jackson was 22 years old and had suffered from "unrequited love" for three years prior to his 1843 commitment.

Harrison, born in 1826, was a farmer. He served as a private in the Virginia First Infantry Battalion and mustered out of the Confederate Army on April 9, 1865, at Appomattox. Like others, the cause of his illness was listed simply as "the war."

After the Civil War, Stribling reported that Western State had been "exposed to trials and difficulties incident to a state of war, and its inmates subjected to privations, in common with families and individuals all around us. . . . Thanks, however, to a kind Providence, the efforts of those upon whom devolved the labor of procuring supplies, were so blessed that we do not believe a single member of our extensive household suffered any time with hunger or cold" (Allis 2011, 63). Attention to nutrition seems especially important as many patients were admitted for mental illnesses and died of malnutrition.

Richard was single and a schoolmaster. He was 27 years old when he was admitted to Western State in 1847. He lived there for two decades, his record noting, "Suicidal. Death from marasmus."

Elizabeth, wife of a miller, was born 1818. Admitted in 1854 at age 35 due to "ill health," she died within the year from marasmus. "Father & 2 aunts insane. Brother in [an] asylum."

James, born in Ireland ca. 1815, was a schoolteacher before being admitted to Western State at age 38. He succumbed 12 years later, dying in 1865. "Blind. Death from marasmus."

Marasmus is a wasting of the body caused by dietary inadequacies bringing about emaciation and severe malnutrition. Perhaps it's reasonable to heed Stribling's claim that "deranged" digestive systems often attended disordered minds. He noted that "a total loss of appetite and loathing of food" often plagued those suffering from psychological ailments (Wood 2004, Appendix C). Perhaps it's also reasonable to question, at some junctures, the sufficiency of diet afforded to patients.

The suffering of Richard, Elizabeth, James, and many others invites thinking about paradigms for illness generally and disability specifically, among them medical and social models. Medical models of disability assume that deficits in individuals are responsible for their inability to function as their "typical" peers do. Social models of disability, on the other hand, suggest that community failures to anticipate and plan for human variation are responsible for individuals' functional challenges. Medical models might attribute deaf people's inability to follow a film clip to a cochlear dysfunction, social models to a lack of captioning. The first would credit spinal cord injuries or congenital conditions for the inability of a wheelchair user to access a restaurant; the latter would look to design failures, such as an absence of ramps as an alternative to steps. To what extent was misery attributed to the body—to blindness, heredity, and melancholy—also a function of the society? As the following section shows, the extent to which communities have been willing to accommodate human variation has varied appreciably over the years.

LIRA: DELIRIUM AND THE SOCIAL FURROW

Theorist Michel Foucault in his classic study *Madness and Civilization* ([1961] 1999) found that in Europe during the early modern era, hospitals often became receptacles "for all the most monstrous and vile things to be found in society" including but not limited to the mentally or physically disabled (Foucault [1961] 1999, 202). Tropes of animality were applied to the poor and dispossessed as well as to the insane, the epileptic, the crippled. A French law passed in 1790 had entrusted to municipal bodies "the care of obviating and remedying the disagreeable events that may be occasioned by madmen set at liberty, and by the wandering of vicious and dangerous animals" (237). A hospital in Germany made the point explicit: "If wild beasts can be broken to the yoke, it must not be despaired of correcting the man who has strayed" (63). Such correction of the insane was thought to necessarily involve brutality, as a French psychological tract explained in 1834:

> Do not employ consolations, they are useless; have no recourse to reasoning, it does not persuade; do not be sad with melancholics; your sadness sustains theirs. . . . What is required is great sang-froid, and when necessary, severity. Let your reason be their rule of conduct. A single string still vibrates in them, that of pain; have courage enough to pluck it. (quoted in Foucault [1961] 1999, 182)

Through their commitment to moral medicine, Dr. Francis Stribling and his colleagues—at Western State and beyond— maintained an alternative. He wrote this of patients in 1837, "We neither starve nor torture them into reason; we meet them as friends and brothers; we cultivate their affections; interest their feelings; arouse their attention, and excite their hopes; we cheer the desponding, soothe the irritated . . .; in a word, we treat them as human beings, deserving of attention and care, rather than as criminals and outlaws" (Allis 2011, 11).

By the 1870s, however, with his career and life drawing to a close, Stribling saw change coming, as cure began losing ground to custody in popular and medical paradigms (Wood 2004). Locally, nationally, and internationally, the weight of opinion began shifting from thoughtful care to containment of danger. Themes of the animality of the insane, the poor, and the disabled sounded with growing volume and frequency in the United States—powerfully in Virginia—during the early twentieth century. Many physicians, educators, social workers, and legislators cited "the menace of the feebleminded," arguing that protecting the nation from the "encroachments of imbecility" and crime was a "matter of self-preservation" (Lombardo 2008, 17; Dorr 2008).

This move reflects an understanding of madness as "delirium," a word "derived from *lira*, a furrow; *deliro* actually means to move out of the furrow, away from the proper path of reason" (Foucault [1961] 1999, 99). Socially prescribed expectations ("furrows") could vary in width over time and across space. In much of Europe and the United States during the nineteenth and first half of the twentieth centuries, culturally condoned paths could be quite narrow, and one could stray from them—slipping out of the furrow—by doing too much or too little. Debauchery and laziness, too much drinking and too little initiative, could both be addressed in the asylum. It "reduces differences, represses vice, eliminates irregularities" and aims for "moral and social uniformity" (258–60).

> Wilton, a 28-year-old lawyer, was committed to Western State in 1850. His difficulties stemmed from "dissipation." He died from cerebral disease 15 days after admission.
>
> Talcott, a physician from a prominent family, was born in 1818. By mid-century, he and his wife held a large enslaved labor force and had built an imposing brick Greek Revival house. By 1860, Talcott was an inmate exhibiting "intemperance."

Solomon was a 65-year-old farmer who, in 1903, was suffering from "excessive use of whiskey, homicidal and suicidal mania."

By the last quarter of the nineteenth century and with increasing force into the first decades of the twentieth, imagining mental illness as hazardous—florid excess, personal failing, dogged immorality—swept into asylums like Western State. Where Stribling had seen himself as a "rational fellow being" gently guiding the ill back onto salubrious paths, his most notorious successor, Dr. Joseph DeJarnette, understood the asylum as a container of danger and himself as guardian of the national moral order (Foucault [1961] 1999, 205).

"THE INSANE BREED INSANE"

DeJarnette, director of Western State Hospital from 1906 until 1943, frequently on public occasions presented a poem that he'd penned in the 1920s.

MENDELS LAW:
A PLEA FOR A BETTER RACE OF MEN

Oh, why are you men so foolish—
    You breeders who breed our men
Let the fools, the weaklings and crazy
    Keep breeding and breeding again?
The criminal, deformed, and the misfit,
    Dependent, diseased, and the rest—
As we breed the human family
    The worst is as good as the best.
. . . .
Go to some homes in the village,
    Look at the garden beds,
The cabbage, the lettuce and turnips,
    Even the beets are thoroughbreds;
Then look at the many children
    With hands like the monkey's paw,
Bowlegged, flat headed, and foolish—
    Bred true to Mendel's law.

This is the law of Mendel,
    And often he makes it plain,
Defectives will breed defectives
    And the insane breed insane.
Oh, why do we allow these people
    To breed back to the monkey's nest,
To increase our country's burdens
    When we should only breed the best?

Oh, you wise men take up the burden,
    And make this you loudest creed,

Sterilize the misfits promptly—
  All not fit to breed!
Then our race will be strengthened and bettered,
  And our men and our women be blest,
Not apish, repulsive and foolish,
  For the best will breed the best.

(quoted in Dorr and *Dictionary of Virginia Biography* 2015)

DeJarnette was a vociferous leader in the eugenics crusade: a movement to regulate the population's "purity" by empowering medical, educational, and legal authorities to decide whether particular people were "fit to breed" (Dorr 2008). He presided at Western State as "a fiscal disciplinarian and iron-fisted manager over a facility that at one point house[d] more than three thousand patients. His role was one part medical patriarch, one part public scientist, and one part political moralist" (Lombardo 2008, 121). DeJarnette was confident in his ability "to navigate the muddy waters between madness and crime, illness and evil."

Among the most striking aspects of the eugenics campaign was the facility with which medical, moral, legal, and political strands of argument intertwined. As a medical doctor, DeJarnette declared that the reproduction of "defectives" was "a crime against their offspring and a burden to their state." He "decried those who constantly invoked 'the so-called inalienable rights of man'" to oppose compulsory sterilization of the "epileptic, imbecile, drunkard," and the poor (Lombardo 2008, 121).

Many American educational authorities joined their peers in law and medicine to advocate for eugenic cleansing of the populace. In the early twentieth century, Professor Harvey Jordan, who would become Dean of the University of Virginia's School of Medicine, found that 5% of the American populace were "seriously defective" and cited "overwhelming" evidence that their deficiencies were hereditable. Doctors could engineer "a perfect society constituted of perfect individuals" by sterilizing the unfit (Lombardo 2008, 210–11). Harry Laughlin, with a graduate degree in science from Princeton University, headed the Eugenics Record Office. At the First National Conference on Race Betterment in 1914, Laughlin presented a plan to eliminate "the great mass of defectives" who were "menacing our national efficiency and happiness." He determined that the lowest 10% of "'human stock' was so poorly prepared for civilization that its survival represented 'a social menace,'" and calculated that purifying the nation required 15 million sterilizations (47).

Similarities between these assertions and those of Nazi Germany are not coincidental. Eugenics movements in the United States—particularly in the Valley of Virginia—and Germany informed each other and shared rhetoric. The Virginia General Assembly authorized "sexual sterilization" of certain inmates in 1924 as part of the "Act to Preserve Racial Integrity." Adolf Hitler became Chancellor of Germany in 1933, and months later a "Law for the Prevention of Hereditarily Diseased Offspring" was passed (Lombardo 2008, 202). Like the physicians championing compulsory sterilization in Virginia to purify its human breeding stock, Hitler criticized his country for allowing the continued procreation of "monstrosities half-way between human and ape" and considered a policy preventing "defective people" from "propagating equally defective offspring" to be "a demand of the clearest reason and if systematically executed represents the most humane aspects of mankind" (201). At Western State, DeJarnette fretted that Nazi policies were more effective in eliminating the "unfit," and that the "Germans are beating us at our own game" (209).

"Education" had been a category rarely used on intake records at Western State during the Stribling era. Its inclusion became standard practice under DeJarnette, doubtless based on the assumption that academic accomplishment scaled with personal quality and fitness to reproduce.

> The intake record for Florence, a 15 year old, characterizes her as an "idiot" with no education (in 1907).
>
> Thirty-five-year-old Wendall had a "poor" education and arrived at Western State suffering from "starvation and acute mania" (1915).
>
> The causes of 37-year-old Emily's problems were "death of child"; she was "feeble minded," and she had no education (1919).

Like many of their peers, Florence, Wendall, and Emily entered through the gates of the asylum but never left. Their remains lie under blank concrete slabs in its cemetery, denigrated in life and anonymized in death.

In addition to education, family histories of "deficit" also weighed heavily on the institutionalized. While during the mid-nineteenth century, notation had sometimes been made that a sibling or parent was "insane," by the early twentieth century—with its focus on the supposed heredity of unfitness—this practice became more regular and extensive. This tendency didn't start with DeJarnette, who became superintendent of Western State in 1906, but he certainly continued and expanded it. Tracking these data was intended to document the role of heredity in perpetuating such social ills as parasitism and pauperism. Remarks on patient forms at Western State included such notations as "one fourth cousin insane," "very distant relatives insane," and "some connection on mother's side insane."

> Liddy suffered from "recurrent mania." Remarks: "Brothers and sister mentally defective" (1901).
>
> Victoria had "spinal disease and chronic mania. Aunt mentally defective. Grandfather epileptic" (1903).
>
> Lenore suffered from "recurrent mania." Her "sister drowned herself and two children. Mother eccentric" (1905).

Jeremiah was "congenitally deficient" and suffered from "imbecility. Great uncle insane and committed suicide" (1906).

Wyatt's difficulties were due to "heredity and melancholia. Uncle insane. Mother mentally defective" (1907).

Cordelia was admitted for "female troubles" and melancholia; nine years later she died from "pellagra and exhaustion from mania." Remarks: "Uncle and aunt now insane. Mother had puerperal insanity. Grandfather was in asylum" (1908).

Linda had "dementia with pellagra," and her "aunt was insane" (1909).

Silas's "imbecility" was "probably hereditary. Four cousins mentally defective" (1913).

Christopher's difficulties were rooted in "heredity and imbecility." Remarks: "Grandmother committed suicide" (1913).

Randall suffered from "melancholia" because of his "separation from wife and child." Remarks: "Uncle was insane" (1914).

These records gesture toward social factors and experiential contributors to patients' difficulties—spinal disease, nutritional deficiencies, the loss of a spouse and child—but still, consistent with medical models of disability, focus on the individual's supposed "defect." The *Oxford English Dictionary* defines the term as an imperfection, a failing, an abnormality. The "defectives" were abnormal: moving away from the norm, not conforming to type or standard. It's no coincidence that the language of eugenics echoes that of statistics. Their emergence and development were intertwined, starting with the foundational work of English polymath Francis Galton in the second half of the nineteenth century. Cousin of Charles Darwin (of "evolution by natural selection" fame), Galton was interested in heredity—including how genius might run in families—and in quantifying basically everything, particularly human intelligence. He's credited with helping to father both eugenics and statistics, twin tools to identify deviation. It's little wonder that so many patients viewed as "defective"—as harboring a hereditary abnormality—ended up numbered rather than named in the Western State cemetery.

THE COLONY: WHAT WAS LOST

Much like DeJarnette at Western State, early twentieth-century Superintendent Dr. Albert Priddy of the Virginia Colony for Epileptics and Feebleminded near Lynchburg combined prevailing medical, ethical, and economic strands of thinking to support compulsory sterilization of people he deemed "unfit." He considered his "feebleminded" charges a "blight on mankind" and warned that, unless "some radical measures are adopted" to prevent their procreation, "non-producing and shiftless persons" would become a "burden too heavy" for the public to bear (Lombardo 2008, 15).

FIGURE 3.5. Building 21, the Halsey Jennings Building, site of compulsory sterilizations. Central Virginia Training Center, formerly the Virginia Colony for Epileptics and Feebleminded, Madison Heights.

Theodore died at age 27 in 1935. The causes were "malnutrition and congenital idiocy."

Elsie was born on Valentine's Day in 1909 and died at the Colony on Christmas day, 1936. She was 27 years old. Principal causes of her death were heart failure and pleurisy; a contributing cause was "feeblemindedness."

Callie was 24 years old when she died at the Colony for Epileptics and Feebleminded in 1938. Records identify "the principal cause of death and related causes of importance" as "idiocy."

When Georgia arrived as a ten-year-old, her "last grade completed" was "none." She died five years later, in 1945, from tuberculosis and idiocy.

Violet had been at the Colony for 11 months when she died, in 1957, at two years of age. The causes were bronchopneumonia and mental retardation. The baby's remains were interred at the Colony cemetery.

Dr. John Bell, subsequent director of the Virginia Colony for Epileptics and Feebleminded and vice president of the American Psychiatric Association, in

1934 praised "the principle of genetic control" provided by Virginia law and called for a federal sterilization law in the United States similar to German law that "applied not merely to institutions but also to the country's entire population." Bell contended that such a far-reaching policy would provide "a vast advantage in the elimination of the unfit" and urged his countrymen to "apply the pruning knife with vigor" (Lombardo 2008, 208).

The eugenicists' dragnet was expansive, and nearly anyone could be trapped in it. In 1909, Virginia's Board of Charities and Corrections had sent teachers a checklist for identifying children "unfit for education in public schools." Telltale characteristics included blinking, cold and clammy hands and excessive pallor or blushing, slight malformation, carelessness, inattention, obstinacy, and imperfections of speech, sight, or hearing (Dorr 2008, 113–14). The survey results strengthened the case for establishing the Virginia Colony for the Epileptic and Feebleminded, designed to segregate and control the rising "army of defectives" (114).

Roy Williams was among those contained. He labored for decades on the farm at the Colony later called the Central Virginia Training Center (CVTC). He picked beans and tomatoes, planted trees, sacked potatoes, and scraped hog hair. Six days a week, his workday ran from 7:00 in the morning until 4:30 in the afternoon. He had one day a week to attend church, and he earned about a dollar a month (Woody 1999). People who knew him recognized him as "a willing worker," a "delight," and a "perfect gentleman" who had a good memory for faces; "his friendliness made him unforgettable" (Pegram, n.d. b.). Sometimes called the "mayor emeritus" of the institution, Williams was "a walking history book," recalling details of buildings and events and people who came and went at CVTC (Pegram, n.d. b.). Williams had arrived at the Colony in 1929 when he was 12 years old (Woody 1999) and remained for more than eight decades, dying in 2012 at age 94 (Laurant 2012).

For many years Williams had kept company with a special young woman who also lived at the institution. He recalled that she "was the same age as me" and that she "had style" (Pegram, n.d. b.). Williams, though, never married or had children. He had been sterilized when he turned 18.

Talking with a reporter late in life, Williams explained, "I've been sterilized. I think that's wrong." But "back in those days, you couldn't say anything about it. You can't say no."

Asked if he would have wanted children, Williams answered: "I don't believe I would. I can't talk. The baby might be like me."

In fact, he had a speech impediment or lisp and a slight limp, the latter perhaps from childhood polio. But he'd come to believe that people like him were better off not being born.

When Williams was a child, his mother had died of pneumonia. His father, a farmer, was left with four children. He kept the two girls, sent one son to relatives in Alexandria, and committed Roy to the Colony (Woolridge 2012). Roy occasionally visited family, but as his niece recalled, "as family members and friends passed away, Roy didn't come home as much. I remember those last few times. He was with us maybe several days when he said, 'I want to go home.' Roy had grown to love everyone at CVTC and considered it his home" (Woolridge 2012). CVTC administrator Mike Bryant agreed, noting that Roy had "had opportunities to leave [but] chose not to." Bryant continued, "It's hard to look at Roy and imagine what potential is not realized."

Roy Williams worked all his life—with sound body, sharp memory, charm, and kindness—but was sterilized without his consent. The "furrow" of social acceptability was so narrow at this time in Virginia history that a speech impediment was sufficient to render an energetically capable person "unfit" for most civic life. The unrealized potential—of Williams and hundreds of others—lies buried in the institution's cemetery.

INIQUITY

A long history interprets physical and mental disabilities as divine retribution for sin. Many have pointed to the Bible: "I the Lord thy God am a jealous God, visiting the iniquity of the fathers upon the children unto the third and fourth generation" (Exodus 20:5[18]). The ritual of the Church of Vienne, in seventeenth-century France, said, "It pleaseth Our Lord that thou shouldst be infected" with a malady as "he desireth to punish thee for thy iniquities in this world" (Foucault [1961] 1999, 6). Many in the eighteenth, nineteenth, and twentieth centuries maintained that "certain crimes . . . must absolutely be thrust into oblivion," along with the sinners, as "the honor of a family requires the disappearance from society of the individual who by vile and abject habits shames his relations" (Foucault [1961] 1999, 67).

> At her admission to Western State, Judie, a "widow's daughter," was 19 years old and had suffered "sexual derangement" for seven years. She remained there for 47 years until her death in 1911 from mitral regurgitation.
>
> Vivian, a married 28-year-old housewife, suffered from "excessive venery"—sexual indulgence (1894).
>
> Micah, 45-year-old farmer, had been afflicted with "alcoholism & sexual excess/acute mania" for "four or five years" before his 1896 admission. Remarks: "Father and uncle were insane."
>
> Jessie was admitted for "sexual excess and acute mania." Remarks: "Aunt & grandmother insane. All are mentally defective" (1902).

American eugenicists viewed poor mental health as "the psychological effect of a moral fault" (Foucault [1961] 1999, 158). They argued that mental defects proved "there must have been sin," a robust, hereditary strain of iniquity (Lombardo 2008, 8). Dr. John Harvey Kellogg (cereal magnate) in 1884 opined that "the throngs of deaf, blind, crippled, idiotic unfortunates" along with the "dwarfed, diseased, and constitutionally weak individuals, are the lamentable results of the violation of some sexual law on the part of their progenitors." Like other eugenicist physicians, Kellogg was self-appointed judge and jury of moral standards. Combining moral and medical language, he asserted that abnormal children had been "begotten in lust" (Lombardo 2008, 10; Foucault [1961] 1999, 261).

Another physician fulminated particularly against masturbation in the *Boston Medical and Surgical Journal* and elsewhere: "From the hand of God himself we receive the noble attributes which distinguish us from the animals around us. This vice reduces us below their level" (quoted in Bainbridge 1984, 230). Many in the medical field pointed to the biblical story of Onan as the source of the injunction against autoeroticism or "onanism":

> Er, Judah's firstborn, was wicked in the sight of the Lord, and the Lord slew him. And Judah said unto Onan, "Go in unto thy brother's wife, and marry her, and raise up seed to thy brother. . . ." And it came to pass, when he went in unto his brother's wife, that he spilled it on the ground. . . . And the thing which he did displeased the Lord: wherefore he slew him also. (Genesis 38:7–10)

This passage seems to describe, not necessarily masturbation, but rather premature ejaculation or coitus interruptus—that Onan intended to deprive his brother's widow of heirs who might have competed with his own for family resources. The part of the story upon which eugenicists as medical moralists seized was not having intercourse with one's dead brother's wife but "spilling seed." If conceiving children in lust resulted in their "abnormality," how much more clearly self-gratification pointed to a depraved, animalistic lack of control or moral compass.

Not all, though, accepted assertions that disability was the cost of moral deviance. In the Valley of Virginia, some were quite clear to the contrary.

BUT THE BERKELEYS

John Hill Berkeley is one of the rare former patients buried at Western State who has a personalized gravestone. In the 1850 federal census, John Berkeley was 15 years old. He had eight siblings. Thomas, the eldest, was 19 and listed as having no occupation. One more brother and six sisters ranged in age from 17 to two, and all lived with their parents in Hanover County. Edmund Berkeley, head of the household, was a farmer.[19]

John Berkeley volunteered for the Confederate cause in 1861. He served in Nelson's and Kirkpatrick's Companies of the Virginia Light Artillery.[20] They were active in Early's Valley Campaign, Cold Harbor, and Gettysburg (National Park Service n.d.) When, years later, Berkeley applied for a pension as a Con-

FIGURE 3.6. Unlike hundreds of anonymous grave markers behind them, the gravestones of Fannie C. Hines (1868–1913) and John H. Berkeley (1834–1913) include their names, birth and death years, and epitaphs. Western State Hospital Cemetery, Staunton.

federate veteran, he said that he'd lived in Virginia all his life and that he had suffered no sickness during the war ("was <u>always</u> with my company"). In answer to the question, "How long were you in the service?" Berkeley responded, "The whole way."[21]

By 1870, John H. Berkeley was back at home, farming. His widowed 60-year-old mother was the head of household, and two of his unmarried sisters also lived with them.[22] The 1880 census was much the same: John was a farmer living with his mother and three unmarried sisters.[23] By 1910, John was 75 years old. He lived with his widowed brother Henry, a public school teacher who at age 70 was listed as head of the household. Living with them were their single sisters: Louise was 73, and Susan was 66.[24]

In 1912, John Berkeley was admitted to Western State. He was 78 years old and died less than a year later of pneumonia.[25] This gravestone was erected over his burial in the asylum cemetery: "John H. Berkeley, 1834–1913. A dutiful son. A fond brother. A kind friend. A good Confederate soldier, always faithful to his duty, however disagreeable, arduous or dangerous. At Peace" (Figure 3.6).

John's older brother, Thomas N. Berkeley, had been laid to rest in Western

State cemetery 13 years earlier (1900). He'd been admitted in 1851, aged 20 and suffering from "disappointed love."[26] Thomas resided at the asylum for nearly 50 years. When he died in 1900, his family erected this stone: "Thomas N., Son of E & S. Berkeley of Hanover Co. Va. Nov. 22, 1830. Neither parents nor this man sinned, but this happened that the works of God should be made manifest in him."

The Berkeley family's move of young Thomas to the asylum was not the casting of a "defective" into social oblivion. Even after he'd been there half a century, siblings still claimed him as part of the fold, linking him to parents and to his home county. They refused any inference that his disability was a function of immorality. Thomas Berkeley's inscription comes from the Bible; when his disciples asked Jesus, "Who sinned, this man or his parents, that he was born blind?" Jesus answered, "Neither" (John 9:2-3).[27] The works of God were manifest in this man. Difference was not punishment for iniquity. It was divine design.

NEGOTIATING LEGACIES:
FALL FROM GRACE AND MARTYRDOM

During their lifetimes, eugenicists like Joseph DeJarnette, superintendent of Western State, and institutionalized patients like Carrie Buck, patient at the State Colony, claimed very different amounts of influence, power, and respect. The apotheosis of DeJarnette—the nearly godlike power he commanded over the fate and freedom of inmates—has suffered a dramatic reversal in recent decades. His fall from grace indeed is the mirror opposite of Carrie Buck's public image, transformed from "defective" to much-loved martyr.

Carrie Buck's mother, Adeline Emma Harlow Buck (1872–1944),[28] had been committed to the Colony as promiscuous and feebleminded (White and Hofland 2004a). Carrie had been placed with a foster family and, at age 17, gave birth to a daughter she named Vivian. It's likely that Carrie Buck had been raped by a relative of her foster parents, but DeJarnette and other eugenicists regarded her pregnancy as evidence that she'd inherited her mother's promiscuity. They arranged for a nurse to examine Carrie's six-month-old daughter, Vivian; the nurse concluded that "there is a look about it that is not quite normal" (Dorr 2008, 131). The evaluation procedure included moving a coin in front of the baby's face. Vivian's eyes focused not on the coin but on the camera documenting her reactions, and thus "was declared an imbecile" (White and Hofland 2004a). Medical authorities averred that the Buck line should not be allowed to continue as they were members of "the shiftless, ignorant, and worthless class of anti-social whites of the South" (White and Hofland 2004a).

The case, knowns as Buck v. Bell (the latter being superintendent of the State

Colony) appeared before the United States Supreme Court in 1927. It centered on the question of whether Carrie Buck of Charlottesville could be sterilized against her will. Affirming the legality of Virginia's compulsory eugenics law, Justice Oliver Wendell Holmes declared, "It is better for all the world, if instead of waiting to execute degenerate offspring for crime or to let them starve for their imbecility, society can prevent those who are manifestly unfit from continuing their kind. . . . Three generations of imbeciles are enough" (White and Hofland 2004b). This decision cleared the way for the institutionalization and compulsory sterilization of tens of thousands of Americans.

DeJarnette pursued the eugenic agenda with gusto at Western State. The Virginia General Assembly honored him in 1932 by naming one division of the institution the "DeJarnette State Sanitarium" (Dorr and *DVB* 2015).

Now in the twenty-first century, the DeJarnette buildings are abandoned and shuttered. They stand high on the landscape along a main entry to Staunton. New construction abounds around them, but the sanitarium remains untouched.

DeJarnette is buried in rural Bath County. His grave marker identifies him as "Dr. Joseph S. DeJarnette, 1866–1957, Physician and Friend of the Mentally Sick." He's "memorialized" on a popular website, Find a Grave (findagrave. com), as "eugenicist," a "proponent and practitioner of compulsory sterilization" whose "lobbying on behalf of eugenics influenced the German Nazi Party's ideology."[29] Joseph DeJarnette has three "flowers" or notes of memory left on his Find a Grave website. His wife, Dr. Chertsey DeJarnette, has one.[30] The couple had no children.

Carrie Buck Detamore died in 1983 and was buried in Charlottesville's municipal Oakwood Cemetery with her husband, Charles A. Detamore. Her online memorial notes that she was "the first of 65,000 Americans . . . sterilized without their own consent or that of a family member. . . . She is loved and dearly missed."[31] Some sixty "flowers" or notes have been left to Carrie online, among them:

God bless you and keep you. I think of you every time I pass "The Colony."[32]

Let us pray that the future undoes all these wrongs to the disabled and they all live dignified lives.[33]

Rest in peace, Carrie. There are many of us trying to make sure that this history is not forgotten and never repeated.[34]

I am sorry.[35]

You are remembered today.[36]

Miss you Carrie.[37]

Death and time have reversed social valuations of Joseph DeJarnette and Carrie Buck. He is, to many, a case study in the fallibility of authority, in the rippling devastation made possible by the presumption to determine who's "fit" for representation in future generations. She is, to many, a case study in suffering from the abuse of authority, from the misguided arrogance of classism, and from the misogyny of blaming girls as promiscuous when sexually assaulted. With the distance of their deaths, it's clear how many deficits were imagined to dwell in one girl, rather than in the social body.

REDEMPTION AT THE COLONY

David Cole was the facility administrator at the CVTC, formerly the Virginia State Colony for Epileptics and Feebleminded, until it closed in 2020. When I visited in 2018, Cole explained, "We often hear from families, 'We're so glad you were here to care for our loved one when we no longer could.'"[38] To him, the cemetery is "interesting, neat, reverent." Staff maintained it through regular mowing and trimming weeds. Nearly all of the headstones are rectangular granite markers, flush to the ground, with the names and birth and death dates of the interred. These were installed beginning in the 1980s (Steenburgh 2016) for new interments and to replace deteriorating stones of people buried earlier. In recent years, per family direction, remains of some former residents have been cremated, and then buried in plots or scattered near the cemetery's focal point,[39] a wooden cross on a small hilltop, surrounded by a low stone wall and, in the spring, flowers. In the majority of cases, the family asked the CVTC campus chaplain to perform a memorial or funeral service, and the deceased was interred on campus. A smaller proportion had their own pastor conduct the ceremony at CVTC, or had the remains returned for burial in their home communities. "We say," Cole observed, "that family and CVTC family" come to patients' funerals. "Staff always attend the funerals conducted on campus, and routinely attend if the family decides to have the person buried at a cemetery closer to their home." One memorial service was so large—so many coming to pay their respects—that it had to be conducted in the campus auditorium.

David Wayne Carter was born in Lexington in 1958.[40] When he was five years old, he went to live at CVTC. Carter's cerebral palsy became more pronounced over time, and a reporter who interviewed him in the mid-1990s—when, at age 36, he'd lived at the Center for 31 years—explained, "He cannot walk. He has almost no control of his hands. His speech is undecipherable to those who don't know him well" (Pegram, n.d. a). A joy in his life had been food—ice cream and roast turkey—but in 1990 surgeons implanted a feeding tube to save his life, meaning that he lost the pleasures of eating and tasting. "I wanted to die," Carter told his psychologist, Wanda Steele. Her office was next to his room, and she worked with him to express his feelings about the feeding tube and other aspects of his life. Together they created a book

painstakingly authored by David, as told to Steele in his difficult speech. Often their collaboration was a matter of his repeating words and of her asking if what he said is what she understood. "If he tells me a sentence, I say, 'I got the first two words. Don't say those words again. Let's work on the next word'—until we've got the whole sentence."

This process enabled David to share what it's like "to be hurt when you can't protect yourself. To make lasting friendships. To live in an institution and love your family" (Pegram, n.d. a.).

Carter passed in 2006 after some 42 years at CVTC. A "Celebration of David's Life" was held in the campus auditorium. His family suggested that attendees wear blue, his favorite color, and that contributions could be made to CVTC for a memorial fund so that a dogwood could be planted on campus in his memory.[41]

People who'd known and loved David Carter—many of them having been his caregivers—wrote messages online. Among them,

> I grew up with David as my special "other brother." My mother was his "Momma Hutch" and David's triumphs and heartaches were as much a part of our family life as were those of the four other children my mother raised. David faced challenges the rest of us could only imagine, but his spirit never flagged and his love and concern for the special people in his life always took precedence over any worry for himself. My siblings and I learned a great deal from David and also from my mother's unflagging devotion to him. . . . And if I ever think that I have a good excuse for sending my Mom's birthday or Mother's Day card late, I'll remind myself that David was ALWAYS on time.[42]

David Carter and Carrie Buck were institutionalized at the same place but at different times and with very different experiences. The contrast demonstrates how plastic understandings of disability are, and how much hinges not on individual difference but on social constructs.

"THE WRONG KIND OF CREATURE"

The Virginia State Colony for Epileptics and Feebleminded: Poems, Molly McCully Brown's award-winning book of poems, imagines the experiences of inmates and the thoughts of their caregivers—nurses, doctors, priests, parents—during the 1930s.

One poem begins, "This child is without a mind," comparing the disabled girl to the skin shed by a cicada—"It's just like that:/ useless approximations of live things/ littered on the beds as I make my rounds." The doctor wonders, "What sin warrants a blown brain,/ a lame body?" (Brown 2017, 13).

In another poem, Brown has parents deciding to baptize their disabled daughter, as "even half-wits might well have a soul to save." Holding her head under water, the parent prays, "Take her up and let her be the end of it./ Put some distance between our bodies and hers. Take her out of our hands." And the narrator wonders about the "force or fate" that "made me like this" (Brown 2017, 36).

In a poem called "The Convulsions Choir," an inmate thinks while in church, "I'd like to take the hands of the other/ epileptic girls & lead them/ up toward the altar,/ humming and weaving/ our arms together/ like chains. I wonder if . . . we could lie down & demand/ to be raptured, or healed, to return/ to safer bodies, or to dust" (Brown 2017, 41). Another narrator concludes, "I am the wrong/ kind of creature/ for this world" (49).

This world, twentieth-century America, was the wrong place for many people with developmental or intellectual disabilities, physical differences or disorders. Brown's poems about "the Colony" are particularly poignant because "by some accident of luck or grace,/ some window less than half a century wide,/ it is my backyard but not what happened/ to my body" (Brown 2017, 4). She says she's her "own kind of damaged . . ./ spastic, palsied and off-balance." Brown grew up with her family some 15 miles from this institution and, given her cerebral palsy (Garner 2017), would likely have been relegated and buried there had she been born just decades earlier.

Instead, Brown attended Stanford and earned an MFA in poetry from the University of Mississippi. Critics find her poems "beautiful and devastating" and compare her work favorably to that of James Agee and Elizabeth Bishop (Garner 2017). Making social space for difference has allowed Brown's intellectual, poetic power to enrich the world.

A LAST GLIMPSE OF WESTERN STATE

In the second half of the twentieth century, new buildings were erected for patients at Western State Hospital. Some of the old spaces were temporarily repurposed as a penitentiary; some have been rehabilitated as a high-end hotel and condominiums. The last patients buried in the Western State cemetery are at the top of the hill, looking down on thousands of their predecessors. The great majority of graves in this viewshed are anonymous—numbers having washed off where names never were—as the cement markers crumble and the iron bars inside them rust.

But four of the final interments included not only the names and dates of the deceased, but also words of kindness in their memory. Two of them were Black; the other two were White. They had lived long lives, never married, and suffered from diverse illnesses.

This is how they are memorialized:

A Place of Rest for Lloyd Y. Berry (1896–1981)
Peace, Dwelling Place for Eternity, James A. Douglas (1909–1981)

Quiet Peace for Ernest N. Jenkins (1895–1980)

Someone Cared for Mary L. Craig (1893–1979) (Figure 3.7)

They sit at the crest of the cemetery's hill, looking over the graves of fellow patients like John and Thomas Berkeley and others we met at the start of this chapter—Ann Carrington Cabell Flournoy and Fannie C. Hines—and thousands of their nameless peers.

Berry, Douglas, Jenkins, and Craig were born as Stribling's compassionate moral medicine lost ground, and DeJarnette's strident eugenics gained it. In the end, though, their resting places were blessed with sentiments that Stribling espoused: Someone cared for them. They were loved.

As an anthropologist, I'm fascinated by the shifting cultural views of cognitive and bodily difference, particularly as articulated so crisply in the Valley of Virginia and adjacent places and burying grounds. Cultural relativism is an intellectual proposition central to the discipline: perceiving diverse cultural constructions of reality enables us to understand actions that might otherwise seem illogical. To take a pair of examples beyond asylum grounds—a wealthy Federal-era civic leader in Harrisonburg has a modest gravestone; a child who was part of a poorer, working family is memorialized more elaborately. These mortuary decisions are explicable as we look toward cultural understandings of

FIGURE 3.7. One of the last burials in Western State Hospital Cemetery affirms that "Someone Cared for Mary L. Craig, Born 1893, Died Nov. 9, 1979." Staunton.

thrift, on the one hand, and the bad death of a little girl on the other. Memorials, like other forms of material culture, are viewed through varying cultural lenses. The first headstone is not intended to represent a life's accomplishments; the second is a manifestation of grief over a great loss. A grave marker in the abstract may have no intrinsic meaning—it can be different things to different people. Meaning is projected onto it, and actions toward it vary accordingly. Perhaps the thrifty eighteenth-century alderman's plain headstone merits a flag on Independence Day, but the two-year-old who succumbed recently to leukemia has a dark, gleaming granite marker shaped like a castle with two turrets. Fabric flowers, angels, crosses, and smooth rocks painted with flowers and bears rest on her grave, as do bottles of bubbles and a battery-powered bubble blower. These two headstones, these resting places, are viewed and treated differently because the two deaths were culturally framed in divergent ways.

FIGURE 3.8. Author's son, Alone Community Cemetery, Rockbridge County.

But what of the man himself, or the girl herself, or the patients at Western State or the Virginia Colony? People—like headstones, like bars of iron, like slabs of cement—can also be culturally constructed. We learn to view each other: how to think of the elderly, of babies, of the disabled. As this chapter has shown, people who lived in the Valley of Virginia during the nineteenth and twentieth centuries and who experienced mental illness or disability were envisioned through different cultural lenses: as fellow travelers lost in the woods, on the one hand, or on the other as "defectives." How far are we willing to extend cultural-relativist analyses of individuals who were committed to, died in, and were buried behind Valley-area asylums? Are people—like stones, grass, and iron—tabulae rasae? If they don't have intrinsic "meaning"—whatever that might be—do they all, equally and inevitably have intrinsic value, independent and regardless of divergent cultural framings?

The American Anthropological Association's "Code of Ethics" suggests some answers. The morality of studying human beings can be complicated and fraught, as anthropologists "are members of many different communities, each with its own moral rules or codes of ethics. Anthropologists have moral obligations as members of other groups, such as the family, religion, and community, as well as the profession. They also have obligations to the scholarly discipline, to the wider society and culture, and to the human species," but our first obligation is "to avoid harm or wrong" (American Anthropological Association 2009). I take these injunctions to mean that cultural imaginings of human beings as less than human—as defective, as abnormal, as being beyond the social furrow—are not ones we simply analyze with dispassionate interest. It's alright, professionally appropriate, and even expected to acknowledge that some cultural constructions have caused harm through dehumanization.

This intellectual position sits comfortably with my view as the mother of a young man who thinks, talks, and moves in ways that diverge from the norm. And my hope for him is that he can enjoy and end his days—long years hence—with the simple statement inscribed on the gravestones of the last people buried at Western State: he was cared for, appreciated, and loved.

CHAPTER 4

"The Colored Dead"

African American Burying Grounds

WHERE THE SOUTH WENT TO DIE

Lexington, Virginia, goes vernacularly by many names: "Lex Vegas" and "Metro Lex," terms used cheekily by college students accustomed to more urban climes. "Mayberry PhD," the small, rural town inhabited largely by professors and retirees and others with lots of letters after their names. More snarkily, "the land of taxidermied horses" and "Confederate Landia" after the southern generals and their respective steeds laid to rest locally.

After General Robert E. Lee surrendered, conceding defeat of the Confederate States of America, he accepted the presidency of Lexington's Washington College, the institution that was rechristened "Washington and Lee University" (W&L) after his death. Today countless visitors amble on campus, many of them Civil War buffs with special interest in the University Chapel—known until recently as "Lee Chapel"—and museum and the Lee family mausoleum. The chapel's focal point is the life-sized marble recumbent Lee; for many of W&L's most revered events—inductions in honor societies, for example, or lectures by visiting international intellectual celebrities—the audience has looked squarely at the carved image of deceased General Lee. He's buried in an adjacent

FIGURE 4.1. Visitors leave coins on Traveller's grave outside of the Lee Mausoleum. Washington and Lee University, Lexington.

vault, along with family members. Just outside is the grave of Lee's faithful horse, Traveller. People leave pennies and apples on the animal's resting place (Figure 4.1). Newcomers to the W&L community are warned that the doors to Traveller's stable—adjacent to the house built for Lee and otherwise known as the University president's garage—must always remain open so that the steed's spirit can come and go at will.

Close by in Lexington rest the remains of General Thomas Stonewall Jackson—all except his left arm that was shot accidentally by his troops, amputated, and buried near Chancellorsville, Virginia, with its own memorial: "Arm of Stonewall Jackson May 3, 1863." The mortal balance of General Jackson survived another week and reposes under the great, fenced, central monument—a full-size bronze version of himself—at a cemetery that was named in his honor: Stonewall Jackson Memorial. In 2020, Lexington City Council voted to change the cemetery's name to "Oak Grove," as it had been known in earlier times. The change invited immense debate, much of it vitriolic, and some of it suggesting the negative impact that removing Jackson's name from the Main Street burying ground could have on tourism dollars. Thousands of people visit the cemetery; some bring him gifts of lemons, as he'd purportedly enjoyed and appropriated, when opportunity arose, lemons from enemy stores. The mounted hide of Jackson's horse, Little Sorrel, enjoys a career nearby at Virginia Military Institute (VMI) Museum; a lovely lane in a high-end part of town carries the gelding's name.

What few sightseers see, what's off radar for most students at Lexington's elite universities, is Evergreen Cemetery: the green, serene resting place of local African Americans since the 1880s. Evergreen is on a on a dead-end street, behind a gas station. Though the town selected a peripheral space for the "colored" cemetery, generations of African American families have beautified, cherished, and sacralized it.

Before Evergreen's establishment in 1881, African Americans were buried in a segregated Lexington city cemetery, near current-day Marble Lane. Among those interred in this "Colored Grave Yard" was enslaved man James Lewis, a "large and handsome mulatto" who had acted as Jackson's cook during the war and cared for him when mortally wounded (Jordan 1995, 194–95). While Jackson's monument towers over the cemetery that was named in his honor, Lewis's grave, across town, is unmarked and its specific location uncertain; in 1880 Lexington Town Council exchanged half of the cemetery for three acres outside of town, banning further burial in the original cemetery. In 1946 the Town of Lexington sold the balance of the old cemetery for development, noting that any human remains encountered would be moved to Evergreen. Controversy persists over how many, if any, remains of the "colored dead" were actually relocated or what happened to them when houses were built (Williams 2007). Undoubtedly, their burying ground was erased from the visible landscape.

Such eradication is not unique to Lexington. In this and other parts of Virginia, many African American burying grounds "have been buried by modern construction or are long forgotten in the surrounding overgrowth" (Rainville 2014, 17). The latter tends to happen when rural economies can no longer support small farmers or business owners, obliging many African American families to move to larger markets. Too few descendants might remain in the

FIGURE 4.2. Grave sites, including those of Confederate veterans, are well maintained at the Fishersville United Methodist Church. Augusta County.

FIGURE 4.3. Grave sites, including that of veteran John Flipping (1894–1967), are obscured by fallen leaves and branches at Ebenezer Methodist Church Cemetery. Augusta County.

area to maintain cemeteries or keep church congregations viable. Dean Amy Tillerson-Brown of Mary Baldwin University notes that municipalities, too, have often expended fewer resources on Black than White cemeteries (Calello 2022).

Fishersville, a town in Augusta County, has a pair of Methodist church cemeteries, one traditionally Black and one White. Confederate veterans are among those buried in the latter (Figure 4.2). The grave of Eppa Fielding (1835–1910), for example, has a shining iron "Southern Cross of Honor" and a crisp American flag. He is remembered, kept present on the landscape. The same isn't true at the nearby Black Methodist church property. Graves are obscured in brambles—including those of John Flipping (1894–1967), who served in World War I,[1] and World War II veteran Hubert William Salisbury (1920–1974)[2] (Figure 4.3). Memorials to these African American veterans and their families—their graveyard—have vanished from the landscape.

The story of Fishersville's churches appears across the length and breadth of the Valley. In the Glasgow area of Rockbridge County, for example, historic Falling Spring Presbyterian Church maintains its perch on a picturesque, manicured hill. The brick church is well known for its architecture and bucolic setting, as well as the prominence of many White people buried there (Figure 4.4).

The nearby African American cemetery is much harder to find. Freed people built a wooden church, Mount Lydia, near Falling Spring soon after the Civil War

FIGURE 4.4. Falling Spring Presbyterian Church Cemetery, Rockbridge County.

ended. For many years they worshiped there, educated children there, socialized, and gathered to mourn and bury the dead. As in so many places, lack of economic opportunity and other factors made remaining in the area difficult or impossible, and when the church burned down, members of the already contracted congregation joined other places of worship. And so, no one was left to cut the grass or pick up branches when they fell. Trees and brambles grew up, fallen leaves covered fieldstone markers, and even some of the professionally carved gravestones tilted or toppled. But in the spring, the baby's breath, periwinkle, yucca, daffodils, and cedar trees planted by headstones still thrive (see Rainville 2014, 49).

STRUCTURE AND AGENCY

We Americans like to think that we occupy a meritocracy: the land of Horatio Alger and countless others who—though born poor—worked hard and "made it." But relationships between effort and success are complicated and don't exist in a vacuum; dynamics of class position, educational opportunity, access to family resources, and others smooth the path for some and make it nearly impassable for others.

Robert E. Lee, for example, was by all accounts brilliant and hard working. He was also the son of General Henry Lee III, Governor of Virginia, and Anne Hill Carter, members of some of Virginia's very most elite colonial families. Henry and Anne had been married in 1793 at her ancestral home, the majestic manor house at Shirley Plantation in eastern Virginia (Korda 2014, 1–26). Robert E. Lee also married well. His wife, Mary Anna Randolph Custis, was a relation of George and Martha Washington; Lee inherited through marriage not only Arlington House (a.k.a. the Custis-Lee Mansion) but also enslaved humans (Korda 2014, 51–57). In other words, Lee had rare advantages in pedigree, connections, and education. That his remains ended up in a mausoleum on a campus bearing his name owed a great deal to this luck of legacy.

Thomas Jonathan Stonewall Jackson's pedigree was rather less illustrious, but nevertheless he enjoyed advantages of education and freedom that his African American contemporaries lacked. Jackson's grandfather had been a colonel in the American Revolution (Jackson and Meyers 2011). His father was an attorney but died young, and Jackson was raised mostly by his uncles before gaining acceptance to the US Military Academy at West Point. There he distinguished himself for his determination and work ethic; later he accepted a teaching position at Virginia Military Institute and married the daughter of the president of Washington College, later named Washington and Lee University (Piston 2021).

Lee and Jackson worked hard and both knew difficulties: Lee's father faced financial problems, and Jackson's father died early. Their grit and smarts were key to their success. But no identical amount of grit and smarts on the part of enslaved Virginians would have resulted in military commissions, university positions, or reverential Main Street tourist venues being named in their memory.

"Agency" means decisions people make and actions they take (Wobst 2000, 41). Agency is tangled up with—it's informed by but sometimes fights against and also affects—structure: the legal, economic, educational, cultural, and political systems into which people are thrust by virtue of birth and luck or tragedy of circumstance (Tarlow 1999, 26; Dobres and Robb 2000). Structures commonly constrain some and disable others, depending on the social positions they happen to occupy (Barrett 2000, 61; Walker and Lucero 2000, 131). Successes are indeed personal successes; individuals can credit their own efforts for determining to stay on the team or with the job, or volunteering to work on weekends, or staying late at the lab or library to get the assignment right. But, too, if honest, these "winners" can cast a grateful eye back to the family, community, and educational or other structures that supported them: parents who drove to school or practice year in and year out, grandparents or teachers or neighbors who tutored or encouraged or provided meals. A good school system, or effective public transportation, or enough food, or a safe place to sleep—not everyone has had those supports or enjoys those structural advantages. Successes are also in part lucky breaks (Johnson 2000).

Anthropologists Philippe Bourgois and Jeff Schonberg (2009) show, in vivid ethnographic and photographic clarity, how intelligent, able-bodied individuals can find themselves homeless heroin addicts through combinations of such structural factors as family instability, food insecurity, physical abuse, and poverty that put childcare, healthcare, transportation, and affordable housing beyond their reach. Anthropologist Jason De León (2015) and photographer Michael Wells similarly create an extraordinarily powerful set of narratives and images in *The Land of Open Graves: Living and Dying on the Migrant Trail*. Readers come to glimpse the enormity of the desperation and brutality that threatens to consume people despite their intelligence, motivation, and devotion to family. Happenstance—the geography of their birth—leaves even the brightest with no good options. Folklorist Henry Glassie (1982), likewise, documented the wit and work ethic among poor Ulster farmers who, given other circumstances, might have become well-heeled attorneys, merchants, or bankers. The same proportion of brilliance to mediocrity appears, Glassie said, around farm tables, and at faculty meetings. The great scientist Stephen Jay Gould pointed to this role of circumstance in enabling or constraining personal capacity when he famously observed, "I am, somehow, less interested in the weight and convolutions of Einstein's brain than in the near certainty that people of equal talent have lived and died in cotton fields and sweatshops" (Gould 1980, 151). When Leila Janah, daughter of Indian immigrants to the U.S., worked in Mumbai and Ghana during 2005, she witnessed the "tragedy of talented and hard-working people struggling in poverty solely due to geographical isolation from well-paying jobs" (The Leila Janah Foundation 2021). Janah is credited with the observation that "talent is equally distributed; opportunity is not."

The following glimpses into lives of African Americans in and around Lexington, Virginia, invite thinking about articulations between agency and structure: about how people worked, evaluated, and planned, and how they were also enmeshed in socio-legal systems that persistently assumed racial inequality. From slavery to segregated schools, from limited economic opportunities to perceptions of young Black men as dangerous, from the Depression to the draft for World War II, enslaved people and their emancipated descendants strove in fields of forces well beyond their own making.

WHEN OTHERS MEMORIALIZE THE "COLORED DEAD"

In the corner of Lexington's Oak Grove (formerly Stonewall Jackson Memorial) Cemetery lie the remains of Davy Buck: "Died Feb. 27, 1855 Agd 85 Yrs[.] Fourty Yrs, Sexton of the Presbyterian Church. Belonged To the Estate of Matthew Hanna Decd."

Buck was buried at a different angle than others (Smith 2020, 163) and on the farthest edge of this cemetery that he had tended, as an enslaved person, for four decades. Before becoming the city's cemetery, this burying ground had been associated with the Presbyterian church. The people with authority to bury him here could only have been White, and doubtless it was their choice to memorialize him by acknowledging the man who legally owned him. The rare "marble markers on the graves of black slaves were undoubtedly" purchased by White people and express cultural values of the owners, not the enslaved community (Little 1998, 36; Fletcher 2020, 133).

This tendency extends into the postbellum era. In rural, mountainous Bath County, the George W. Cleek Cemetery includes a headstone for the "Colored Servants of John & Jane Gwin Cleek & John & Sallie Kime Cleek. Jerry 1821–1863. Dafney 1812–1873" (Figure 4.5). Neither Jerry nor Dafney are mentioned as having last names (see Smith 2020, 168–74). Decades later in Augusta County just north of Rockbridge, another stone acknowledges White agency: "Luly Walker Smith. Died Oct 24, 1923 Aged About 65 years. Erected by her White Friends." Smith's gravestone is in a small historically Black cemetery behind a bank and trust parking lot. The Reconstruction-era church associated with the cemetery no longer survives, and visitors can only access the cemetery—or bury the recently dead—with some difficulty, as no maintained road exists. Here on Smith's stone, as in much of the South, epitaphs for African Americans "stress attachment to employers or masters but rarely to family, friends, or black institutions" (Baugher and Veit 2014, 171).

FIGURE 4.5. George W. Cleek Cemetery, Bath County.

Cedar Hill Church and Cemetery in Murat, in Rockbridge County (southwest of Lexington), was established in 1874, and its cemetery remains in use. The congregation and community thrived until the 1920s, when many members moved to larger towns hoping for better educational and economic opportunities (Pezzoni 2001). Although the church is not regularly used, members of the historically Black First Baptist Church in Lexington hold an annual homecoming at Cedar Hill, and in 2009 they welcomed to its cemetery remains of thirty people whose resting place had been disrupted by highway expansion. A single large stone was erected:

> The remains reinterred here/ Are from one of the many/ Unmarked African-American/ Cemeteries in Virginia. It was/ Located on land owned by/ The Gibson and Lackey/ Families. Archaeologists/ Excavated 30 burials dating/ Circa 1855 to 1895. Based on/ Census records, it appears/ That the African-American/ Families in the nearby Timber /Ridge Community may have/ Been employed as day/ Laborers at the Gibson/ Distillery or as farmers on/ One of the Gibson's many/ Properties. It appears burials/ Ceased when the land on/ Which the cemetery is/ Located was sold to the / Lackey family in 1895[.]/ The descendants of Cedar Hill/ Church offer this historic/ Cemetery as a final resting/ Place for these burial remains[.] REST IN PEACE / Erected 2009."

The thirty African American people buried here are anonymous. The White Gibson and Lackey families are each named three times. The contrast stems from White people's greater visibility in historic records, but the stone, ironically and unintentionally, foregrounds them in memorializing their Black neighbors.

Excavation revealed thirty grave shafts, but the preservation conditions were very poor (Louis Berger Group 2009). In many cases, the bone had deteriorated altogether, and only in a minority of burials did skeletal material suggest the age or sex of the deceased. Excavators made a strong case, based on archaeological as well as archival materials, that this cemetery was used during the second half of the nineteenth century.

The remains had been interred in a cemetery at an intersection of parcels owned by the interrelated Gibson and Lackey families in Rockbridge County (Louis Berger Group 2009). John Beard Gibson (1806–1890) owned one of these tracts ca. 1829–1892; his son John Alexander Gibson (1833–1906) married neighbor Georgeanna Lackey and bought an adjoining parcel from her parents, Phebe and William Lackey (Louis Berger Group 2009). These families owned significant additional acreage and were among the most socially prominent of this antebellum community. Indeed their households were often, to varying extents, merged.[3] Almost certainly, many of the individuals enslaved by John A. and his father John B. Gibson also lived on or near the Maple Hall property and supported the Gibsons' diverse financial activities: agriculture, livestock, dairies, distilleries, a ferry, merchandizing, and shipping (15–18).

The 1860 slave schedule records 22 enslaved people in the extended Gibson household.[4] This document lacks names of the enslaved, but many households preceding and following the Gibsons in the 1870 federal census were Black. As enumerators typically recorded families in the order encountered, proximity in census records generally implies geographic proximity as well. Thus, the Gibsons' closest neighbors in 1870 included the African American families of Hy and Ann Washington, Henry and Elizabeth Madison, Peter and Lucinda Carter, Cesear and Hannah Weeks, and William and Eliza Willson. The men were listed as "laborer" or "laborer on farm," the women as "keeping house," and the children as "at home." All were recorded as having been born in Virginia, and none had any value listed under categories of real or personal estate; certainly, they occupied houses that others owned.[5] It is very likely that some, if not all, of these freed people had belonged to the antebellum Gibson household. Moreover, a number of them remained in the area for decades. Members of the extended Washington and Carter families, for example, appear in this vicinity into the early twentieth century (Louis Berger Group 2009, 137–41). The 1900 census for example finds "Peater and Lucindy Carter" still in the vicinity, the former at that time "mining ore." Henry Washington (born ca. 1825) no longer appears, but his son Charlie Washington was there as a blacksmith, and daughter Phoebe had married John Davis, a farmer (Louis Berger Group 2009, 141). Members of these extended African American families are almost certainly represented among those buried in the "Gibson-Lackey" cemetery.

Artifacts from the graves themselves provide poignant insights into the lives of these African American families who lived through the slavery, emancipation, and Reconstruction eras. Just over a thousand artifacts were recovered, the majority being coffin hardware from the second half of the nineteenth century: machine-cut and wire nails, screws, ornamental thumbscrews, coffin tacks, and escutcheons (Louis Berger Group 2009). These objects, as well as remnants of coffin wood, point to the expense and honor that attended these burials. Personal effects also communicate the dedication to sending loved ones into the hereafter with comfort, affection, and solemnity. The deceased were dressed in shirts and other clothing secured with a total of 78 buttons; most of them were "china" (or "Prosser") buttons, including one with a calico print (120). Others were made of rubber, copper alloy, and other metals, often covered in cloth (124–25). Some burials revealed surviving pieces of cloth and shoe leather; others included a hair comb, hair pins, a belt buckle, and cuff links. Several people were also buried with copper alloy brooches: one shaped like a horseshoe, one a butterfly, one a frond with berries (126–29). They set off for the next life well dressed, well cared for, well loved. Archaeologists who excavated the Freedman's Cemetery in Dallas, Texas—also to clear the way for highway expansion—found similar accoutrements, reflecting the African American community's determination to confer on the deceased the honor, respect, and value often denied them in life (Baugher and Veit 2014, 57).

When able to erect enduring memorials of their own design—after hundreds of years with burials marked by fieldstones or pieces of wood, or with epitaphs chosen by "white friends"—what did African Americans inscribe on them?

INSCRIBING LOVE AND ACCOMPLISHMENT

At Evergreen Cemetery in Lexington, grave markers are postbellum testimonies to family devotion, aspiration, accomplishment, and loss. Some markers memorialize people who spent much of their lives before the Emancipation Proclamation. Many of those simply list names and dates: "James and Kizzie Jackson Died 1921." James Jackson's death certificate identifies him as "colored" and a barber. Date of birth? "Don't know exactly." Age? "About 85."[6] Kizzie Anna Jackson's death certificate suggests her date of birth was "about 1840."[7] The informant for both certificates was Thomas J. Jackson, likely their son; he reported that both had been born in Lynchburg (in Amherst County that borders Rockbridge). Given the circumstances of African American life before the Civil War, though, he could not know some information about his family. He knew that his maternal grandmother was Eliza Merchant of Lynchburg, but he answered "don't know" when asked for Kizzie's father's name and place of birth. Likewise, he listed John Jackson of Lynchburg as his paternal grandfather but did "not know" his father's mother's name.

In this context, early Evergreen grave markers that point to relationships seem especially poignant: "Our Parents/ Warner Mack 1820–1894/ Louise Mack 1839–1904," or "Jane E. Holmes/ Died October 14 1897 Aged 76 years/ Erected by her son W. H. Holmes." Or Charles Humble (1889–1929): "He has gone to a mansion. At rest. Erected by his adopted sister Lucy Jackson."

What was it like for parents who'd lived during slavery to have children born free? Epitaphs suggest optimism and hope. For example, "Ulysses Grant Fisher" was born in 1869, while General Robert E. Lee was president of Washington College and racial tensions ran high. Naming an African American baby after General Ulysses S. Grant, to whom Lee had surrendered at Appomattox Court House, must have been an act of immense courage. Fisher lived nearly 70 years. Other children born in the first free generations were less lucky—Mary E. Robinson (1885–1908): "She faltered by the wayside and the angels took her home." Or "William R./ Son of W.A. & S.E. Clark/ Born Oct. 12, 1873/ Died Mar. 22, 1895/ How many hopes lie buried here."

Many early grave markers at Evergreen acknowledge professional accomplishments and community connections: "Rev. Milton Smith Died 1872/ Julia Smith Died 1886/ Servants of God well done." The first postbellum generations contain memorials not only to ministers but also to physicians: "Alfred W. Pleasants MD

1877–1940"; the marker of Dr. Sam Wooldridge (1892–1980) also memorializes his daughter (Ramona Moonbeam Wooldridge 1935–1952). Scores of men are commemorated with military markers attesting to their service in World Wars I and II.

An image commonly included on grave markers for men born in the last quarter of the nineteenth century is a chain with three links, a symbol of the Grand United Order of Odd Fellows, a fraternal organization dedicated to "Friendship, Love, and Truth." Fellows "relieve members when sick, assist with the burial of members and their families, protect the widows of Odd Fellows, and educate orphans" (Grand Order of Odd Fellows in America and Jurisdiction n.d.). The Odd Fellows symbol appears on the grave marker for Rufus O. Miller (1895–1978) and Fern Miller (1898–1967); descendants recognized their dedication and efforts on their behalf with the epitaph: "They gave their today for our tomorrow."

John B. Thompson (1867–1942) is buried with his second wife, Mary (1881–1945). Next to him is the resting place of first wife, Nannie A. (1869–1910): "She has left us. Her soul has fled. Her body now slumbers Along with the dead." John and Mary's daughter, Lillian Elizabeth (1912–1925), is next to Nannie. The inscription reads, "An angel visited the green earth and took the flower away." John B. Thompson was a sought-after caterer for social functions. When, during the Depression, members of the local African American fraternal organization Knights of Pythias could not maintain payments on their lodge, Thompson won it at auction on the courthouse steps; his ownership ensured its use by the Knights, and it served as a center for African American social life throughout much of the twentieth century (Green and Reed 2012).

A US military marker honors the resting place of "Alexander L. Banister, Kansas. Corpl., U.S. Army. December 21, 1926." Alexander Banister was born ca. 1878 in Rockbridge County to Thornton and Nancy Bannister. The 1880 census lists them as "mulatto." Thornton was a farm hand born ca. 1849. It's not known whether he had been enslaved; the Lexington area had a sizeable population of free African Americans who suffered, nonetheless, from material privation and omnipresent threats.

Alexander Banister was born in the first generation after the Civil War. In 1899 at age 21, he left his job as a waiter in Lexington.[8] Like many other Black men in this era, he might have served meals to White cadets at Virginia Military Institute. He traveled to Washington, DC, and enlisted in the US Army. For the next twenty years, Banister served in the American West. Army records show him at Fort McDowell on Angel Island near Oakland, California, and at Fort Riley in Kansas. He was a private in Company H of the 25th Infantry Regiment and a private first class in the Mounted Service School Division at Fort Riley. In the latter capacity, Banister taught horsemanship and cavalry skills to enlisted soldiers. After he was honorably discharged on June 20, 1919, Banister re-enlisted and was assigned to the United States Military Academy at West Point.[9] He and other

African Americans—so-called "Buffalo" soldiers—in a detachment from Fort Riley were tasked with supporting "cadet riding instruction and mounted drill, which was conducted on the ground now called Buffalo Soldier Field, formerly known as the Cavalry Plain" (Buffalo Soldiers Association of West Point, n.d.). Alexander L. Banister of the first free generation ended his military career in 1926 as an instructor and corporal at the U.S. Military Academy.[10]

INSCRIBING WONDER AND TRAGEDY

Another veteran buried in Evergreen Cemetery has a quite different story (Figure 4.6). A tapered marble column is topped with carved, drooping flowers and inscribed with the following: "Wonderful P. Pettigrew/ Born Feb. 10, 1895/ A victim of the World/ War shot to death at/ Charleston West VA/ Sept. 8, 1923/ Being deaf/ He was a Christian Soldier/ Rest from his labors."

On another side of the column is the following inscription:

"My parents/ Alfred W. Pettigrew/ Born Jan. 18, 1833/ Died April 29, 1900/ Peaceful sleep/ Frances Louisa/ His wife/ Born Aug. 23, 1839/ Died May 13, 1887/ To live is Christ [.] To die is her gain."

FIGURE 4.6. Gravestone memorializing Wonderful P. Pettigrew (1895–1923), a "victim of the World War shot to death at Charleston West VA." Evergreen Cemetery, Lexington.

This stone was erected by Johnson Pettigrew, son of Alfred and Frances, and father of Wonderful. Because Johnson's wife predeceased Wonderful, the epitaphs can be understood as his own perspectives and terms.

Wonderful Price Pettigrew appears in the 1900 federal census for Lexington as five-year-old "Wunderfull"; index preparers transcribed his name as "Winterspell Pettinger" in 1900[11] and "Wonchrful Pittinger" in 1910.[12]

The 1900 return shows Wonderful as the only child of Johnson and Virginia "Pettigner," who had been married for 12 years. In response to the question, "mother of how many children," Virginia had seven; "number of these children living" was one. The couple had lost six children.

The 1880 federal census in Lexington had listed Virginia Franklin as a 19-year-old (born ca. 1863) attending school and living with her mother, Emily Robinson: "mulatto," widow, head of household who could neither read nor write.[13] Virginia C. Franklin married Johnston A. Pettigrew in 1888.[14] Their marriage certificate identifies her father as Smiley Franklin, about whom the records seem otherwise silent.

Johnson (sometimes "Johnston") A. Pettigrew appears in the 1870 federal census as an eight-year-old "mulatto" who could not read or write.[15] He lived in "Buffalo," the Buffalo Creek area of southern Rockbridge County, quite possibly in the vicinity of Buffalo Forge Plantation or Cedar Hill, mentioned previously. The 1880 census lists Johnson Pettigrew as an 18-year-old "black servant" working as a laborer in the Lexington household of a prominent White physician.[16] After marrying Virginia in 1888, they lived in the African American neighborhood of Diamond Hill in Lexington and started a family. The 1900 federal census classifies Johnson, Virginia, and their son Wonderful— along with nearly all their neighbors—as "black."[17]

Johnson's occupation was a cook, a relatively common calling in this neighborhood. Neighbors worked as day laborers. Others were hotel waiters, teachers, butlers, washer women, barbers, plasterers, and farm laborers, and many children were "at school." The 1900 record indicates that Johnson and Virginia could read and write, as could some two-thirds of their Black neighbors. He owned their house, as did roughly half of the Black heads of household near them in the census. Pettigrew continued to work as a cook almost until the day he died (Figure 4.7). His dedication to family extended also to community, as his grave marker is inscribed: "Deacon J.A. Pettigrew/ Founder of Lodge 2461/ GUO of Odd Fellows/ June 14. 1862–Sept. 23, 1937."

Born during slavery times in Rockbridge County, Johnson A. Pettigrew moved to town and worked to forge an empowered, supportive African American community—by founding a local branch of a fraternal organization and through serving as a deacon in the First Baptist Church. A framed photograph of Deacon Pettigrew still hangs in the church, honoring him as one of its founders. We'll now seek to understand the words on his son's gravestone.

FIGURE 4.7. Deacon J. A. Pettigrew, First Baptist Church, Lexington.

WONDERFUL PRICE AND THE GREAT WAR

In the summer of 1917, Wonderful Price Pettigrew registered with the Selective Service.[18] The card lists his race as "Negro" and his trade as "Waiter" at Virginia Military Institute, serving cadets meals. He was 22 years old, single, "tall," and with a "medium" build. In response to the question, "Has person lost arm, leg, hand, foot, or both eyes, or is he otherwise disabled?" the answer was "No."

Wonderful's military-issue footstone indicates that he served as a private in the US Army. The headstone that his father designed calls him a "victim of the World War," but he did not die until 1923, and then in West Virginia, "Being Deaf." Wonderful could have been a victim of the war in many respects, psychological and physiological; quite likely he suffered from noise-induced hearing loss (Traynor 2014; Conroy and Malik 2018). Certainly, he was able to hear when he left for the war.

In 1973, a fire destroyed millions of World War I personnel documents. There were no duplicate copies, making some information about service impossible to reconstruct (National Personnel Records Center 2019). No record has been found of Wonderful Pettigrew's experience in the Army. The closest available proxies are his peers—other African American men who were drafted for the Great War and later buried in Evergreen Cemetery.

In World War I, the great majority of Black soldiers were assigned to "Services of Supplies (SOS) units and labor battalions," and tens of thousands "served in the 16 Pioneer Infantry Regiments . . . [that provided] engineering support as well as logistical support to the combat divisions" (Virginia WWI and WWII Commemoration Commission 2020). Some draftees from the Lexington area remained stateside, working in depot brigades at forts such as Camp Lee in Petersburg, Virginia, a vast mobilization and recruit training facility (Rainville 2018:94-97; Wineman 2010). Many others were deployed abroad (Scott 1919).

One African American veteran buried in Evergreen was Lewis Bolen (1894–1948). He enlisted July 29, 1918, and was assigned to the 808 Pioneer Infantry,[19] organized at Camp Meade (Maryland), moved overseas in August 1918, and served in France with the First Army September into November 1918. These pioneers "march[ed] at the head of each battalion to clear a passage for it through woods or other obstructions, improve roads, make bridges and generally do any minor engineering or construction work that may [have been] necessary" (Davis 1919). For Pioneer divisions, the Personnel Bureau of the War Department looked to assign men who were "experienced in life in the open, skilled in woodcraft and simple carpentry—substitute occupations, rancher, prospector, hunter, scout" (Davis 1919). After the war,[20] Bolen was a boiler fireman at Washington and Lee University, a "skilled worker who operated high pressure boiler and auxiliary equipment" in the institution's coal-fired power plant.[21]

Other Black Lexington draftees were assigned to segregated combat units in World War I. Brothers Preston Hinton (1895–1953) and William Henry Hinton (1894–1955) served in the 367 Infantry of the 92nd Division. William was in a Machine Gun Company; Preston was in Company A.[22] The 92nd Division "fought with distinction under French Army command" (Virginia WWI and WWII Commemoration Commission 2020). In what would turn out to be the last two days of the war (November 10–11, 1918), the 367 Infantry was positioned in the valley of Ruisseau Moulin, on the west bank of the Moselle River south of the city of Metz in northeastern France. This location was on the front line in an area of very heavy enemy fire (Kaiser's Cross n.d.). The 367th held its position until the armistice was announced. Preston and "Willie" Hinton were honorably discharged on March 24, 1919, and returned to Lexington. The former worked as a plasterer, the latter as "machinist" in a garage, meaning an automobile mechanic.[23] Thus, while the particular role that Wonderful Pettigrew played in the Great War is not known, given his peers' experiences, he likely encountered combat conditions—trenches, shells, mortar fire—along the western front and, for this reason, came home deaf.

The 1920 census lists Wonderful as a 24-year-old "mulatto" living in his father's house on Diamond Hill, with occupation "none." Johnson Pettigrew Sr. was a "cook" at Virginia Military Institute; 15-year-old brother, Johnson Jr. attended school, and 19-year-old sister, Thelma, resided with them.[24]

The 1923 Lexington City Directory simply identifies Wonderful as "(Col.)" for "colored." Unlike his father, no occupation is listed,[25] confirming the sense that he had entered the war educated, employed, and able-bodied—but returned home deaf and had difficulty reestablishing a vocation. In September of that year, Wonderful was in Charleston, West Virginia. His father's brother, John Pettigrew, lived in Charleston,[26] and it seems likely that Wonderful was looking for work there.

As Wonderful's grave marker says, he "was shot to death at Charleston West VA Sept. 8, 1923." According to the death certificate,[27] the cause was "a gun-shot of lung," a contributing factor being "hemorrhage." He lingered a day, having been shot on September 8 and dying on September 9.

Wonderful's niece never met him. Della Evans, daughter of Thelma Pettigrew Evans and David Gray Evans, was born in 1937, some fourteen years after his death. She remembers her mother saying that Wonderful was in Charleston and was walking in a rail yard. A night watchman told him to stop, but Wonderful didn't stop because he didn't hear him. And so, he was killed.[28] Wonderful Price Pettigrew: A victim of the World War shot to death at Charleston, West Virginia, being deaf.

The death certificate identifies him as "James Pettigrew," and probate materials confirm that James and Wonderful were one and the same. Information on the death certificate was supplied by John Pettigrew ("accurate to the best of my knowledge") and describes a "colored" male "laborer," son of Johnson and Virginia Pettigrew, who was shot on September 8, 1923, and whose "place of funeral or removal" was "Lexington VA." Apparently Wonderful, in some contexts, used not his given name but the chosen one of James.[29]

He was known in many ways, and unknown in many others.

To the thousands of tourists streaming into Lexington, many to pay respects to Confederate General Thomas Stonewall Jackson in the cemetery on Main Street, he is invisible: his grave marker and Evergreen Cemetery out of sight and out of mind, even as they abut bustling businesses.

To VMI cadets he was a waiter.

To the US Army he was a private.

To a night watchman, he was a Black man imagined to pose a threat.

But to those who knew and loved him—his parents who welcomed him after having lost six children—he was Wonderful (Figure 4.8).

FIGURE 4.8. Footstone of Wonderful P. Pettigrew taken on Memorial Day, 2019. Evergreen Cemetery, Lexington. Photograph courtesy of Eric Wilson.

It's impossible in 2020 to think about Wonderful without also thinking about Ahmaud Arbery, Breonna Taylor, Philando Castile, Tamir Rice, Michael Brown, Trayvon Martin, Eric Garner, and George Floyd, and to wonder how many other Black men, boys, women, girls, and even unborn babies have been killed because armed officials imagined threats, or didn't believe—or didn't care—when dying people said, "I can't breathe." Wonderful Pettigrew's story is a heart-wrenching one, all the more as iterations of it spin from the headlines day after day. We don't know what Wonderful said, but George Floyd's dying words were recorded and watched millions of times. Writer Lonnae O'Neal didn't want to watch but, as a "black mother," felt obligated to witness:

> "Please, man!" Floyd begs as he is ground into the pavement. His pleas mix with the ambient noises around him. They are the disjointed sounds from the clash of belief systems and competing visions of sovereignty, of ownership, of authority over black bodies compressed into the narrow frame of Floyd's last moments.
>
> "Momma!" Floyd, 46, calls out. "Momma! I'm through," the dying man says. . . . A call to your mother is a prayer to be seen. Floyd's mother died two years [earlier], but he used her as a sacred invocation.

As bystanders scream at Minneapolis officers, "He's dying. You're f—ing killing him," Floyd is no longer moving, he is perhaps already dead. In the ways black people have trained themselves to look at these things, in his final breaths, he has already won. (O'Neal 2020)

Historian Kami Fletcher (2020, 133) explains that, often, "death meant freedom to the enslaved." Short of death, what freedom from racism and brutality might Black Americans be certain of today?

ANCIENT JANE, MISS JANE, UNKNOWN AFRICAN AMERICAN WOMAN

Uphill from Wonderful Pettigrew's resting place is a new grave for a woman who died before he was born, and who was buried nearly a century after his death.

In December of 2008, construction of a parking lot for the new county courthouse in Lexington revealed a set of human remains. This site is about a mile from Evergreen Cemetery and, during the twenty-first century, was not known to be a burying ground. Police contacted forensic scientists at Radford University, Cliff Boyd and Donna Boyd, who examined the bones and site. They recorded a "gray stain" in the wet clay; no coffin hardware or personal items (such as buttons or pins) were recovered, making it likely that this person had been buried in a cloth shroud.

The site form labels this set of human remains "Ancient Jane": an anonymous Jane Doe from another century. She was likely between 5 feet 6 inches and 5 feet 9 inches tall, between 17 and 23 years of age, and African American. She had at least six untreated cavities and other dental conditions—an abscess, tooth loss, dentin exposure, and enamel hypoplasia—that can have multiple causes.[30] In historic African American populations, they often relate to compounding environmental, "systemic nutritional and disease stresses" (Blakey et al. 1994, 371).

This young woman had been buried on a hill behind a livery and blacksmith shop. Well into the twentieth century this hill was still labeled on maps "vacant sloping ground," perhaps a kind of potter's field. Despite appreciable activity in this vicinity—most recently construction of a sizeable parking lot for the courthouse—a carpet of periwinkle covers the bank. Periwinkle is an extremely common ground cover in historic cemeteries; often the more extensive the periwinkle, the older the cemetery. It's quite possible that "Ancient Jane" was not the only person buried on that hillside.

This little lot in Lexington bears some structural similarities to the much larger African Burial Ground in New York City. In use during the late seventeenth century and nearly all of the eighteenth century, it might have contained the graves of some 15,000 Africans and African Americans. As with much of the New York burial ground, the Lexington burial ground lay in a ravine. Mourners might therefore have "achieved privacy and seclusion" from White surveillance.

Despite the extraordinary structural forces arrayed against them, people of African descent carved out spaces and ways to affirm their full humanity. Until the 1780s, maps depicted the New York burying ground as being on undeveloped, open land: "on the outskirts of the city floating in empty space, with few landmarks in its vicinity" (Frohne 2015, 48). Surveys document the "division of the African Burial Ground into lots, blocks, and streets between 1787 and 1795, with buildings and streets constructed on it afterwards. Thus, a sacred space was obliterated from visible sight and, over the period of two hundred years, was erased from public memory" (Frohne 2015, 1).

The name of the woman buried in "vacant sloping ground" on what was then the edge of Lexington has been similarly erased (Figure 4.9). It has not been possible through documents to ascertain her identity. Late nineteenth-century Sanborn maps show in the area a blacksmith shop, "tenements" (likely rental properties), "shanties" (small wooden houses), a wagon shed, and a livery (a stable where horses could be kept temporarily) (Sanborn Map Company 1886). Many visitors to Lexington would have boarded their horses at the livery. Thus,

FIGURE 4.9. View toward the original burial place of a young African American woman whose remains were disturbed in the 2008 construction of the Rockbridge County Courthouse in Lexington. Wright's Livery Stable, Rockbridge Historical Society Photograph Collection. Courtesy of Special Collections Department, Leyburn Library, Washington and Lee University.

the burial ground was downhill from, but in the midst of, spaces for physical labor, animal husbandry, and mobility, with visitors and renters regularly cycling through. Because her name is not known, twenty-first-century Lexingtonians are unsure what to call her. Some find the label on her forensic report, "Ancient Jane," moving. Others prefer "Miss Jane," a title more in keeping with African American tradition. Still others resist inventing a name for her, opting to refer to her as a nineteenth-century African American woman.

The remains were housed at Radford University's Forensic Science Institute, some 90 miles southwest of Lexington, for just over a decade. Many in Lexington wanted to see their return, and the pieces came into place during the spring of 2019. Officers from the Lexington Police Department traveled to the laboratory at Radford, where Dr. Clifford Boyd had prepared the bones for transport. A bank account for reburial and commemoration was established, and in addition to individual citizens, organizations contributed: Rockbridge County, Washington and Lee University, Virginia Military Institute, and others. The City of Lexington donated a plot in Evergreen Cemetery and costs for opening and closing. Avocational woodworkers crafted a coffin, based on nineteenth-century models, from area oaks, and a local memorial company donated a gravestone: "Unknown African American Woman/ Died ca. 1800's/ Exhumed During Construction of Rockbridge County Courthouse In 2008./ Reinterred May 19, 2019."

On the morning of her reburial, several of us gathered in Randolph Street United Methodist Church (RSUMC), one of Lexington's historically African American churches. Poised on a trestle, the unvarnished oak coffin lay open. Ted DeLaney, Marylin Alexander, and Maria Quillin—deeply rooted, prominent members of the African American community—donned gloves and, with support from anthropologists and reference sources, carefully laid each piece of each bone in its proper anatomical place (Figure 4.10). They rested on a bed of foam and fabric and, once complete, were covered in the same. Those assembled took turns driving nails into the coffin lid, and then pallbearers from the Lexington Police Department carried the coffin from the sanctuary. Outside waited a caisson pulled by two powerful black Percherons. The officers loaded the coffin onto the caisson and provided an escort to Evergreen Cemetery, less than a mile away. There scores of people awaited and witnessed the arrival—the powerful, matched horses, the reverberations of their hooves, the driver's erect spine, the solemnity and propriety of the slender black wagon (Figure 4.11). Silently, men serving as pallbearers and representing VMI, W&L, the City, and the County carried the coffin from the caisson to the grave. The Reverend Reginald Early of RSUMC lead, with sonorous voice, the singing of "Amazing Grace." Deacon Irene Thompson of the historically African American First Baptist Church invited all to join her in the Lord's Prayer. Those assembled

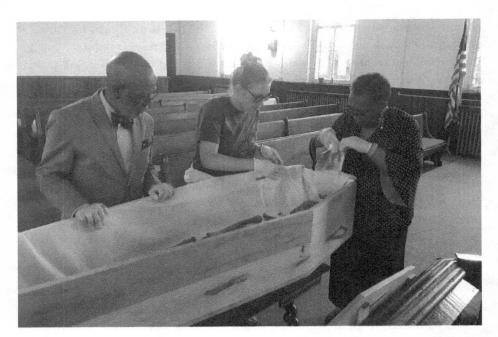

FIGURE 4.10. May 19, 2019, Ted DeLaney, Erin Schwartz, and Maria Quillin lay out the remains of the anonymous woman found in 2008. Randolph Street United Methodist Church, Lexington.

FIGURE 4.11. A pair of Percherons, guided by India Nichols, brings a caisson bearing the young woman's remains in the oak coffin to Evergreen Cemetery, Lexington. Photograph courtesy of Richelle Alexander.

FIGURE 4.12. Locally grown flowers on the coffin of anonymous African American woman. May 19, 2019. Evergreen Cemetery, Lexington.

brought flowers cut from their yards and gardens—lilies, peonies, climbing roses—to lay on the coffin (Figure 4.12).

The crowd was diverse, Black and White, and people who claim other ethnicities. The speakers were African American. W&L Professor of History, Dr. Theodore Carter DeLaney, remarked that this young woman

was just as likely to have been a free woman as an enslaved person. . . . Mid-nineteenth-century Lexington was home to both enslaved people and free people of color. . . . Often desperately poor, free Blacks lived on the brink of starvation. . . . After the Civil War, racial hostilities increased, and Blacks became part of a permanent caste as Jim Crow segregation defined the nature of race relations. We do not know the decades of the nineteenth century in which this woman lived, or how she negotiated the racial landscape. All we know is that construction workers brought her skeletal remains into the twenty-first century. . . . In return for pulling her remains into our time, we offer this memorial service, a handmade coffin, a new grave, and a gravestone.

City councilor and vice mayor of Lexington, Marylin Evans Alexander, also spoke:

African Americans don't have famous war heroes buried in Lexington to pay homage to, nor have practically every street or historic building named after them or their ancestors—all which are so much the norm, it's taken for granted that it's significant for all, but it's not. . . ! African Americans have Lylburn Downing School, Richardson Park, and possibly churches for some. Therefore, when we heard that an African American female's skeletal remains were discovered at the courthouse construction site, we took notice. Miss Jane can certainly be the ancestor of someone standing here today. This discovery may not have been a war hero, but we know she was certainly someone's child! So, she was certainly someone's hero. We really don't know how she arrived at her first place of interment. Did she die of disease or natural causes and was buried in the potter's field? Did she perhaps even die at the hands of the Klan who rode through Lexington one night in 1867, an event described as a "bloody hour" with a report that ended in the word "death"? We don't know, and because we don't know, we are here today. . . . Miss Jane represents all of our ancestors.

This young, anonymous woman seized the imagination and hearts of many. In her anonymity, she represented the unknown ancestry of local African Americans. In her burial, the community gained a powerful symbol: a Black woman who died young, poorly nourished, wrapped in a cloth, and buried in vacant ground was exhumed and reburied with respect and affection.

In Confederate Landia, in this "Shrine of the South," with the meccas of Stonewall Jackson's grave and Robert E. Lee's family mausoleum, with seemingly every stretch of pavement named for White heroes—who were also slaveholders—Jefferson, Washington, Jackson, Lee—in a city that was designed as a White space and that has offered little harbor to African Americans, a small claim has been struck: Unknown African American Woman. Died ca. 1800s. Reinterred 2019. Her new grave site asserts her humanity, encouraging us to envision not anonymous bones but, to paraphrase Ta-Nehisi Coates (2015, 69–70),

a particular, specific woman, whose mind was active as your own, whose range of feelings was as vast as your own; who may have preferred the way the light fell in one particular spot in the woods, who enjoyed fishing where the water eddies in a nearby stream, who loved her mother in her own complicated way, thought her sister talked too loud, had a favorite cousin, exceled at dress-making and knew, inside herself, that she was as intelligent and capable as anyone.

Perhaps the opportunity to contribute toward Miss Jane's burial enabled some donors and participants—particularly White residents—to feel good about themselves, or I should say "ourselves." It provided a chance for White people like me to show that I recognized her humanity, that I care, that I want to do the right thing. Like sharing Wonderful's story. But the past is, in a way, easy.

Miss Jane and Wonderful Pettigrew are "safe" to memorialize affectionately. No one could imagine them now—deceased as they've been these many years—as threats. But what about the young Black women and men who were alive just recently, like Breonna Taylor and Ahmaud Arbery? What about those alive today? Are those of us who help memorialize the nineteenth-century innocents as willing to see our Black contemporaries as equally vulnerable, valued, and wonderful?

CHAPTER 5

"The Bivouac of the Dead"
Military Conflicts and Cemeteries

THE SOCIAL, GRATEFUL DEAD

The muffled drum's sad roll has beat
The soldier's last tattoo;
No more on life's parade shall meet
That brave and fallen few.
On Fame's eternal camping-ground
Their silent tents are spread,
And Glory guards, with solemn round,
The bivouac of the dead.

The lines are from a poem that Captain Theodore O'Hara wrote in memory of Kentucky troops killed in the Mexican War (O'Hara 1847). They're also used on plaques and inscriptions to commemorate the Civil War dead in Arlington, Winchester, and many other Virginia cemeteries (Sanders 2003) (Figure 5.1). O'Hara imagines dying soldiers heeding their final "tattoo," a signal in the evening for soldiers to retire, and gathering in encampments for the night in open air, a bivouac of the dead.

FIGURE 5.1. National Cemetery, Winchester.

American history is written through thousands of headstones in the Valley of Virginia. Nearly every cemetery includes the war dead. Burying grounds in the Valley abound with earthly remains of veterans of the American Revolution and "Indian Wars," the War of 1812, the Spanish American War, the Great War, World War II, Korea, Vietnam, Iraq, and Afghanistan. Many were killed in combat; others succumbed to disease on duty. Some came home only to die in short order; others survived for decades and were finally buried with military honors. Some were conscientious objectors. Some were civilians for whom war was the defining experience of their lives.

On one level "cemeteries are about the pasts we bury in them. But on another they are inherently future-oriented," directed at those "who will look upon them and be called to remember" (Eggener 2010, 10). Graves can generate, revive, or underscore a sense of obligation "to both the dead and the unborn" (Eggener 2010, 22), reminding viewers that they're integral to a society that came before them and will outlast them. In this way, domains of the dead serve as "a massive mnemonic device" (see Glassie 1994, 965).

Remembering the dead as a gesture of commitment to the social whole is an ancient theme and appears in many contexts (Eggener 2010, 9). Among them is the tale of the "Grateful Dead," a story that's been told for some two thousand years in Europe and beyond (Trist 1989). Elements of the folktale vary, but in many versions the king is ill, and the kingdom is ailing: the fields are barren; the sun won't shine. The king's eldest son sets out ostensibly to find a cure for king and kingdom but actually to secure the throne for himself; he disregards a beggar at the city's gate and soon finds himself trapped in a canyon. The second son follows suit, but the third and youngest son stops at the city gate to give the beggar alms. In turn the beggar gives him advice and several magic objects. When the prince comes to a crossroads, he notices a corpse on the ground. Villagers tell him that the deceased was a debtor and doesn't deserve the courtesy of a burial. The prince uses his last coins to pay the dead man's bills, and he himself digs the grave. Turning then into the woods, the prince meets Jack, a minstrel who happens to be headed to the castle that holds the water of life. With Jack's help the young prince succeeds in his quest. The water of life restores the king to health and the land of the kingdom to life. The thankful prince offers to give Jack all he owns. Jack declines, explaining that his assistance to the prince had been repaying a kindness: "I am the spirit of the corpse you buried at the crossroads."

The dead, here and often, stand in for society. In this tale told through unknown generations, extending respect to the deceased—much like showing kindness to the poor—expresses commitment to the health of the social whole.

These gestures can be especially important with the war dead. Mortuary rituals—attending funerals, visiting cemeteries, laying wreaths on graves of unknown soldiers—encourage participants to envision the social whole of which they're part (Bloch and Parry 1982, 6). Commemorating veterans sets "in motion the symbolic resources that can be mobilized to create society" (Árnason 2013, 21). They're part of a larger communal "us," and ways in which they're memorialized convey understandings of shared values. Their grave sites can be a powerful source of identity, making claims about who "we" are, what we value, to whom we owe debts, of what sorts, and how we pay them back, forward, or both (Doss 2010, 17–60).

Burial sites of the military dead can be recruited as resources, materials that people mobilize to frame the past in ways conducive to their present goals and future aspirations (Crossland 2014, 144). The cemetery is an area in which cultural values, social relationships, and claims to truth are "negotiated and (re)produced" (Tarlow 1999, 12). They might call viewers to imagine or remember in particular ways, foregrounding some aspects of the past and omitting others. They might portray war as valorous, tragic, or sinful. They might praise the majesty of the United States, or they might assert the glory of the Confederate States, or both—even on single stones.

Reflecting on the "practice and purpose of history," folklorist Henry Glassie (1994, 961) concluded that historic narratives serve to charter society. People look to the past to identify values and stories that will equip them "for their trip into the future" (961). Being open to the past's complexity "prevents witless assent to political order, calling people into understanding of themselves so that they will act knowledgeably, deciding whether to acquiesce, rebel, or withdraw into isolation for imaginative discourse with the shades of their choice" (966). Glassie provides the example of Hugh Nolan, aged member of a small community in Northern Ireland during the 1970s. Before electricity came to the village, neighbors would gather

> in his tiny home, its interior smoked to every shade of black, [and] Mr. Nolan would pluck one story off a hilltop to speak of the heroes of their place. Old warriors would come alive in their minds to fight again for Irish freedom. Then he would reach out, collect another, and tell it to show how people at war risk damnation for breaking Our Lord's commandment to love. And they would stop to think. And that is history's purpose (967–68).

The stories that Valley cemeteries tell are like these. Many gravestones look to Jesus—who blessed the peacemakers, the merciful, the meek—and also exalt combat. Many gravestones praise the patriotic and moral virtues of the dead, though in life they held people in bondage. To adapt a phrase from anthropologist Claude Levi-Strauss, the past is "good to think with." Cemeteries encourage people to reflect on who they are or hope to be, individually and communally; what values they cherish and which they repudiate; and how they might gather up some parts of the past and renounce others as they craft their communities and futures.

THE AMERICAN REVOLUTION

Memory of the American Revolution is reverently curated in many Valley cemeteries. They often reference ways that these soldiers and settlers civilized a "wilderness." Memorials characterize Revolutionary-era settlers as rugged, independent, honest immigrants from northwestern Europe—Scots-Irish, English, German—arrived to tame this mountain-ringed region.

At Falling Spring Presbyterian Church Cemetery in Rockbridge County, a Sons of the American Revolution (SAR) marker recognizes Captain or "Soldier John Grigsby" as he was (and is) commonly known, having commanded a company in the 13th Virginia Regiment. His headstone is "Sacred to the memory of John Grigsby,/ who was born 1720,/ and departed this life Apl./ 7th 1794./ Pause, reader, here and look with solemn dread/ Upon the last lone dwelling of the dead./ Tho' num'rous graves appear on every hand,/ This was the first of all the silent band" (Figure 5.2). Soldier John and his wife Elizabeth Grigsby indeed founded a prosperous, prodigious family, many members of which are memorialized for contributions to later military, political, and civic efforts. Another Rockbridge County memorial to Revolution-era founders of enduring family

lines is "Sacred to the memory of John Paxton who died October the 3rd 1787 Aged 44 years. And also his wife Phebe Paxton who died the 13th of February 1821, aged 76 years." Accompanying their grave markers is a plaque installed by the Daughters of the American Revolution (DAR) in memory of "Captain John Paxton a Revolutionary War Soldier and Phoebe Alexander Paxton his Wife who Rode Horseback through the Wilderness to Carry Food and Clothing to him at Valley Forge." Like the Grigsbys, the Paxtons are remembered not only by their many descendants but also lauded more widely as exemplifying the determination to forge American independence in the "wilderness."

In adjacent Augusta County, the Tinkling Spring Presbyterian Church Cemetery features a large granite memorial "Sacred to the Memory of the Immigrants to this Valley who Turned the Wilderness into Habitations." It lists the heads of households who paid 12 shillings per family in 1744 to build the first meeting house at this location: a Presbyterian congregation that Anglo-Virginia authorities permitted as part of the colonial strategy to encourage White,

Protestant settlement in the Valley as a buffer against the French and indigenous peoples. At Thornrose Cemetery in nearby Staunton, a bronze tablet calls on visitors to remember "the settlers of the Great Valley of Virginia, who had courage to lead the way beyond the mountains and give what Governor Gooch desired for his province, a line of defence against the savages." These memorials celebrate settler colonialism, the replacement of native peoples as part of global imperial strategies, and encourage an understanding of who "we" are—who Americans are—as capable, honest, determined fighters in the struggle for civilization.

One Revolutionary War veteran's experience illustrates, with nuance and clarity, how community members inflected cultural values through memory. The headstone for Peter Haught bears a star, his name, and date of death: "February 12, 1853, aged 98." An SAR marker accompanies it, and the DAR recently installed a marker on the grave of Haught's second wife, Sarah Jones, recognizing her as the wife of a patriot (Berg 2013). He's buried near their home place in Monongalia County, West Virginia (during their lives part of Virginia) and she's interred at Western State Hospital in Staunton, where she spent the last years of her life. Sarah was Peter's second wife; they married after his first wife[1] with whom he'd had at least five children, died.[2] Although Sarah (1805–1857) was apparently fifty years younger than Peter (1755–1853), they had four children together, the last apparently being born in 1839 when Peter was 84 years old.[3]

Peter Haught's status as Revolutionary War veteran sparked some controversy, and the resulting court records shed light on the values of his time and community. Between 1832 and 1835, Haught received a military pension of $40 per year, but then a US Attorney for the Western District of Virginia suspended payments and sought reimbursement, claiming fraud. Apparently, an attorney had found inconsistencies in Haught's history of service and pension application. So, some 50 years after the Revolution, Haught was called to testify, and he said, "I am in my 80th year of age. I was drafted in Fayette County, Pennsylvania," then part of Virginia, but he could not recall or "tell in what year." He marched "under Lieut. Catt to Fort McIntosh" and then to Fort Laurens on the Tuscarawas River in Ohio. Haught "remained there about six weeks" then returned to Fort McIntosh where he "was discharged having been in service five months. I left home after harvest. Returned about Christmas. In the summer preceding the above mentioned tour I lived at Duncan Fort," in Monongalia County. He continued:

> The people assembled at the Fort for their mutual defence and protection—they cultivated their corn patches and cleared their lands, and scouted & watched and guarded alternately, whilst some were working others were scouting & guarding. All the settlers at these Forts done the duty of watching and guarding by turn—and in this way I was employed at the Fort for the above three months. (Harris, n.d.)

Instead of signing his name, Peter Haught made his mark, an act suggesting that he was not literate.

Following the deaths of Peter and Sarah Haught, their two youngest children were minors and in 1857 sought the land bounty and money withheld from their father. Testimony on their behalf by neighbors is candid. Joseph Tennant, for example, said that he had been "well acquainted" with Peter Haught. Tennant's farm "adjoined the farm upon which said Haught resided for the space of near seventy years," and his father had served with Haught in the Revolution (Harris, n.d.). Another neighbor explained that some local men,

> now between 75 and 80 years of age, . . . have heard their fathers talk a thousand times about the campaign to the Tuscarawas in the then northwestern territory, and of their services in the Fort in the neighborhood. The old man said he was well acquainted with General McIntosh, at Tuscarawas, according to the representation of his children. Captain Michael Catt would frequently come to see Tennant, and on such occasions . . . Haught would be sent for and the old Indian Fighters would have a reunion, drink grog, and have a good time of it. (Harris, n.d.)

Another neighbor underscored the community's anger about the withholding of Haught's pension, saying that the government

> through the indiscreet zeal of a third rate lawyer by the name of W. G. Singleton, at the time United district attorney, has done the old soldier, and his numerous and respectable family irreparable injustice. This is the universal conviction of this whole neighborhood, now and at the time, not so much in the trifling pecuniary loss of withholding the annuity it had allowed him, as in the efforts that were made to question his veracity and impugn his motives. (Harris, n.d.)

This neighbor went on to say that Haught didn't need the money. "He had a competency and could live without a pension," but his minor children deserved restitution. Moreover, the matter of Haught's honor was at stake; "his numerous & respected children and grandchildren . . . desire to have their ancestor's character vindicated from the aspersions cast upon it." Several people acknowledged that Haught "was a man of moderate mental endowments," or a "weak, uneducated man" and perhaps even a "coward." But "that does not affect the well settled conviction of the neighborhood that he was in the service," and that he was a "man of excellent moral character, and especially for truth, and knowingly, under oath, or otherwise, would not make a declaration he did not believe to be true." By 1858, Peter Haught, deceased, had been restored to the pensioners list and arrears paid to his heirs (Harris, n.d.).

Peter Haught is not remembered as a military standout, but long-resident families defended him in the face of aspersions that some "third-rate lawyer" cast against his character. Haught was one of them—one of "us" American patriots—recognized by neighbors, the courts, and Sons of the American Revolution. These processes of memory illuminate the values that most mattered to members of his community. It seemed of little consequence that he was "uneducated," that he made his mark rather than signing his name, or that he might have had "moderate mental endowments." He was considered honest, he had a competency—the ability to provide adequately for his family (Hofstra 2004)—and the restoration of his pension was a matter less, they contended, of acquisitiveness than of honor. As a soldier in Virginia forts, he'd contributed to the "mutual defence and protection" of colonial settlements, clearing acreage, cultivating patches of corn, scouting and watching and guarding against the land's native people. Thus, Haught was remembered and recognized as belonging among the old soldiers who "would have a reunion, drink grog, and have a good time." Undoubtedly, indigenous people, to whom the Valley had been home for more than ten thousand years, held deeply divergent views on their displacement as providing cause for celebration.

THE WORLD WAR

William Roy Nicholas (b. 1891) is buried in Highland County's Blue Grass Cemetery with views of the Allegheny Mountains stretching for miles in every direction. The county has one of the lowest population densities in the Valley (approximately five people per square mile). It's hard to imagine a greater contrast between this rural majesty—this sweep of ancient forested mountains in the crisp autumn air, a red-tailed hawk on the wing—and the European theater of war in which Nicholas died, with its shattered masonry buildings and lines of men in bowl-shaped "doughboy" helmets inching, on their bellies, across a desolate deathscape of mud, trenches, gas, and looping barbed wire.

Nicholas seems to have wanted to stay in Virginia. He'd been a toddler when his father died.[4] He was 26 years old on June 5, 1917, when he appeared before the draft board to register along with thousands of other men, aged 21 to 31, throughout Virginia in accordance with the new Selective Service Act (Rainville 2018, 41). Nicholas identified himself as a farm laborer and asked for exemption from military service "on acct. mother" (on account of his mother), a widow who depended on him for support.[5] His request must have been denied, as the inscription on his headstone in Highland County reads, "Killed in Action in the World War, Oct. 4, 1918."

Some Virginians, like Nicholas, were conscripted, others volunteered, and still others were already members of the armed forces when the United States declared war on Germany in April of 1917. Anthropologist and historian Lynn Rainville finds that many Virginians—including those in the southwestern part of the commonwealth—had been opposed to American involvement in the European war until Germany's attacks on US ships fomented a spirit of mobilization and defense. She cites the opinion of the *Lynchburg News* that this was "a war against mankind, against all nations" (Rainville 2018, 40). In the Valley, gravestones dedicated to the dead from the Great War mourn losses to families and communities, hail the sacrifices of those who succumbed to injury or disease, and recognize the part that young men from country corners of Virginia played in the global contest (150). They suggest that to be an American is to be integral to dynamics far beyond Valley horizons and to be ready—through volunteer service or conscription—to be, in the words of one veteran, "of some service to suffering humanity" (46).

A marble obelisk in Lexington's historically African American Evergreen Cemetery commemorates Mitchell Douglas Gooch (1895–1918). Mitchell's father Richard Gooch (b. 1856) first appeared in federal census returns as a mulatto farm laborer in Amherst County, to the south of the Valley in 1880. The senior Gooch became a landowning farmer in Rockbridge County (1900 census) and a university custodian who owned a home in Lexington (1910 census). Mitchell, son of Richard and Signora Gooch, complied with Selective Service requirements by registering on June 5, 1917. He reported being 22 years old and employed as a "houseboy" for a White woman in Lexington. Mitchell Gooch was sent with some 8,000 men to build a new boot camp, Camp Greene, in Charlotte, North Carolina (Morten 1920, 454). He and other members of the Pioneer Infantry worked as "stevedores, dug trenches, graves, and latrines, and built hospitals, roads, bridges, and railroad lines" (Lefferts 2012, 2). Camp Greene eventually had "2,000 buildings, including a 60-acre hospital facility with 2,000 beds. It had more than a mile of horse stables" and "a bakery that produced 40,000 loaves of bread a day" (Perzel 1993). Gooch died at Camp Greene in October 1918 (Morten 1920, 454), very likely in the influenza epidemic of 1918 and 1919. Researchers estimate that "half of the 80,000 people who lived in Charlotte and at Camp Greene were infected, causing more than 1,200 deaths in a few short months. One funeral home had sixty bodies awaiting burial, and citizens told of coffins stacked like wood at the train station, waiting to be shipped home" (Perzel 1993). Back in Lexington, Private Gooch's remains rest under a marker: "Brief, brave, and glorious was his young career."

This same epitaph honors the resting place of a young White man, Alvie M. Adams, who was buried in a family plot in Paint Bank, a crossroads in Craig County, Virginia (with about 13 people per square mile). In 1917, 21-year-old Adams reported on his service registration form that he worked in "lumbering." On August 22, 1918, he left Virginia, heading for service in France.[6] Adams survived the war. He returned to Paint Bank, taking up work in "common labor," but in 1920 died of "phthisis pulmonia," likely tuberculosis. He was single and 23 years old.[7] Even though Private Adams arrived in Europe shortly before the armistice, when he died of disease at home, he was remembered as a soldier of the Great War. His gravestone identifies him as a private in Company E of the

FIGURE 5.3A AND B. A gravestone honoring Oscar T. Almarode (1897–1918), who "gave his life" in France. Calvary United Methodist Church, Augusta County.

110 Infantry Regiment of the 28th Division; "In Battle Skirmishes from Aug 17, 1918 To Mar 24, 1919. Brief Brave and Glorious Was His Young Career."

Oscar T. Almarode was another White 21-year-old who met requirements to register for conscription on June 5, 1918. His draft card says he was a farmer: tall, his eyes blue and his hair "light."[8] He's buried in Calvary United Methodist Church Cemetery, Augusta County (Figure 5.3). His headstone says that he was "Killed in Battle at Romagne France Oct 31 1918," and includes this epitaph: "He heard humanity's clear call, and knew the voice divine. He gave his life, he gave his all in deadly battle line. The silent stars in love look down where lies this loyal son. In frost and dew they weave a crown of honor he has won."

Like other World War memorials, Almarode's grave marker weaves care for country, humanity, and God into unitary obligation. Even celestial nature—"the silent stars"—lovingly honor the loyal son and fallen soldier (see Rainville 2018, 144).

Brown Colbert Borgus was, like Almarode, 21 years old when he registered

MILITARY CONFLICTS AND CEMETERIES

with the Selective Service on June 5, 1918, but his experiences before, during, and after the war were quite different, in part because he was Black. On his draft paperwork, Borgus noted he was working in Nitro, West Virginia, and identified his employer as the United States of America.[9] Almost certainly, he was among those laboring in ammunition factories gearing up for the war effort. During the war, Borgus served in a depot brigade at Camp Lee in Petersburg, Virginia.[10] The work of the depot brigades focused on receiving recruits, providing them equipment, and supporting them during preparation for deployment. His gravestone in Lexington's Evergreen Cemetery recalls this service: "Virginia Pvt 13 Co, 155 Depot Brigade, World War I, April 18, 1897–October 10, 1963." Borgus descends from a famous Virginia family: the Hemings of Monticello, President Thomas Jefferson's home in Albemarle County (Getting Word n.d. d.). Matriarch Elizabeth Hemings (1735–1807) reportedly

> was the daughter of an English sea captain named Hemings and an enslaved woman. She came with her children to Monticello about 1775, part of the inheritance from John Wayles, Jefferson's father-in-law. There she was a valued domestic [enslaved] servant. Over seventy-five of her descendants lived and worked at Monticello as butlers, seamstresses, weavers, carpenters, blacksmiths, gardeners, and musicians. Elizabeth Hemings had twelve known children (Getting Word n.d. c.).

Among her children was Betty Brown (b. 1759, d. post-1831), who had a son named Brown Colbert (1785–1833). He worked as a nail maker at Monticello, and in

> 1805, he asked to be sold to a free workman leaving Monticello, so that he and his wife would not be separated. Jefferson reluctantly agreed and the Colberts lived in slavery in Lexington, Virginia, until 1833, when they took a momentous step. In exchange for freedom, they agreed to leave Virginia for a new colony in Africa. Colbert, his wife, Mary, and their two youngest sons boarded a ship for Liberia, leaving behind three grown children who could not be freed (Getting Word n.d. a.).

Brown and Mary Colbert , along with one son, died shortly after arriving in Liberia (Getting Word n.d. a.). However, three of their children, including Robert Colbert (1806–1883), remained in Virginia, and this is the line through which Brown Colbert Borgus descends.[11]

When the war ended, Borgus settled in Lexington, married Laura Holloway, and began work as a waiter at the Virginia Military Institute.[12] His daughter, Emily Borgus Adamson, recalled:

> My father was something like the maître d', headwaiter, down at VMI. He hired and fired and had his own office. That was the time the waiters were all black and they wore black-like tuxedo pants with that stripe down the leg and waiter jackets

and black bow ties and white shirts. They waited on the Keydets [VMI cadets/students]. . . . There is a plaque there in Crozet Hall on the wall with his picture in it. There was a big ceremony and the whole family was invited (McClung 2012).

The plaque says, "In honor of Mr. Brown Colbert Borgus, 'Bogus,' VMI Head Waiter 1919–1955. A sympathetic ear for cadets. Always a diplomat. Always a gentleman."

Like many veterans of the Great War and other conflicts, Borgus lived a rich life with extensive family and community ties, and work with responsibility and respect. But at the end, at the grave site, he like many other veterans is remembered for the role he played in America's military. For some, service is memorialized as the most meaningful part of their brief, brave, and glorious young lives. Others seem to have gone reluctantly, citing duty to family but recruited for duty to country. Whether they died in the war or survived, whether they were Black or White, whether they volunteered or were drafted, soldiers' gravestones mark them as integral to the nation, and the nation to the world.

WORLD WAR II

Memory of the Second World War winds out diversely, poignantly, and complexly in Valley burying grounds. The general history is familiar to most: the Holocaust, the atomic bomb, the millions of deaths, city, town, and countryside in ruins. On the ground in Valley cemeteries, the international conflagration materializes on headstones through personal experiences that gesture toward many perspectives. What is it to be an American? Who are "we"? Memorials suggest that we are liberators, we are survivors of nuclear war, we are remnants of ancestral lines that barely survived concentration camps to find some freedom but also prejudice in the US. We are families with members lost to the Pacific or to skies over Italy. Epitaphs of Americans in these generations heed their greatness but often acknowledge, too, enduring costs of conflicts.

Kim Yoshiko Wright died in Virginia at age 70, but the accomplishment highlighted on her grave marker[13] occurred when she was six years old: "Hiroshima Survivor. Loving wife and mother." She predeceased her husband, Randolph William Wright, whose marker describes him as a chief warrant officer retired from the US Navy and "devoted husband."

Robert Leroy Gangwer was 21 years old and working as a truck driver when he got married on September 5, 1942.[14] Two days later he enlisted in the Army.[15] His gravestone says that he was "Killed in Burma, Oct. 20, 1944."[16] Other gravestones record other losses. Private Earl G. Pauley was "Killed in Action 1944 Anzio Beach Head, Italy."[17] Andrew G. Hancock "Died at Sea" (Figure 5.4). Staff Sergeant Billy S. Thomas was "Killed in Action Feb. 5, 1944 in the North African Area."[18] Thorold J. B. Sharitz is "Buried in St. Avold France."[19] Willis Jennings Comer is "Missing in B-29 over Tokyo."[20]

FIGURE 5.4. Grave marker of Andrew G. Hancock (1923–1945), who "died at sea," Morning Star Temple Hill Cemetery, Bland County.

Sergeant Lyle W. Fitzgerald was "Killed Over Belgium. Dec. 30, 1943." Lyle Fitzgerald's father, Hansford Fitzgerald, owned a general store in the crossroads town of Riverheads.[21] Hansford and his wife, Mary Julia Fitzgerald, had five children, Lyle being the oldest.[22] Lyle's 1942 military registration card indicates that he had completed four years of high school and was working in the manufacturing of textiles. It lists his weight as 131 pounds and his height as 65 inches, or 5 feet 5 inches.[23] His relatively short stature and slight build were doubtless key factors in his being assigned the position of a ball turret gunner on a B-17 (Together We Served n.d.). He deployed to England in November 1943 and joined a combat crew within the 360th Bomb Squadron. On December 30, 1943, this crew was part of a raid on a chemical works in Germany. According to reports "Flak was . . . light, and only a few encounters with enemy aircraft were noted. After the bomb run, the B-17 dropped from formation, and was losing altitude as 3 German fighters began an attack. The aircraft reached cloud cover, and the enemy aircraft broke off the attacks. Damage had been done, however, and the aircraft crash-landed in an open field near the French-Belgium border" (Together We Served n.d.).

The ball turret gunner was among the most vulnerable positions: these men "were protected only by a glass bubble jutting out from the bowels of the plane. Permanently fixed and unable to be retracted, there was no hiding from enemy attack. It was an enclosure that at any time could become an airman's coffin. And often did" (Pastor 2017). The tragedy of such ends was famously captured by Randall Jarrell in his five-line poem, "The Death of the Ball Turret Gunner." The poet imagines falling from his "mother's sleep" into "the State" and being awoken to flak and "nightmare fighters." It concludes starkly: "When I died they washed me out of the turret with a hose" (Jarrell 1980).

Numerous writers have offered analyses of and commentary on this poem. Among them, Frances Ferguson (1974) observes that the

> poem so thoroughly manifests the lack of a middle between the gunner's birth and his death—in the life and in the brevity of the poetry—that the time between birth and death is lost. . . . Jarrell pays his shocked tribute to the indeterminate forces that produce mere circumstance, which in turn become a kind of grisly determinism as it overtakes the speaker, along with his counterparts, the nameless and faceless soldiers who died along with him.

This poem and interpretation, however, don't seem really to capture Sergeant Lyle Fitzgerald's experience. Together We Served (TWS) is an "online community connecting and honoring every American who has worn the uniform of the United States military" (Foster n.d.) A page on the Air Force TWS website explains that

> a group of [Belgian] civilians attempted to assist the airmen, but Sgt Fitzgerald died of wounds received in the fighter attacks soon after the crash. Other crew members were captured, while others managed to evade. The dead crew members were buried in a local cemetery, and later returned to the U.S. An application for a headstone was signed by Fitzgerald's father on August 28, 1949. Sgt Fitzgerald lies today in the Calvary United Methodist Church Cemetery in Riverheads, Virginia (Together We Served n.d.).

Most of his flight mates survived. Memorialization—from the Belgians' efforts to his affectionate hometown burial to Air Force histories—strives to honor the human sacrifice enmeshed in the seeming inhumanness of a ball turret gunner's death.

Other gravestones—particularly those in the Valley's Jewish cemeteries—also underscore the tragedy of people lost to dehumanizing forces. Albert Diener (1906–1996) and his wife Sari Diener (1908–1992) are buried at Beth Israel Cemetery in Roanoke. Above the last name on their shared stone is a menorah and this epitaph: "Survivors of Concentration Camps." The back of their marker memorializes Albert's father, mother, and two brothers, as well as his two sisters and their husbands and three children. It also lists Sari's father and mother and her two brothers. All, the stone says, were "From Csenger, Hungary. Perished in Auschwitz."

The grave of Max Trompeter (1920–1996) is nearby at Temple Emanuel Cemetery in Roanoke (Figure 5.5). Both faces of the marker feature the Star of David, and the rear reads, "In loving memory of his family members who perished in the Holocaust." It lists the names of his father, stepmother, paternal grandparents, and nine brothers and sisters who were killed. Max Trompeter and his wife Geraldine[24] were well-known in Pulaski, Virginia, where they ran Max's Bakery for many years (Horn 2006).

FIGURE 5.5. Gravestone of Max Trompeter (1920–1996), also memorializing his parents, grandparents, and siblings who "perished in the Holocaust." Temple Emanuel Cemetery, Roanoke.

Max and Geraldine's son, Jacob A. Trompeter, recorded memories of his father in an oral history interview with Ferrum College professor Marcia Horn (2006). Jacob emphasized that his father, Max Trompeter, had talked frequently with him and his sisters about his experiences in the Holocaust: "It was very important to him. To educate us about it. To tell us about the atrocities." And Jacob committed to sharing his father's story because Max had "wanted people to know, so people wouldn't forget. It was important to him. He wanted to bear witness." Jacob explained:

My dad was a baker. Ten generations in the bakery business. So we had a bakery in Pulaski. It was called Max's Bakery. . . . We were Jewish. We kept kosher. It was different in a small town because sixty miles was the closest synagogue, in Roanoke. We had to travel to Roanoke to synagogue. My dad taught us Hebrew because we couldn't travel to Roanoke regularly. We had services at home, on Shabbat. We'd always light our candles on Friday night and say our prayers. . . .

I remember many times, people would break my dad's store windows. They'd throw a rock through them, or they'd paint a swastika on the windows. In the sixties. They painted a swastika on the sidewalk in front of our house once. . . . My father said the more you stir something that stinks, the worse it gets. He didn't trust the government. He wouldn't go to them. So we just survived.

When the Nazis occupied Poland [in 1939], they took over all the Jewish companies and bakeries and stores, and made them continue baking. And that's why he stayed til '43 there [before being sent to a series of concentration camps]. . . . He had a younger brother with him, through all the camps, til January of '45. . . . My dad used to smuggle food to him. . . . He said he saved his food and tried to get extra food to him, and a friend of his was the one who guarded that [building], another Jew. And [one day my dad] asked him, "Where's Moshe?" And he said, "He's not here." And my dad said, "Where is he? Where?" He kept pressuring him. And he said, "He's over there." And he pointed across, and there was a big pile of naked bodies, stacked up like wood my father said. There was snow, and he went over there and the top guy, he knocked the snow off, and it was his brother. He said they took him to the crematorium and burned them.

My father used to mash coal to get a little oil out of it, for nutrient. He told me he crushed bones he found in the dirt, to eat the marrow out of them, because he was starving. He weighed 82 pounds when he was liberated.

I just wonder how he kept his sanity and kept his faith in God. It did not make him bitter. . . . They didn't believe in violence. They thought God would save them. And He did save a lot of them. A lot He didn't. (Horn 2006)

Freed by the US Army on May 5, 1945 (Pynn 2014), Max Trompeter lived in Italy before immigrating to the United States. He resided in Virginia nearly half a century—but, looking toward the end of his own life, he remembered on his grave marker the brother he'd tried to save, Moshe, as well as their siblings who'd died—Rivkah, Sholom, Rosa, Abraham, Simchah, Netta, Mordechai, and Samuel. Max Trompeter was not a veteran but a victim of the war. Though he physically survived it, his family members' suffering stayed with him all his life, and in the end—on his gravestone in Roanoke, Virginia—he's reunited with them through memorialization.

Members of some other religious persuasions in the Valley similarly "didn't believe in violence" and declined to fight. On the edge of a Mennonite church cemetery near Harrisonburg is a memorial reading, "Posm Twist Earth Commitals. Look Ye on High. We Are Not Here" (Figure 5.6). This gravestone commemorates Nathan E. Showalter (1926–2018) and Mary E. Witmer Showalter (1928–2009). It appears that "Possum Twist" is an old colloquial name for this part of Rockingham County. The balance of the Showalters' epitaph refers to their understanding that their bodies had been committed to the earth but they themselves—their immortal souls—were "on high," in Heaven. As a Mennonite and religious conscientious objector to the war, when drafted, Nathan Showalter was assigned to a Soil Conservation Service base camp located in a Civilian Conservation Corps camp northeast of Powellville, Maryland. . . . The men performed dangerous work cutting and cleaning drainage channels of the Pokomoke River to limit erosion of low lying farm land. . . . The river flowed south through the peninsula, falling about an inch to a mile. The channel, choked by silt and trees, prevented the ditches from draining the low lying farm land along the river. Farmers had abandoned the land. The dangerous work required use of axes, saws, slogging through acres of mucky soil, heavy machinery and dynamite. . . . By autumn 1946, the water table had lowered sufficiently making it possible to farm an additional thirty-seven thousand formerly unproductive acres (Mennonite Central Committee n.d.)

Refusing to take human life, Nathan Showalter's wartime legacy was creating land on which crops would be grown to sustain it.

FIGURE 5.6. Grave site of Mary E. Witmer Showalter (1928–2009) and Nathan E. Showalter (1926–2018)— "Look ye on high/ We are not here." Adjacent to Weavers Mennonite Church Cemetery, Harrisonburg.

If mortuary spaces make claims about social identity and cultural values, gravestones dedicated to Valley residents who had varied involvement in the Second World War suggest multifaceted relationships to American involvement. Markers remember Virginians who survived Hiroshima and whose relatives didn't survive Auschwitz, those freed through conflict and those who would not take up arms. In this complexity, memorialization is like myth, like history. It can charter societies—telling us who "we" are and what beliefs we should embrace and defend—even as it offers discrepant claims: fighting for freedom is noble, and war breaks the Lord's commandment (Glassie 1994, 967–68). As we the living face questions of morality, obligation, and community, cemeteries can be, recalling Levi-Strauss' phrase, "good to think with."

KOREA AND VIETNAM

Memorialization of the dead from conflicts in the second half of the twentieth century also extends invitation to think about what ethical courses of action might look like in complicated times. Cemeteries in the Valley of Virginia record family lost to battles—military and ideological—on a global scale. To be an American, these burial grounds seem to suggest, is to be prepared to sacrifice children for the nation in contests with superpowers on the earth's other side, to show determination even when all seems lost, and to come home, sometimes, to deep disappointment.

"Funeral services for Cpl. Charles W. Dameron, 20, who died in action in Korea on Sept. 19, 1950, will be held Sunday. . . . Military rites will be conducted by the Waynesboro Veterans Burial Team. . . . The body arrived with military escort" (*Staunton News-Leader* 1951). Dameron enlisted when he was 18 and died at 20.[25] He'd served in the US Army's Medical Department and was killed as the "result of missile wound received in action."[26] Corporal Dameron (1930–1950) is memorialized on a three-person marker with his parents Sarah and William Dameron, a carpenter, in a Methodist church cemetery (Augusta County). It includes a photograph of him in uniform, young and somber. His memorialization, like many others from the Korean War, frames the deceased as a young man who—doing his duty for the nation—lost opportunity to move into fuller adulthood with work, a life in the community, or a family of his own. His parents brought him into the fold of their family in death, as he had been during his young life, with a gravestone dedicated to the three of them. His father died in 1965, and his mother in 1985.

A memorial to Howard Lovin Campbell (1926–1953) in the same cemetery is strikingly similar, as was his experience (Figure 5.7). His father, Talmage Lovin Campbell, was a laborer in a nursery.[27] Howard had worked at the DuPont manufacturing plant in Waynesboro, "mostly in the maintenance department," before joining the Army (*Evening Leader* 1953). He arrived in Korea in September, 1952

FIGURE 5.7. Gravestone memorializing Howard L. Campbell (1926–1953), killed in Korea, and his parents who died years later. Calvary United Methodist Church, Augusta County.

and became "chief gunner of a heavy mortar company with the 40th Division" (*Evening Leader* 1953). Some eight months later, in May 1953, he was killed in action in the North Korean Sector.[28] Staunton's *Evening Leader* (1953) reported, "The Defense Department . . . notified Mr. And Mrs. T. L. Campbell of Stuarts Draft that the body of their son, Howard L. Campbell, is on the way back to the United States from Korea." Corporal Campbell shares a grave marker with his parents, his father dying in 1969 and his mother in 1984. The gravestone is engraved with modest sprigs of ivy and grapes, and a photograph of Howard Campbell in uniform. Both Dameron and Campbell were awarded the Purple Heart.

US Marine Corps Sergeant Charles A. Gregory (1928–2011) survived his tour in Korea.[29] At his death some 60 years later, Gregory's grave marker in Southwest Virginia Veterans Cemetery, Dublin (Pulaski County), remembers him with the inscription "The Frozen Chosin." The Battle of the Chosin Reservoir

> was one of the defining battles of the [Korean] war and of the Marine Corps. Today, the events of that battle serve as a major history lesson for young Marines. Throughout boot camp, recruits will hear all about the heroics of this battle, instilling that "never-give-up" mentality that defines a Marine. From this battle comes some of the Corps' greatest . . . quotes. Sayings such as, "We're surrounded. Good, that simplifies the problem" and, "We're not retreating; we're attacking in a different direction." (Baker 2019)

In November 1950, the US and its allies had moved into North Korea, and the war seemed to be coming to a close. Unexpectedly, however, tens of thousands of Chinese soldiers arrived to support and defend North Korea (Seelinger, n.d.). It was bitterly cold, the terrain was mountainous, and the US Marines and Army were outnumbered and virtually surrounded:

> The fighting lasted 17 days. By the battle's end, the fighting was hand-to-hand. Men were using their teeth, rifle butts, and anything else they could get their hands on to fight the Chinese onslaught. . . . With the ground frozen and foxholes impossible to dig, Marines used the bodies of the Chinese attackers as sandbags to help protect them from incoming fire. . . . Marines were forced to start fighting back towards South Korea. Still surrounded and with elements of the [Chinese Army] in the way, Marines had to fight their way out against a 360-degree front as they moved south. (Baker 2019)

Chosin "was technically a loss for the Marines. But it was a Pyrrhic victory at best for the Communists" because they lost more soldiers—untold thousands.

> Despite the loss, this battle instills in every Marine the ability to find strength. "You never give up, did those men give up?" This statement is made by almost every Marine who has ever served since. When faced with overwhelming odds, we use the thoughts of the Frozen Chosin to remind us to never retreat, never surrender, and raise hell. (Baker 2019)

In 1966, Winfred Lee Smith was an 18-year-old service station attendant in Greenville (Augusta County).[30] He started a tour with the Army in Vietnam in May 1970 and only survived three weeks.[31] Smith was a "ground casualty," dying from "gun shot or small arms fire." Sergeant Smith's remains were returned home and interred at Pines Chapel Presbyterian Church.

Another young Augusta County man survived the war but not the aftermath. A 1960 graduate of Wilson Memorial High School in Fishersville, he included his motto next to his senior picture: "Fortune and fame follow the brave." He served in the US Air Force 1960–1964, including in Vietnam. By 1965 he was back home, working in a manufacturing plant and getting married. Ten years later his wife sued for divorce. Three months after it was granted, he died from a self-inflicted gunshot wound to the chest. He's buried in a church cemetery with both a brass military marker and an upright headstone bearing peaceful arboreal images.

Moving through nearly any cemetery in the Valley of Virginia brings America's history of war to view and to mind. Visitors to burial grounds encounter reminders: killed in Italy, in France, over Tokyo. Died under fire in Vietnam; died afterward from suicide. Whole families obliterated through starvation and radiation. Not giving up, fighting despite all odds. Not taking up arms, choosing pacifist service. Remembering these many dead prompts the living to perceive themselves as part of the diverse national whole, and to encourage thinking "about moral problems and human potential" (Glassie 1994, 966).

We've saved the Civil War for last because, in the Valley of Virginia, it's treated emotively, qualitatively differently than other conflicts' experiences and fallout. The difference is rooted partially in outcome, as a proud people were beaten. Countless White Virginians went all in, and lost. Headstone after stone after stone after stone mourns this defeat, the loss of young man after young man after young man (Figure 5.8).

FIGURE 5.8. The dead, named and unknown, along "Confederate Lane" in the Stonewall section of Mount Hebron Cemetery, Winchester.

This war is also different in its palpability. I live in the crossroads town of Fishersville where on March 2, 1865, Union Brigadier General George Armstrong Custer encountered a small Confederate sentry positioned to keep watch for Confederate troops who were six miles to the east in Waynesboro. The road Custer used closely parallels the main corridor through Fishersville. Marching east toward Waynesboro, Custer's forces encountered the remainder of the Army of the Valley commanded by Lieutenant General Jubal Early. A good friend of mine lived on Pine Street in Waynesboro, the road where Early aligned his Confederate forces. Their backs to the South River, they watched for the North coming from the west. The grocery we use is on part of the battlefield where Custer's Union troops routed Early's men. The pizza restaurant my son likes is near the train tracks over which the rebels tried to retreat in panic.

Where I work in Lexington, I recently sunk a shovel into the ground and hit a Civil War–era Minié ball. I look out of my office window onto the chapel where Robert E. Lee worshipped and the mausoleum where he's buried. My University, Washington and Lee (W&L), bears his name. W&L's campus adjoins Virginia Military Institute (VMI). After VMI cadets helped turn back a Union offensive at the Battle of New Market in Shenandoah County (1864), General David Hunter successfully moved south, wreaking havoc in the Valley. It all seems both spatially and temporally present. Sites seem to hold these memories (Fletcher 2020).

I talked with a man in his seventies, a lifelong resident of Rockbridge County, about the continued embedding of the Confederacy in living communities. He raised an eyebrow, took a breath, shrugged, and said simply, "The war was here. I remember sitting on my grandfather's front porch, and he would tell how Union troops came over that hill" on an ancient road now called the "Lee Highway." His grandfather could still see in his mind's eye the blue wave crashing over the ridge, pouring down the Valley, as he stood on the pine boards of his porch, his wife and children in the house at his back. His grandson came to see it, too, in his imagination, inherited memory anchored to the landscape.

This was the route taken by General Hunter in 1864, when under order from Union commander General Ulysses S. Grant, he and some 18,000 soldiers moved south through the Valley laying waste to the "breadbasket of the Confederacy." Reaching Lexington, Hunter ordered the torching of the governor's home and of VMI. A Union officer remarked that the "burning of the Institute made a grand picture, a vast volume of black smoke rolled above the flames and covered the horizon." Meanwhile a Lexington resident recalled that "we remained as quiet as possible all the afternoon while the town was alive with soldiers plundering and robbing the inhabitants" (Williams 2013). Later General Philip Sheridan followed General Grant's order to "make the Shenandoah Valley so desolate that crows flying over it would have to carry their own provender." Sheridan claimed to have slaughtered thousands of sheep, hogs, and cattle, and laid in ashes "2,000 barns filled with wheat, hay, and farming implements [and] over seventy mills filled with flour and wheat" (Anderson 2015).

The Civil War remains raw in the Valley of Virginia, and tensions run high over the meaning and future of Confederate memorials. Like some other objects, they "operate much more at the level of the mythic and totemic than that of a linear historicism or memorialization" (Dawdy 2016, 144). Stonewall Jackson's grave site, Robert E. Lee's resting place, the burials of Confederate soldiers up and down the Valley of Virginia are totemic: a symbol seen as the sacred emblem of a group. Confederate memorials possess a kind of "mana," an "evocative force that runs through some objects that makes people feel like they belong to a collectivity" (Dawdy 2016, 154). Cemeteries remain ideological battlegrounds in fights over identity, community, and morality (Baugher and Veit 2014, 163), as well as politics and power (Blair 2004). Every February in honor of "Lee-Jackson Day," Confederate reenactors—with uniforms, swords, pistols, and battle flags—muster near Jackson's grave and from there launch a march through Lexington. Such staging illustrates ways in which cemeteries can be "part of the active manipulation of people's perceptions, beliefs and allegiances" (Parker Pearson 1999, 32). The observation that archaeologist Mike Parker Pearson made of ancient Europe holds again in the Valley: "The dead are everywhere." Through treatment of their mortal remains, we "reaffirm and construct our attitudes" toward the deceased, place, and social identities today (Parker Pearson 1999, 124).

Among the countless Confederate dead is James Wilson Poague (1834–1864); he was wounded in action at Todd's Tavern in Spotsylvania County on May 7, 1864,[32] and died weeks later, on May 22, 1864 according to his headstone at Falling Spring Presbyterian Church Cemetery (Rockbridge County). His epitaph says, "I had hoped to live to preach the gospel but there is a brighter prospect before me now."

At the same cemetery is a stone in memory of "John Poague Moore Co. I 4th Regt. Liberty Hall Volunteers" who was "Killed at Appomattox 9th April 1865." Moore, 24 years old, died on the last day of the war on the field where Lee surrendered.

At Fincastle Presbyterian Church (Botetourt County), a Confederate States of America (CSA) cross and granite stone remember Major Joseph Washington Anderson, mortally wounded during battle in Mississippi.[33] Anderson was scion of a prominent family: the son of Colonel John T. Anderson, well-to-do attorney and long-time member of the Virginia Legislature, and the nephew of Judge Francis T. Anderson who served on the Supreme Court of Virginia (*Richmond Dispatch* 1879). In its announcement of Colonel Anderson's death, the *Richmond Dispatch* (1879) noted that, "educated under the old *regime*, he [had] inherited the sterling qualities that characterized the ruling class in the better days of the republic." It concluded by remembering his son, Major Joseph W. Anderson, "who fell in defence of Vicksburg, Miss, in 1863."

At Mt. Carmel Presbyterian Church Cemetery in Steeles Tavern, among the Confederate dead are two soldiers who "Fell at the Battle of Manassas July 21 1861": 20-year-old Benjamin A. Bradley and 22-year-old Charles William Bell. In the same cemetery lie the remains of 18-year-old John Bolar McGuffin who in 1864 "fell a victim to desease in defence of his country. By his Captain: He was a gallant soldier, noble, brave and generous and the idol of his company."

Just down the road in the McDowell family cemetery (Fairfield in Rockbridge County) is a marker dedicated to "Samuel Wallace, Lieutenant in the Confederate Army Born Feb. 23, 1834 Killed at Petersburg Apr. 1, 1864. Death is swallowed up in Victory."

In addition to the ubiquity of the Confederate dead from Winchester in the north to Wytheville in the south, the enormity of the conflict's impact on the Valley is manifest in individual burying grounds. At Tinkling Spring Presby-

FIGURE 5.9. In the foreground is a gravestone honoring First Lieutenant Joseph S. Coiner of the 52nd Virginia Infantry Regiment, "killed at the Battle at Spotsylvania Court House." Tinkling Spring Presbyterian Church Cemetery, Augusta County.

FIGURE 5.10. Union soldiers, National Cemetery, Winchester.

terian Church Cemetery (Fishersville, Augusta County), one surging marble obelisk after the next remembers the death of a young man in gray:

Joseph S. Coiner "killed in the battle of Spotsylvania Court House May 12, 1864, aged 29 years" (Figure 5.9).

William Luther McComb was fatally injured at Second Manassas (Bull Run) in 1862.[34] "Aged 19 Years & 29 days. If to die for liberty be right, remember me. If wrong forget me."

William W. Finley "Died in the service of his country Feb. 13, 1862, aged 19 Yr. 10 Mo. 13 ds. Dear William."

Another memorial is "Sacred to the memory of My Husband Jas. W. Hamilton Who was killed in the Second Battle of Manassas Aug. 29, 1862. in the 29 Yr. Of his age. Asleep in Jesus. Jimmie."

And another: "Sacred to the memory of My Husband Capt. Jas. A. Dold, C.S.A who was Killed in the Battle of Cold Harbor May 30, 1864 in the 27 Yr. of his age. I shall go to him but he will not return to me."[35]

Though many of the dead are named and known, thousands of others aren't. Row after row of Confederate resting places are simply numbered at Mount

Hebron's Stonewall Section in Winchester: "260," "261." On the other side of a wall in Winchester National Cemetery lie the Union dead, some remembered by name: "Solomon Bequeath Co. F. 12 PA. Cav." and "In Memory of James Ford 21st NY Calvary Civil War Killed Jul 1 1864 in Winchester at Age 38." The names of many of their fellow Union soldiers are not known but marked by numbers (Figure 5.10).

The same is the case at Staunton National Cemetery, where 518 of the 749 Civil-War era interments are unknown (National Cemetery Administration 2019). Hundreds of gravestones are simply inscribed "Unknown," or in some cases "Two Unknown U.S. Soldiers," or "Three Unknown U.S. Soldiers." Among the named dead are Corporal Peleg Beals (New York), Private William Dove (Ohio), and Sergeant A. K. Gilmore (West Virginia). Soldiers here were killed on (and originally buried near) various Virginia battlefields and, after the war, gathered for interment in the National Cemetery.

Many people who survived the war were memorialized years later for their roles in it. At Tinkling Spring Presbyterian Church Cemetery, the epitaph for Henry C. Carter (1844–1929), for example, is simply "Confederate Veteran." George W. Finley, DD (doctor of divinity), was "Pastor of Tinkling Spring Church from Feb. 1892 to April 1909. Devoted husband and father, faithful minister, gallant Confederate soldier."

Allie Beverley Pence (1886–1982) died while Ronald Reagan was in the White House, but her gravestone recalls her as "Wife of Civil War Veteran David Pence."

FLAGS, CATECHISMS, AND FRUIT

Confederate Captain William Randolph is buried in a cemetery formerly associated with a Presbyterian congregation. One face of his gravestone reads: "Wm. H. Randolph/ Capt. Co. D. 5 Va. Regt./ Stonewall Brigade/ who fell in battle at Gaines Mill near Richmond/ June 27, 1862/ aged 28 yrs. 8 Mo. & 21 ds." Another face includes a line from Horace—"Dulce et decorum est pro patria mori"—or "It is sweet and fitting to die for the homeland," and continues: "No more he'll grasp the warrior's sword,/ But lies all mute and low./ Where comrade's kindly word/ No more will wake him now./ But God who willed the spark of life/ To be both faint and brief,/ In mercy to our world of strife/ Gave memory as relief."

The nearby church building is now a private home, but the cemetery is beautifully maintained, and new American flags mark the resting places of all veterans, including those who fought against the United States. When I visited one July day in 2017, an older man who lives nearby came over to talk. He said he takes care of the grass in the cemetery and drew my attention to some substantial Confederate gravestones. I said I was surprised to see American flags on these graves and asked him who put them there. He smiled. I said, "Is it a secret?"

FIGURE 5.11. A footstone recently marked with both the Confederate States of America's Southern Cross of Honor and the United States of America's flag. Godwin Cemetery Fincastle.

He smiled. I ventured, "That wasn't the flag they fought for." He nodded and smiled.

The phenomenon of honoring Confederate soldiers' burial places with American flags is widely spread in the Valley (Figure 5.11). At Sharon Union Baptist Church in Clifton Forge, Peter M. Nicely (1844–1923) has a gravestone recognizing him as "Pvt Co. C 22 VA Inf." An iron Southern Cross of Honor is on one side of his marker, and a cloth American flag is on the other. This pairing appears, too, at St. James Lutheran Church Cemetery in Augusta County, the municipal Godwin Cemetery in Fincastle, Elk Run Cemetery in Elkton, and countless others.

For many, there's no discrepancy in embracing both the Confederacy and the United States. The Civil War to them was the second American Revolution, and they sought freedom's cause as surely in the 1860s as American patriots had 90 years earlier. Believing that the Confederates were the true Americans, the Stars and Stripes can partner with the Stars and Bars on Confederate burials.

The Sons of Confederate Veterans (SCV) make this understanding explicit:

> The citizen-soldiers who fought for the Confederacy personified the best qualities of America. The preservation of liberty and freedom was the motivating factor

in the South's decision to fight the Second American Revolution. The tenacity with which Confederate soldiers fought underscored their belief in the rights guaranteed by the Constitution. These attributes are the underpinning of our democratic society and represent the foundation on which this nation was built (Sons of Confederate Veterans 2019).

In 1906 the Commander General of the United Confederate Veterans charged the SCV with vindicating the cause for which they'd fought: "To your strength will be given the defense of the Confederate soldier's good name, the guardianship of his history, the emulation of his virtues, the perpetuation of those principles which he loved and which you love also, and those ideals which made him glorious and which you also cherish" (Sons of Confederate Veterans 2019).

The United Daughters of the Confederacy (UDC), similarly, is "dedicated to the purpose of honoring the memory of its Confederate ancestors; protecting, preserving and marking the places made historic by Confederate valor; collecting and preserving the material for a truthful history of the War Between the States" (United Daughters of the Confederacy n.d.b.). They maintain that, in the words of the "Children of the Confederacy Creed," the "War Between the States was not a rebellion nor was its underlying cause to sustain slavery" (Wilson and Millweard 2019).

The UDC's website includes the Confederate catechisms, "part of the culture and history" of the Children of the Confederacy. "Members are encouraged to recite basic beliefs and elements of Confederate history. Children compete at all levels to display excellence" (United Daughters of the Confederacy n.d.a.). UDC members have produced a number of catechisms since 1904 (Heyse 2008).

A Confederate Catechism (1929) written by Lyon Gardiner Tyler, son of US President John Tyler and himself president of the College of William and Mary, emphasized that the root of the war was not slavery but abolitionism:

Q. "Was slavery the cause of secession or the war?"

A. "No. Slavery existed previous to the Constitution. . . . It was not slavery, but the vindictive, intemperate antislavery movement that was at the bottom of all the troubles" (Tyler 1920, 2).

Confederate catechisms penned by others echoed this point and similar themes that continue in current-day circulation:

Q. "Were the sufferings of the South ended by the surrender?"

A. "No; they suffered from poverty, negro rule, and military domination" (quoted in Heyse 2008, 427–28).

In 1901, UDC member Adelia A. Dunovant clearly framed the intent of these question-and-answer lists, and by extension, the intent of much of the project of the Lost Cause supporters. She explained that an error would lie in embalming, as it were, historic truths and putting them away in the tomb of the Confederacy—making them as devoid of energizing influence as an Egyptian mummy—instead of bringing them and keeping them ever before us in the vital, living present. Memory is not a passivity, but an ever active faculty. . . . History should be made to serve its true purpose by bringing its lessons into the present and using them as a guide to the future. (quoted in Heyse 2008, 408)

The UDC and SCV are without peer in the efficacy and longevity of their determination to bring Old South ideology into twenty-first century social life. Their erection and maintenance of grave markers and cenotaphs to honor Confederate veterans, as well as their installation of Southern Crosses and new flags over Confederate remains, keeps the past as they understand it "vital," an "energizing influence" and guide to future action. By designs such as these, the Civil War is cultivated as a powerful presence on memorial landscapes, including gravestones historic and contemporary.

The Confederate dead are kept in living memory even more doggedly than most other veterans in part through the placement of iron crosses, flags—both American and Confederate—and gifts. Devotees of General Thomas Stonewall Jackson, regularly leave fresh lemons on his grave site in Lexington. An apocryphal story suggests that Jackson loved lemons and, though his preferred treat was probably a peach, the tradition of leaving lemons for him holds fast. In fact, the lemons have become integral to competing contemporary cultural projects.

In 2015, several town residents started leaving on Jackson's grave lemons on which they'd written "Black Lives Matter." I interviewed participant Coye Heard. He explained, "On Lee-Jackson Day in 2015, I got four or five friends together and inscribed some 300 lemons. The Friday night, we dumped them at midnight. All lemons were gone by 10:00 the next morning. On Easter, I inscribed a dozen lemons and left them that morning. By that afternoon someone had taken them out and stomped on them." He said that he wasn't defacing the Jackson memorial but was asserting the humanity of African Americans, past and present. Heard's intent was

to restore what is obscured, erased in remembrance of the Confederacy, the suppressed memory of enslaved people Jackson owned. Hetty was his wife's nursemaid. They received George, Cyrus, Emma, and Albert as wedding presents. Jackson rented Albert to Virginia Military Institute; Albert did the work and Jackson got the money. Jackson bought Amy as a gift for his wife. Hetty, George, Cyrus, Emma, Albert and Amy matter. The humanity of Black people still has an asterisk around it, as if they're not truly human.[36]

Cemeteries—sites of memory tied intimately to the buried bodies of culturally-charged figures—are also sites of contest in civic belonging, collective identity, and cultural values.

There's a good case to be made that interest in the Civil War—drawing it into current civic life—is increasing. One indication is the appearance of Confederate references etched into gravestones. The marker for Ricky Lee Sheffer (1966–2006), for example, in Staunton's Thornrose Cemetery features the "Bonnie Blue" flag with a single star: a Confederate flag flying over Fort Sumpter at the start of the war. The back of Sheffer's gravestone says, "Let us cross over the river, and rest under the trees. Thomas Jonathan "Stonewall" Jackson, last words, 10 May 1863." A memorial page for Scheffer notes that he was a tool and die maker, husband, father, and member of the Fifth Virginia Company E Confederate reenactors, and that "he was laid to rest in his uniform minus his brogans because they hurt his feet." Sheffer's wife left him a note on the memorial page: "My Rebel I hope you are making gravy for Stonewall and the boys."[37]

Roy Albert Cole (1959–2002, Winchester) was a US veteran and has a flat military-issued marker. He also has an upright black granite headstone with images of an eagle and Confederate battle flag. In Lexington, Russell "Cliff" Clifton Flournoy (1977–2004) was a Lieutenant in the US Navy. He and his father, Mitchell Wayne Flournoy (1950–), share a stone. The back of the gravestone memorializes the younger Flournoy as a 1999 graduate of Virginia Military Institute, and an etched Confederate battle flag covers most of the surface.

Harry E. Kibler, Jr. (1971–1993, Woodstock, Shenandoah County) has a flat bronze marker with images of a motorcycle and battle flag. The marker for Jeffery Wade Perdue (1957–2009, Giles County) includes his photograph, bronze trees in relief, and the Stars and Bars. Women, too, have Confederate motifs on their graves. In Winchester, the gravestone for William Harrington Smith, Jr. (d. 2004) and wife Barbara Gray Armistead Smith, "Boogee," (d. 2015) includes a full-color Confederate battle flag. Her obituary recalls her as "a quiet and highly intelligent woman, who was an avid student of history," and "her passion was the Civil War."[38]

Passion about the Civil War indeed runs high in the Valley of Virginia— doubtless in large measure because so much of it transpired here and because so many of those who fought in it are laid to rest here. But it's also more: for many the battle flag and the American flag are symbols of local self-determination and freedom. For many others, the battle flag, the Lost Cause, and the Old South are symbols of a heritage founded on enslavement. Questions of who "we" are persist, pressing the dead and their memorial markers into action.

The gravestone of Andrew Hale Snyder (1956–1998, Bland County) includes an etched image of the Confederate battle flag and the epitaph—"Sic Semper Tyrannis," or "Thus Always to Tyrants"—with an image of a classical warrior, Virtue, standing over the defeated Tyranny. It has a long history, some say dating back to the assassination of Julius Caesar. John Wilkes Booth reportedly yelled this phrase when he shot President Lincoln in Ford's Theater, along with "The South is avenged!"

"Sic Semper Tyrannis" is the official motto of the Commonwealth of Virginia. What would this phrase mean from the mouths of the enslaved? Or in the voices of Black soldiers who proudly served in uniform during the First and Second World Wars, but came home to segregated businesses, busses, schools, and cemeteries, and to the terrors of Jim Crow? When is the defeat of tyranny celebrated, and who decides?

When might the Valley's Civil War soldiers truly be laid to rest? And what would their retirement imply about the ways that Valley residents understand who they are, or who we Americans believe ourselves to be?

CHAPTER 6

"Don't Forget about Daddy and Me"
Reunions of the Quick and the Dead

COMMUNITY LIKE A PHOENIX

In the mountains of western Maryland, a gravestone erected to a man who died in 2000 features a grinning winged skull and the words, "Remember me as you pass by. As you are now, so once was I. As I am now, soon you shall be. Prepare for death and follow me."

This inscription derives from the medieval European tradition of *memento mori*: a reminder that death is inevitable and an encouragement to make life choices accordingly. A fourteenth-century European version reads, "Good people who pass this way, to God unceasingly please pray for the soul of the body that lies below" (Ariès 1981, 219).

The formulation implies a worldview in which living and dead are responsible to each other, part of a community that transcends the grave. A "two-way communication was being established, a message to the deceased for the repose of his soul, and from the deceased for the edification of the living" (Ariès 1981, 218). *Memento mori* represents a classic gift exchange—remembrance or prayers flow in one direction, advice in the other (Mauss 1950). These transactions both express and maintain social connections among members of a community that includes the quick and the dead.

The *memento mori* poem in western Maryland, appears on the gravestone of renowned anthropologist James Deetz (1930–2000). The words chosen to fete Deetz have a familiar ring to the many of us who've read his work about the cultural import of changes in historic gravestone design. He and others showed how material culture—gravestones as well as dishes, furniture, and houses—documented pervasive cultural changes during the eighteenth and nineteenth centuries in the eastern United States (Deetz and Dethlefsen 1967). Earlier assemblages expressed assumptions about communal ties and responsibility. Advice would be shared across generations; mugs would be shared around a table; benches would be shared among members of a household. Turn-of-the-nineteenth-century material culture reflects different expectations. The dead would be buttoned up in a private grave, the headstone neither offering counsel to nor requesting remembrance from passersby. Isolation in death followed a life that emphasized the individual over the community or family: one person per mug; chairs replaced benches. Social ties thinned. A sense of communal responsibility became attenuated. In the words of folklorist Henry Glassie, the society began "to curl in upon itself like a dying spider" (Glassie 1975, 188).

Having driven the length of the Valley of Virginia—winding along side roads and seeking out cemeteries of all sizes, affiliations, and types, from little family burying grounds to hearty congregational cemeteries and vast municipal memorial parks—I see evidence that the cultural pendulum is swinging back in the direction of maintaining social ties. There's a rapprochement, I believe, between living and dead, as well as a selective strengthening of bonds within communities. Starting in the 1980s, social ties started to reknit. If they died like spiders two centuries ago, communities have in some ways begun, phoenix-like, to regenerate. This chapter explores evidence for this selective regathering by considering epitaphs and motifs on grave markers, gifts left on grave sites, and messages to the deceased in newspapers and on social media.

DEETZ, GLASSIE, AND COMMUNITY

In their analyses of centuries of American material culture, James Deetz ([1977] 1996) and Henry Glassie (1975) detected the emergence of an atomistic, isolated individualism over the course of the eighteenth and nineteenth centuries, and they recognized it as an outgrowth of the Renaissance. Deetz perceived a movement from a more communal to a more fragmented social orientation through many types of material culture, as much that had been shared became the province of one individual.

Deetz ([1977] 1996, 123) contended that burial practices in colonial America mirrored those of late medieval Europe in that a burial shaft did not belong to any one person in perpetuity, being rather "a finite space that would hold all the deceased members of a parish regardless of how congested the space became."

A spot in the cemetery was a temporary place in which the body transformed to a skeleton. Gravediggers often encountered bones of those who had died in living memory. Sometimes they treated them as unremarkable inclusions in soil excavated for new burials. A 1655 Dutch painting depicts gravediggers preparing for a burial: "the earth that has been dug out and piled to one side contains a disorderly collection of bones and skulls, the remains of older graves. Such was the familiar appearance of a Protestant church in the middle of the seventeenth century" (Ariès 1981, 49). Deetz ([1977] 1996,123–24) pointed out that this practice informed Hamlet's famous consideration of a skull encountered in a graveyard: "Alas, poor Yorick! I knew him, Horatio; a fellow of infinite jest, of most excellent fancy; he hath borne me on his back a thousand times." Yorick had been a court jester and close companion of young Prince Hamlet.

During the seventeenth century, many European communities also continued the practice, collecting the "enormous mass of bones that was perpetually being heaved up by the earth" and displaying them "artistically" in charnels and chapels (Ariès 1981, 60). These displays formed a backdrop for daily life, encouraging Christians—as in a Breton hymn—to "see the bones of our brothers. . . . Let us see the pitiful state that they have come to. . . . You see them broken, crumbled into dust. . . . Listen to their lessons, listen well" (61). Thus bones—whether left in graveyards and incorporated in the fill of new burials, or collected and arrayed in charnel houses—continued to be part of the community's life. The dead remained integral to the collective both physically, as the newly deceased joined their predecessors, and socially, as bodily remains acted as *memento mori* to encourage viewers to live well.

In colonial New England, death's-heads—winged skulls—were popular symbols, as were verbal forms of *memento mori*: "My youthful mates both small and great / Come here and you may see / An awful sight, which is a type / Of which you soon must be" (Deetz [1977] 1996, 98). The community's dead retained responsibility for advising the living. By the early nineteenth century, however, many cemeteries consisted of "carefully designed lots and only one body per grave pit" (see Eggener 2010, 17–18). This shift from communal to individual graves accompanied a transformation in grave marker imagery and epitaphs. By the turn of the nineteenth century, American gravestones more often featured neoclassical urn-and-willow designs with "in memory of" inscriptions that simply commemorated the individual (Deetz [1977] 1996, 99). Epitaphs were usually limited to the name and age of the deceased (Deetz [1977] 1996, 97). The dead no longer spoke to the living.

Deetz saw in this evolution a social and cultural transformation. Earlier gravestones reflected a sense of community, but later gravestones suggested a dissolution of solidarity. There's no indication of a continuing social contract, no obligation to advise or to listen. Gravestone design was one indicator of a pervasive change in worldview from one that assumed communal responsibility to one that assumed appreciable social distance among individuals (Deetz [1977] 1996, 183). Mortuary practice paralleled changes in other categories of material culture. Houses became more private, with central passages protecting residents from outsiders and individual rooms separating residents from each other (156–64). Ceramics exhibited the same process, as shared trenchers and mugs gave way to individual plates and glasses (85–88).

While Deetz's study focused on New England, Henry Glassie identified these dynamics in central Virginia. His study of "folk houses" centered on the Piedmont but represented a larger region (Glassie 1975, 15). Glassie found an increasing insistence on privacy and individualism (among other, related trajectories) in houses of "middling" farmers and their families during the eighteenth and nineteenth centuries: "individualism is found in the desire for privacy and in separation at every level of the architectural particularistic context" (182). Whereas visitors to earlier houses had "entered directly into the house's main room" where "the family might be eating or chatting by the fire," later visitors encountered a passage or hallway that blocked off sight and immediate entry into living spaces (120–21). "The change for the person crossing the threshold was great, for he was standing in a dark, unheated hallway, not within the hearthside glow. The house types effected a greater distancing between the family and outsiders" (121). Stairways moved away from front doors; sleeping spaces migrated upstairs (121–22). Glassie sees this transition as "the point at which the face-to-face community dies" (190). Architectural changes track social and cultural currents: "families broke down into smaller and smaller components as the social unit contracted from the community to the family to the individual. . . . The pattern is the evolution of individualism . . . the evolution of alienation" (193).

As one reviewer of *Folk Housing in Middle Virginia* effused, "Henry Glassie has once again proved himself the leader in American studies of folk architecture. . . . With this book the nascent subfield of material culture has achieved the threshold of maturity" (Vlach 1978, 134). *Folk Housing*, much like *In Small Things Forgotten*, was a scholarly breakthrough, as both authors demonstrated the possibility of detecting historic mind in matter. Deetz, said a reviewer of the latter book, "has demonstrated the importance of looking at certain classes of artifacts" like gravestones as "potential carriers of information significant for anthropological studies of cultural systems" (Price 1979, 392).

Deetz's research on cemeteries has also been critiqued. Archaeologist Harold Mytum (2004, 116–21) suggested that Deetz had overlooked plain stones and unmarked graves and had neglected a wider range of meanings that symbols could have held. Some challenged the validity of the temporal patterns in gravestone stylistic variation that Deetz identified, and others suggested that the changes had less to do with an evolving world view than with "fashion," some people opting for new styles en vogue among the well educated or well heeled as a statement of (or aspiration to) social standing (Baugher and Veit 2014, 88–99).

These points, however, don't weaken Deetz's fundamental finding that changing mortuary practices reveal changing cultural expectations about social relationships. Between the seventeenth and nineteenth centuries, many people became less vested in their communities—focusing more on the family and the individual—not only in New England but also in Virginia (e.g., Glassie 1975; Isaac 1982; Morgan 1975), and indeed, much of North America (e.g., Larkin 1988; Ulrich 1994) and beyond (e.g., Mercer 1975). Many scholars have linked weakening social ties among the living to excluding the dead from ongoing social life (Ariès 1981; Eggener 2010; Tarlow 1999; Yalom 2008).

Cemeteries in the Valley of Virginia, though, reveal that something different started happening during the last decades of the twentieth century. Headstones again began offering advice from the dead to the living. The living reciprocated through remembrance. Among the copious, diverse indications of social reunion are treatments of grave sites like domiciles of vital, if invisible, souls.

THE DEAD IN RESIDENCE

Today in the Valley, the living often decorate burial sites as if the deceased were at home, as if the grave were the front porch of their residence. It's not unusual now to see small flags, designed for gardens or mailboxes, that say, "Welcome!" (Figure 6.1). Since 2015 I've documented dozens of grave sites with welcome flags. Along with the greeting, they bear images of butterflies, for example, cardinals, hummingbirds, bird houses, tulips, geraniums, pansies, dogwood flowers, sunflowers, fallen oak leaves, pumpkins, deer, and sea turtles.[1]

Figurines left on graves also often welcome the living to the space of the dead. The grave site of Ernest Allen Hardin (1982–2015) at Dublin Cemetery in Pulaksi County contains a headstone with photographs of Hardin and his children. Perpendicular to it is a bench, a Virginia Tech flag, and a figurine of a bird on a fence that says, "Welcome." Similarly, at Prospect Hill Cemetery in Front Royal, the grave site of Mae E. Boyd (1931–2008) is decorated with a flag—"Welcome Friends"—as well as potted flowers, solar lights, ceramic angels, and approximately a dozen small signs and plaques (e.g., a rock painted with a flower and a bee that says, "bee happy"; Figure 6.2).

Countless grave sites are decorated in the very ways front porches commonly are—signs of welcome being only the beginning (Figure 6.3). They have benches, monogrammed flags and mats, solar-powered lights, bird feeders, wind spinners, and wind chimes. L. V. "Randy" Randall (1928–2005) has a grave site with a white wrought-iron bench, wind sock, and bird feeder full of seed, as well as pinwheels, an American flag, and live marigolds—all things commonly seen in front of Valley houses. Another grave has a flag that says, "Grandkids spoiled

here," and yet another has an image of University of Delaware's mascot, YoUDee the Fightin' Blue Hen.[2] Hummingbird feeders with red syrup hang over some headstones.[3] Wind spinners keep others lively, breezes flapping a cardinal's wings and driving the wheels of a blue New Holland tractor.[4] In some cases, the dead "invite" the living to spend time with them. A gravestone in Rockingham County offers a companionable ear: "Talk to Me. I will listen."[5] A bench in a

FIGURE 6.2. Autumnal decorations on the grave site of Mae E. Boyd (1931–2008) include flags ("Welcome friends"), scarecrows, wooden pumpkins ("hello fall"), fresh flowers, angel figurines, and solar-powered lights, Prospect Hill Cemetery, Front Royal.

Winchester cemetery suggests what people on Virginia porches have long said: "Come Sit with Me."[6]

Once, as I was walking along the fenced edge of a cemetery in the Valley—the sun setting and the moon rising—a trio of gravestones drew my attention (Figure 6.4). They seemed to form a family group, in part because of their design similarities—black granite with a colored photograph in the center and paired images on either side, roses in one case, bluegrass string instruments in the two others. Each grave had white gravel at the head and solar-powered lights at the foot. To the far right was a bench, so that someone could sit facing into the space—this family's space—created by stone and light.

From left to right, the stones are dedicated to family members of three generations. The first is the matriarch, "Beloved Mother" and grandmother

FIGURE 6.3A AND B. Grave sites include objects often displayed on area porches including wind chimes, wind spinners, bird houses, and lights. Augusta Memorial Gardens, Augusta County.

FIGURE 6.4. Members of the Roach/Mowbray family buried together. Headstones include images and demarcate the space on one end; footstones line the other end, and a bench on the side enables the living to visit. Elk Run Cemetery, Elkton.

(1916–2008); it bears a laser-etched image of a small church. The central stone memorializes her grandson (1963–2005) with the epitaph, "I'm Using My Bible for a Road Map." Images etched into this grave marker include a banjo, guitar, angel, pickup truck, and motorcycle. His footstone is military issued. The last gravestone, closest to the bench, is for the father (1936–2004) and mother (1945–) of the second decedent (the mother also being the daughter of the first person buried in the family row). This couple's gravestone includes their date of marriage, their children's names, and images of Jesus, a barn, silo, pickup truck, guitar, and beagle. The husband's foot marker acknowledges his service with the US Army in Korea.

This family plot felt something like a living room. Bounded, maintained, and conducive to visiting; it communicated both family unity and each member's interests. As I snapped photographs, an SUV zoomed up the cemetery's gravel path. A young woman hopped out and asked if she could help me. I explained that I was writing a book on cemeteries in the Valley of Virginia, and—as in so many of my encounters—she seemed pleased with my interest in the gravestones. Like others I met in Valley cemeteries, she was proud of these grave assemblages for both their symbolic and aesthetic properties. She enthusiastically explained who each person there was, how they were related to her, and how each image on each stone and each object on each grave was special. Her grandmother had been an ardent Christian, and the images of church and Jesus praying were right for her marker. Her brother had died in a trucking accident. He'd loved playing in his bluegrass band and riding his Harley. He was buried next to his father, also a bluegrass musician and a horse enthusiast. This friendly woman mentioned several times the name of the person who'd created the artwork on the grave markers, saying that he was the best and that he'd come out to touch them up as needed. She explained that she usually visits every day, sometimes multiple times a day, just to check in or touch base with her family. A pickup truck pulled up just outside of the cemetery fence; the woman went over to chat with the driver—a man I took to be her husband—and a little boy I assumed was her son, as she lifted him in her arms over the fence. And so, the family was there: some alive, some dead, still together, passing the time.

DEAD AND ALIVE

If many Virginians seem to think of grave sites as a kind of residence for the deceased, they also imagine the departed as mobile and lithe. Victoria Britton's son, Kyle Brennan, died tragically at age twenty. She brings her own topsoil and grass seed to his grave: "We have to do things for our loved ones, to go and care for family plots, and not expect someone else to do that. When I go to Kyle's grave site, I think of it as tending to his room at home. It's what mothers do." On Kyle's birthday, Britton often takes a cake to the cemetery workers, "the people who are spending the whole day with him."[7] Britton thinks of Kyle as being both resident in the cemetery and widely mobile: "Ireland was Kyle's ancestral family home, and he was planning to visit with his brothers. This was a wish that was never going to be. Spiritually, I feel like Kyle lives in Ireland now. He's in the wind."

Conceptually the beloved can be both dead and alive, here and there, all around us and up above. Any seeming inconsistency of beliefs should not be surprising. In her study of the cultural history of death and the body in early modern Ireland, Sarah Tarlow (2011, 15) found that "it is possible for people to hold a number of incompatible or incommensurable beliefs simultaneously." Especially when thinking about death, people's inferences can be multiple: "the brain 'Balkanizes'—sets up boundaries between beliefs so that they are not all called upon at the same time" (198–202).

Many objects on grave sites express a sense of the continuing vitality and social engagement of the deceased (Eggener 2010, 2). A flag on one grave speaks for the person interred there, saying, "Do not stand at my grave and weep, I am not there, I do not sleep. I am a thousand winds that blow, I am the diamond glints on snow, I am the sun on ripened grain, I am the gentle autumn rain. . . . Do not stand at my grave and cry, I am not there, I did not die."[8]

The grave site of a young woman buried in Augusta County (Mt. Carmel Presbyterian Church Cemetery) contains a plaque: "Though you cannot see or touch me, I will be near and if you listen with your heart, you will hear all my love around you, soft and clear." Perhaps most moving is the grave of Kyle D. Stullenburg (1988–2013). The back of his gravestone includes a partial transcription of his suicide note: "I just hope I am remembered as being brave, that taking my own life was a sacrifice I had to make to salvage my heart, which is my family. I know I'll be all around you all. I love you" (Figure 6.5).

Epitaphs, too, convey imaginings of the dead as alive. They're still doing the things they most loved to do. At a Methodist Church cemetery in Augusta County,[9] a gravestone for Clinton Dale Loan (1955–2006) includes images of a hound treeing a raccoon, and a car with the inscription "Making My Rounds." David L. Abbott Sr. (1928–2009) in Craig County's Brickey Cemetery is "Cruising in Heaven." Cody R. Breeden (1989–2013) in Elkton is "Riding with Angels," and Alyse Sisson Ashwell (1924–2010) in Botetourt County is "Singing Among Angels." Others are understood to be "Walking with God on the Mountain" or "Gone sailing with Jesus, who strengthened me." Simon (1903–1993) and Loraine (1909–1996) Birdsong share a gravestone; his side has an image of drums, "He Keeps on Beating," and hers an organ, "She Keeps on Singing."[10] A former pilot's stone has images of a trumpet and airplane; he's "Flying Angels on High."[11]

Ralph T. Martin's obituary notes that he "was employed by Bobby's Trash Service and Waste Management for 21 years. Ralph was a loving husband,

FIGURE 6.5A AND B. Gravestone for Kyle D. Stullenburg (1988–2013). The front face depicts him in a mountainous setting with a wolf; the back features part of his suicide note. Riverview Cemetery, Waynesboro.

father, and grandfather."[12] Martin's grave marker (1944–2005)[13] declares him a "Waste Management Driver Forever."

THE COGNIZANT DEAD

Not only do many people in the Valley of Virginia think of the deceased both as "living" in the cemetery and as moving widely, but they also treat the dead as cognizant and socially connected. The cemetery can be a "place where the dead are kept alive. . . . [The living] bring flowers or gifts, they gaze upon the grave marker, and they conduct conversations with it, treating it as a substitute for the deceased" (Eggener 2010, 11–12).

The living send news to the dead; they leave souvenirs, photographs, and other updates. A 2003 bowling trophy sits on a headstone for a man who died in 2001. A photo from a 2014 soccer tournament is secured to the gravestone of a woman who passed in 2013. A clear fiberglass box sits on the grave of a teenage girl who died in 1996. Inside is a light purple Easter rabbit holding an open album of photographs toward the headstone, as if showing recent family images to the deceased girl (Figure 6.6). A widow explained that, when she goes to the

FIGURE 6.6. A plush purple rabbit in a Plexiglas box holds photographs of children and adults toward a headstone. Lebanon Presbyterian Church Cemetery, Rockbridge County.

FIGURE 6.7. Teddy Brent Davis (1973–2016) is remembered in the fall with mini-pumpkins, a scarecrow, and seasonally colored flowers on his grave marker. Morning Star Temple Hill, Bland County.

grave of her husband, "Hootie," she just says, "'Hey Hootie, how're you doing?' and I talk to him and tell him everything is okay. As far as I'm concerned, I'm still married to him. He's my husband" (Ledbetter and Sharman 2015).

A historically African American cemetery in Augusta County is difficult to access, but recently someone climbed its hill with a baby in a car carrier (which, as caregivers know, is unwieldly and heavy). The infant in his carrier was put on the grave site of a woman (1948–2004) and a photo was snapped. It was printed and then placed on the grave site: a picture of the baby on the grave is on the grave. When I mentioned this example to a friend, she related a similar experience, saying that when she discovered that she was pregnant, she went to her grandmother's grave to share the news. As with my other interlocutors, she smiled to acknowledge that this move was not "logical," but that on some level she wanted her ancestors to know about continued births in the family.

The deceased are also positioned as conscious and connected in social networks with the living through their inclusion in holidays. For years, Colleen

Baber has taken a turkey leg to the cemetery. Her 19-year-old son Andrew died suddenly, choking on a piece of candy en route to a New Year's Eve party. She told me that she often visits his grave site, bringing balloons for his birthday, a tree at Christmas, and turkey at Thanksgiving. Baber explains that these gifts enable her "to still mother Andrew. I can still care for my child. I'm able to give something to him. I know that he's still around. It's like there's a veil here, and he's just on the other side of it."[14]

Countless other Virginians register their remembrance of deceased loved ones on holidays (see Mytum 2004, 175). A new grave had no formal marker, but someone had tacked to it a "Happy Valentine's Day" balloon, card, and teddy bear. The Fourth of July is enthusiastically marked with red-white-and-blue pinwheels, bunting, American flags, and stars-and-stripes solar lights. At one grave site in October, someone installed a flag depicting a smiling witch with her cauldron. A nearby headstone was decorated with rubber spiders and rats. Fall is widely marked on grave sites with pumpkins and scarecrows (Figure 6.7). "Be Thankful" flags with turkeys in Pilgrim hats appear during November. A boy who lived for six months in 1950 has a gravestone with an upright angel. Now some 65 years later, someone attached to it a stuffed Santa Claus. Elsewhere, the grave site of a teenage girl has a shrink-wrapped Nativity and a poinsettia. People also remember personal benchmarks: a "Happy Anniversary" balloon depicting a pair of clinking champagne glasses, for example, and "Happy Birthday" balloons with stars or smiling face emojis.

LETTERS TO THE DEAD

In addition to bringing news to the cemetery and observing holidays with the dead, many people in the Valley write to deceased loved ones. They act as if the dead, being cognizant and connected to the community, can read.

Paper cards and notes are frequently affixed to grave sites. A bright green garden hose coiled into a wreath with fabric jonquils and floral ribbon, a geranium flag, solar-powered hanging lanterns, and in a baggie, a pink envelope, "Mom" (Figure 6.8). A clear glass jar sits on another headstone. The rusting top says, "Pickled Beets." Inside, safe from the weather, are folded pieces of paper, doubtless letters to the deceased. Sometimes cards or notes are left sealed on graves, often in honor of a holiday, birthday, or "angel-versary": an anniversary of someone's death. In other cases, messages are affixed to graves so that any passerby can read them. For example, the very same card was laminated and left on a grave in Prospect Hill Cemetery in Front Royal and some 250 miles to the south at West End Cemetery in Wytheville: "Thinking of you. . . . I hope you know how much I love you and even though you have passed from this life you are forever in my heart." At Wheatland Lutheran Church Cemetery in Botetourt County, a card was recently affixed to a grave of a woman who'd passed nearly

FIGURE 6.8A AND B. This gravesite includes a wreath made out of a garden hose, flowers, a flag, a lamp, and notes to "Mom" sealed in plastic baggies. Augusta Memorial Gardens, Augusta County.

twenty years earlier: "Love and miss you. Your friend, Ann." Back at Riverview Cemetery in Waynesboro, a young man who died was, per his gravestone, a "Loving husband, father & son"—and his epitaph is "Love you so much. Love you too much." At the base of the gravestone is a laminated message in a child's penmanship: "I miss you I do not haet [hate] you I love you with all my hearts." Also at Riverview, a hand-painted sign: "Grandma, We know your watching over us everywhere we go, we wish you was here."

Some gravestones are inscribed with messages to the dead, a practice that frames the grave marker itself as a letter (see Tarlow 1999, 131). Many messages are from children to their parents or grandparents. The epitaph for William Dallas Bethea Jr. (1918–2006) reads, "From the Depression to the Battle of the Bulge to sun swept Shores of California and Hawaii, you and Mom taught us how to live and savor life."[15] Descendants of Teri Trayman (1918–2009) wrote, "Your love embraced us. Your strength empowered us. And your will inspired us."[16] Sometimes the relationship between living writer and the deceased is not clear. The epitaph for Kathleen O. "Jimmie" Neighbours (1924–2002) reads, "I brought you home again Kathleen."[17]

Parents, too, write to their children. One mother inscribed a headstone for her son (1980–2013): "I tucked you in and said Good night/ I love you/ See you in the morning. Never dreamed that would be our last night together." One boy who died before he'd turned two years old has a teddy bear grave marker. It includes his photograph in a heart-shaped frame and an engraved message from his mother: "Jakie you are the light that brightened my world. You will always be my little heartbreaker. So sweet Jakie don't forget about Daddy and me."

THE DEAD ON SOCIAL MEDIA

Many newspapers in the Valley of Virginia print messages from the living to the dead. On a holiday or anniversary of a death, family members may take out an "advertisement" in the paper addressed to a deceased loved one.

This notice was published, for example, in a Valley paper: "In loving memory of our father, Buck Stone, on Father's Day. From your Children, Grandchildren & Great Grandchildren." Many newspapers also offer "memorials" or "memoriams" in their classified sections. This example refers to the deceased in both the third and second person: "In Loving Memory of our father, James I. Clark (Bill). August brings sad memories of our loved one gone to rest, but he will always be remembered, by the ones who love him best. Sadly missed by your loving daughters, Linda and Wanda and all of your grandchildren."

Other published messages are addressed to children, even if they passed on before learning to read. This is certainly the case with infants, and perhaps with Delaney Faithe Crowder Bishopriggs, a four-year-old who had been killed in a vehicle accident: "Happy Birthday, Delaney 7 years old. 'You are turning seven in heaven.' . . . We miss and love you so very much, Mommy, Daddy, Madison, Bri, PawPaw, Mimi, Nana, Pap, family and friends." They address Bishopriggs, too, on her grave marker: "If love could have saved you, you would have lived forever." Other popular forms of commemoration that could be considered "broadcast media" include memorial decals—seen very frequently now on the rear windows of cars—and memorial tattoos.

Social media have facilitated such public expressions to the deceased. Facebook, Instagram, and other platforms are used so widely not only to "keep in touch" with the dead, but also for the living to remain in close communication with each other (Sofka et al. 2012).

Bralyn Matthew Davis-Vest (2013–2014) is buried at Riverview Cemetery in Waynesboro. His family created a Facebook page, "R.I.P. Bralyn Matthew Davis-Vest," where people post messages to him: "Happy First Birthday in Heaven Today!" Also uploaded are photographs of family members at Bralyn's burial site. One shows a young woman in cap and gown kneeling behind his gravestone. To her right is a large photograph of baby Bralyn and to her left her high school diploma. The caption says, "Aunty Morgy Made it Bralyn! . . . I Wish You Would've Been Here In Person To See Aunty Morgy Graduated But I Know You Were Still There Watching Down At Me."[18]

At Thornrose Cemetery in Staunton, a gravestone for Richard Allen "Buddy" Winkelspecht (1964–1998) remembers him as "Father, Brother, Friend." Dead at age 33, he had been the drummer for the rock bands The Dead End Kids and Asylum. An extraordinary multi-year, multi-authored conversation about and directed to Buddy is publicly available online at Find a Grave, a website that allows the uploading of pictures and messages. All manner of fans, friends, and family members write to Buddy on the page. Someone posted an image of a can of Pringles on Super Bowl Sunday. Another uploaded a picture of drums: "Here's a drum set for you to play in heaven." Others simply touch base: "Well Buddy, I guess all good things come to an end and 'my weekend' just did. Guess I better get some sleep. . . . I'll check back in with you next weekend." Or "Hey man, I just dropped in to say hello."[19]

GIFTS TO THE DEAD

Social bonds depend on reciprocity: obligations to give, to receive, and to reciprocate join individuals in relationships that constitute the very core of society (Mauss 1950). A "gift that does nothing to enhance solidarity is a contradiction" (Douglas 1990, x). The volume of exchange underway between the quick and the dead suggests the cultivation of a robust solidarity indeed. The living give countless things to the dead (Mytum 2004, 97). Some grave markers themselves are understood as presents to deceased loved ones.

Victoria Britton explained that with her son's grave marker, "I took my time and was very thoughtful and particular about Kyle's grave site. It was the last gift I was going to give to my child. I wanted to make it lasting and special." On his gravestone rest about half a dozen small rocks that "people have sent from their travels, especially from Ireland—places he would have liked to have visited if he had lived. Someone recently sent one from Norway. They often write a poignant word or the place where the stone is from on it."[20] They are gifts on a gift (Figure 6.9).

I was at a cemetery when a young man came by; he sat quietly by a grave for a few minutes and left a Snickers bar. Another time, a woman brought a card and bouquet of flowers to a grave. She remained for some time. After she left, I walked by and realized that it was the tenth anniversary of the death of the girl buried there.

Other presents left recently on Valley grave sites include golf tees, Red Man Loose Leaf Chewing Tobacco, a Batman t-shirt, a wristwatch, dog tags, a Rubik's cube, a Washington Nationals baseball cap, a Virginia Tech mug, a gilt

FIGURE 6.9. Grave site of Kyle T. Brennan (1986–2007) with stones from Ireland, Norway, and other places he had hoped to visit. Monticello Memorial Park, Albemarle County.

porcelain teacup ("Mother"), a Bristol Motor Speedway flag and "Pre Race Pit & Driver Intro Pass" card, and a losing lottery ticket ($1 for a chance to win a "$3,000,000 Cash Payout").

Last but by no means least, people leave beer on grave sites. In Rockbridge County on the grave of a veteran killed in Afghanistan are bottles of Devil's Backbone Vienna Lager. The fiancée of a soldier deployed in Iraq told me

> with modern day veterans, there's a very real sense of duty to keep their buddies "alive" by remembering them. When they go to their graves they speak their names (because "a man isn't dead as long as someone speaks his name") and also, on various anniversaries or holidays such as Memorial Day, Budweiser is purchased, combat buddies are rounded up, and everyone meets in the cemetery.

People also leave objects on the graves of children. In February 2017, I visited a memorial park that contained the grave of a boy who'd lived for about seven months (May 2006–January 2007). On his grave were fresh red roses, white snapdragons, and two presents wrapped in checked paper. Through a weatherworn hole in the paper appeared a stuffed animal's chestnut-colored fur. A football, baseball, and mitt rest on the grave of another boy who lived for less than a month in 2012. In a church cemetery, someone left a deceased teenager a paperback copy of *Harry Potter and the Sorcerer's Stone*.

At Angels Rest Memorial Gardens in Giles County, some 350 grave sites populate an idyllic hilltop where wide oaks shade some areas and sunshine warms the grass in others. Many grave sites are edged with decorative cement, rubber, or wooden borders. Some are then filled with mulch and planted with live roses and lilies, as well as many fabric flowers. Gifts left on the graves include angels, crosses, rosaries, wreaths, and solar lights. One small burial plot stands out. Outlined in concrete edging pavers (the kind made for garden borders) is a rectangle of about three-by-five feet. The inside looks like a child's room or chest, with scores of toys. Along one wall is a line of little green and yellow tractors, Thomas the Tank Engine trains, matchbox cars, helicopters, and airplanes. Along another side are toy construction vehicles—a cement mixer, dump trucks—and along another, lines of rubber dinosaurs. In the middle are toy owls, turtles, snails, dogs, and bears. Solar lanterns secure each corner, and interspersed among all are resin angels and painted butterflies. There is no headstone, but the metal plate supplied by the funeral agency shows that this child was born and died in 2014. Propped up against a small baseball mitt is a bear in a blue-and-white striped tunic; it has a red heart and this message written in permanent marker: "I Love You Baby Boy/ Hugs and Kisses to You in Heaven."

THE DEAD DO THEIR PART

If the living give, the dead are believed to receive and to reciprocate. They accept messages, news, and gifts. In return, they send signs of their presence and orchestrate positive outcomes for the living. Many Valley residents seem to understand themselves as "people with a strong sense of community, and being dead is no impediment to belonging to it" (Metcalfe and Hays 2005, 4).

Signs on grave sites, some of them hand painted, or printed flags register expectations of communication from the dead. "A cardinal can be a special sign from [your] loved one in heaven," says one. Another notes that "Butterflies are the heaven sent kisses of an angel."

Participants on drummer Buddy Winkelspecht's Find a Grave website often express the belief that he can send messages and assistance. One person wrote, "Hey, let something come by me every now and then that will say its from you." Another averred, "Our loved ones let us know in many ways that they are alright and safe with God in Heaven." One writer said, "To you, Buddy. I am a huge fan. Watch over your brother and his new wife." He then expressed his belief that Buddy had "probably played a hand" in his brother's meeting the woman he would marry. The page administrator wrote to one contributor, "You left the 500th message on Buddy's site, so I know that he will do something nice for you today!" (Find a Grave 2002).

Indeed, the deceased now—much like the dead in medieval Europe and the American colonies—are frequently thought to proffer guidance. One widow explained that the significance of visiting her husband's grave is "talking to him. I know he's not there, but this is where we put him and was the last time I saw him. Sometimes I come here at 3 o'clock in the morning and I'll turn the car where the lights will shine here, and I get out a blanket and lie down on it and stay the night. I can talk to him and I feel like I get some answers or something comes about that answers my problems" (Ledbetter and Sharman 2015).

The dead have started talking again. Rarely seen since the colonial era in the US and the medieval period in Europe, some headstones in the Valley of Virginia have resumed the responsibility to dispense advice. The Southwest Virginia Veterans Cemetery (Pulaski County) offers much counsel through grave markers. They fought in Korea, for example, and Vietnam, and now urge passersby to "Pray for Others," to "Keep Smiling," or to "Let Your Faith Move Mountains." These suggestions are gifts from the dead to the living, for whose wellbeing they seem to care.

In a Methodist cemetery,[21] Glen Allen Price's (1936–1999) gravestone is inscribed with a poem he wrote: "There is a time within our life/ When time seems to stand still/ Old Satan tries to tempt us/ To pull us from God's will./ He offers money, booze, sex, and fun,/ He say that's what we lost./ But what he didn't realize,/ You are in the shadow of the cross./ So when he comes to offer you/ Refuse him with a grin./ In doing so you defeat him,/ Your soul will surely win."

Of the thousands upon thousands of gravestones I've seen, Price's is the only one to reference booze and sex (at least on the same stone). He did so to warn those who would come after him about pitfalls to avoid and godly ways to seek—*memento mori*.

The gravestone of William Bradshaw Beverley[22] (1938–2005) has different advice for passersby: "When you can, follow a woodland trail, climb a high mountain, sleep beneath the stars, swim in a cold river, chew the thoughts of some book which challenges your soul. I shall be with you." Eric Evine Sutphin's marker (1966–2006) urges the living, in words often attributed to early Methodist John Wesley, to "Do all the good you can by all the means you can in all the ways you can in all the places you can at all the times you can to all the people you can as long as ever you can."[23]

On their gravestone, Wingini Ferraba Dean Lindamood (1959–) and Lewis Allen Lindamood (1957–2013) recommend cultivating a sunny disposition: "Have a Happy. Have Two! They're Small."[24] They explain that

if you change your mind, you change the world—or at least the way you experience it. . . . If you thought the world was a hostile, ugly place filled with awful people doing awful things, that is what you'd see. Your mind would naturally seek out confirmation for its preconceived ideas. (E.G. if you're intent on buying a Volkswagen, as you go about your day you'll see lots of Volkswagens). If, however, you were able to sincerely change your mind and see that we are all the conscious aspects of a perfect universe which had to create us so that we could bear witness and stand in awe before its loving magnificence, then that is the soul-shaking reality you'd be greeted with each and every moment of each and every day. . . . It is entirely your choice as to what kind of world we live in. With a simple decision we can suffer in the darkness or play in the light. We can be angry, frightened and enslaved, or loving, joyous and free. I know. It's a toughie. . . . Adapted from Chuck Lorre.

Other recent inscriptions express even more clearly the ancient *memento mori* formulation. A 1973 epitaph reads, "For all who pass by, I hope to meet you in Heaven,"[25] and one from 1997 says, "Don't just stand there, Get ready!"[26] These phrases echo those of past centuries, with the dead communicating to the living and recommending that they act in ways that benefit their souls.

Inscriptions on the stones of two women who died some 250 years apart in Augusta County suggest how far the cultural pendulum has swung back toward a sense of lasting community and obligation. Mary Trimble died in 1770. Her remains are in the Glebe Burying Ground under a coffin-shaped body stone that says, "to all you that Come My Grave To See/ As I am Now So Must you Bee/ . . . . Repent In Time. Make No Delay. . . . In The Bloom of Youth I Was Snatched

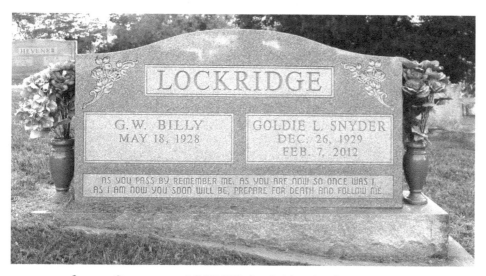

FIGURE 6.10. Gravestone of G.W. Billy Lockridge (1928-) and Goldie L. Snyder Lockridge (1929–2012). Though erected in the twenty-first century, its inscription was familiar in the eighteenth century and earlier: "As you pass by, remember me." Tinkling Spring Presbyterian Church Cemetery, Augusta County.

FIGURE 6.11. "Here lyes Buried/ James Deetz/ born to this world Feb 8 1930/ departed for another Nov 25 2000/ remember me as you pass by/ As you are now so once was I/ As I am soon you shall be/ prepare for death and follow me/ I told you I was sick." Westernport, Maryland. Photograph courtesy of Dave Wheelock and Eric Deetz.

Away." Goldie L. Snyder Lockridge died in 2012. Her remains are in Tinkling Spring Presbyterian Church Cemetery, and her upright gravestone says, "As you pass by remember me. As you are now so once was I/ As I am now you soon will be. Prepare for death and follow me" (Figure 6.10).

Perhaps, then, James Deetz's 2000 gravestone, "Remember me as you pass by," is not anachronistic but rather on the leading edge of a cultural movement working to reknit the social fabric. Certainly, it asserts a sense of connection and history.

Deetz's stone also offers levity. Under the *memento mori* poem is one line: "I told you I was sick" (Figure 6.11). Sharing a laugh with the dead is surely a gift to the living.

CHAPTER 7

"She Had an Affinity for Snowmen and Roosters"
Relational Identities

THE INDIVIDUAL RECONSIDERED

Deborah Ann Parker was the "World's First Living Stranger to Stranger Liver Recipient. Thank you, Ken Schuler of Linville, Va. A Stranger No Longer."[1]

Mary Catherine Alexander was the "Last of Seven Generations to live at Riverside Plantation from 1749 to 1991."[2]

Eugene ("Gene") and Sue Alley Dickerson were "Proud Parents and Grandparents, Harley Riders and Beach Lovers."[3]

The gravestone for Larry Sambrook (1948–2009) features the logo of his company, the Indoor Air Quality Network[4] (Figure 7.1). Sambrook's obituary recalls him as an "active leader of the Air Conditioning Contractors of America (ACCA). . . . He was a true embodiment of what makes ACCA great—passionate, knowledgeable professionals who are happy to connect with others and share what they've learned." A "valuable member of the ACCA family," Larry will be missed but "his good work created a legacy that will have impact on the . . . industry for many years to come."[5]

Who were Parker, Alexander, the Dickersons, and Sambrook? Their identities were infused with people, places, family, and work. The departed were a diverse lot, and of course, these five represent just the tip of the iceberg. Other grave

FIGURE 7.1. The gravestone of Larry Daniel Sambrook (1948–2009) features the logo of the Indoor Air Quality Network. Thornrose Cemetery, Staunton.

markers in the Valley of Virginia memorialize the deceased as Dallas Cowboy fans, Trailways bus drivers, descendants of the Pilgrims, or in one case, a "loving farmer, husband and father."

Wide ranging on one level, on another these memorials share an understanding of identity as relational. Social personhood inhered in links to other people, communities, ancestors, animals, places, objects, and events. Countless recent epitaphs position the deceased not as discrete, bounded individuals alienated from society and nature—but quite the reverse.

The notion of the individual as self-determined and separate from all else—including other humans and the natural world—emerged in and is often equated with Western modernity. Developing in much of Europe beginning in the seventeenth century, a framing of the person as profoundly separate contrasted with medieval models that imagined the person as organic, knitted into and inseparable from family, community, congregation, and landscape. This chapter reads grave markers in the Valley of Virginia as expressions of reconnection: a backing away from modern, alienated individualism and a claiming of self that exceeds the body as it extends to farms and vehicles, family and work, recreation and beloved places. Evidence from cemeteries suggests that this turn began, at a grassroots level, in the 1980s and has accelerated since then. People are building bridges beyond themselves to define themselves.

THE MODERN, ALIENATED INDIVIDUAL

As archaeologist Chris Fowler (2004, 1) explains, in the model of Western individualism often associated with modernity, "Each of our bodies is understood as our own property, our own project, our own business. Personal concerns are understood as private concerns centering around the knowledgeable actions of each individual." He identifies "mass production, capitalism, internalized reflection, privatized concerns, [and] social technologies" as having "individuated each person and alienated people from both the wider community and nature." In European prehistory, however, identities were "temporary, contextual, and community concerns" (Fowler 2004, 1). Fowler interprets mixtures of "material culture, human and animal bones" at some sites as representing cultural framings of identity that differed "from the body-as-individual model" (Fowler 2002, 55). The social person was not isolated and discrete, but rather combined "people, animals, and things" (Fowler 2002, 57). He encourages archaeologists to envision European prehistoric landscapes as having been populated by "personified places, objects, communities, ancestors, and spirits" (Fowler 2004, 161).

Philosopher Mikhail Bakhtin ([1968] 1984, 27) famously contends that in medieval European imaginings, the individual body was always open. It was "not separated from the world by clearly defined boundaries," but instead was "blended with the world, with animals, with objects." It was "cosmic." With the Renaissance came the invention of a lonely individualism, as people began to conceive of the person as "isolated, alone, fenced off from all other bodies." All signs of its "proliferation were eliminated" (29; see also Bakhtin 1982, 216–217).

Archaeologist Sarah Tarlow (1999) has traced this evolution through mortuary practice and emotion in early modern Ireland and Britain. Drawing on cemetery data as well as historic and contemporary scholarship, Tarlow observes that the medieval "self was never truly severed from its familial and social context—it was always relational" (Tarlow 2011:120–21). The Renaissance witnessed a "more atomistic conception of the relationship in which members of a society stood to each other" (Tarlow 1999, 87; Tarlow 2002a, 91). A specific way in which this difference in the conception of the person manifests is in models of the afterlife. In medieval times, most people "expected that after death they would go to one of three places: Heaven, if very blessed; Hell, if very sinful; or Purgatory for nearly everyone else" (Tarlow 2011, 45). Purgatory was "envisioned as a sort of antechamber of judgement where sins could be atoned for," particularly through the prayers of the living (Tarlow 2011, 22–23). Survivors remained responsible for the wellbeing of the deceased's soul. Purgatory, however, was a casualty of the Protestant Reformation beginning in the sixteenth century: "For Protestants there was no interval between the moment of death and the general resurrection, no space which Purgatory could occupy" (Tarlow 2011, 24). No one could act on behalf of a deceased person's soul. The dead were on their own.

From an economic perspective, historian Joyce Oldham Appleby (1978, 24) agrees on a profound shift in thinking about the person in the early modern era. She explained that "the weight of English social thought shifted to its modern foundations during the course of the seventeenth century." Before this time, English law and custom had controlled economic practices for the good of the social whole (27–30):

> [The] growing and marketing of corn, the milling of flour, and the baking of bread were principally social rather than economic activities. Grain was not seen as a commodity to be moved through the countryside in search of the best price, nor was it ever absolutely possessed by the produced. The farmer who grew it . . . did not really own the corn; he attended it during its passage from the field to the market. . . . He must load up his carts with his grain, proceed to the nearest market, and offer his year's harvest to his traditional customers. Similarly, the miller and the baker were constrained to push the grain processing along in an orderly fashion to its final form as a loaf of bread selling at a price set by the local court. . . . At a time when the tiller of the soil had God to thank for the weather and the king to thank for his land, manipulating the fruits of the two could easily be viewed as wicked and ungrateful (28).

These farmers and bakers were not modern individuals: their identities, choices, and ways of thinking were not understood as being centered in themselves, but rather in the social web of which they were part.

In *Essays on Individualism: Modern Ideology in Anthropological Perspective*, anthropologist Louis Dumont (1986, 216) contends that the "sociological discovery of modern societies begins" when "the Individual is accepted as an ideological fact." Here, "Individual" means not the "empirical subject, indivisible sample of the human species, as encountered in all societies," but rather the "independent, autonomous moral and, thus, essentially nonsocial being, as encountered first of all in our modern ideology of man and society" (Dumont 1986, 279; see also Davenport and Lloyd 2016, 5–8). In this imagining, the individual is profoundly distinct: through isolated, internal will, a person evaluates right and wrong, navigates relationships with the Divine, and charters a life path. We imagine these modern individuals as self-determined, their identities lodged in their personal narratives they've forged of accomplishment, scandal, or tedium.

An indispensable foundational analysis of modern individualism is Alexis de Tocqueville's study, *Democracy in America*. A French diplomat and historian—as well as a forerunner of sociology—Tocqueville traveled widely in the United States in the early 1830s. His contrasts between European aristocracy and American democracy generated profound, even prescient, insights into American cultural dynamics. He understood individualism as "a reflective and tranquil sentiment that disposes each citizen to cut himself off from the mass of his fellow men" (Tocqueville [1840] 2004, 585). In democratic contexts, devotion among people "becomes rarer: the bond of human affection stretches and slackens" (586). Whereas "aristocracy linked all citizens together in a long chain from peasant to king," democracy "breaks the chain and severs the links," inclining people to "become indifferent to one another and treat one another as strangers" (586). Political equality, Tocqueville observed, encourages people to believe that they owe nothing to, and can expect nothing from, anyone; they "become accustomed to thinking of themselves always in isolation and are pleased to think that their fate lies entirely in their own hands" (586–87). "Again and again" the American system leads the person "back to himself and threatens ultimately to imprison him altogether in the loneliness of his own heart" (587). Eventually people even become alienated within their own families: "The fabric of time is forever being ripped, and vestiges of the generations disappear. People easily forget those who went before them and have no idea of those who will come after. . . . Not only does democracy cause each man to forget his forebears, but it makes it difficult for him to see his offspring and cuts him off from his contemporaries" (586–87).

Sociologist Robert Bellah and his colleagues (1985, 277) describe modernity as "the culture of separation." They see social fragmentation in twentieth-century America as just "the latest phase of that process of separation and individuation that modernity seems to entail" (275). They point to English poet John Donne who in 1611, "at the very beginning of the modern era," perceived an emergent alienated individualism:

'Tis all in peeces, all cohaerence gone . . .

Prince, Subject, Father, Sonne, are things forgot,

For every many alone thinkes he hath got

To be a Phoenix, and that then can bee

None of that kinde, of which he is, but hee (quoted in Bellah et al. 1985, 276).

Political scientist Robert D. Putnam (2000, 25) perceives a series of "ups and downs in civic engagement" over the course of American history in his widely read book, *Bowling Alone: The Collapse and Revival of American Community*. He concludes, however, that during the last third of the twentieth century, "active involvement in face-to-face organizations" plunged (63). The "classic institutions of American civic life, both religious and secular, have been 'hollowed out,'" as "decay has consumed the load-bearing beams of our civic infrastructure" (72). Putnam takes his title from the observation that "given population growth, more Americans are bowling than ever before, but league bowling has plummeted" during the 1980s and 90s (112). He describes Americans' "silent withdrawal from social intercourse" and their "growing sense at some visceral level of disintegrating social bonds" (115, 287).

Putnam (2000, 402) concludes that at the dawn of the twenty-first century, it was "past time to begin to reweave the fabric of our communities." Doing so requires a recommitment to social networks and reinvestment in social capital—the latter being the value people generate through community engagement, mutual obligation, and reciprocity. Living requires various sorts of capital, economic and social being among them. While traveling, we can use economic capital (money, credit) to rent a hotel room or social capital to stay in a friend's guest room. If we have children, we can pay a sitter or call in a favor from a neighbor. Social capital is a kind of currency created through positive interaction. It's being able to rely on friends, family, neighbors, or others for assistance and companionship, and it's generally created through spending time with others: playing, praying, protesting, working, serving together, and much else.

Cemeteries in the Valley of Virginia document the reinvestment in social capital and the reweaving of social ties for which Putnam called. Indeed, given the apparent changes beginning in the last quarter of the twentieth century, this transformation was underway at a grassroots level even as Putnam was writing. Countless epitaphs, inscriptions, and motifs on Valley grave markers from ca. the 1980s to the present position the person in webs of interconnection. Rather than isolated, "unitary, totalized, and indivisible" persons (Fowler 2004, 8), the dead are depicted as having deeply relational identities. Who they were—their social personhood—was not bound in a discrete human body but extended to places, animals, objects, and other people.

Symbols on grave markers point to a model of personhood diffused through motorcycles and Jeeps, cats, horses, houses, barns, roads and mountains, tools, musical instruments, and sports gear. Grave markers convey the identity of the dead, too, through logos and mascots of teams—high school, college, professional—sometimes as players, sometimes as fans. These symbols of distributed personhood also point to a fostering of social capital and a pushback against alienation as people claim identity in bands of Harley riders, Steelers fans, cattle farmers, or "a Family that Loved Labrador Retrievers."[6] In Virginia, many people seep into landscapes; their pets and livestock shore up their identities; they entangle themselves in generations moving to the future and back to the past. Some are, much as Bakhtin said of the medieval dead, "cosmic."

Notions of distributed personhood (see Strathern 1988, 13) expressed on recent Valley grave markers take four primary forms: consanguinity, affinity, synecdoche, and metonymy (see Hamilakis et al. 2002, 11; Tarlow 1999, 39). Anthropologists have long explored the power of these tropes to encapsulate cultural beliefs or positions (Sapir and Crocker 1977; Turner 1984), and indeed, they serve as worthy guides through contemporary Virginia cemeteries.

Consanguinity connotes biological relationships: heredity, descent. Affinity can imply sense of deep connection; it can also refer to relations by marriage. With synecdoche, a part stands for the whole, and in metonymic relationships, one thing connotes another because of their regular co-occurrence. These categories are not exclusive nor exhaustive, but they do offer order and pattern to the great plethora of ways that grave markers suggest forms of identity that implicate much beyond the self (Crocker 1977).

CONSANGUINITY

Anthropologists love kinship; our aphorism is that family systems structure social, economic, and religious life in much of the world, particularly small-scale, farming or foraging communities. We traditionally distinguish two main means through which kinship relations form: consanguinity and affinity. The former—derived from the Latin term for "blood"—indicates relationship by ancestry or descent. Your parents, children, and siblings are your consanguines. Relationship by affinity is through marriage: your spouse and in-laws are affines. Adoption is a third category in which someone assumes a position normally reserved for consanguines.

For many in the Valley of Virginia, the deceased's social identity is expressed in relation to ancestors, living or dead. On the grand end of the scale are massive family memorials in municipal cemeteries. Members of the Echols family, for example, in Staunton's Thornrose Cemetery rest in a marble Greek Revival mausoleum with fluted columns and filigree brass doors. In front of the mausoleum are massive memorials to family members, most commandingly a soaring obelisk honoring John Echols (1823–1896), who was a Confederate brigadier general, attorney, and banker. Its pediment includes the opening stanza of Scottish poet John Knox's poem, "Mortality"—"He passes from life to his rest in the grave"—and then, rather more enigmatically, "He knows the great secret." Nearby are other memorials to Echols's descendants, including a column—carved to appear broken and draped, symbols of life cut short—for son John Percy Echols (1861–1881).

On smaller scales, family plots in municipal and church cemeteries are common, including in historically African American burial grounds. An upright marble gravestone in Staunton's Fairview Cemetery memorializes "Marshall's Estate," consisting of Plesant Marshall and wife Roberta Clark Marshall and nine additional names (eight Marshalls and one Hill).

Others express the deceased's identity through values believed to inhere in the family name. The back of Edward Lee Wilt's (1948–2000) stone, for example, includes an explanation of "Being a Wilt" by Amanda Leigh Wilt: "It means to never settle for less than perfection. You are the best without anyone else's little corrections. It means to let the fire run through your eyes, do not be so weak the fire is put out with foolish cries. It means to stand up for what you know is right. If you know you are wrong still do not let go without a fight."[7] The person here is subsumed, defined by the fighting family spirit that courses through the veins, like fire through the eyes.

A mausoleum for Wilden F. Van Sweringen IV (1906–1979) and Nora Spotswood Van Sweringen (1906–) highlights key events in his ancestral line[8] (Figure 7.2). With a Van Sweringen coat of arms at the top, it alludes to the Second Crusade during the twelfth century in which an ancestor apparently participated. It then lists places and years corresponding to actions of Wilden's ancestor, Garrett Van Sweringen (Historic St. Mary's City, n.d.). Born in Holland, during the 1650s Garrett Van Sweringen served as deputy commander of the Dutch colony of "Nieu Amstel" in present-day Delaware (Anonymous 1906). He was later a prominent businessperson in St. Mary's City, Maryland. Wilden F. Van Sweringen's 1979 grave marker also cites the "Battle of Fallen Timber 1794" and "Ft. Van Sweringen, FL 1837," the former referencing ancestors' participation in Northwest Indian Wars and the latter in the Seminole Wars. The mausoleum's list ends with "AKIA," a code term that generally means "A Klansman I Am" and refers to the Ku Klux Klan (Southern Poverty Law Center, n.d.). It seems

FIGURE 7.2A AND B. The memorial for Wilden F. Van Sweringen IV lists events in which his ancestors participated, from the Crusades to the Seminole Wars, and concludes with "AKIA," or "A Klansman I Am." Monticello Memorial Park, Albemarle County.

that the grandfather of Wilden Fisk Van Sweringen IV—whose name appears spelled in widely varying ways on available records, including as Wilbur and Wilber Fisk Swaringen (b. 1843)—enlisted in 1862 as a private in Company K of the 28th North Carolina Infantry of the Confederate Army.[9] He was 19 years old.[10] He served in key campaigns, including the Battle of Second Manassas (Bull Run) and the Siege of Petersburg, and was injured during Pickett's Charge at the Battle of Gettysburg. Swaringen survived and only mustered out of the Army with Lee's surrender on April 9, 1865, at Appomattox Courthouse.[11] By some accounts, his son W. F. Swaringen III was "active in various CSA veterans' organizations and causes."[12] In framing his identity for posterity, Wilden F. Van Sweringen IV imagined a straight line from the crusades against the "Moors" or Muslims in Europe, to the seizing of native people's land in North America, to the Klan.[13] That's who "I Am," set in stone.

Inconsistencies in spelling are very common in historic records; variations do not necessarily connote different people or families. Census enumerators and other officials tended to phonetically transcribe names given to them verbally. Moreover, there seems to have often been a general tolerance for variation in spellings. As a case in point, the gravestone of Samuel I. Petrie (1900–1978) identifies him as the son of "J. M. and Hannah R. Patrie" and grandson of "Samuel & Susannah Petry." On the back was added, "Also Grandson of Jacob & Elizabeth Senger/ Great Grandson of Joel & Sarah Sanger."[14]

Some people conjure a vital kinship to define themselves, and others use their grave markers to claim links to honored ancestors. John Warren Porter (1833–1901) and his wife, Helen Mar Stoddard (1836–1894), for example, are identified as "Descendants of John Alden, Pilgrim."[15] The gravestone for Christopher Columbus Pleasants (1867–1921) lists patrilineal ancestors on one side: "Pleasants Family Lineage/ John (1 of 6 Children) Norwich, England 1644—Henrico Co. VA 1698/ Joseph (3 of 3) Henrico Co. VA/ Richard (6 of 8) Goochland Co. VA." The list continues through two more Richards and a Joseph before arriving at Christopher himself, "(8 of 9) Albemarle Co. VA."

Recently, many Valley residents tend to express their identities in relation to their children and grandchildren. For example, in a Mennonite church cemetery, a gravestone for Shari Lynn Graber (1971–2007) says two things: "In Loving Memory" and "Daughter Stormy Dawn."[16] In Roanoke's Evergreen Burial Park, a stone for Jay Edwin Rauch (1907–1970) simply says, "He carried on though his heart was broken." Next to him are his wife and daughter who died together in an automobile accident in 1967.[17]

ONE KIND OF AFFINITY: THE COUPLE

As the foregoing examples celebrated largely consanguineous relations, the following showcase the affinal, particularly through celebration of the married couple. Of course, the landscape doesn't parse into clean categories—the Bickeys, described below, offering a case in point.

Some memorial parks offer "private family estates": tracts, usually bounded by bushes or low columns or walls, intended for the burial of multiple family members. They usually contain a large central obelisk with the family name,

FIGURE 7.3. A welcome flag and fresh floral spray honor the grave of Daniel Bickey (1946–2014). The adjacent space waits for his wife Cynthia (1948-) to join him, "reposing without pain in the place of darkness." Sunset Memorial Park, Beckley, West Virginia.

FIGURE 7.4. On this couple's gravestone, the American Sign Language sign for "I give my life to you" accompanies Roy T. Stephenson's name (1930–2014); that of "I love you" is next to Wanda N. Stephenson's name (1934–). Mt. Hermon Cemetery, Augusta County.

and small, uniform grave markers radiating from it, as well as ornamental trees and benches. Some with their circles of white marble remind of Stonehenge. The Bickey estate in Sunset Memorial Park (Beckley, West Virginia) centers on a gray granite pedimented obelisk (Figure 7.3). At the base of the monument is a mulched bed with hostas; a walkway brings visitors to this central memorial, around which are grave markers for individuals and couples. Among the latter is a flat granite marker for Daniel Bickey (1946–2014) and Cynthia Bickey (1948–). The inscription on their grave marker comes from Donald Hall's poem "The Painted Bed." Lying on a painted bed, the poet concentrates on "the journey I undertake to repose without pain in the palace of darkness, my body beside your body" (Hall 2006). On the day I visited, an elegant spray of flowers and a "welcome" flag with pineapple decorated Daniel Bickey's grave. It seems that, until she undertakes the journey to repose "in the palace of darkness," her body beside her husband's, Cynthia Bickey beautifies his grave.

Nearby, the couple bond is celebrated as warmly although in a different key. On a mausoleum, a pair of plates read: "Eddie Preston Thornton is 'Booger'/ Sandra Ann Thornton is the one I love and wish to spend eternity with." And "Sandra and Booger. Together forever in Heaven's embrace."[18]

Harold Herman (1932–2016) and Linde Hayen Herman (1924–2013) are buried in Winchester.[19] Their grave marker exhibits tragedy-comedy theater masks, stage curtains, and this inscription: "How the world can change. It can change like that,/ Due to one little word: 'married.' See a palace rise/ from a two room flat, Due to one little word 'married.'/ And the old despair that was so often there/ Suddenly ceases to be. For you wake one day,/ Look around and say, 'Somebody wonderful married me.'/ Fred Ebb, *Cabaret*."[20]

In Augusta County, Wanda N. Stephenson (1934–) and Roy T. Stephenson (1930–2014) share a gravestone (Figure 7.4). Under her name is the image of a hand with thumb, index finger, and pinkie extended, the American Sign Language sign for "I love you." Under his name is a hand, open with the palm up; it means, "I give my life to you."[21]

Even some burials in military cemeteries privilege affinal affection. T. Wayne Hewett (1947–2015) "SP5 US Army Vietnam / Loved Sarah Country and God."[22] This epitaph reverses (if inadvertently) the more common order of the terms.

In these many ways—a quote from a play and a poem, signed sentiments— some in the Valley of Virginia convey their social identities on their grave markers most profoundly as part of a pair. The individual here is not isolated, but rather—in life and death—half of a cherished whole.

"SEVERAL OF HIS AFFINITY"

Carolyn Hite Fitzgerald (1943–2012) and John Steven Arehart (1949–) have a gravestone featuring a snow woman and snowman looking into each other's

FIGURE 7.5. According to her obituary, Carolyn Hite Fitzgerald (1943–2012) had "an affinity for snowmen," and a "special relationship that few people will ever know" with John Steven Arehart (1949-). Their gravestone reflects both of these affections. Mt. Hermon Cemetery, Augusta County.

FIGURE 7.6. The gravestone of Charles Lee Breeden (1936–2007) and Brenda Kay Breeden (1944-) depicts him with his emu and water truck, her with their front-yard pond. Elk Run Cemetery, Elkton.

coal eyes and hugging with branch arms (Figure 7.5). Her obituary explains that Carolyn and Steve "had a 'special' relationship that few people will ever know," and that she had "an affinity for snowmen and roosters," conferring a name on each of them.[23]

Carolyn's affinity for snowmen and roosters suggests a definition of the term "affinity" or "affinial" that is different from that of being related through marriage. This use denotes a "liking for or attraction to a person or thing; natural inclination towards something; sympathy and understanding for something; the state of being closely connected or mutually dependent; a link, a connection; similarity of characteristics or nature; resemblance; common ground," or even a "state of being psychically or spiritually connected" to someone or something else (*Oxford English Dictionary* 2021). An affinity can imply a close alliance (as with pets) or a liking of or attraction toward something (an affinity for snowmen and roosters). It's less important to fit particular grave markers into one or another category than to use these terms in tracing varieties of ways that people express personal identity through associations with animals and objects.

During the last few decades in the Valley of Virginia, countless pets have been invoked through word or image on grave markers. Their prominence on many stones suggests that they were among the deceased's affinity: their close confederates. Certainly, the United States broadly has seen an explosion of material culture that positions pets as companions; the marketing of rain gear, whole wardrobes, and Halloween costumes for dogs and cats caters to a widely spread perception of pets as allied closely to the self.

FIGURE 7.7A AND B. The gravestone for Robert Lee Coffey (1930–1996) and wife Martha Ann Coffey (1934–2013) is topped by a porcelain picture of Mr. Coffey and a dog wearing sweaters. Riverview Cemetery, Waynesboro.

Walking through Elk Run Cemetery in Elkton (Rockingham County), you'll see images of Bibles, crosses, doves—and an emu. Charles Lee Breeden (1936–2007) and Brenda Kay Breeden (1944–) have a gravestone with images of the couple in their yard; she's standing by a small pond with a waterfall, and he's next to a water truck and pet emu (Figure 7.6). According to an obituary shared on a family history page, Charles Breeden had been employed by Lofton Manufacturing as a polisher and finisher. Later he "began hauling water," and "he raised a variety of birds including chickens and Emu's" (Klein n.d.).

Cats also make appearances on grave markers—perhaps most commonly with women. In a Presbyterian church cemetery, the headstone for Ruth Hall Miller (1905–1995) includes a cat and the epitaph, "All God's Critters Got a Place in the Choir."[24] A cat adorns the marker for Mary Margaret Lescalleet (1917–2003), remembered with this epitaph: "Our Miss Mary Did It Her Way."[25] Sometimes cats and dogs are paired on markers.

Dogs, though, seem to be the most common companion included on grave markers. They appear in municipal cemeteries and religious burying grounds, in town and country, in affluent and economically marginal communities. Poodles pop up on gravestones in Bland County and Winchester. A Chihuahua adorns the stone of a "Loving Son" in Elkton. Tappy the pug appears on a marker in Page County. In a Methodist burying ground, Linda Moyer (1951–) remembers her dog Chanel Moyer (2000–2014) as "The Love of My Life."[26]

Sometimes the dog seems to stand for the couple or to epitomize their bond. Thomas W. Marshall (1944–2013) and Linda J. Marshall (1947–2011) share a stone. At top center is an enamel photo of "Our Dog Bear."[27] Other married couples have a grave marker with pictures—not of the Mr. and Mrs.—but of man and dog. Robert Lee Coffey (1930–1996) and his dog, both wearing sweaters, are pictured in an enamel oval at the top of the headstone Robert shares with his wife, Martha Ann Coffey (1934–2013)[28] (Figure 7.7). The headstone for Helen L. Pence (1922–1992) and Martin R. Pence (1908–1979) likewise includes (only) the photograph of Martin and man's best friend.[29] In most cases, when a masculine image prevails on a couple's headstone—a man and his dog or his truck—the husband predeceased his wife, and it's possible that the marker was originally designed with him primarily in mind.

AN AFFINITY FOR BOWLING

A final connotation of "affinity" is that of a confederation, with common interests, values, and dispositions drawing people together. The *Oxford English Dictionary* provides examples of a successful man gathering his affinity about him and of a session being presided over by a leader "and several of his affinity." In this way affines are your "people," your band, the ones who share ways of thinking if not also interpersonal histories. Innumerable recent grave markers in the Valley of Virginia convey people's affinities for hobbies, teams, or organizations that integrate them into social collectives.

Jeffrey "Hippie" Earhart's (1975–2014) gravestone features images of a bowling ball and pins.[30] His obituary mentions his church membership (Memorial Baptist), vocation (in a company manufacturing automated loading systems for the food processing industry), and membership in community organizations (like the Moose Lodge). And it emphasizes the passion depicted on his gravestone: Jeff "was an avid bowler." Indeed, he and his brother had been inducted into "the Shenandoah Valley Bowlers Hall of Fame where Jeff was also recently elected to serve as a Board Member."[31] Far from "bowling alone," Hippie created extensive social ties through work, worship, and play.

A common form of affiliation on recent grave markers is with sports teams, from little league to professionals. Sometimes this association is direct, the deceased having been players. The family of Remington Colt Bortell, "Remmy," created a very detailed gravestone for him: "God gave us you on November 10, 1982/ God needed you on July 7, 2002/ Son of Mark and Mary/ Brother Rock." The back of Remmy's large upright gravestone is filled with details of his high school and college athletic accomplishments—among them "Shady Spring High School Hall of Fame," member of "The Most Winningest Team to Ever Wear Blue & Gold," "First Team All-State Running Back 2000 . . . Career Rushing Yardage – 4,200 yds.,"[32] and his placement in three years of West Virginia State Track Championships, along with achievements in motocross and in the "National Top Gun Racing Championship." Clearly his family—along with "the crew" as referenced on Remmy's grave marker, were devastated when he died at age 19, "a result of an accidental drowning."[33]

FIGURE 7.8. William J. "Bill" Linkous is one of many people at rest in the Valley with a grave marker that reflects their dedication to Virginia Tech. Westview Cemetery, Blacksburg.

Countless markers include references to colleges. Among them, the inscription for Joe M. Fix II (1963–2001) references James Madison University: "JMU Forever."[34] Others mention Virginia Military Institute[35] or invoke the University of Virginia through its unofficial chant, for example: Gardiner M. Haight (1930–2016), "Captain US Navy, Wahoowa."[36] Judging from cemeteries, Virginia Tech may have the most ardent fans and alumni. The "VT" symbol and the school's turkey-like mascot, a Hokie, have become familiar sights on Valley grave markers[37] (Figure 7.8). In a veterans' cemetery, for instance, is a gravestone dedicated to Michael L. Smith Sr. (1949–2015): "SP4 USA Vietnam. We Love You. Go Hokies."[38]

References to the Washington football team, the professional football team in closest proximity to the Valley, and until recently known as the "Redskins," are also common. The memorial for James W. Sword (1979–2006) exhibits a photo of him and images of football helmets, one for Virginia Tech and one for the Washington Redskins.[39] Brian Patrick Blythe (1980–2010) has a Redskins image affixed to his marker and four other Redskin logo objects on his grave: a flag, hat, painted stone, and flowerpot.[40] Other Valley gravestones feature logos from the New York Yankees, Pittsburg Steelers, Atlanta Braves, LA Dodgers, and Baltimore Orioles.

And then there's NASCAR—beloved, it would seem, by many. A memorial to a "Sister, Mother and Grandmother," Rhonda Joann Mosser, "Dodie," (1964–2006) includes a Washington Redskins logo and number 24, a reference to NASCAR driver Jeff Gordon.[41] Ann Houston Snell's marker (1935–2009) features the image of racecar number 28 for Davey Allison; her husband's side of the stone includes the Atlanta Braves logo.[42] Another marker says "Asleep in Jesus" on the front and "Grand Nationals Race Fan" on the back, with racecar numbers 9 (Chase Elliott) and 43 (Richard Petty).[43]

Jabe Thomas's marker identifies him as the 1958 Radford Speedway Track Champion and a 2010 inductee into the Racers Reunion Memory Lane Hall of Fame. Moreover, "5 NASCAR Hall of Fame Drivers have driven Jabe's cars: Ned Jarrett, Bobby Allison, Cale Yarborough, Wendell Scott, and Richard Petty. 4 were Grand National / Winston Cup Champions. 2 of Richard's 200 wins came driving Jabe's Plymouth."[44]

Music also often offers bridges to others and construction of the self. A stone memorializing Mayo Scott Nininger Jr. (1928–2013) features the outline of a man playing the trumpet.[45] Nininger was the retired bursar of Mary Baldwin College and "a jazz enthusiast" who had "traveled all over the East Coast attending jazz events and met many of the great jazz musicians, including Louie Armstrong."[46]

Nancy Ann Lorencki's (1958–2008) cenotaph in Harrisonburg features an image of a grand piano. Lessons "were a part of Nancy's childhood and she was an accomplished musician and vocalist as an adult. Her musical ability was a delight to her family and she was a member of the Otterbein United Methodist Choir as well as the local community band known as 'Just Jazzin.'"[47]

Of course, in this valley bordered by the Alleghenies and the Blue Ridge, bluegrass music references abound. An early example of musical instruments' representation on grave sites, David Charles Ritter's marker (1927–1983) includes a small fiddle, bow, and Bible.[48] In Southwest Virginia Veterans Cemetery, among the dead is James M. Phillips (1928–2016), "SN US Navy/ Korea/ Fiddle Man." Phillips's obituary omits any reference to his military service or occupation, but it does mention his family members and "music friends at River City Grill."[49]

Staunton's Thornrose Cemetery contains a gravestone for Wilson L. Fielding (1939–1998), "WD4FOZ," and Judy H. Fielding (1944–2012), "KM4NX." Wilson was an automotive internist and Judy a licensed practical nurse, but it was their affinity for amateur (or "ham") radio that appears on their gravestone—this association both a profound aspect of their identity and deeply social. WD4FOZ and KM4NX, their call signs, were members of the Valley Amateur Radio Association (VARA), an organization "dedicated to service to our community by providing radio communication whenever possible in times of emergency" or "public events where radio communications can facilitate the safety of the general public." VARA also aims to further the "exchange of information and cooperation between members, to promote radio knowledge, fraternalism and individual operating efficiency, and to so conduct club programs and activities as to advance the general interest and welfare of amateur radio in the community" (VARA, n.d.). An association newsletter in February 1997 reported that "Amateur Radio operators in the Shenandoah Valley proved once again that they are ready, willing, and able to respond to assist the public when necessary." One rider became separated from her group of cyclists in a national forest along Virginia's border with West Virginia:

> Running downhill on a particular stretch of forest road, the main part of the group got considerably ahead of one female biker. By the time they stopped to wait for her, she was nowhere to be seen. After waiting an extended length of time with the biker still not showing up, the group reported her missing. Since she was not dressed to survive a night in the mountains, a search was begun. . . . Because the search area straddled the state line, officials requested assistance from Rockingham County [Virginia] to cover the east side of the mountains. To allow communications between the West Virginia and Virginia operations, amateur radio operators were called in. Plans were quickly formulated to place hams in strategic locations to enable the searchers to communicate with one another and with command posts, located on opposite sides of the signal-blocking mountains. (Massanutten Amateur Radio Association [MARA] 1997)

The cyclist was found "cold, but not hypothermic, and otherwise in good health." Among volunteer operators assisting in this effort had been WD4FOZ (MARA 1997).

The next year, the newsletter reported that the "ham radio community in the valley has been rocked" by "major losses this month," including that of "Wilson 'Tiny' Fielding, WD4FOZ, [who] passed away suddenly on Sunday, August 23. . . . Tiny was the trustee and president of the Elliot's Knob repeater association, sponsor of the 147.045 repeater which recently returned to full power and coverage. Tiny is survived by his wife, the former Judy Cowardin, who is an advanced class ham KM4NX. Both Judy and Tiny are active members of the VARA club" (MARA 1998).

Other organizations that feed interconnection and identity are fraternal, and those symbols are common on grave markers in the Valley. Among them the Freemasons, Kiwanis, Rotary, and the Order of the Eastern Star often appear. Less common are badges of patriotism such as bronze markers identifying those who served in the Revolutionary War or War of 1812. The military affinity most commonly expressed in Valley cemeteries is promulgated by the Sons of Confederate Veterans and Daughters of the Confederacy. They include upright marble markers for veterans (typically pointed on top, not rounded like those of Union soldiers), the iron "Southern Cross of Honor" installed on countless graves, and—at least once a year—new Confederate flags, usually the familiar battle flag of the Army of Northern Virginia, less commonly the original version of the Confederate States of America (the Stars and Bars with two red stripes, one white stripe, and a blue square with a ring of white stars in the top left).

FIGURE 7.9A AND B. Paul Raymond Tully (1944–1992) is remembered as "A Democrat." His gravesite includes a bronze chair, coffee cups, and *New York Times* from the day Bill Clinton was elected president five weeks after Tully died. Rock Creek Cemetery, Washington, DC.

George R. Hite (also spelled "Hight") was a farmer who enlisted at age 34 in May of 1861, just weeks after the war began, as a private in Company E, Fifth Regiment, Virginia Infantry.[50] As part of the "Stonewall Brigade" serving under General Thomas J. "Stonewall" Jackson, the Fifth Infantry participated in some of the most pitched and important battles of the war, including First Manassas (Bull Run), Chancellorsville, Gettysburg, and the Wilderness (Rafuse 2011). Muster rolls identify Hight as a "prisoner of war, captured" on May 12, 1864, at the battle of Spotsylvania Courthouse.[51] He was sent to the prison camp at Fort Delaware. Hight was released on June 12, 1865, having signed an Oath of Allegiance to the United States.[52] When he died, though, in 1913 at age 87, his remains came to rest under a stone identifying him as a "Confederate Soldier and a Democrat." In his era, Republicans dominated the Union; Southern Democrats were the party of secession.

The political platforms had virtually reversed, of course, by the time Paul Raymond Tully (1944–1992) was buried in Washington DC's Rock Creek Cemetery, abutting the Valley to the north (Figure 7.9). His extraordinary grave marker identifies him simply as "Democrat." On the flat marble slab rest full-size bronze replicas of a wooden chair, paper coffee cups, and a folded copy of the *New York Times* from November 4, 1992: "Clinton Captures Presidency with Huge Electoral Margin, Wins a Democratic Congress." Tully had served as an advisor to Clinton and died five weeks before Clinton won.

To be a Democrat in the late 1800s was unlike being one in the late 1900s. The party stood for different values in Hite's time than in Tully's, but it was a term that tags both in death: claiming a party membership as constitutive of the self.

TROPES: SYNECDOCHE

The foregoing examples of affinity—confederations of people with common interests or dispositions—emphasize human-to-human connection. To understand expressions of human-to-object relationships, the concept of synecdoche is also useful. With synecdoche, a part stands for the whole. It "separates out" or draws attention to one aspect of an entity (Sapir 1977, 4). A classic example is referring to a sailor as a "hand." A "brain drain" describes outmigration as the loss of well-educated residents. Getting "boots on the ground" means moving soldiers into place.

Jerry W. Talbott's gravestone (1943–2006) features a single image: a pair of loafers.[53] We can understand the shoes as a part that represents the whole person, as it was a salient part of his identity. Talbott held membership in a Methodist church, was a US Navy veteran, and had retired from "Georgia-Pacific with 35 years service, having worked in sales and warehouse operations." He was also "a founding member of the Roanoke Valley Shag Club. Jerry will be remembered for his love, knowledge and dedication to shag music. His activities centered around an adoring wife, son, family and friends who understood his love of life, music and shag activities."[54]

Carl Michael Gainsback (1982–2002) has a grave marker with an image of his face and a depiction of his hand holding a pencil; his epitaph is "I Trust in You, O Lord, My Times are in Your Hands."[55] According to an online memorial, Gainsback

was a sophomore at George Mason University, where he was an honor roll student and a member of the lacrosse team and rowing crew. He was a photographer and artist. He was a 2000 graduate of Sherando High School and a member of the soccer team, Spanish Club, National Art Honor Society, Outdoor Club, Varsity Club, and Leo Club. . . . He was a member of Winchester Church of God.

He died from massive head trauma after falling off a balcony at an off-campus apartment while visiting friends in Charlottesville at the University of Virginia. He was 19 years old.[56]

Gainsback's family, of course, had a choice of ways to memorialize him: they could have created a bricolage representing his many activities. They could have chosen an image such as a lacrosse stick that, metonymically, called him to mind through his long association with it. But the trope to which the Gainsback family turned was synecdoche: "he was an artist," and his hand appears on his grave marker with a pencil, as if he's drawing the slender vine border of his own gravestone.

Some synecdochical practices today echo earlier memorial traditions. Much like Victorians who spun hair of the deceased into bracelets and brooches (Ariès 1981, 542), some people—well beyond the Valley of Virginia—now have cremains of their loved ones incorporated into synthetic diamonds, vinyl records, or paint for portraits (Zox and Dawdy, n.d.). The creator of Life Gem, a company casting human ashes into forms the living can continue to see or wear, explains the sense of relief many feel when they realize that they can retain a portion of their beloved. Journalist Lisa Takeuchi Cullen (2006, 73) interviewed a man who had turned some of his daughter's ashes into a gem. Cullen described a "vibrant, generous man, driving alone down an Illinois highway, sobbing as he tells a stranger about the daughter he lost, the daughter who now sparkles from his left ring finger. It is not Valerie, but it is part of her, and that is something."

The fluid lines between people, places, and things is clear in the tragedy of days following September 11, 2001. Of nearly 2,800 who died in the attacks in New York City, "no trace was ever found of about 45%. That's 1,268 families with nothing at all of their loved one left." One couple waited two years before resorting "to burying a vial of blood their son had donated" (Cullen 2006, 30). That tiny part of the body had to stand in for the whole missing person. Many others lacked any biological representation of their deceased loved ones. One such widow explained that her family came to feel the need for a funeral, a rite to say that her husband's life

> had been lived. In the Catholic doctrine, you're not supposed to go to into a church with an empty casket. That's a vessel for somebody. Because this was such a unique situation, the church and cemetery allowed it. . . . We chose a casket. My husband was a motorcyclist. He had a Harley, a Corvette. He liked his toys. He always told me he wanted a black-and-chrome casket. . . . Not a lot of people knew it wasn't Ken in the casket. It didn't seem important. We put his motorcycle helmet in it. . . . Just to know that there was some part of him in there (12–14).

The "part of him in there" was not biological. Nevertheless, it represented him to the satisfaction and relief of his family—so much so that when Ken's remains were found—in January, in the concourse of Tower Two—his family held another funeral. While "it meant a lot to have a part of him" physically in the casket, "we had the mementoes again in the second service" (Cullen 2006, 14).

These relationships to materiality are constitutive. Objects facilitate our construction as social beings, enabling us to make claims to identity, associations with others, and connections with a world that many experience as unalienated.

METONYMY: MAY MY WORK SPEAK FOR ME

Another trope often used in Valley cemeteries, metonymy is a formulation that "replaces or juxtaposes contiguous terms that occupy a distinct and separate place within what is considered a single semantic or conceptual domain. Homer will often be used instead of *The Iliad* ('you will read in Homer . . .'), where agent replaces act; or the phrase 'deep in his cups,' where 'cups' as container stands for the sherry or wine that is contained" (Sapir 1977, 4).

In metonymy, one thing evokes another because of their close, regular association. A classic example is the term "the bench" used to represent a judge (who sits on the bench). When we hear that the "White House has made an announcement," the building refers metonymically to the US president.

The gravestone of Marie Lety Niece (1926–2008) depicts an empty rocking chair and a porch swing with a blanket[57] (Figure 7.10). These objects represent

FIGURE 7.10. Marie Lety Niece (1926–2008) is memorialized with a rocking chair and porch swing. Mount Hebron Cemetery, Winchester.

Niece in much the way that the "bench" represents the judge. Habitual relationships—between people, objects, activities, and places—can form the groundwork for metonymic expressions that foreground a sense of "wholeness" (Sapir 1977, 21). The idea of metonymy, two things in such long association that one can invoke the other, offers inklings of what people are "up to" when they have a cow or a cement mixer engraved on a headstone.

Much as we can mention Homer and mean *The Iliad*, so a number of recent gravestones in the Valley of Virginia suggest that the deceased and their works are indistinguishable. Their labor represents them as social beings. Joseph Clay Stewart Sr. (1915–2006) was a Montgomery County supervisor, auctioneer, and farmer. Stewart's epitaph reads, "His Character and Contributions to the Community Will Be Forever Remembered," and "May the Work I've Done Speak for Me."[58] The latter is from John 10:25; when crowds around him were trying to understand whether Jesus was the Messiah—trying to figure out who he really was—some said, "'He is demon-possessed and raving mad. Why listen to him?' But others said, 'Can a demon open the eyes of the blind?' Jesus observed, 'I did tell you, but you do not believe. The works I do in my Father's name testify about me.'" In other Bible versions, Jesus said, "May the work I've done speak for me." A person's deeds, contributions, labor, and accomplishments "testify" to their essence.

Ronald Lee Lucas's gravestone (1949–2013) adopts words from Scottish churchman Horatius Bonar to make this very point: "My name and my place, and my tomb, all forgotten. The brief race of time well and patiently run. So let me pass away, peacefully, silently, Only remembered by what I have done."[59]

Images on Lee Elizabeth Pesti's gravestone (1930–1992) include a sickle, hammer, and barbed wire. Her inscription reads, "*On the Edge of the Volcano.* Hungarian Revolution. In 1956 the earth quaked. The great rivers overflowed. Life was in motion. New grain spikes rustled. The earth is quiet. Rivers again have bounds. But life moves on! Freedom is boundless."[60] These words and images reference a book about the Hungarian Revolution, *On the Edge of the Volcano* (1966), on which Lee Elizabeth Pesti and her husband József Pesti collaborated. This work, and relationship, represents her in death.

Tools often appear on recent memorials—mostly when commemorating men. Billy Kibler (1946–2004) in Page County has a grave marker with images of a cross, flowers, a saw, and a hammer.[61] Billy Shelton's stone (1941–2015) in Wytheville has a saw, a plane, and a hammer.[62]

It's not unusual now to see couples' grave markers decorated primarily—or even exclusively—with the husband's occupational vehicle, as if his work represents the couple and their connection. Virgil and Revonda H. Dedrick's resting place features a tractor trailer named "BIG MOE."[63] Stuart B. Hensley Jr. (1933–1978) worked for the railroad.[64] The stone memorializing him and his wife, Gladys (1935–2011), features an angel, stairway to Heaven, and a

FIGURE 7.11. A bench beside the gravesite of Linda C. Lemon (1948-) and Larry Earl Lemon (1949–2004) depicts an overturned 18-wheeler and a man pulling a chain from a tow truck. Sunset Memorial Park, Beckley, West Virginia.

locomotive.[65] Images on Benny and Becky Hite's stone include a tractor trailer on a road winding toward the mountains.[66] Benny was "a self-employed truck driver for 33 years."[67] Linda and Larry Lemon each have a flat bronze marker; she's memorialized as a "beloved wife and mother" and he as having earned a Bronze Star and Purple Heart in Vietnam. The Lemons also have a memorial bench that shows, in full color, a wrecked, crushed tractor trailer laying on its side while a man pulls a chain from a tow truck[68] (Figure 7.11).

Sometimes couples' stones feature work-related vehicles only on the husband's side. For example, on their 1954 marriage certificate, Sam Cummins was identified as a bus driver for Trailways, and Beulah Jeanette Meneffee as a typist for Pearl Assurance Company.[69] His side of their shared gravestone features a Trailways bus, hers grazing sheep.[70] Wanda F. Good (1947–2014) and Millar V. Merica Jr. (1945–2010) were "Two Hearts One Love." On her side of the memorial are images of flowers, on his side a CAT bulldozer.[71] The back of the marker for Mary Lou Little Gordon (1936–) and Clarence Henry "C. H." Gordon (1937–2006) names their four children on her side and depicts a riding lawn mower on his.[72] His obituary notes that Mr. Gordon "was owner and operator of Gordon's Lawnmower Service."[73]

Single memorials for men also often conjure their identity through association with work vehicles. One marker has images of flowers, a butterfly, and a cement mixer.[74] Another one features a cross flanked by a grader and skid steer[75] (Figure 7.12). Another has a deer, trees, and a log truck.[76]

Side-by-side markers in a church cemetery remember father Ray Borden Corbin (1943–2012) and son Michael Ray Corbin (1969–2014).[77] Both stones have images of tractors that pull trailers. Not only their gravestones but also their

RELATIONAL IDENTITIES

FIGURE 7.12. On the gravestone of Harry Edward Pauley, Sr. (1929–2006), images of a grader and a skid steer flank a cross. Morning Star Temple Hill Cemetery, Bland County.

obituaries point to the Corbins' deep, proud association with their vocation. "Ray Borden 'Hustlin Hillbilly' Corbin" had 45 years of service as a truck driver and "earned a Million-Mile Safe Driving Award from the National Transportation and Safety Board in Washington, DC for being the fourth safest driver in the nation."[78] Son Michael Corbin "drove over 3 million miles in the past 24 years as an over the road tractor trailer driver."[79]

The fusion between man and machine—with pride in an honest day's work together—also seems evident on the gravestone for Donald C. Jenkins (1936–1993) and Shelvy M. Jenkins (1939–). It features a landscape image of their house, barn, fields, garden, silo, garden, and farm tractor. When I visited the cemetery, a neighbor commented on the tractor, saying that Donald Jenkins's grandson has it now and still shows "Granddaddy's tractor" in fairs and other community gatherings.[80] Jenkins and his tractor are metonymically related. Who he was socially exceeded his biological bounds, linking to machines, architecture, and landscapes.

TWO WHEELS MOVE THE SOUL: METONYMY IN MOTION

An endless array of vehicles adorn grave sites in the Valley of Virginia, suggesting a common rendering of a social personhood that involves cars, Jeeps, motorcycles, and more. For example, in Giles County, Billy Junior Bowles (1929–2014) has a flat bronze marker with pine trees, mountains, an angel, a Bible, and a motorcycle, along with a bench featuring a colored picture of a NW 1776 train engine.[81] His obituary underscores the centrality of vehicles to his enjoyment, his vocation, and his identity as part of a family and community:

> Bill had over 40 years of service to the Virginian, Norfolk & Western and Norfolk Southern Railway Companies. Bill was a Roadmaster on the Radford Division. . . . He worked his way to that position having started as a water boy on the section crew of the Virginian Railway Co. Bill always provided for his family by working two jobs. After a day on the railroad he would work the evening shift and weekends at Pynes Store in Eggleston. After leaving Pynes Store, he worked at Akers Motor Co. in Narrows, and then Hendrickson Motor Company in Pembroke. . . . His hobbies in his earlier years were riding Harley-Davidson motorcycles and attending motorcycle races and field meets or the hill climb every Sunday outside of Princeton, W.Va. Today, Bill still has a motorcycle, a Honda which he rode at age 81 and received an award for oldest rider at a poker run. Bill and Hogie loved NASCAR racing and have attended all the tracks on the east coast.[82]

Donald Lee Woolfrey (1962–2011), too, has a Harley-Davidson Motorcycle logo at the top of his stone.[83] Jason Matthew Vaughan's stone (1973–2015) includes images of a dog, morel mushrooms, and a motorcycle. His obituary observes that "He was a loving father, son and brother. Jason loved his Harley."[84]

Vehicles sometimes suggest that the ride has come to an end; other times, the suggestion is that the road goes on. Brad Earhart (1982–2008) seems in motion on his gravestone enlivened with color images of a dune buggy, four-wheeler, and motorcycles.[85] The gravestone for Cindy J. Moore (1971–2003) includes the image of a man driving a motorcycle with a woman on the back. They ride away from the viewer, though the epitaph assures she will be "Forever With Me."[86] The convention of a riderless motorcycle points to absence. Examples from Elkton[87] and Winchester[88] feature motorcycles bereft of riders accompanied by images of mountains, fields, trees, roads, and flying eagles—suggestions of the open road. A cycle sans rider centers the gravestone of "Cotton" James L. Thompson (1940–2011) and "Lucy" Donna R. Thompson (1959–); their epitaph is a refrain among motorcycle enthusiasts: "Four Wheels Move the Body. Two Wheels Move the Soul."[89]

Other memorials feature popular four-wheel vehicle brands. The gravestone of Teresa Downey Hart (1958–2015), buried in a Methodist church cemetery, is inscribed with a Jeep[90] (Figure 7.13). "T" was "well known in the Troutville and Buchanan communities always wearing blue jeans, flannel shirts, and boots as she sported around in her red Jeep Wrangler."[91] Volkswagen Beetles also appear on some recent graves. One is that of Shannon Briscoe Branche (1981–2013), "Beloved Son, Brother & Uncle," and former employee of Washington and Lee

FIGURE 7.13. An image of her Jeep Wrangler adorns the gravestone of Teresa Downey Hart (1958–2015). Calvary United Methodist Church, Augusta County.

University. His epitaph is paired with images of praying hands and a VW Bug.[92] Chevrolet adherents seem especially passionate. In Bland County, Thomas M. King (1947–) and Joyce Harman King (1944–) plan to be "Together Forever." The back of their gravestone features their last name inside the Chevrolet chevron.[93] Similarly in Elkton, Kevin and Laura Meadows's stone consists of paired hearts, with a Chevrolet symbol at the top.[94]

Pickup trucks are also frequent sights on recently erected memorials. Maynard L. Will's stone (1948–2008) has a pickup truck flanked by crosses and flowers. James Lewis Humphries (1923–2004) and Eunice Henson Humphries's stone (1921–2007) includes their wedding photo on the front and, on the back, a pickup truck with this assurance: "My children, I'll meet you in the rapture."[95]

THE LAND ALIVE AND STORIED

Perhaps nothing points to a rapprochement between humanity and materiality more profoundly than expressions of identity as being inextricable from the land (see Mytum 2004, 153). This fusion—this seepage of the self from the body to the community to the soil itself—is beautifully illustrated by the grave site of James R. DePoy (1935–2014) and Mary Elizabeth DePoy (1935–) in Rockingham County. Their black granite gravestone is inscribed with the image of a wooden house that has a sheet metal roof and long porch. The landscape also includes trees, a stump with an axe, and a man on a riding lawn mower[96] (Figure 7.14). According to his obituary, James "Big Jim" Russell DePoy went to work at age 12 "at the Silver Grill to help support his family" and "dedicated his life to community service. He enjoyed preparing steak for various groups, organizations and family" and was a town councilor, little league coach, and member of the Ruritan Club, a Masonic lodge, a hunt club, and "Bud's Doghouse Social Club."[97] Jim's son, Clint DePoy, talked with me about the choices he and his mother made for the grave site. He explained:

> We own land in Highland County, and we have a cabin on that land. Dad fought a battle with cancer for three months and decided he wanted to be buried there at the cabin, but it turned out not to be an option. We went to a place where tombstones are sold, and we saw one with a cabin carved on it, and a lake. We thought that could be good for dad's tombstone, except without the lake. The person helping us there asked if we had a picture of our cabin. We showed it to her, and she said they could take that image and put it on his headstone. It was a way to get Dad part of what he wanted. On the headstone we also put a stump with an axe and a lawn mower. My dad was an avid collector of axes. We're still sorting through his collection of two or three thousand axes. We wanted to recognize that on his tombstone. And when he retired, he took over my mowing business. People in this area called him "the Mowing Man." We wanted

FIGURE 7.14. The gravestone of James R. DePoy (1935–2014) and Mary Elizabeth DePoy (1935-) features their house in Highland County and him on a lawn mower. Mount Crawford Cemetery, Rockingham County.

to recognize that [on the gravestone as well]. Almost up until he died, he was mowing grass. He probably mowed 30 to 40 acres per week.[98]

Clint DePoy emphasized that although mowing was a business, it was also a passion. Having thought through each meaningful motif to add to his father's gravestone, Clint and his mother still hoped they could grant Jim's wish to be buried at the cabin in Highland County—and so they did the next best thing:

We did steps out of order at my father's funeral. First, we had a graveside service, then we went to the church. Then we came back as family and friends and we covered the grave with dirt from Highland County. We did that ourselves. We'd hauled soil from Highland County. The whole fill of the grave is dirt from the land in front of the cabin. He had a really strong connection to it.[99]

Countless recent grave markers in the Valley of Virginia depict houses as part of larger rural landscapes. In Winchester, a couple's grave marker depicts "Featherwood Farm" with its cows and a pond, an image of a tractor at the top.[100] In Bland County, a couple's stone features a barn, a silo, cows, a fence, a road, trees, hills, a tractor, and an all-terrain utility vehicle.[101] In Botetourt County married "High School Sweethearts" share a gravestone: above his name are a tractor and fields, above hers a barn and cows.[102]

Couples depicted in landscapes usually have their backs toward the viewer. Visitors to the cemetery see wife and husband viewing the places they loved, the landscapes to which they understood themselves as being integral. The visual focus is less on the deceased themselves than on their being part of a pastoral scene. For example, in Rockbridge County, a couple's grave marker depicts them leaning on a fence, looking toward a pasture and mountains. A little dog between them shares their view, while a squirrel poses on a fence post. Two by two—pairs of deer, cows, and turkeys—and a barn also share in the landscape.[103] In Christiansburg, a gravestone memorializes a couple through an etched color landscape featuring two houses, a barn, silo, tractor, road, and fence. Husband and wife stand on a rock bridge over a creek with swans, ducks, and a rowboat.[104] In Buena Vista, another couple—holding hands with their backs to the viewer—look toward their house. Also featured in this domestic and agricultural rendering are a barn, silo, windmill, buck, doe, fawns, two horses, and six dogs.[105] While still alive, some couples design such ensembles—including themselves, architecture, livestock, wildlife, and pets—to represent them to posterity. Who they were, their social personhood, was distributed in these landscape elements.

At his death, Joe Stewart owned some 4,000 acres; as a reporter observed, Stewart "liked land. He collected it the way some people collect cut glass or old coins" (Thornton 2008). His heirs placed over a third of it under a conservation easement, ensuring that it will remain open space. Images on Stewart's gravestone at Christianburg's Sunset Cemetery include mares with their colts, a hen with her chicks, puppies, long-horn cattle, horses, fields, hills, a barn, and his massive, early nineteenth-century brick Colonial Revival house known as the Barnett House on Big Spring Farm (Worsham 1988). Stewart enjoyed the view from his Big Spring Farm "so much that he had a likeness of it depicted on his grave marker." His funeral was held on the porch (Thornton 2018). His fond association with the house is not about conspicuous display but personal and family history. Stewart's daughter recalled this house as "the first place Daddy said he ever saw electric light." Later he purchased it in an attempt to convince his wife to move from Salem (near Roanoke) back to the country. Stewart "bought Mill Creek trying to entice her to move. It didn't work. He bought White Sulfur Springs. That didn't work, either. But Big Spring was close enough to Salem to suit her. So the family moved into the old Barnett house." Their daughter recalled that Stewart was unconcerned with "creature comforts," saying that "as long as he had his land and a good pickup truck," Joe Stewart was happy (Thornton 2018).

This concept of metonymy helps make sense of some grave imagery that, otherwise, might seem odd. Many motifs recently carved into gravestones are metonyms: trucks, for example, horses, and dogs were in such close, long association with the deceased that the former call the latter to mind. One example from the Valley illustrates not only this process, but also ways in which current death practices resist alienation. The landscape is animate and intimate, inalienable. The boundaries between person, place, and animal are gauzy.

CONCLUSION: "HE'S AT HOME"

Dale Lyle, now in his late 50s, was the youngest of six children. He recalls that his father, Henry Mason Lyle (1931–2014), worked at Stillwater, Inc., a fabric factory, in the Goshen area of Rockbridge County "for 34 and a half years. In retirement he made $77.16 a month." Henry always supplemented his income with cattle: "All his life he raised cattle. He had a truck and on each side was an image of polled Hereford cattle. That's what he loved to do."[106]

Dale continues the tradition of cattle raising on the Lyle land in Goshen, where his family has lived for over a century. "When I'm doing cattle in Goshen, I always think about Dad. I still talk to him. Sometimes," Dale explains, smiling:

> I get teary eyed, and then I can hear him say, "Don't you be crying, boy!" In all the years, I never saw the man cry at all. There's a certain stone on the edge of the woods where he would sit and watch me work. Dad said, "That's where I want to be buried." Where he wanted his ashes spread.
>
> I didn't really mourn when Dad passed because we knew it was coming. I'd asked him, "Dad, when you pass, do you mind if we have a bottle of wine?" He loved Little Debbie cakes. When he passed, just close family had Little Debbie pumpkin rolls and a little bit of wine. I said, "It doesn't matter how old you are, if you want some and your parents say OK." It was our way of saying goodbye, for now.[107]

Henry Lyle died in January 2014, and as Dale recalled:

> Most of his friends were elderly people. We didn't want them coming out into the cold. So, in the spring, we put an announcement in the paper that there would be a celebration at Little River Presbyterian Church. We had a celebration of life, not a funeral. We provided the hot dogs and hamburgers. People brought side dishes, and we had a good time.[108]

Henry had been cremated. Dale bought clay jars, filled them with his father's cremains, and sealed them with caps he'd made. The jars were different colors, and he asked his siblings to take one that "represents you, and talk to Dad."[109] Then they put the clay jars in an ammo can that Dale had bought at an antique mall. He encased the box in concrete and buried it in their field at Goshen.

Above his cremains, Henry's grave marker has images of a cow on one side and a horse on the other: cattle and horses were "what Dad was into," Dale explained. "We always had ponies and one donkey. The last pony we had died of old age when I went into the service. When I came back from the service, Dad had two horses. His horses were hay burners"—doing nothing productive, just eating hay. His horses were "his babies. He would get out there every evening and stand out there and comb them and give them sugar cubes and grain. He loved them." The horse on the grave marker reminds the family of Henry. Dale says, "When I look at the headstone, I think 'That's really nice.' I wanted Dad to be in the place where he was happiest, and that rock was where he was happiest. He's at home. He is at home."[110]

Like Henry Lyle's homecoming in the pasture he loved and worked, Valley deathscapes offer diverse, copious claims of relational identity informed by association with tasks, events, people, places, objects, communities, and ancestors. Many intimate a sense of identity as located not in the atomized, biological individual, but in associations. The social persona is distributed through relationships to other people, pets, and places; through work and accomplishments; and through material culture including objects, brands, and hobby paraphernalia (see Tarlow 1999, 67). Through countless expressions of connection—reckoning consanguineous ancestry and descent, and affinity of marriage, close association, alliance, and inclination—current identities are deeply relational.

On the ground in country cemeteries, rejection of alienation abounds. So much about late twentieth-century and contemporary death practices implicates relational identity—the social self uncontained in the biological body—and seems to echo medieval assumptions that we might ask if we were, indeed, ever modern (Latour 1993) or if "modernity" was an experiment with estrangement that many are coming to reject.

CHAPTER 8

"The Grasshopper Not the Ant"
The Ludic, Populist Cemetery

Walk over the hills in Thornrose Cemetery, on the west end of Staunton, Virginia. You pass the towering monument to thousands of Confederate dead, headstones dedicated to little children, old gravestones sharing the wisdom of philosophers and poets. You notice a new marker for "Joe" and "Gigi" Kelly. On one side it says, "Put the kettle on luv," and on the other, "Time for a long English cuppa." Then you come to an especially striking gravestone. Dennis Lee Clatterbaugh (1956–2010) is buried under black granite inscribed with "Monsters from the Vault": the Wolf Man, Dracula, Creature, Frankenstein's Monster, and the Mummy[1] (Figure 8.1).

I became committed to researching cemeteries in 2015 when I saw Clatterbaugh's gravestone. I'd casually observed many other surprising markers—one with a gas station, one with a VW Bug, a thousand (it seemed) with pickup trucks. I suspected there must be a cultural shift informing these novel expressions. Seeing the "Monsters from the Vault" stone confirmed that suspicion and put me on the road to scores of cemeteries.

In *The Vital Dead*, we've surveyed burial grounds in the Valley of Virginia—histories of racism and self-determination, local experiences and legacies of

FIGURE 8.1. Dennis Lee Clatterbaugh (1956–2010) was a "monster kid." An online post suggests that his "favorite monsters will always be watching over him." Thornrose Cemetery, Staunton.

war, shifting definitions of "who counted" as fully human in and after the eugenics era. We've also considered recent developments in cemetery practice, as many people treat graves as front porches of the dead, and many express their identities as having been distributed among places, animals, organizations, and objects. This final chapter draws on these themes to suggest "what's going on" with the idiosyncrasy, novelty, and informality exhibited on markers like "Monsters from the Vault."

TECHNOLOGY, FAITH, FAMILY

Several factors seem to be in play with these developments but are unable in themselves to account for them. Among them are changes in grave marker technology; laser etching, for example, has greatly expanded the range of images that can be affordably applied to memorials. Technology has made it easier to get a Harley on a grave marker but doesn't explain why a couple identifies themselves on it as Harley riders. Inscriptions in past eras could have said—as some contemporary ones do—that the deceased intended to be a "Waste Management Driver Forever,"[2] or recommended that passersby "Read the Directions,"[3]

FIGURE 8.2.
Motifs like this delicate flower on the grave of J. Frank Walker, M.D. (1865–1890) exhibit the expertise and craftsmanship of nineteenth-century stone carvers. They possessed the technology and skill to carve vehicles, for example, or pet dogs on headstones, but they didn't do so because of cultural norms. East End Cemetery, Wytheville.

or suggested that "God Needed a Baritone."[4] Carvers in the mid-twentieth century and earlier could have easily inscribed pithy, playful epitaphs—like "I told you I was sick"[5]—on stones, but didn't. Those with training and talent carved extraordinary peonies, roses, weeping willows, and angels[6] (Figure 8.2). It was not skill but the power of cultural expectation that kept them from carving dogs, deer, and silos on grave markers. Technology in itself can't explain the effervescence of expression in cemeteries: culture has shifted too. Valley residents have "Gone Fishin" for centuries, but only in recent decades have some inscribed that phrase on their headstones.

Similarly, decline in religious belief and participation in organized religion may inform but cannot explain changes in cemetery expression (see Tarlow 2002). Innumerable recent grave markers combine sacred and secular images, suggesting that they coexisted as aspects of the deceased's life and were not at odds. In Rockbridge County, a pair of gravestones colorfully commemorate one widow's husbands. On the stone for Kenneth E. "Zip" Burch (1940–2000), Jesus watches over him as he's fishing, with house and pickup "Clyde" nearby[7] (Figure 8.3). Jesus also smiles benevolently on a scene of two men playing horseshoes on a stone for Dennis James Davis (1953–2004). Davis belonged to the Buena

FIGURE 8.3. The grave marker of Kenneth E. "Zip" Burch (1940–2000) and Faye Coleman Burch (1948-) depicts Jesus watching over a scene with deer, a man fishing, and a pickup truck ("Clyde"). Green Hill Cemetery, Buena Vista, Rockbridge County.

Vista Pentecostal Holiness Church, and he was a member of the Churchville Horseshoe Club, the Virginia Horseshoe Pitchers Association, and the Virginia Horseshoe Pitchers Association Hall of Fame.[8]

In a Presbyterian church cemetery, Garlet M. Hostetter (1939–) and Rev. Phyllis L. Hostetter (1944–) have a stone with a buck and a butterfly; the inscription is, "We lived for God."[9] In Giles County, Bobby G. Sanders's stone (1951–) includes images of a chicken and praying hands.[10] In Wythe County, James Landon Simmerman (1979–2006) is buried under a stone with images of a farm tractor and horse: "Blessed are the pure in heart for they shall see God."[11] Other markers combine a football and praying hands,[12] a pickup truck and crosses,[13] and the Star of David with a baseball, a dog, and butterflies.[14] In these expressions, people have not fallen away from God; their faith coexists comfortably with quotidian hobbies and interests (Figure 8.4).

A final potential impetus for recent changes in cemetery practice is the demise of the family. Could people be putting their Jeeps, cats, and favorite NASCAR racers' numbers on gravestones as substitutes for formerly valued ties to spouses, parents, or children? Again, while this suggestion may account for some particular decisions, the preponderance of expression is in the other direction: a celebration and foregrounding of kin relations.

As mentioned in the previous chapter, many gravestones now position the deceased in the context of both ancestors and descendants. David "Lloyd" Trissel (1920–2018) and Alice Blosser Trissel (1924–2019) grew up a mile apart in Rockingham County and lived in the area all their lives. They were married

FIGURE 8.4. The back of a gravestone memorializing James Lewis Humphries (1923–2004) and Eunice Henson Humphries (1921–2007) combines the image of a work truck with religious statements. Green Hill Cemetery, Buena Vista, Rockbridge County.

for 73 years and are buried in a Mennonite church cemetery. Alice "helped early on with the farm work, until [their] five sons were old enough to help with the morning and evening chores of milking cows to feeding and caring for the turkeys."[15] Lloyd and Alice Trissel's headstone lists "our parents" as well as "our children," with the names and birthdates of the five boys.[16] In a Presbyterian

FIGURE. 8.5. Dorothy Lorene Carr Brooks (1937-) is memorialized as a grandmother of four and a mother of five, two of them stillborn. Mt. Carmel Presbyterian Church Cemetery, Augusta County.

church cemetery, the gravestone for Dorothy Lorene Carr Brooks (1937–) lists her first and second husbands, her three daughters, and six grandchildren including two "stillborn"[17] (Figure 8.5). Though these two boys died on the days they were born, though they'd never drawn breath, they were nevertheless family. Brooks defined herself here through relatives, living and dead. Memorials without religious contexts or references also often highlight relations. Scott (1960–) and Marie (1949–) Straub's marker in a municipal cemetery features a pair of hands clinking champagne flutes and an inscription: "To the Family."[18]

MONSTER KIDS

If these factors—technology, secularization, and strength of the family—don't in themselves offer adequate explanation for the remarkable recent developments in commemoration, we can look to "Monsters from the Vault" for indication of other currents. In 2016, I found a discussion about this marker online, on the "Classic Horror Film Board"(Clatterbaugh 2010b). The post included a photo of Dennis Clatterbaug's gravestone and a message from his brother Jim Clatterbaugh, editor and publisher of *Monsters from the Vault* fanzine/magazine of classic horror and sci-fi films:

> Growing up we both loved the classic monsters, and continued to do so to this day. [Dennis] was always so proud of *Monsters from the Vault* and couldn't believe his brother could publish such a fine magazine. He showed off copies and bragged to friends constantly about it. For his 50th birthday he got a large tattoo of the Frankenstein Monster, along with the Mummy, Dracula, Creature (his favorite), and the Wolf Man (with a film strip winding through them that said *Monsters from the Vault*) on his shoulder in honor of the magazine. I always loved to bring him the latest classic horror and sci-fi DVDs (and cool monster toys) when I visited because he was like a kid at Christmas when he opened the boxes. Dennis, you'll be missed and I love you. May you be in a better place now! (Clatterbaugh 2010a).

Nearly a hundred people posted responses to Jim's message. They wrote, "The memorial is stunning," and "I think Dennis would be proud to spend eternity under such an awesomely cool tombstone." Another remarked, "Seeing that beautiful headstone brought tears to my eyes. It's absolutely wonderful." And still another: "What a beautiful tribute for a . . . monster fan."[19]

Jim Clatterbaugh describes himself as "a 'Monster Kid' who grew up in the 1960s loving horror and sci-fi films and the monsters that starred in them." Jim said that his brother Dennis, too, was a Monster Kid. Their sister Doris worked for over 30 years at Woolworth's in Staunton and

> on many a Saturday while downtown with my mother, my brother Dennis and I would stop in to see her and use her employee discount to pick up the latest

monster toys she had stashed away for us. . . . Like me, Dennis was a HUGE fan of classic horror (especially Universal) and was just as proud of *Monsters from the Vault* as [my wife] Marian and I are. So when his wife approached us with the idea of the memorial stone, we were speechless. . . . It brought tears to my eyes when we saw it, and we feel great comfort in knowing that Dennis' favorite monsters will always be watching over him. RIP, brother.

This gravestone is unprecedented, and its novelty can't be explained by the factors considered above. Technological developments facilitated the execution of this design, but depicting a Wolf Man was not beyond the capacity of stone carvers in previous generations. Werewolves are absent from Valley cemeteries earlier for cultural, not mechanical, reasons. This stone also illustrates the ease with which the sacred and the secular can coexist. Members of the Classic Horror Film Board responded to Jim Clatterbaugh's post with blessings: "I'm praying for you, Jim," and "I'll keep you and your family in my prayers," and "My family and I are praying for you and remember, when the pain seems overwhelming, *rest in Him*." These comments, too, point to a strength and intimacy among family members: "I'm very sorry to read this, Jim, but you have some great memories of your mutual love of monsters with Dennis." And this: "Monster Kids are united, Jim, because we are a unique group. My deepest condolences to you and your family. . . . What a stunning tribute to your brother. God bless."[20]

Indeed, these responses bring us to dynamics that do, I contend, inform a great deal of the novelty apparent in recent cemetery practice: the cultivation of social capital in the context of emergent populist sentiments.

BANDING TOGETHER

As sociologist Robert D. Putnam (2000, 18) explained, the core idea of "social capital theory is that social networks have value." The encouragement job seekers receive to network is a function of this notion, as "networks involve (almost by definition) mutual obligations. . . . Networks of community engagement foster sturdy norms of reciprocity: I'll do this for you now, in the expectation that you (or perhaps someone else) will return the favor" (20). Social capital is bankable: connections can provide substantial financial, personal, and social benefit. Importantly, however, it can work in two ways—bridging, or inclusive, and bonding, or exclusive:

> Some forms of social capital are . . . inward looking and tend to reinforce exclusive identities and homogenous groups. Examples of bonding social capital include ethnic fraternal organizations, church-based women's reading groups, and fashionable country clubs. Other networks are outward looking and encompass people across social cleavages. Examples of bridging social capital include the civil rights movement, many youth service groups, and ecumenical religious organizations. (22)

Putnam (2000, 23) acknowledges that "bonding social capital, by creating strong in-group loyalty, may also create strong out-group antagonism." It can be "directed toward malevolent, antisocial purposes, just like any other form of capital" (Putnam 2000, 20). Members of the Ku Klux Klan, for example, may have strong internal bonds and cultivate virulent distinctions from African Americans, Jews, Muslims, and others (Kennedy 1990).

This bonding social capital is, I think, in large measure the dynamic that developments in death practices intimate. Having lost much faith in authorities and institutions, people are building their own posses: groups of people "who have a common characteristic, occupation, or purpose" (Lexico 2021). They're creating social bonds and bands, taking some matters into their own hands, forging a "do-it-yourself" (DIY) culture, and devising their own forms of memorialization (see Dawdy 2021).

French historian Pierre Nora (2011, 437–38) perceives a "memorialist trend" internationally, starting in the late twentieth century, as "every social, ethnic or family group has undergone a profound change in the relationship it traditionally enjoyed with the past." The change often involves "criticism of official versions of history," increasing "interest in 'roots' and genealogical research," and "a kind of tidal wave of memorial concerns" that unite "respect for the past" with a "sense of belonging" (437). This movement is populist and democratizing:

> Unlike history, which has always been in the hands of the public authorities, of scholars and specialized peer groups, memory has acquired all the new privileges and prestige of a popular protest movement. It has come to resemble the revenge of the underdog or injured party, the outcast, the history of those denied the right to History. What is new . . . is the demand for a truth more "truthful" than that of history, the truth of personal experience and individual memory. (440)

Forms that this DIY impulse takes include vernacular memorials in public spaces. For example, material tributes appear throughout the United States on the shoulders of roads where people died in traffic accidents. In the Valley of Virginia, hundreds of wooden crosses, fabric flowers, Mylar balloons, and notes commemorate sites of sudden death. Whether or not legally permitted in different localities, the "abundance and agency" of roadside memorials act as "expressions of alternative authority drawn from the intensity of grief and from a belief in the spiritual presence of the deceased" (Doss 2010†, 84–85). Spontaneous community memorial assemblages also often appear on sites of homicides and other tragedies. National examples include the outpouring of grief and immense ensembles of mementoes—flowers, cards, ribbons, toys, and personal effects like t-shirts and shoes—following the bombing of the Alfred P. Murrah Federal Building in Oklahoma (1995), the murder of students at Columbine High School in Colorado (1999), and the Columbia space shuttle disaster memorialized at the Johnson Space Center in Texas (2003; Doss 2010, 61–66) In the Valley of

Virginia, reporter Alison Parker and photojournalist Adam Ward, who worked for CBS affiliate WDJB in Roanoke, were killed on live television in 2014 while conducting an interview. Community members assembled an ad hoc memorial of teddy bears, candles, cards, and flowers outside of the TV station then and again on the first anniversary of their deaths (Chan 2016).

As an example of the trend toward people taking matters into their own hands rather than awaiting authoritative guidance: One summer day I was with three students, surveying cemeteries in Rockingham County. We pulled up to a small nondenominational church where, as it turned out, the minister was up on a ladder, painting a gutter. He climbed down and greeted us cordially. He offered us water and church literature, and then gave us a tour of the little building and its cemetery. While walking he inquired into the wellbeing of our souls, asking us whether or where we each attended church. He emphasized that the important thing was to find an independent church, one not associated with any denomination, so that the local congregation would enjoy control and self-determination. He didn't trust "truth" imposed by outside authority. Indeed nationally, countless churches are struggling with attendance, but nondenominational (unaffiliated) congregations are on the rise (Stetzer 2015). Americans are increasingly unlikely "to identify with an official or formal religion in recent decades, and nowhere is this more evident than in the dwindling percentage who identify with a specific Protestant denomination. In 2000, 50% of Americans identified with a specific denomination; by 2016 that figure had dropped to 30%" (Newport 2017).

A turn away from external authority and toward local determination appears, too, in treatments of the past. In recent decades, many history museums in Virginia and elsewhere have struggled to maintain visitorship (Vagnone and Ryan 2016). In 2017, the president of the Colonial Williamsburg Foundation announced that this flagship museum was attracting "half the visitors we did 30 years ago." The Foundation "loses significant amounts of money every year," he noted, citing as an example 2014 when they "lost a total of $62 million, or $176,000 every day. This is . . . not sustainable" (Wise 2017). Vernacular history, however, is surging. Interest in genealogy—through archival records and home DNA kits—is soaring, with people of many backgrounds working to "find their roots." Many Virginians are sharply attentive to history, as municipalities, schools, and citizens wrestle over names and monuments. Proposals to move the Lee and Jackson statues from squares in Charlottesville provided much of the impetus for the rallies and counterrallies in recent years. Many people care deeply about history, but "history" as past that is personally meaningful and not delivered to them as passive visitors by docents in Georgian mansion museums (Vagnone and Ryan 2016).

A particularly moving example of this preferred direct relationship with the past occurred on a crisp fall day in 2017. Roughly twenty people gathered

FIGURE 8.6. Attendees at a ceremony honoring Captain John Young as a veteran of the American Revolution include a young couple and their baby. They live close by and help maintain the cemetery. Glebe Burying Ground, Augusta County, September 30, 2017.

at one of Augusta County's oldest cemeteries, the Glebe Burying Ground, to honor Revolutionary War soldier Captain John Young (Figure 8.6). Young hailed from Scotland. Descendants wore kilts and tartans to the ceremony, listened to patriotic remarks and the powerful voice of a bagpipe, and watched a new "Sons of the American Revolution" marker being pounded into the ground next to Young's headstone.

A blonde baby sat quietly near the grave. His parents stood behind him, a young couple who had renovated and made their home in an old house near the burying ground. They don't have a genealogical relationship to the property but told me that they considered themselves its stewards; they encouraged visitors to the land and spoke warmly about their intent to care for it, given its historic significance to so many. This is why they brought their baby to the ceremony for Captain Young. They're showing him to care for the burial ground, to curate the past. They regularly visit to remove fallen limbs and pull weeds and are teaching him to do the same (Cavallaro 2017).

Many people, then, are deeply engaged with historical and contemporary others—but in selective, DIY manners. Setting this trajectory in the sociocultural and political contexts of the late twentieth and early twenty-first centuries, along with anthropological theory, illuminates its emergence.

In 1909, anthropologist Arnold van Gennep published a book, *The Rites of Passage*, that exercised profound influence on the field. Drawing on observations of communities around the world, van Gennep observed that funerals are very commonly structured around rites of separation, rites of transition, and rites of incorporation. The deceased is separated from the community, placed according to local custom on the ground; on a table, trestle or platform; or in a morgue or funeral home. Some traditions include "burning the tools, the house, the jewels, the deceased's possessions," putting to death favorite animals, or "washings, anointings," and other purifying efforts (van Gennep 2018, 40). The dead and those who loved them then enter a "liminal stage," a period when the old way has not truly passed, and the new reality has not been cemented. During "mourning, the living mourners and the deceased constitute a special group, situated between the world of the living and the world of the dead" (van Gennep 2018, 35). In this period, "social life is suspended for all those affected" by the death. People might not work, for example, eat, or wear their normal clothes. The usual social structures are temporarily upended. The third rite incorporates the deceased into the realm of the dead: through a funeral or other ceremony, they become ancestors, spirits, or other kinds of beings who occupy the afterlife. Likewise, survivors reintegrate into their communities as widows, for example, or orphans. The whole rite of passage—separation, transition, and incorporation—serves to solidify in minds the changing of identities and community composition that comes with death.

An anthropologist who famously extended van Gennep's model was Victor Turner. Among his many contributions was Turner's analysis of liminality, the transitional state, *limen* being Latin for "threshold":

> The attributes of liminality or of liminal personae ("threshold people") are
> necessarily ambiguous, since this condition and these persons elude or slip
> through the network of classifications that normally locate states and positions
> in cultural space. Liminal entities are neither here nor there; they are betwixt
> and between the positions assigned by law, custom, convention, and ceremonial.
> As such, their ambiguous and indeterminate attributes are expressed by a
> rich variety of symbols in the many societies that ritualize social and cultural
> transitions (Turner [1969] 1995, 95).

Funerals exist in liminal times and spaces. They're part of transitioning, the dead being "betwixt and between" the living community and the buried crypt. In their ambiguity, cemetery commemorations represent a space conducive to established ritual and its reassuring sense of order, certainty, and connection. The liminal is deeply social and usually, by design, familiar. Participants often experience a sense of *communitas*, or profound equality and oneness, as a member of the group transitions to a new status while the group affirms its identity and reality.

Being "betwixt and between" can also, however, offer opportunity for innovation. With the social order in flux, people might "'play' with the elements of the familiar and defamiliarize them. Novelty emerges from unprecedented combinations of familiar elements" (Turner 1982, 27; see also Rosaldo et al. 1993, 3). In this "free or 'ludic' recombination" of extant symbols and cultural practice, new arrangements and expressions, "however weird," can emerge (Turner 1982, 28; see also Rosaldo et al. 1993, 3). This freedom, playfulness, and strangeness characterize recent trends in many Valley grave markers, as for the first time an emu appears on one and a garbage truck on another, along with an endless procession of cats, bucks, jon boats and pickups. Turner describes moments when tradition and obligation give way to creativity and choice as "liminoid" (43; see also Schnecher 1993). Liminoid phenomena

> develop apart from the central economic and political processes, along the margins, in the interfaces and interstices of central and servicing institutions— they are plural, fragmentary, and experimental in character. . . . [They] tend to be . . . idiosyncratic, quirky . . . [and] are often parts of social critiques . . . exposing the injustices, inefficiencies, and immoralities of the mainstream economic and political structures and organizations. (54–55)

The liminoid tends especially to emerge "at certain historical junctures" when "the societal value-consensus has broken down" (Turner 1982, 71). People who feel that social, economic, and political systems are arraying against them may seek redress through rebellion, mobilizing cultural elements in novel ways to register a rejection of mainstream and valorization of alternate ways of being.

The liminoid, then, can articulate with populist movements. Although the term has several definitions, populism generally connotes a "critique of the establishment and an adulation of the common people" (Mudde and Kaltwasser 2017, 5). A notion of the pure, common people "vindicates the dignity and knowledge of groups who objectively or subjectively are being excluded from power due to their sociocultural and socioeconomic status. This is the reason why populist leaders and constituencies often adopt cultural elements that are considered markers of inferiority by the dominant culture" (10). A populist impulse opposes "political correctness" and breaks "taboos" imposed by the elite (19). It challenges "the establishment" and gives "voice to groups that feel unrepresented" (51). Populist social movements are examples of "bottom-up mobilization," their power and pervasiveness lying dormant until an actor is "able to exploit the existing context to mobilize the amorphous anti-establishment sentiments and to appeal to the population by promoting 'common sense' solutions" (47, 104).

Many will perceive in this description of populism strains of politics in the Trump era. I interpret the liminoid spirit of gravestones, beginning in the 1980s, as expressions of populist sentiment (see Mitford 1998) that moved from quiet corners like the Valley of Virginia to national prominence with the 2016 presidential election. The rejection of taboos and elite authority, the embrace of cultural elements "considered markers of inferiority by the dominant culture" are clear—literally carved in stone—for decades before an emergent leader perceived, enunciated, and capitalized on them, riding the populist wave he released to the White House.

"GONE HUNTIN FOR THE LORD"

A rejection of elite ascribed norms appears nowhere more clearly than in Southwest Virginia Veterans Cemetery on the gravestone of John C. Henry (1934–2016): "SP3 US Army, Korea. The Grasshopper Not the Ant"[21] (Figure 8.7). This epitaph is a twist on Aesop's fable, "The Ants and the Grasshopper." On a sunny day in the late autumn,

a family of ants were bustling about in the warm sunshine, drying out the grain they had stored up during the summer, when a starving Grasshopper, his fiddle

FIGURE 8.7. John C. Henry (1934–2016) served in Korea and is remembered as "the grasshopper, not the ant." Southwest Virginia Veterans' Cemetery, Pulaski County.

under his arm, came up and humbly begged for a bite to eat. "What!" cried the Ants in surprise, "haven't you stored anything away for the winter? What in the world were you doing all last summer?" "I didn't have time to store up any food," whined the Grasshopper; "I was so busy making music that before I knew it the summer was gone." The Ants shrugged their shoulders in disgust.

The moral of the story: "There's a time for work and a time for play."
(Aesop n.d.)

Henry's stone aligns him with the grasshopper, one who played and rejected injunctions for hard labor, striving, and future planning. This marker is liminoid, as it plays with existing cultural elements (in this case, a fable with long history) to express values at odds with prescription.

Numerous grave markers in the Valley champion rural lifeways and links to the local. They don't list accomplishments. In some cemeteries—like Riverview in Waynesboro—a few references appear to the ways people made a living. There are some images linked to livelihoods, almost exclusively masculine—a firefighter's hat, a food truck, the logo for a sign-making business—but much more common are references to wildlife, agrarian scenes, mountain landscapes, and images of modest home places.

Twenty-year-old Samuel McCown died on the fourth of July 2004. His headstone features a waterfall, pine trees, fish, an eagle, and deer.[22] His epitaph references two Lynyrd Skynyrd songs: "Simple Man – Free Bird, fly high." The lyrics of "Simple Man" reject the rat race in favor of plain, rural living, as the singer recalls advice that "Mama" gave him when he was young: "Take your time, don't live too fast. . . . You'll find a woman and you'll find love. And don't forget, son, there is Someone up above. . . . Forget your lust for the rich man's gold. All that you need is in your soul. . . . All that I want for you, my son, is to be satisfied." The chorus emphasizes the goal to be "satisfied" by being "a simple kind of man," something "you love and understand" (Lynyrd Skynyrd 1973). Life's goal is not wealth or fame, but family, God, and honest work. "Free Bird" portrays a different kind of departure from standard expectation, with the singer leaving the woman he loves simply because his spirit requires freedom: "I must be traveling on, now. Cause there's too many places I've got to see. But, if I stayed here with you, girl, things just couldn't be the same. Cause I'm as free as a bird now, and this bird you cannot change" (Lynyrd Skynyrd 1974). In the context of a gravestone, this Southern rock anthem gestures toward an idealized way of living and envisions the soul as flying high and free.

References to rural pleasures populate countless markers beginning in the 1980s, among them fishing poles, lines, and boats. The fish seem often to be large-mouthed bass, shown as a second away from grabbing the bait. Images of fishers reeling in a catch are also common. Single women and men, as well as couples, frequently have these motifs.

Deer are extremely common images on grave markers, sometimes with overt references to the deceased hunting them. For example, the headstone for Anthony "Tony" W. Patterson (1965–2005) in a Presbyterian church cemetery shows him smiling, wearing camouflage, and kneeling with a freshly killed buck.[23] His obituary noted that he coached little league, attended the Bible Church at Rockbridge, and was a "loving husband and devoted family man." Patterson was also "an accomplished hunter and fisherman" who "loved the out-of-doors."[24] Similarly, the stone for Mark Richard Futch (1965–2015) features a log cabin, sun setting behind hills, a buck, and pine trees.[25] It also includes a colored, enamel photograph of him, and at the top an image of a rifle. He "was a member of the Christ United Methodist Church," a mechanic, a Dobro player in a bluegrass band, "and he enjoyed deer and bear hunting. He loved animals, always caring for strays. His dogs, Ralph, Frank, and Woody, along with his cats, Sam, Floyd, and Sylvester will surely miss Mark."[26] Thomas L. and Melinda Fix share a headstone inscribed with mountains, pines, and deer. Their epitaph: "Gone Huntin for the Lord."[27]

The outdoors, the agrarian, the down home are also foregrounded on memorials through farm and domestic references. The stone for June Gayle Armstrong (1961–2013) includes a cow and a cat and remembers her as "Our Farm Girl."[28] Pricilla Kern Redd (1939–2002) predeceased her husband. Their grave

FIGURE 8.8. Among images on the gravestone of Leonard Ray Nida, Sr. (1943–2013) and Bettie Jane Nida (1945-) are a bulldozer and fireworks. Lone Star Cemetery, Alleghany County.

marker features turkeys, deer, and a log cabin.[29] She was "a retired manager for the National Rifle Association and a member of the Burnt Chimney United Methodist Church."[30] The marker for John T. Clowser (1924–2004) and Hazel E. Clowser (1927–2009) likewise depicts mountains, barns, fields, cartwheels, a barrel and a milk can, a buck and doe, and male and female ring-necked pheasants.[31] Other couples, like Leonard Ray and Bettie Jane Nida, share gravestones with etched images of their houses and—in the Nidas' case—also of the couple, a bulldozer, a truck, and fireworks (Figure 8.8). Leonard was remembered as having "loved the mountains and outdoors and gathering at the picnic shelter for the famous Nida July 4th celebration. He loved a bargain, yard sales and flea markets and enjoyed hunting and fishing and spending time with friends and family."[32] Obituaries and grave markers in these and countless other cases celebrate populist themes of the quotidian, the frugal, the rural, the local.

INFORMALITY

A denunciation of elite establishment tradition often appears as informal presentations of the self on grave markers in the Valley of Virginia. According to the *Oxford English Dictionary*, the word "form" means "proper figure," the "orderly arrangement of parts, regularity, good order." "Informal" means "not done or made according to a recognized or prescribed form; not observing established procedures or rules; unofficial; irregular." Applied to the economy, informality refers to activity carried out in "self-employed, casual, or irregular basis." In connoting "proper order," formality gestures toward authority, particularly when contrasted with informality that implies self-determination and defection from established norms.

In social relations, formality tends to "enable the preservation of social distance and structures of power," while informality facilitates "group feeling" and social integration (Misztal 2000, 18, 21). Informal relationships "rely more on tacit knowledge than on prescribed norms" (19). Informality tends to support bonding social capital and to maintain distance between groups:

> [It] plays a dual role. On one hand, informality ensures the preservation of distinctions between groups. The phenomenon of "old boy networks" or informal talks in the corridor are often quoted, for example, by many professional women in academia as the principal factor restricting their access to important resources such as information, grants or teamwork projects. On the other hand, informality also reinforces the emotional and moral ties within the respective groups. (45)

"Informal," of course can also mean "casual," and all of these meanings explicate novel expressions on gravestones.

A number of men appear on their headstones casually (or minimally) clad. Wiley Eugene Thomas (1963–2003), for example, wears a cowboy hat and over-

FIGURE 8.9A AND B. The gravesite of Jason Lee Shifflett (1984–2015) includes images of him with a tattooed torso and face ("Mama Tried . . . Outlaw"). Holly Memorial Gardens, Albemarle County.

alls.[33] Leonard "Lenny" Ray Nida Jr. (1961–2008) looks out from under an "Advanced Auto Parts" cap.[34] Robert Lee Shifflett (1937–2007) holds an axe.[35] Thomas "Tommy" Preston Lunsford II (1981–2005) is bare-chested.[36] Killed in a car accident, "Tommy was a caring and loving father, son and brother. He was employed by Brickwood Builders. He enjoyed hunting, fishing, and spending time with his family and friends. Tommy was a talented craftsman and took pride in his trade."[37]

Jason Lee Shifflett (1984–2015) has a flat bronze marker with a nickname, "Daddy Rabbit," and two enameled photos of him (Figure 8.9). One shows him shirtless driving a boat, grinning clear-eyed at the camera, tattooed all over with skulls and spider webs, and much else. The other image is a close-up of his heavily inked face: playing cards inked onto his forehead, "OUTLAW" on his chin, "Mama Tried" beneath his eyes.

Jason Lee Shifflett, age 31, went to be with the Lord. . . . He was a devoted son, father, brother and friend. . . . His family was his life and his son was number one to him. He loved his son Justin with all of his heart and soul. . . . Jay loved his boat and being on the water with his son, family, and friends. Jay would brighten the lives of whoever he came in contact with and if they needed money he would give his last penny and he would starve just to make sure nobody else would. He was a good hearted man. He is now in Heaven helping the Lord.[38]

Lunsford and Shifflett are memorialized—sent into the public and the future—bare chested. Their nicknames go with them: Tommy and Daddy Rabbit. While most area residents represented on their grave markers are fully clothed, countless recent stones include nicknames. The *Oxford English Dictionary* defines "nickname" as a "usually familiar or humorous name which is given to a person, place, etc., as a supposedly appropriate replacement for or addition to the proper name." This attention to nicknames as familiar, humorous, and "supposedly" acceptable in place of a "proper" name points to them as an expression of informality.

Samples of couples' nicknames from Valley grave markers in recent years include Spot and Puff, Pop and Muffett, Buck and Pee Wee, Rabbit and Sis, Tooter and Wifey, and Fuzzy and Liz. Husband Aubrey Russell Humphries Jr. "Junior" (1946–2007) and Beverly Ann "Butch" Humphries (1944–) share a marker in a Presbyterian cemetery.[39] Shirley "Dumpy" Ellinger (1946–2018) and Garland "Nubby" Ellinger (1939–2005) are buried in an Augusta County municipal cemetery.[40] Their marker is decorated with images of pine trees and mountains. Under her name is a fish on a line, under his masonry tools. "Shirley Ann 'Dumpy' (Wade) Ellinger, 71, widow of Garland Glenn 'Nubby' Ellinger . . . passed away. . . . She worked as a waitress and cook for Harry's Lunch and prior to Harry's, she was a laborer in her husband['s] business, 'Nubby's Masonry.' She enjoyed fishing and playing bingo."[41]

People buried singly are remembered, in addition to their given names, as Baby Doll, Boogie, Chum, Coach, The Colonel, Cornie, Butterball, Goofy, Mr. Ag, Mule, Preacherman, Ruru, Sketchy, Sparkey, Sheep, Squirrel, and Toad. The marker for Jane Martin, "Pudding" (1931–2001), includes an angel and a flower. That for Albert Stanley Peterson, "Pistol Pete" (1936–2005), urges passersby to "Have Faith in God."

LEVITY

We've seen that hallmarks of a liminoid populism on Valley grave markers include the rejection of elite authority, the embrace of cultural elements that economically dominant groups may consider markers of inferiority, and celebrations of informality—in self-presentation, language, cultural references, and motifs. A related, and indeed often integral, characteristic of this movement is humor. As Turner (1982, 27) observed, the liminal and especially the liminoid are grounds for play, for the "subversive and the ludic." The liminoid is "idiosyncratic or quirky," a space of social critique, rebellion, levity, and laughter.

The Valley has seen the emergence of funny epitaphs recently—among them: "Stuff It."[42] "Viet Nam Vet 1969–1970 / I Told You I Was Sick."[43] "It's been real. It's been fun. But it hasn't been real fun."[44] "Be Right Back."[45] "'Me Mudder' One of a Kind."[46] Humor "in any form, whether blatant or in more subtle guises such as whimsy or even delicately playful wit, is simply not a significantly identifiable element" in American cemetery expression throughout its history, but the "interjection of humor" into the "final material testament" is a growing trend in modern commemoration (Meyer 2003, 141–43).

The dawn of wit on Valley headstones since the 1980s is part of the expressive, cultural turn toward populism. The laughter of the "common people"—what Bakhtin called "universal laughter"—"builds its own world versus the official world, its own church versus the official church, its own state versus the official state" (Bakhtin [1968] 1984, 88). It represents "an element of victory not only over supernatural awe, over the sacred, over death; it also means the defeat of power, of earthly kings, of the earthly upper classes, or all that opposes and restricts" (92). The "function of laughter in the historical development of culture and literature" rejects the "form," the strictures of imposed authority, and "purifies from dogmatism, from the intolerant and petrified; it liberates from fanaticism and pedantry, from fear and intimidation, from didacticism, naiveté, and illusion, from the single meaning, the single level" (123). Laughter is revolutionary.

RIOTS AND BONDING SOCIAL CAPITAL IN CHARLOTTESVILLE

I was in Charlottesville in July 2017 when the Ku Klux Klan came to town. As an anthropologist I wanted to watch, witness, and listen. My friend, the late Douglas Turner Day IV, was alive and well that morning, leading a cacophony of "Musicians Against the Klan" (Figure 8.10). Many intended to drown out Klan speeches with guitars, cymbals, drums, songs, chants, and a host of kazoos. I was near the front of a huge crowd of counter protestors. Young adults to my right wore yarmulkes. Others held Black Lives Matter posters, one with an image of Bree Newsome dressed as Wonder Woman, high on a pole removing the Confederate flag from the South Carolina State House. There's no doubt that the hooded Klansmen—separated from the crowd by fences and police—used the flag to mean "white supremacy." They waved others identifying them as the "Loyal White Nights of the KKK" and posters that claimed Bible verses in support of the contention that "Jews are Satan's Children."

I was there, too, in August 2017 during the Unite the Right Rally, when self-proclaimed neo-Nazis and their allies massed. The air was filled with sounds of helicopters, singing, yelling, chanting, and in some places the air was filled with pepper spray, urine hurled in bottles, and aerosol containers used as fiery weapons. The festive and the violent swarmed together. Celebratory lines of people protesting the rally chanted slogans like "We're here, we're gay, we fight the KKK" (Spencer 2018, 13). Delighted marchers in tutus and clown suits paraded by, smiling, waving, holding balloons. There were no "two sides" in

FIGURE 8.10. Douglas Turner Day IV playing his guitar as a member of Musicians Against the Klan. July 8, 2017, Charlottesville.

FIGURE 8.11. Virginia State Police remain in formation on the Downtown Mall and watch fights in nearby parking lots. Unite the Right Rally, August 12, 2017, Charlottesville.

Charlottesville, but instead many groups and constituencies—self-proclaimed militias, Antifa, Vanguard America, and members of diverse faith communities.

I stood for some time on the downtown pedestrian mall, near hundreds of city and state police officers in paramilitary uniforms; an armed vehicle rumbled past, and the din of circling helicopters was constant. An officer told me that they'd been ordered to secure the businesses on the mall. I watched them as they watched fights break out on adjoining blocks, but they had not received orders and didn't move to intervene (Figure 8.11). Sometimes I heard the crackle of instructions come across their radios, and they'd muster and move en masse like soldiers, not nimble urban officers.

Cornel West, Professor Emeritus at Princeton University and longtime political activist committed to "telling the truth and bearing witness to love and justice,"[47] came to Charlottesville in support of the counter protestors. "We were there to get arrested," West said on the news program *Democracy Now* two days after the rally. He and other faith leaders had planned to lock arms around an entrance to the park where Unite the Right planned to rally, preventing them from gathering, and peacefully accepting arrest (Spencer 2018, 77). Members of the alt-right, though, "just pushed their way through." This was one reason West "couldn't get arrested." Another was that "the police had pulled back and were just allowing fellow citizens to go at each other" (81).

When I walked away from the pedestrian mall back toward my vehicle, police presence disappeared. It was chaos: dozens facing off in one parking lot; half a dozen in a garage; a long, loud, marching, chanting line of protestors; cars revving engines. An officer who was stationed by herself at an intersection expressed concern because of the "violent skirmishes" breaking out. She was repositioned, and no one took her place. That's why a White supremacist could gun his Dodge Challenger through a line of counter protestors, injuring 35 and killing one young woman.

The street where she died has been named Honorary Heather Heyer Way. Mementoes and flowers continue to be left there, as well as messages written in chalk over walls and sidewalks. One says, "The City did not defend us. They

FIGURE 8.12. Messages in chalk and paint urge passersby to protect each other: "Love = Guard Your Neighbor." Honorary Heather Heyer Way, Charlottesville.

abandoned us. The community protected itself instead." The sense of being unable to rely on authorities as safeguards seemed new to most White participants, but not to Black, Indigenous, and People of Color who knew through generational experience that—as a chalked message read— "Love = Guard Your Neighbor" (Figure 8.12).

The writing is both literally and figuratively on the wall, just as it is in cemeteries. In a DIY, populist spirit, many are finding "their people." They're shoring up group bonds to support and "guard" each other (see Metcalf and Huntington 1991:24-28). As Charlottesville 2017 showed, that movement can have life and death consequences.

"The Smallest Sprout"

What do you think has become of the young and old men?
And what do you think has become of the women and children?
    They are alive and well somewhere;
The smallest sprout shows there is really no death,
And if ever there was it led forward life . . .
    All goes onward and outward . . . and nothing collapses,
And to die is different from what anyone supposed, and luckier.

—Walt Whitman, *Leaves of Grass*

We might feel familiar now with some of the dead in the Great Valley of Virginia—the "young and old men," the "women and children." In the pages of this book we've gleaned inklings of their stories, their tragedies, their celebrations, their humor. The dead humanize the land on which we live (Eggener 2010, 10), the spaces we've inherited from the past and will pass on to the future as we ourselves become shades: "all goes onward and outward."

Driving the length of the Valley; walking through scores of burying grounds; looking at epitaphs and images and gifts left on graves; researching obituaries, census returns, and death records; talking with people about the ones they love who've died, I've tried to glimpse "the shades of those" who once lived here. We've seen struggles against disease and devastation: a solider succumbing to influenza, a pair of "sweetly sleeping fire victims."

Global contests reached into the Valley, often mingling with lingering local prejudice: the baker whose family "perished in Auschwitz" and faced anti-Semitism in Virginia; the Black veteran of the Great War "shot to death" in West Virginia, "being deaf." His family knew him as Wonderful. Like many others in the Valley, they accorded their loved ones the dignity they deserved, even if the society at large sought to deny them full equality.

We've remembered the young man who requested exemption from military service to support his widowed mother but was instead "Killed in Action in the World War." One grave marker honors a "Hiroshima Survivor." Another memorializes a young man "Missing in B-29 over Tokyo."

Lexington—"where the South went to die" but declined to do so—persists, we've seen, as a staging ground for conflict about the Civil War. Spatial memory is among the dynamics maintaining the spirit of the Confederacy in Lexington and the balance of the Valley. General Jackson's admirers leave lemons on his grave; detractors mark them "Black Lives Matter."

We've tried to gain some insight into experiences of thousands of former patients buried behind a "Lunatic Asylum" and at a Colony for the "Feebleminded." Some having had a "slight malformation" or imperfections of speech, sight, or hearing were caught in eugenic campaigns to "purify" the populace through compulsory sterilization. Compassion for disabled people waxed and waned and waxed again, its fluctuation a reminder that acceptance of difference is culturally constructed and not guaranteed.

The person and the community, too, are historically variable. If Deetz, Glassie, and others read the "evolution of alienation" in historic material culture, our attention to cemeteries has revealed some contemporary efforts to reverse it. Many in the Valley of Virginia are increasingly expressing their identities as being distributed among other people and places. Who they are, their grave markers suggest, is inextricable from the landscapes, wildlife, vehicles, pets, teams, and hobbies they loved. As sociologist Pierre Bourdieu observed, "Taste is what brings together things and people that go together" (Bourdieu 1984:241). Since the 1980s, Virginians have tended increasingly to find the people and things that "go together" with them. They've cultivated bonding social capital, creating and strengthening in-group relationships. Bridging social capital, forging ties among groups, seems thinner on the ground. Indeed, a kind of Balkanization seems manifest in cemeteries, as people use word and symbol to claim association with particular others. Often these declarations evince a populist spirit: rejecting outsider authority, embracing the rural, the known, the local, the do-it-yourself.

A lesson of these many stories from cemeteries in the Valley of Virginia is among the great lessons of anthropology: "it could be otherwise." It has been otherwise.

People with mental illness were met "as friends" in need of tenderly rendered assistance in one generation. In another they were a "feebleminded menace" to be expunged from society. In yet another "someone cared" for them.

The anonymous woman whose remains were encountered during construction and reburied respectfully in 2019 shows it can be otherwise: bones can move from "vacant sloping ground" to a laboratory shelf to a handcrafted oak coffin interred with honor—both to herself and the African American community.

The strength of social ties, too, has ebbed and flowed. Alienation is not inevitable. Nor is meaningful commitment to others.

In the early twenty-first century, many people seem to be finding their bands: identifying the likeminded and gathering close. If boundaries between "us" and "them" are hardening, we can look to the dead—to the past in the Valley of Virginia and beyond—and remember that options and possibility for other ways have existed, and do exist.

POSTSCRIPT

I drafted most of this manuscript in 2018–2019. Polishing it up and off now in 2020—a year plagued with death—its themes seem amplified and complicated. As I write this paragraph on October 4, 2020, the nation and world have struggled for months in the grip of COVID-19. To date, more than 3,000 Virginians have died from COVID, more than 200,000 Americans, more than a million people globally. The virulence of the virus has most affected the poor, the disabled, and the socially marginalized. For nearly everyone it has upended virtually every aspect of life: shopping for food or clothes, playing sports, attending classes and religious services and weddings, and funerals. Loved ones succumb to COVID as medical staff do their best, sealed head to toe with personal protective equipment, to comfort them—sometimes holding up cellphones so that the dying person's spouse or children can send at least some goodbye. The usual subsequent rites of passage are throttled too: sitting with the body, sitting with the widow, gathering around the casket, standing shoulder to shoulder as the casket descends into the vault, gathering then for a meal, visiting the bereaved in following days, weeks, and months. With such familiar rituals impossible, people make do: they gather via Zoom or Google Hangouts, or stand alone on a back porch and raise a glass to the departing soul.

On Friday the 13th of March 2020, my university like many others announced a sudden move to online teaching. Our community was fraught, frightened, plagued with uncertainty and with some disagreement. Is shutting down campus an overreaction? How deadly really is COVID, and to whom? Following months saw politicians at rancorous odds over the value of human life generally, of particular human lives (the insured, the White, the well-to-do), the economy, and relationships between them. Some said the virus was just slightly hastening the end of life for those already on death's doorstep: not only the elderly but also younger folks, too, who were poor, or disabled, or Black or Brown, the people for whom structural forces of inequality had raised the bar of access to resources needed for healthy food and quality healthcare. Some intimated that the vulnerable had only themselves to blame. Some suggested the elderly should sacrifice themselves for the good of the economy. Here in the Valley, this call sounds somewhat familiar. Many, many lives—whether Native American, of African descent, or considered "unfit" and "defective" due to differences—have been offered to the altar of an imagined greater good: for the good of taming a wilderness, of national and economic progress, of purifying the White race and safeguarding the nation (Dorr 2008).

Nationally, 2020 has focused attention on death, social structures, and cultural values not only through the pandemic but also through Black death: Black death after Black death in the United States. Children gunned down, even fetuses—unborn babies who died when their mothers were killed—boys and girls, women and men, young and old, the emergency room technician, the jogger. In Virginia death attends, too, nearly daily to overburdened, underdeveloped infrastructure through accidents on roads like Interstate 81, the corridor running the length of the Great Valley that often follows trails established by Native Americans on foot over thousands of years. Death stalks into the Valley today through other routes too: opioid addiction, violence and homicide, cancer, heart disease, diabetes, stroke, and suicide.

Here on the morning of October 4, 2020, the President of the United States is hospitalized with COVID-19. The leader is ill but the nation and its constituent parts—including residents of varied political stripes in the Valley of Virginia—remain fractious and divided as seen in social media posts, news outlet reports, and the signs of protestors with diverse persuasions on the streets abutting Walter Reed. Death's rites of passage—those liminal moments, days, weeks, or longer of suspensions between what was and what will have to be—usually usher in a sense of *communitas*: a feeling of common cause, of togetherness, sameness, fusion, mutual understanding, profound connection among peers who comprise a polity of whatever scale.

I look to wise people—especially the poets, the novelists, the artists—for inklings about how our communities might knit, how compassion might be cultivated. One of these sage creators is Amira Hegazy—a 2015 alumna of Washington and Lee University where she studied anthropology, sociology, and studio art, and a 2020 graduate of the Art Institute of Chicago. Amira "creates art, books, poems, and interactive experiences that manipulate cultural symbols and domestic spaces to produce art that addresses political and social issues" (Hegazy 2020) including, most recently, death in the time of COVID. She recently talked, over Zoom, with students in my Anthropology of Death class about a loss close to her, about mourning, and about quarantine and isolation.[1] And she talked with us about plants.

Part of Amira's MFA thesis is a set of instructions outlining how to involve live plants to "make ruins and preserve a pathway for revisiting those we have lost" (Hegazy 2020, 3). Following the steps she lays out, we might "solidify the remnant qualities of a person who has died. In small and intimate individual gestures, these artworks are easily made at home and can be kept close."

These artworks are plants, and here are some steps to create a work of art:

> Take a moment to think of a person who was close to you who has died.
>
> Think of a plant they loved. It may be a plant they cared for, or a plant they liked to eat, or a plant they liked the smell of. . . .
>
> Get seeds or seedlings to grow this plant.
>
> Remember a place this person loved . . . Go to that place or a similar place and collect . . . soil. . . .

FIGURE E.1. "The Ruins," Liberty Hall Academy House, ancestor of Washington and Lee University. Image c. 1890, Michael Miley. Miley-Burns Photograph Collection, courtesy of Special Collections Department, Leyburn Library, Washington and Lee University, Lexington.

FIGURE E.2. Elizabeth McGee '24 and Jamie Winslett '21, students in the Anthropology of Death course, with their freshly potted plants. Washington and Lee University, Fall 2020.

> Plant the seed or seedlings of the plant they loved into the soil from a place they loved.
> Care for it. (Hegazy 2020, 12)

With directions from Amira, I visited a family-run greenhouse in an exquisitely beautiful part of the Valley: you can feed the goats, chat with the parrot, pick among a seeming million pumpkins, and wander through hothouses bursting with leaf, vine, tendril and blossom. I bought pothos, spider plants, ferns—one for each student in the Anthropology of Death class—along with pots and soil.

Back on campus, I brought soil from an ancestral part of our university: dirt that been archaeologically excavated near "the Ruins," a pair of limestone walls surviving from the eighteenth century (Figure E.1). For class we met outside, each student masked, each choosing a plant and an earthen pot, mixing soil from the greenhouse, rich in nutrients, with soil from the old campus, rich in history (Figure E.2).

And so, students in the Anthropology of Death class went back to their dorm rooms or apartments with a plant from the Valley rooted in soil that students at this institution trod 250 years before. We followed Amira's advice for investing memory in a growing thing: "Take your time, claim it, and know it is yours. For now, you are here and you have this" (Hegazy 2020, 8).

I didn't ask students to remain for a full class meeting that day. I recommended instead that they stay outdoors to enjoy being alive in the Valley on an autumn afternoon, and I suggested this for the day's reading:

> All things belonging to the earth will never change—the leaf, the blade, the flower, the wind that cries and sleeps and wakes again, the trees whose stiff arms clash and tremble in the dark, and the dust of lovers long since buried in the earth . . . these things will always be the same, for they come up from the earth that never changes, they go back into the earth that lasts forever. . . . The tarantula, the adder, and the asp will also never change. Pain and death will always be the same. But under the pavements trembling like a pulse, under the buildings trembling like a cry, under the waste of time, under the hoof of the beast above the broken bones of cities, there will be something growing like a flower, something bursting from the earth again, forever deathless, faithful, coming into life again like April.
>
> —Thomas Wolfe, *You Can't Go Home Again*

APPENDIX: LIST OF CEMETERIES VISITED
(A SAMPLE OF VALLEY BURYING GROUNDS)

CEMETERY NAME	COUNTY	CITY	TYPE	DENOMINATION/ AFFILIATION	NOTES
African American Woman, Unknown	Rockbridge	Lexington	unknown		Also known as "Ancient Jane" and "Miss Jane"
Alone Community	Rockbridge	Lexington	religious affiliation	Lutheran	Also known as Bethany Lutheran Church Cemetery
Andrews	Rockbridge	Bells Valley	religious affiliation	Methodist	
Angels Rest Memorial Gardens	Giles	Narrows	private company		
Arbor Hill	Augusta	Staunton	religious affiliation	Brethren	
Arlington National	n/a	Arlington	military		
Augusta Memorial Gardens	Augusta	Waynesboro	private company		
Beth El	Rockingham	Harrisonburg	religious affiliation	Reform Jewish	
Beth Israel	Roanoke	Roanoke	religious affiliation	Jewish	
Bethlehem Lutheran	Augusta	Waynesboro	religious affiliation	Lutheran	
Bethlehem Methodist	Augusta	Swoope	religious affiliation	Methodist	
Birchlawn Burial Park	Giles	Pearisburg	private company		
Blue Grass	Highland	Blue Grass	private company		
Brickey	Craig	Abbott	family		
Cavalry United	Augusta	Stuarts Draft	religious affiliation	Methodist	
Cedar Grove	Shenandoah	New Market	religious affiliation	Brethren	

CEMETERY NAME	COUNTY	CITY	TYPE	DENOMINATION/ AFFILIATION	NOTES
Cedar Hill	Rockbridge	Lexington	religious affiliation	Baptist	African American
Central Virginia Training Center	Amherst	Madison Heights	hospital		Formerly Virginia Colony for Epileptic & Feebleminded
Collierstown	Rockbridge	Collierstown	religious affiliation	Presbyterian	
Colored Grave Yard	Rockbridge	Lexington	municipal		African American; Marble Ln. and N. Lewis St.
Coverstone	Page	Shenandoah	religious affiliation	Adjacent to Lutheran Church	
Daughters of Zion	Albemarle	Charlottesville	municipal		African American
Dayton	Rockingham	Dayton	nonprofit		
Dayton Mennonite	Rockingham	Dayton	religious affiliation	Mennonite	
Dublin	Pulaski	Dublin	municipal		
Duck Run	Rockingham	Penn Laird	private company		Natural/green cemetery
East End	Wythe	Wytheville	municipal		
Ebenezer	Augusta	Fishersville	religious affiliation	Methodist	
Elk Run	Rockingham	Elkton	municipal		
Elk Run Church	Augusta	Churchville	religious affiliation	Brethren	
Emmanuel	Albemarle	Greenwood	religious affiliation	Episcopal	
Evergreen Glasgow	Rockbridge	Glasgow	nonprofit		African American
Evergreen Lexington	Rockbridge	Lexington	municipal		African American
Evergreen Memorial Gardens	Page	Luray	private company		
Evergreen Roanoke	Roanoke	Roanoke	private company		
Fair View	Roanoke	Roanoke	nonprofit		
Fairview	Augusta	Staunton	religious affiliation	Baptist and Methodist	African American
Fairview	Augusta	Waynesboro	religious affiliation	Methodist	African American
Falling Spring	Rockbridge	Glasgow	religious affiliation	Presbyterian	
Fincastle Presbyterian	Botetourt	Fincastle	religious affiliation	Presbyterian	
Fishersville United Methodist	Augusta	Fishersville	religious affiliation	Methodist	

CEMETERY NAME	COUNTY	CITY	TYPE	DENOMINATION/ AFFILIATION	NOTES
Friedens Church	Rockingham	Mount Crawford	religious affiliation	Reformed, Lutheran, Church of Christ	
Furrow	Craig	Craig Creek	family		
George W. Cleek	Bath	Warm Springs	family		
Glasgow	Rockbridge	Glasgow	nonprofit		
Glebe Burying Ground	Augusta	Swoope	religious affiliation	Anglican	Owned by county; maintained by historical society
Godwin	Botetourt	Fincastle	nonprofit		
Green Hill	Rockbridge	Buena Vista	municipal		
Greenville	Augusta	Greenville	religious affiliation	Baptist and Methodist	African American; a.k.a. Mount Ead Cemetery
Greenville Baptist	Augusta	Greenville	religious affiliation	Baptist	
Greenville United	Augusta	Greenville	religious affiliation	Methodist	
Greenwood/Ames	Rockingham	Bridgewater	religious affiliation	Methodist	Black and White sections
Hebrew Cemetery	Albemarle	Charlottesville	religious affiliation	Jewish	
Hebrew Cemetery	n/a	Richmond	religious affiliation	Reform Jewish	
Highland Memory Gardens	Pulaski	Dublin	private company		
Hillsboro	Albemarle	Crozet	religious affiliation	Baptist	
Holly Memorial Gardens	Albemarle	Charlottesville	private company		
Hollywood	n/a	Richmond	nonprofit		
Immanuel	Rockbridge	Zack	religious affiliation	Presbyterian	
Ivy Road	Albemarle	Ivy	religious affiliation	Baptist	
Knick	Rockbridge	Collierstown	family		
Lebanon	Rockbridge	Goshen	religious affiliation	Presbyterian	
Lee Family Mausoleum	Rockbridge	Lexington	family		At Washington and Lee University
Lincoln	Albemarle	Charlottesville	private company		African American
Lone Star	Alleghany	Covington	religious affiliation	Baptist	
Maplewood	Albemarle	Charlottesville	municipal		
McDowell	Rockbridge	Fairfield	family		

CEMETERY NAME	COUNTY	CITY	TYPE	DENOMINATION/ AFFILIATION	NOTES
McDowell Presbyterian	Highland	McDowell	religious affiliation	Presbyterian	
McKinley	Augusta	Middlebrook	religious affiliation	Methodist	
Meadow	Rockbridge	Lexington	private company		Natural/green cemetery
Mill Creek	Rockingham	Port Republic	religious affiliation	Brethren	
Monticello Memorial Park	Albemarle	Charlottesville	private company		Also known as Monticello Memory Gardens
Mossy Creek	Augusta	Mount Solon	religious affiliation	Presbyterian	
Mount Crawford	Rockingham	Mount Crawford	religious affiliation	Reformed and Methodist	
Mount Hebron	Frederick	Winchester	nonprofit		Complex of five cemeteries
Mount Hermon	Augusta	Newport	religious affiliation	Lutheran	
Mount Lydia	Rockbridge	Glasgow	religious affiliation	Baptist	
Mount Plain	Albemarle	Crozet	religious affiliation	Baptist	Also known as Mountain Plain
Mount Vernon	Augusta	Waynesboro	religious affiliation	Brethren	
Mt. Carmel	Augusta	Steeles Tavern	religious affiliation	Presbyterian	
Mt. Union	Botetourt	Troutville	religious affiliation	Presbyterian	
Mt. Zion	Rockbridge	Glasgow	religious affiliation	Methodist	
Natural Bridge	Rockbridge	Natural Bridge	religious affiliation	Baptist	
Neriah	Rockbridge	Buena Vista	religious affiliation	Baptist	
New Hope	Rockingham	Harrisonburg	religious affiliation	Christian	
New Providence	Rockbridge	Brownsburg	religious affiliation	Presbyterian	
Nowlin	Rockbridge	Buena Vista	municipal		African American
Oak Grove	Rockbridge	Lexington	municipal		Formerly Stonewall Jackson Memorial
Oak Grove	Rockingham	Dayton	religious affiliation	Mennonite	
Oak Lawn	Rockingham	Bridgewater	private company		

CEMETERY NAME	COUNTY	CITY	TYPE	DENOMINATION/ AFFILIATION	NOTES
Oakwood	Albemarle	Charlottesville	municipal		Black and White sections
Oakwood Memorial Gardens	Wythe	Wytheville	municipal		
Old Presbyterian	Augusta	Waynesboro	religious affiliation	Presbyterian	
Oxford	Rockbridge	Lexington	religious affiliation	Presbyterian	
Panorama Memorial Gardens	Warren	Strasburg	private company		
Paxton	Rockbridge	Mechanicsville	family		
Piedmont	Albemarle	Crozet	religious affiliation	Baptist	African American
Pines Chapel	Augusta	Greenville	religious affiliation	Presbyterian	
Prospect Hill	Warren	Front Royal	municipal		
Rest Haven Community	Page	Shenandoah	private company		
Riverview	Albemarle	Charlottesville	private company		
Riverview	Augusta	Waynesboro	municipal		
Rock Creek	n/a	Washington, DC	municipal	Nondenominational	St. Paul's Episcopal steward
Rockbridge Memorial Gardens	Rockbridge	Lexington	private company		
Serenity Garden	Augusta	Waynesboro	municipal		Cancer awareness garden
Sharon	Alleghany	Clifton Forge	religious affiliation	Baptist	Also known as Union Baptist
Shemariah	Augusta	Middlebrook	religious affiliation	Presbyterian	
Shockoe Hill	n/a	Richmond	municipal		
Smith	Craig	Paint Bank	family		
Southwest Virginia Veterans	Pulaski	Dublin	military		
St. Andrews Diocesan	Roanoke	Roanoke	religious affiliation	Catholic	
St. James	Augusta	Fishersville	religious affiliation	Lutheran	
St. John	Wythe	Wytheville	religious affiliation	Lutheran	
St. Matthews	Shenandoah	New Market	religious affiliation	Lutheran	Also known as Reformation Cemetery
St. Pauls	Albemarle	Ivy	religious affiliation	Episcopal	

CEMETERY NAME	COUNTY	CITY	TYPE	DENOMINATION/ AFFILIATION	NOTES
St. Peters	Augusta	Churchville	religious affiliation	Lutheran	
Staunton National	Augusta	Staunton	military		
Sunset	Montgomery	Christiansburg	municipal		
Sunset Memorial Park	Raleigh	Beckley, WV	private company		
Sunset View Memorial Gardens	Shenandoah	Woodstock	private company		
Temple Emanuel	Roanoke	Roanoke	religious affiliation	Reform Jewish	
Temple Hill, Morning Star, Bland	Bland	Bland	nonprofit		Complex of three cemeteries
Temple House of Israel	Augusta	Staunton	religious affiliation	Reform Jewish	
Thornrose	Augusta	Staunton	nonprofit		
Timber Ridge	Rockbridge	Fairfield	religious affiliation	Presbyterian	
Tinkling Spring	Augusta	Fishersville	religious affiliation	Presbyterian	
Trinity	Augusta	Staunton	religious affiliation	Episcopal	
Trinity	Botetourt	Troutville	religious affiliation	Brethren	
University of Virginia	Albemarle	Charlottesville	campus		
Verona United Methodist	Augusta	Verona	religious affiliation	Methodist	
Walnut Springs	Shenandoah	Strasburg	religious affiliation	Church of Christ	
Weavers	Rockingham	Harrisonburg	religious affiliation	Mennonite	
Wesley Chapel	Rockbridge	Mechanicsville	religious affiliation	Methodist	
West End	Wythe	Wytheville	municipal		
Western State	Augusta	Staunton	hospital		Formerly Western State Lunatic Asylum Cemeteries
Westview	Montgomery	Blacksburg	municipal		
Wheatland	Botetourt	Buchanan	religious affiliation	Lutheran	
Williams Memorial Park	Roanoke	Roanoke	private company		
Winchester National	Frederick	Winchester	military		
Windy Cove	Bath	Millboro	religious affiliation	Presbyterian	
Woodbine	Rockingham	Harrisonburg	nonprofit		
Woodland Union	Bath	Millboro	religious affiliation	"All denominations welcome"	

NOTES

Chapter 2

1. Memorial page, George R. Magary, March 2, 2017, Find a Grave (website), https://www.findagrave.com/memorial/176902905/george-r.-magary

2. Paraphrasing the thirteenth-century Persian poet Mawlana Jalal ad-Din Rumi (2011).

3. Death Records, Virginia, 1912–2014, (Richmond: Virginia Department of Health), Ancestry.com, https://www.ancestry.com/.

4. Lional A. Herrald, Obituary, February 26, 1999, *Register-Herald* [Beckley, West Virginia], Newspaperarchive (website), https://newspaperarchive.com/

5. Death Index, 1862–1877, Rockingham County, Virginia (Richmond: Bureau of Vital Statistics), Ancestry.com, https://www.ancestry.com/.

6. Death Index, 1862–1877, Rockingham County, Virginia, (Richmond: Bureau of Vital Statistics), Ancestry.com, https://www.ancestry.com/.

7. Calvary United Methodist Church Cemetery, Augusta County.

8. 1860 US Census, District 1, Rockingham County, Virginia, NARA microfilm publication M653, (Washington, DC: National Archives and Records Administration), Ancestry.com, https://www.ancestry.com/.

9. U.S., Civil War Soldier Records and Profiles, 1861–1865, American Civil War Research Database (Duxbury, Massachusetts: Historical Data Systems, Inc.), Ancestry.com, https://www.ancestry.com/.

10. 1870 US Census, Franklin Township, Rockingham County, Virginia, NARA microfilm publication M593, roll M593, page 136A, (Washington, DC: National Archives and Records Administration), Ancestry.com, https://www.ancestry.com/.

11. Memorial page, Capt. Philander Herring, August 9, 2012, Find a Grave (website), https://www.findagrave.com/memorial/95055027/philander-herring

12. Gerald P. (Jerry) Bunton, Obituary, October 25, 2005, *Alleghany Journal* (website), http://www.alleghanyjournal.com/obits/obit.php?action=3&id=1145

13. Samuel A.L. Hall, Obituary, May 12, 2009, *Sun News* [Myrtle Beach, South Carolina], Legacy.com (website), https://www.legacy.com/us/obituaries/myrtlebeachonline/name/samuel-hall-obituary?pid=127199520

14. 2006, Lone Star Baptist Church Cemetery, Covington; 2011, Calvary United Methodist Church Cemetery, Augusta County

15. Josh Fox, May 6, 2016, personal communication.

16. Death Records, Virginia, 1912–2014, (Richmond: Virginia Department of Health), Ancestry.com, https://www.ancestry.com/.

17. New International Version (often used in Mennonite churches)

18. 2009, Calvary United Methodist Church Cemetery, Augusta County

19. 2009, Thornrose Cemetery, Staunton

20. Mount Hebron Cemetery, Winchester

21. Evergreen Cemetery, Roanoke

22. Woodbine Cemetery, Harrisonburg; Mill Creek Church of the Brethren Cemetery, Rockingham County (for husband and wife burials 1918 and 1923)

23. Former example from Sunset Cemetery in Beckley, West Virginia; the latter from Thornrose Cemetery in Staunton

24. Bethlehem United Methodist Church Cemetery, Augusta County.

25. 1982, Falling Spring Presbyterian Church Cemetery, Rockbridge County; 1974 Mt. Hermon Cemetery, Augusta County; 1928, Calvary United Methodist Church Cemetery, Augusta County

26. Examples: Glebe Burying Ground, Augusta County; Mount Hebron, Winchester; Hollywood Cemetery, Richmond; Fincastle Presbyterian, Botetourt County

27. New International Version (often used in Presbyterian churches)

Chapter 3

1. 1810 US Census, Prince Edward County, Virginia, roll 70, page 567, image 00471, Family History Library Film 0181430, NARA microfilm publication M252, (Washington, DC: National Archives), Ancestry.com, https://www.ancestry.com/.

2. 1830 US Census, Prince Edward County, Virginia, NARA microfilm publication M19, roll 201, page 128, Family History Library Film 0029680, (Washington, DC: National Archives), Ancestry.com, https://www.ancestry.com/.

3. Flournoy, Thomas Stanhope 1811–1883, accessed January 15, 2021, Biographical Directory of the United States Congress (website), http://bioguide.congress.gov /scripts/biodisplay.pl?index=F000216

4. 1850 US Census, Prince Edward County, Virginia, National Archives Microfilm Publication Series M432, roll 970, page 34b (Washington, D.C.: Records of the Bureau of the Census), Ancestry.com, https://www.ancestry.com/.

5. 1860 US Census, Regiment 22, County of Mecklenburg, Virginia, NARA microfilm publication M653, page 156 (Washington, DC: National Archives and Records Administration), Ancestry.com, https://www.ancestry.com/. Virginia Marriages, 1785–1940, (Salt Lake City: FamilySearch), Ancestry.com, https://www.ancestry.com/.

6. Memorial page for Ann Carrington Cabell Flournoy, September 22, 2009, Find a Grave (website), https://www.findagrave.com/memorial/42273284/ann -carrington-flournoy.

7. 1870 US Census, Madison, Shenandoah County, Virginia, NARA microfilm publication M593_1678, page 762B, (Washington, DC: National Archives and Records Administration), Ancestry.com, https://www.ancestry.com/.

8. 1880 US Census, Madison, Shenandoah County, Virginia, roll 1390, page 449D, Enumeration District 086, NARA microfilm publication T9, (Washington, DC: National Archives and Records Administration), the Church of Latter-day Saints and Ancestry.com, https://www.ancestry.com/.

9. 1900 US Census, Lee District, Shenandoah County, Virginia, page 2, Enumera-

tion District 0078, Family History Library microfilm 1241728, NARA microfilm publication T623, (Washington, DC: National Archives and Records Administration), Ancestry.com, https://www.ancestry.com/.

10. Memorial page for Fannie C. Hines, September 22, 2009, Find a Grave (website), https://www.findagrave.com/memorial/42273499/fannie-c-hines

11. Death Records, Virginia, 1912–2014, (Richmond: Virginia Department of Health), Ancestry.com, https://www.ancestry.com/.

12. 1850 US Census, District 22, Harrison County, Virginia, roll 950, page 223a, National Archives Microfilm Publication M432, (Washington, DC: National Archives), Ancestry.com, https://www.ancestry.com/.

13. Memorial page for Peter Hinkle, Find a Grave (website). https://www.findagrave.com/memorial/8523129/peter-hinkle

14. Memorial page for Peter Hinkle, Find a Grave (website). https://www.findagrave.com/memorial/8523129/peter-hinkle

15. 1850 US Census, Northern Division, Bedford County, Virginia, roll 935, page 145b, National Archives Microfilm Publication M432, (Washington, DC: National Archives), Ancestry.com, https://www.ancestry.com/.

16. Memorial page for Margaret Rice McGhee, September 5, 2009, Find a Grave (website), https://www.findagrave.com/memorial/41588591/margaret-mcghee

17. "asylum, n.". OED Online, December 2020, Oxford University Press (website), https://www-oed-com.ezproxy.wlu.edu/view/Entry/12340?rskey=cZnAv7&result=1

18. King James Bible.

19. 1850 US Census, West District, Hanover County, Virginia, roll 949, page 372b, National Archives Microfilm Publication M432, (Washington, DC: National Archives), Ancestry.com, https://www.ancestry.com/.

20. Confederate Pension Rolls, Veterans and Widows, Collection CP-5_130, roll 130 (Richmond: Library of Virginia) Ancestry.com, https://www.ancestry.com/.

21. Confederate Pension Rolls, Veterans and Widows, Collection CP-5_130, roll 130 (Richmond: Library of Virginia) Ancestry.com, https://www.ancestry.com/.

22. 1870 US Census, Upper Revenue District, Hanover County, Virginia, roll M593_1651, page 108B, NARA microfilm publication M593, (Washington, D.C.: National Archives and Records Administration), Ancestry.com, https://www.ancestry.com/.

23. 1880 US Census, Beaver Dam, Hanover County, Virginia, roll 1370, page 109A, Enumeration District 065, NARA microfilm publication T9, (Washington, DC: National Archives), the Church of Jesus Christ of Latter-day Saints and Ancestry.com, https://www.ancestry.com/.

24. 1910 US Census, Madison, Orange County, Virginia, roll T624_1640, page 13B, Enumeration District 0089, Family History Library microfilm 1375653, NARA microfilm publication T624, (Washington, DC: National Archives), Ancestry.com, https://www.ancestry.com/.

25. Memorial page for John Hill Berkeley, September 22, 2009, Find a Grave (website), https://www.findagrave.com/memorial/42272825/john-hill-berkeley

26. Memorial page for Thomas N. Berkeley, September 22, 2009, Find a Grave (website), https://www.findagrave.com/memorial/42272813/thomas-n-berkeley

27. King James Bible.

28. Memorial page for Adeline Emma Harlow Buck, May 25, 2016, Find a Grave (website), https://www.findagrave.com/memorial/163262942/adeline-emma-buck.

29. Memorial page for Dr. Joseph Spencer DeJarnette, January 20, 2009, Find a

Grave (website), https://www.findagrave.com/memorial/33089671/joseph-spencer
-dejarnette.

30. Memorial page for Dr. Chertsey Hopkins DeJarnette. September 26, 2012, Find a
Grave (website), https://www.findagrave.com/memorial/97818523/chertsey-dejarnette.

31. Memorial page for Carrie Elizabeth Buck Detamore, April 3, 2007. Find a Grave
(website), https://www.findagrave.com/memorial/18751764/carrie-elizabeth-detamore.

32. Message on "Memorial: Carrie Elizabeth Buck Detamore." September 6, 2020,
Find a Grave (website), https://www.findagrave.com/memorial/18751764/carrie
-elizabeth-detamore.

33. Message on "Memorial: Carrie Elizabeth Buck Detamore." September 18, 2016,
Find a Grave (website), https://www.findagrave.com/memorial/18751764/carrie
-elizabeth-detamore.

34. Message on "Memorial: Carrie Elizabeth Buck Detamore." October 22, 2009,
Find a Grave (website), https://www.findagrave.com/memorial/18751764/carrie
-elizabeth-detamore.

35. Message on "Memorial: Carrie Elizabeth Buck Detamore." May 10, 2014, Find
a Grave (website), https://www.findagrave.com/memorial/18751764/carrie-elizabeth
-detamore.

36. Message on "Memorial: Carrie Elizabeth Buck Detamore." February 4, 2010,
Find a Grave (website), https://www.findagrave.com/memorial/18751764/carrie
-elizabeth-detamore.

37. Message on "Memorial: Carrie Elizabeth Buck Detamore." January 3, 2016, Find
a Grave (website), https://www.findagrave.com/memorial/18751764/carrie-elizabeth
-detamore.

38. David Cole, personal communication, January 10, 2018.

39. David Cole, personal communication, January 10, 2018.

40. US Social Security Applications and Claim Index, 1936–2007. Ancestry.com,
https://www.ancestry.com/.

41. David Wayne Carter, 2006, Obituary, *News and Advance* [Lynchburg], June 28,
2006. Legacy.com (website), https://www.legacy.com/us/obituaries/newsadvance
/name/david-wayne-carter-obituary?n=david-wayne-carter&pid=18279681.

42. Barbara Hutcherson, message posted on memorial site for David Wayne Carter,
News & Advance [Lynchburg], Legacy.com (website), June 29, 2006, https://www.legacy
.com/us/obituaries/newsadvance/name/david-carter-obituary?pid=18279681.

Chapter 4

1. Death Records, Virginia, 1912–2014, (Richmond: Virginia Department of
Health), Ancestry.com, https://www.ancestry.com/.

2. Death Records, Virginia, 1912–2014, (Richmond: Virginia Department of
Health), Ancestry.com, https://www.ancestry.com/.

3. John A. Gibson might have lived with his new bride and mother-in-law in the Civil
War era (Berger 2009, 18); certainly John A. Gibson lived at the stately brick mansion
Maple Hall (Coffey 1985) with his parents virtually all of his life. 1850 US Census,
District 51, Rockbridge County, Virginia, roll 973, page 380a, National Archives Micro-
film Publication Series M432. 1870 US Census, Natural Bridge, Rockbridge County,
Virginia, roll 1675, page 555A, Family History Library Film 553174, National Archives
Microfilm Publication Series M593. 1880 US Census, South River, Enumeration District

070, Rockbridge County, Virginia, roll 1388, page 209A National Archives Microfilm Publication T9, (Washington, DC: National Archives), Ancestry.com and the Church of Jesus Christ of Latter-day Saints, https://www.ancestry.com/.

4. 1860 US Census, Slave Schedules, District 6, Rockbridge County, Virginia, Series Number M653, Records of the Bureau of the Census, Record Group Number 29 (Washington, DC: National Archives and Records Administration), Ancestry.com, https://www.ancestry.com/.

5. 1870 US Census, Natural Bridge, Rockbridge County, Virginia, roll M593_1675, page 555A, (Washington, DC: National Archives and Records Administration), Ancestry.com, https://www.ancestry.com/.

6. Death Records, Virginia, 1912–2014, (Richmond: Virginia Department of Health), Ancestry.com, https://www.ancestry.com/.

7. Death Records, Virginia, 1912–2014, (Richmond: Virginia Department of Health), Ancestry.com, https://www.ancestry.com/.

8. Army Register of Enlistments, 1798–1914. Fold3 by Ancestry (website), https://www.fold3.com.

9. Register of Enlistments in the U.S. Army, 1798–1914, National Archives Microfilm Publication M233, Records of the Adjutant General's Office, 1780's-1917, Record Group 94 (Washington, DC: National Archives), Ancestry.com, https://www.ancestry.com/.

10. Applications for Headstones for U.S. Military Veterans, 1925–1941, NAID: M1916, NAID 596118, Record Group Number 92, Records of the Office of the Quartermaster General, U.S., Ancestry.com, https://www.ancestry.com/.

11. 1900 US Census, Lexington, Rockbridge, Virginia, NARA microfilm publication T623 (Washington, DC: National Archives and Records Administration), Ancestry.com, https://www.ancestry.com/.

12. 1910 US Census, Lexington, Rockbridge, Virginia, NARA microfilm publication T624 (Washington, DC: National Archives and Records Administration), Ancestry.com, https://www.ancestry.com/.

13. 1880 US, Lexington, Rockbridge, Virginia, roll 1387, page 25A, enumeration district 065, NARA microfilm publication T9 (Washington, DC: National Archives), Ancestry.com and the Church of Jesus Christ of Latter-day Saints, https://www.ancestry.com/.

14. Virginia, Marriages, 1785–1940, Virginia, U.S., Select Marriages, 1785–1940, Ancestry.com, https://www.ancestry.com/.https://www.ancestry.com/.

15. 1870 US Census, Buffalo, Rockbridge, Virginia, roll M593_1675, page 424B, (Washington, D.C.: National Archives and Records Administration), Ancestry.com, https://www.ancestry.com/.

16. 1880 US Census, Lexington, Rockbridge, Virginia, Roll 1387, page 30C, enumeration district 065, NARA microfilm publication T9, (Washington, D.C., National Archives), Ancestry.com and the Church of Jesus Christ of Latter-day Saints, https://www.ancestry.com/.

17. 1900 US Census, Lexington, Rockbridge, Virginia, page 22, enumeration district 0097, NARA T623, (Washington, DC: National Archives and Records Administration), Ancestry.com, https://www.ancestry.com/.

18. United States, Selective Service System, World War I Selective Service System Draft Registration Cards, 1917–1918, NARA M1509, (Washington, DC: National Archives and Records Administration), Ancestry.com, https://www.ancestry.com/.

19. Applications for Headstones for U.S. Military Veterans, 1925–1941. Microfilm

publication M1916, ARC ID 596118. Records of the Office of the Quartermaster General, Record Group 92, (Washington, DC: National Archives), Ancestry.com, https://www.ancestry.com/.

20. 1940 US Census, Lexington, Rockbridge, Virginia, roll m-t0627-04290, page 14B, enumeration district 82-9, NARA T627 (Washington, D.C.: National Archives and Records Administration), Ancestry.com, https://www.ancestry.com/.

21. Thomas Kalasky, personal communication, July 5 2017.

22. Applications for Headstones for U.S. Military Veterans, 1925–1941, NAID A1, 2110-C, Record Group Number 92, Records of the Office of the Quartermaster General, (Washington, D.C.: National Archives), Ancestry.com, https://www.ancestry.com/.

23. 1930 US Census, Lexington, Rockbridge, Virginia, page 2B, enumeration district 0005, FHL microfilm 2342192, NARA T626, (Washington, D.C.: National Archives and Records Administration), Ancestry.com, https://www.ancestry.com/.

24. 1920 US Census, Lexington, Rockbridge, Virginia, roll T625_1906, page 9A, enumeration district 122, NARA microfilm publication T625, (Washington, D.C.: National Archives), Ancestry.com, https://www.ancestry.com/.

25. 1923 Lexington, Virginia, City Directory, U.S. City Directories, 1822–1995, Ancestry.com, https://www.ancestry.com/.

26. Bonds, County Court, Kanawha, West Virginia, U.S., Wills and Probate Records, 1724–1985, Ancestry.com, https://www.ancestry.com/.

27. Certificate of Death, (Charleston, Kanawha County: West Virginia State Department of Health), West Virginia Department of Arts, Culture & History (website) http://www.wvculture.org/vrr/va_view.aspx?Id=414007&Type=Death.

28. Della Evans, personal communication, July 26, 2016.

29. Certificate of Death, (Charleston, Kanawha County: West Virginia State Department of Health), West Virginia Department of Arts, Culture & History (website) http://www.wvculture.org/vrr/va_view.aspx?Id=414007&Type=Death.

30. Kristina Killgrove, personal communication, March 27, 2017.

Chapter 5

1. U.S. and International Marriage Records, 1560–1900, Ancestry.com, https://www.ancestry.com/.

2. West Virginia Deaths, 1853–1970. Ancestry.com, https://www.ancestry.com/.

3. 1850 US Census, District 37, Monongalia, Virginia, roll 961, page, 333a, Records of the Bureau of the Census, Record Group 29, (Washington, DC: National Archives), Ancestry.com, https://www.ancestry.com/. See also memorial page for Peter Haught II, August 8, 2009, Find a Grave (website), https://www.findagrave.com/memorial/40412483/peter-haught.

4. 1900 US Census, Blue Grass, Highland, Virginia, page 1, enumeration district 0078, FHL microfilm 1241713, NARA T623, (Washington, D.C.: National Archives and Records Administration), Ancestry.com, https://www.ancestry.com/.

5. World War I Selective Service System, Draft Registration Cards, 1917–1918, NARA M1509 (Washington, DC: National Archives and Records Administration), Ancestry.com, https://www.ancestry.com/.

6. Lists of Outgoing Passengers, 1917–1938, U.S., Army Transport Service Arriving and Departing Passenger Lists, 1910–1939, Records of the Office of the Quartermaster

General, 1774–1985, record group 92, roll or box number 540, (College Park, Maryland: National Archives at College Park), Ancestry.com, https://www.ancestry.com/.

7. Death Records, Virginia, 1912–2014, (Richmond: Virginia Department of Health), Ancestry.com, https://www.ancestry.com/.

8. World War I Selective Service System, Draft Registration Cards, 1917–1918, NARA M1509 (Washington, DC: National Archives and Records Administration). Ancestry.com, https://www.ancestry.com/.

9. World War I Selective Service System, Draft Registration Cards, 1917–1918, NARA M1509 (Washington, DC: National Archives and Records Administration). Ancestry.com, https://www.ancestry.com/.

10. Brown Colbert Borgus's successful application for a military veteran headstone notes that he served in the 13th Company, 4th Battalion, 155th Depot Brigade Training Center August 15, 1918 until January 11, 1919. Applications for Headstones, 1/1/1925–6/30/1970, NAID 596118, record group number 92, Records of the Office of the Quartermaster General (St. Louis, MO: National Archives), Ancestry.com, https://www.ancestry.com/. Many newspaper accounts place the 155th Depot Brigade at Camp Lee during this period (e.g., *Shepherdstown Register* 1918).

11. Brown Colbert (1785–1833) was the father of Robert Colbert (1806–1883; Getting Word n.d. b.). Robert Colbert was the father of Brown Colbert (1849–1913; death certificate of Brown Colbert, Death Records, Virginia, 1912–2014, (Richmond: Virginia Department of Health). Brown Colbert was the father of Mattie Jane Colbert (b. 1876; 1880 US Census, Lexington, Rockbridge, Virginia, roll 1387, page 38D, enumeration district 065, NARA microfilm publication T9, (Washington, DC: National Archives). Mattie Jane Colbert married Edward Thornton Borgus in 1894 (Virginia, Marriages, 1785–1940). Mattie Jane Colbert Borgus and Edward Thornton Borgus were the parents of Brown Colbert Borgus (Brown Colbert Borgus's death certificate, Death Records, Virginia, 1912–2014, (Richmond: Virginia Department of Health)). Ancestry .com, https://www.ancestry.com/.

12. 1920 US Census, Lexington, Rockbridge, Virginia, roll T625_190, page 9A, enumeration district 122, NARA microfilm publication T625, (Washington, D.C.: National Archives), Ancestry.com, https://www.ancestry.com/.

13. Augusta Memorial Gardens, Augusta County

14. Virginia, Marriages, 1936–2014, roll 101168520, (Richmond: Virginia Department of Health), Ancestry.com, https://www.ancestry.com/.

15. World War II Draft Registration Cards Young Men, 1940–1947, Virginia, Records of the Selective Service System 147, Box 268 (St. Louis, Missouri: The National Archives), Ancestry.com, https://www.ancestry.com/.

16. Dayton Cemetery, Rockingham County.

17. Morning Star and Temple Hill Cemeteries, Bland County.

18. Evergreen Cemetery, Roanoke.

19. St. John Lutheran Church, Wytheville.

20. Coverstone Cemetery, Page County.

21. 1930 US Census, Riverheads, Augusta, Virginia, page 7A, enumeration district 0014, FHL microfilm 2342169, NARA microfilm T626, (Washington, DC: National Archives and Records Administration), Ancestry.com, https://www.ancestry.com/.

22. 1940 US Census, Riverheads, Augusta, Virginia, roll m-t0627-04247, page 12B, enumeration district 8-19. Ancestry.com, https://www.ancestry.com/.

23. World War II Draft Registration Cards Young Men, 1940–1947, Virginia, Records of the Selective Service System 147, Box 248 (St. Louis, Missouri: The National Archives), Ancestry.com, https://www.ancestry.com/

24. Marriage record of Geraldine McHenry to Max Trompeter, 17 October 1950. *Pennsylvania, U.S., Marriages, 1852–1968*, Ancestry.com, https://www.ancestry.com/.

25. Applications for Headstones for U.S. Military Veterans, 1925–1941, NAID A1, 2110-C, Record Group Number 92, Records of the Office of the Quartermaster General, (Washington DC: National Archives), Ancestry.com, https://www.ancestry.com/.

26. Records of U.S. Army officers and soldiers killed or wounded in the Korean War for the period 2/13/1950–12/31/1953 (created, 1950 - 1970, updated December 21, 2012), (Washington, DC: National Archives), Fold 3, https://www.fold3.com.

27. 1940 US Census, South River, Augusta, Virginia, roll m-to627-04247, page 22A, enumeration district 8-32, NARA T627, (Washington, DC: National Archives and Records Administration), Ancestry.com, https://www.ancestry.com/.

28. Records of U.S. Army officers and soldiers killed or wounded in the Korean War, for the period 2/13/1950–12/31/1953 (created, 1950–1970, updated December 21, 2012), (Washington, DC: National Archives), Fold 3, https://www.fold3.com. See also Applications for Headstones for U.S. Military Veterans, 1925–1941, NAID A1, 2110-C, Record Group Number 92, Records of the Office of the Quartermaster General, (Washington DC: National Archives), Ancestry.com, https://www.ancestry.com/.

29. US Veterans' Gravesites, ca.1775–2019, (Washington, DC: U.S. Department of Veterans Affairs), July 15, 2020, Fold 3, https://www.fold3.com.

30. Virginia Marriages, 1936–2014, roll 101144520, (Richmond: Virginia Department of Health), Ancestry.com, https://www.ancestry.com/.

31. US Vietnam War Military Casualties, 1956–1998, Combat Area Casualties Current File, Records on Military Personnel Who Died, Were Missing in Action or Prisoners of War as a Result of the Vietnam Conflict, 1/20/1967–12/1998, Office of the Secretary of Defense, record group 330, (College Park, MD: National Archives at College Park), Ancestry.com, https://www.ancestry.com/.

32. US Civil War Soldier Records and Profiles, 1861–1865, *American Civil War Research Database* (Duxbury, MA: Historical Data Systems, Inc.), Ancestry.com, https://www.ancestry.com/.

33. US Civil War Soldier Records and Profiles, 1861–1865, *American Civil War Research Database* (Duxbury, MA: Historical Data Systems, Inc.), Ancestry.com, https://www.ancestry.com/.

34. US Civil War Soldier Records and Profiles, 1861–1865, *American Civil War Research Database* (Duxbury, MA: Historical Data Systems, Inc.), Ancestry.com, https://www.ancestry.com/.

35. 2 Samuel 12:23, King James Version: "But now he is dead. Wherefore should I fast? Can I bring him back again? I shall go to him, but he shall not return to me."

36. Coye Heard, personal communication, May 26, 2017.

37. Memorial page for Ricky Lee Sheffer, October 11, 2007, Find a Grave (website), https://www.findagrave.com/memorial/22109301/ricky-lee-sheffer.

38. Barbara Armistead Smith, Obituary, July 22, 2015, Jones Funeral Home and Cremation Service (website), https://memorials.jonesfuneralhomes.com/barbara-smith/2198912/obituary.php.

Chapter 6

1. At Augusta Memorial Gardens in Augusta County, a flag with deer welcomes visitors to one grave site, one with sea turtles to another. A welcome flag with pansies flutters over a grave at Rest Haven Cemetery in Page County, and another with a cardinal in Christiansburg's Sunset Cemetery. A welcome flag with an image of fallen oak leaves is planted next to a memorial bench in a Warren County cemetery: "In Loving Memory of Todd Nichols/ Love, Mom, Mamaw and Family" (Panorama Memorial Gardens). One with tulips waves over a grave in a Baptist church graveyard in Clifton Forge (Sharon Union Baptist Church). Welcome flags with hummingbirds flutter over two graves at a Presbyterian church cemetery in Rockbridge County.

2. Mount Hebron Cemetery in Winchester.

3. Green Hill Cemetery in Buena Vista.

4. Sunset View Memorial Gardens in Shenandoah County.

5. Mount Crawford Cemetery, Rockingham County.

6. Mount Hebron Cemetery, Winchester.

7. Victoria Britton, personal communication, 1 December 2017.

8. Augusta Memorial Gardens, Waynesboro.

9. Calvary United Methodist Church Cemetery.

10. Riverview Cemetery, Waynesboro.

11. Jeffrey Lane Williams, Oak Lawn, Bridgewater, Rockingham County.

12. Ralph Thomas Martin, Sr., Obituary, *News Virginian* [Waynesboro], October 22, 2005, Legacy.com (website), https://www.legacy.com/us/obituaries/newsvirginian/name/ralph-martin-obituary?pid=15448917.

13. Augusta Memorial Gardens, Augusta County.

14. Colleen Baber, personal communication, November 10, 2017.

15. Oak Grove Cemetery, Lexington.

16. Temple Emanuel Cemetery, Roanoke.

17. Riverview Cemetery in Waynesboro.

18. R.I.P. Bralyn Matthew Davis-Vest, April 16, 2014, Facebook (website), https://www.facebook.com/RIP-Bralyn-Matthew-Davis-Vest-863041820391132/.

19. Memorial page for Richard Allen "Buddy" Winkelspecht, February 28, 2002, Find a Grave (website), https://www.findagrave.com/memorial/6224716/richard-allen-winkelspecht.

20. Victoria Britton, personal communication, December 1, 2017.

21. Fishersville United Methodist Church Cemetery, Augusta County.

22. Thornrose Cemetery, Staunton.

23. Sunset Cemetery, Christiansburg.

24. Elk Run Cemetery, Elkton.

25. Frances Diehl Miller (1904–1973), Mill Creek Church of the Brethren, Rockingham County.

26. Ralph William Shank (1921–1997), Weavers Mennonite Church Cemetery, Harrisonburg.

Chapter 7

1. Advent Cemetery, Stanley, Page County.

2. Tinkling Spring Presbyterian Church Cemetery, Augusta County.

3. Sunset Cemetery, Christiansburg.

4. Thornrose Cemetery, Staunton.

5. Larry D. Sambrook, Obituary, *News Leader* [Staunton], August 2, 2009, Newspapers.com (website https://www.newspapers.com/.

6. Monticello Memorial Park, Charlottesville/Albemarle County.

7. Riverview Cemetery, Waynesboro.

8. Monticello Memorial Park, Charlottesville/Albemarle County.

9. Memorial page for Wilbur Fisk Swaringen, September 27, 2008, Find a Grave (website), https://www.findagrave.com/memorial/30125302/wilbur-fisk-swaringen.

10. US Civil War Soldier Records and Profiles, 1861–1865, *American Civil War Research Database* (Duxbury, MA: Historical Data Systems, Inc.), Ancestry.com, https://www.ancestry.com/.

11. US Civil War Soldier Records and Profiles, 1861–1865, *American Civil War Research Database* (Duxbury, MA: Historical Data Systems, Inc.), Ancestry.com, https://www.ancestry.com/.

12. Memorial page for Wilden Fisk Van Swearingen, November 25, 2014, Find a Grave (website), https://www.findagrave.com/memorial/139240978/wilden-fisk-van_swearingen.

13. Van Sweringen seems to have put funds in trust for the United Klans of America, Knights of the Ku Klux Klan (Orlando Sentinel, Orlando, Florida. October 17, 1989, pg. 94).

14. Mill Creek Church of the Brethren, Rockingham County.

15. Oakwood Cemetery, Charlottesville.

16. Dayton Mennonite Church Cemetery, Rockingham County.

17. Death Records, Virginia, 1912–2014, (Richmond: Virginia Department of Health), Ancestry.com, https://www.ancestry.com/.

18. Sunset Memorial Park, Beckley, West Virginia.

19. Mount Hebron Cemetery, Winchester.

20. Mount Hebron Cemetery, Winchester.

21. Mt. Hermon Cemetery, Augusta County. Thanks to Nat Faulkner for assistance reading this grave marker.

22. Southwest Virginia Veterans Cemetery, Dublin/ Pulaski County.

23. Carolyn Joan (Hite) Fitzgerald, Obituary, January 31, 2012, Dignity Memorial (website), https://www.dignitymemorial.com/obituaries/waynesboro-va/carolyn-fitzgerald-4978672.

24. Tinkling Spring Presbyterian Church Cemetery, Fishersville/Augusta County.

25. Holly Memorial Gardens, Charlottesville/Albemarle County.

26. Cavalry United Methodist Church Cemetery, Augusta County.

27. Riverview Cemetery, Waynesboro.

28. Riverview Cemetery, Waynesboro.

29. Coverstone Cemetery, Page County.

30. Thornrose Cemetery, Staunton.

31. Obituary, Jeffrey Scott Hippie Earhart, March 1, 2014, Tribute Archive (website), https://www.tributearchive.com/obituaries/3050160/Jeffrey-Scott-Earhart.

32. Sunset Memorial Park, Beckley, West Virginia.

33. Remington Colt "Remmy" Bortell, Obituary, Accessed January 29, 2021, WVGenWEb (website). http://www.wvgenweb.org/raleigh/obit37.htm.

34. Hillsboro Cemetery, Albemarle County.

35. Oak Grove Cemetery, Lexington.

36. Monticello Memorial Park, Charlottesville/Albemarle County.

37. For example, Stuart Moncure Dillon, Trinity Brethren Church Cemetery, Botetourt County.

38. Southwest Virginia Veterans Cemetery, Dublin/Pulaski County.

39. Thornrose Cemetery, Staunton.

40. Prospect Hill Cemetery, Front Royal, Warren County.

41. Advent Cemetery, Stanley, Page County.

42. Mt. Carmel Presbyterian Church Cemetery, Augusta County.

43. Glasgow Cemetery, Rockbridge County.

44. Sunset Cemetery, Christiansburg.

45. Riverview Cemetery, Waynesboro.

46. Mayo S. Nininger, Obituary, June 18, 2013. *News Leader* (Staunton), Newspapers
.com (website), https://www.newspapers.com/image/115598287/?terms=mayo%20
nininger&match=1.

47. Memorial page for Nancy Ann Lorencki, October 9, 2008, Find a Grave (website),
https://www.findagrave.com/memorial/30433756/nancy-ann-lorencki.

48. Panorama Memorial Gardens, Warren County.

49. James Maynard "Fiddle Man" Phillips, Obituary, Accessed January 29, 2021,
Legacy.com (website). https://www.legacy.com/obituaries/name/james-maynard
-phillips-obituary?pid=183117772.

50. US Civil War Soldier Records and Profiles, 1861–1865, *American Civil War Research Database* (Duxbury, MA: Historical Data Systems, Inc.), Ancestry.com, https://
www.ancestry.com/

51. Compiled Service Records of Confederate Soldiers Who Served in Organizations
from the State of Virginia, August 13, 2013, Civil War Service Index, record group 109,
NARA M382, (Washington, DC: National Archives), Fold 3, https://www.fold3.com/.

52. Compiled Service Records of Confederate Soldiers Who Served in Organizations from the State of Virginia, September 15, 2010, Civil War Service Records, record
group 109, NARA M324, (Washington, DC: National Archives), Fold 3, https://www
.fold3.com/.

53. Evergreen Cemetery, Roanoke.

54. Jerry W. Talbott, Obituary, *Roanoke Times*, Accessed January 29, 2021, Legacy.
com (website), https://www.legacy.com/us/obituaries/roanoke/name/jerry-talbott
-obituary?pid=18457181.

55. Mount Hebron Cemetery, Winchester.

56. Memorial page for Carl Michael Gainsback, April 27, 2004, Find a Grave
(website), https://www.findagrave.com/memorial/8693868/carl-michael-gainsback.

57. Mount Hebron Cemetery, Winchester.

58. Sunset Cemetery, Christiansburg.

59. Godwin Cemetery, Fincastle.

60. Riverview Cemetery, Waynesboro.

61. Advent Cemetery, Page County.

62. West End Cemetery, Wytheville, Wythe County.

63. Oak Lawn Memory Gardens, Staunton.

64. *Records of the Railroad Retirement Board, 1934–1987*, record group number *184*,
U.S., Railroad Retirement Pension Index, 1934–1987, (Morrow, Georgia: National Archives
at Atlanta), Ancestry.com, https://www.ancestry.com/.

65. Mt. Carmel Presbyterian Church Cemetery, Augusta County.

66. Riverview Cemetery, Waynesboro.

67. Memorial page for Benjamin "Benny" Calvin Hite, Jr., November 28, 2006, Find a Grave (website), https://www.findagrave.com/memorial/16818668/benjamin -calvin-hite.

68. Sunset Memorial Park, Beckley, West Virginia.

69. *Virginia Marriages, 1936–2014*, roll *101168289*, (Richmond: Virginia Department of Health), Ancestry.com, https://www.ancestry.com/.

70. Timber Ridge ARP Church Cemetery, Rockbridge County.

71. Advent Cemetery, Page County.

72. Mt. Hermon Cemetery, Augusta County.

73. Memorial page for Clarence Henry "C.H." Gordon, October 3, 2011, Find a Grave (website), https://www.findagrave.com/memorial/77570891/clarence-henry-gordon.

74. Sunset View Memorial Gardens, Woodstock, Shenandoah County.

75. Morning Star and Temple Hill Cemeteries, Bland County.

76. Lone Star Baptist Church Cemetery, Covington.

77. Mt. Carmel Presbyterian Church Cemetery, Augusta County.

78. Memorial page for Ray Borden Corbin, May 29, 2012, Find a Grave (website), https://www.findagrave.com/memorial/90941960/ray-borden-corbin.

79. Memorial page for Michael Ray Corbin, April 2, 2014, Find a Grave (website), https://www.findagrave.com/memorial/127321891/michael-ray-corbin.

80. Coverstone Cemetery, Page County.

81. Birchlawn Burial Park, Pearisburg, Giles County.

82. Memorial page for Billy Junior Bowles, January 20, 2014, Find a Grave (website), https://www.findagrave.com/memorial/123778786/billy-junior-bowles.

83. Glasgow Cemetery, Rockbridge County.

84. Green Hill, Buena Vista. Jason Matthew Vaughan, Obituary, November 29, 2015, *Roanoke Time*s (website), https://roanoke.com/obituaries/vaughan-jason-matthew /article_04f92c0b-baa1-5ce4-b099-5a8198c08970.html.

85. Mt. Carmel Presbyterian Church Cemetery, Augusta County.

86. Calvary United Methodist Church Cemetery, Augusta County.

87. Elk Run Cemetery, Elkton.

88. Mount Hebron Cemetery, Winchester.

89. Sunset Cemetery, Christiansburg.

90. Calvary United Methodist Church Cemetery, Augusta County.

91. Teresa Downey Hart, Obituary, January 1, 2016, *Roanoke Times* (website), http:// www.roanoke.com/obituaries/hart-teresa-downey/article_4e2ad813-3dcd-5f87-bb12 -fcea87cad202.html.

92. Nowlin Cemetery, Buena Vista.

93. Morning Star and Temple Hill Cemeteries, Bland County.

94. Elk Run Cemetery, Elkton.

95. Green Hill Cemetery, Buena Vista.

96. Mount Crawford Cemetery, Rockingham County.

97. Memorial page for James "Big Jim" Russell DePoy, Find a Grave (website), August 19, 2014, https://www.findagrave.com/memorial/134562043/james-depoy.

98. Clint DePoy, personal communication. May 30, 2018.

99. Clint DePoy, personal communication, May 30, 2018.

100. Mount Hebron Cemetery, Winchester.

101. Morning Star and Temple Hill Cemeteries, Bland County.

102. Trinity Church of the Brethren, Botetourt County.

103. Collierstown Presbyterian Church Cemetery, Rockbridge County.

104. Sunset Cemetery, Christiansburg.

105. Green Hill Cemetery, Buena Vista.

106. Dale Lyle, personal communication, May 22, 2018.

107. Dale Lyle, personal communication, May 22, 2018.

108. Dale Lyle, personal communication, May 22, 2018.

109. Dale Lyle, personal communication, May 22, 2018.

110. Dale Lyle, personal communication, May 22, 2018.

Chapter 8

1. Dennis Clatterbaugh, Monster Kid (1956–2010) and Doris Clatterbaugh, Beloved Sister (1940–2010), November 2010, Classic Horror Film Board (website), https://www.tapatalk.com/groups/monsterkidclassichorrorforum/dennis-clatterbaugh-monster-kid-1956-2010-and-dori-t32522.html.

2. Augusta Memorial Gardens, Waynesboro.

3. Monticello Memorial Park, Albemarle County.

4. Southwest Virginia Veterans Cemetery, Dublin, Pulaski County.

5. Calvary United Methodist Church Cemetery, Augusta County.

6. For example, East End Cemetery, Wytheville, and Tinkling Spring Presbyterian Church Cemetery, Augusta County.

7. Green Hill Cemetery, Buena Vista.

8. Green Hill Cemetery, Buena Vista. Memorial page for Dennis James Davis, March 20, 2012, Find a Grave (website), https://www.findagrave.com/memorial/87089330/dennis-james-davis.

9. Collierstown Presbyterian Church Cemetery, Rockbridge County.

10. Birchlawn Burial Park, Pearisburg/Giles County.

11. West End Cemetery, Wytheville/Wythe County.

12. Sunset Cemetery, Christiansburg.

13. Mount Crawford Cemetery, Rockingham County.

14. Temple Emanuel Cemetery, Roanoke.

15. Memorial page for Alice Trissel, February 6, 2019, Find a Grave (website), https://www.findagrave.com/memorial/196656751/alice-trissel.

16. Weavers Mennonite Church Cemetery, Harrisonburg.

17. Mt. Carmel Presbyterian Church Cemetery, Augusta County.

18. Mount Hebron Cemetery, Winchester.

19. Various authors, Dennis Clatterbaugh, Monster Kid (1956–2010) and Doris Clatterbaugh, Beloved Sister (1940–2010). August - November 2010. Classic Horror Film Board (website). https://www.tapatalk.com/groups/monsterkidclassichorrorforum/dennis-clatterbaugh-monster-kid-1956-2010-and-dori-t32522.html.

20. Various authors, Dennis Clatterbaugh, Monster Kid (1956–2010) and Doris Clatterbaugh, Beloved Sister (1940–2010). August - November 2010. Classic Horror Film Board (website). https://www.tapatalk.com/groups/monsterkidclassichorrorforum/dennis-clatterbaugh-monster-kid-1956-2010-and-dori-t32522.html.

21. Southwest Virginia Veterans Cemetery, Dublin, Pulaski County.

22. Immanuel Presbyterian Church, Rockbridge County.

23. Collierstown Presbyterian Church Cemetery, Rockbridge County.

24. Memorial page for Anthony Wayne "Tony" Patterson, March 18, 2012, Find a Grave (website), https://www.findagrave.com/memorial/86944096/anthony-wayne-patterson.

25. Elk Run Cemetery, Elkton.

26. Memorial page for Mark Richard Futch, February 10, 2015, Find a Grave (website), https://www.findagrave.com/memorial/142426642/mark-richard-futch.

27. Riverview Cemetery, Waynesboro.

28. Tinkling Spring Presbyterian Church Cemetery, Augusta County.

29. Trinity Brethren Church Cemetery, Botetourt County.

30. Memorial page for Priscilla Ann Kern Redd, December 7, 2010, Find a Grave (webpage), https://www.findagrave.com/memorial/62645925/priscilla-ann-redd.

31. Mount Hebron Cemetery, Winchester.

32. Memorial page for Leonard Ray Nida Sr., December 14, 2013, Find a Grave (website), https://www.findagrave.com/memorial/121735813/leonard-ray-nida.

33. Advent Cemetery, Stanley, Page County.

34. Lone Star Baptist Church, Covington.

35. Elk Run Cemetery, Elkton.

36. Green Hill Cemetery, Buena Vista.

37. Memorial page for Thomas Preston "Tommy" Lunsford II, March 17, 2012, Find a Grave (website), https://www.findagrave.com/memorial/86908927/thomas-preston-lunsford.

38. Memorial page for Jason Lee Shifflett, September 8, 2015, Find a Grave (website), https://www.findagrave.com/memorial/152039489/jason-lee-shifflett.

39. Mt. Carmel Presbyterian Church Cemetery, Augusta County.

40. Oak Lawn Memory Gardens, Staunton/Augusta County.

41. Memorial page for Shirley Ann "Dumpy" *Wade* Ellinger, January 21, 2018, Find a Grave (website), https://www.findagrave.com/memorial/186789891/shirley-ann-ellinger.

42. Thornrose Cemetery, Staunton.

43. Calvary United Methodist Church Cemetery, Augusta County.

44. Augusta Memorial Gardens, Augusta County.

45. Riverview Cemetery, Waynesboro.

46. Serenity Garden, Waynesboro.

47. "About Dr. Cornel West." n.d. Dr. Cornel West (website), http://www.cornelwest.com/bio.html#.XPrK88hKg2w.

Epilogue

1. Amira Hegazy, personal communication, September 22, 2020.

WORKS CITED

ABC News. 2006. "Exclusive: Mother of 'Tears in Heaven' Inspiration Shares Story." September 7, 2006. ABC News (website). https://abcnews.go.com/2020 /Entertainment/story?id=2404474&page=1.

Aesop. n.d. "The Ants & the Grasshopper." *The Aesop for Children.* Library of Congress (website). Accessed January 29, 2021. http://read.gov/aesop/052.html.

Allis, Ashley A. 2011. *Old Western State Hospital: Staunton, Virginia.* Richmond: Garden Club of Virginia.

American Anthropological Association. 2009. "Code of Ethics." American Anthropological Association (website). February 2009. http://s3.amazonaws.com/rdcms-aaa /files/production/public/FileDownloads/pdfs/issues/policy-advocacy/upload /AAA-Ethics-Code-2009.pdf.

Anderson, Paul C. 2015. "Shenandoah Valley during the Civil War." October 27, 2015. *Encyclopedia Virginia* (website). Virginia Humanities. https://www.encyclopedia virginia.org/Shenandoah_Valley_During_the_Civil_War.

Antrosio, Jason. 2018. "Science in Anthropology: Humanistic Science and Scientific Humanism." February 12, 2018. *Living Anthropologically* (blog). https://www .livinganthropologically.com/science-in-anthropology/.

Appleby, Joyce Oldham. 1978. *Economic Thought and Ideology in Seventeenth-Century England.* Princeton, NJ: Princeton University Press.

Ariès, Phillippe. 1981. *The Hour of Our Death.* New York: Alfred A. Knopf.

Árnason, Arnar. 2013. "Anthropology." In *The Encyclopedia of Death and Dying,* edited by Glennys Howarth and Oliver Leaman, 21–23. New York: Routledge.

Bainbridge, William Sims. 1984. "Religious Insanity in America: The Official Nineteenth-Century Theory." *Sociological Analysis* 45 (3):223–39.

Baker, Donald. 2019. "Why the 'Frozen Chosin' is the Defining Battle of the Modern Marine Corps." January 28, 2019. We Are the Mighty (website). http://www .wearethemighty.com/history/why-the-frozen-chosin-is-the-defining-battle-of-the -modern-marine-corps.

Bakhtin, Mikhail M. (1968) 1984. *Rabelais and His World.* Bloomington: Indiana University Press.

———. 1982. *The Dialogic Imagination: Four Essays by M. M. Bakhtin.* Austin: University of Texas Press.

Barber, Michael B., and Eugene B. Barfield. 1997. "Native Americans on the Virginia Frontier in the Seventeenth Century: Archaeological Investigations along the

Interior Roanoke River Drainage." In *Diversity and Accommodation: Essays on the Cultural Composition of the Virginia Frontier*, edited by Michael J. Puglisi, 134–58. Knoxville: University of Tennessee Press.

Barret, John C. 2000. "A Thesis on Agency." In *Agency in Archaeology*, edited by Marcia-Anne Dobres and John E. Robb, 61–68. London: Routledge.

Battle-Baptiste, Whitney. 2011. *Black Feminist Archaeology*. New York: Routledge.

Baugher, Sherene, and Richard F. Veit. 2014. *The Archaeology of American Cemeteries and Gravemarkers*. Gainesville: University Press of Florida.

Behar, Ruth. 1996. *The Vulnerable Observer: Anthropology that Breaks Your Heart*. Boston: Beacon Press.

Bell, Alison, Donald Gaylord, and Kristin Sharman. 2019. "'All My Little Might of Money': Signaling, Structure, and Mobility among the Middling in Nineteenth-Century Virginia and Kentucky." *Historical Archaeology* 53 (2):372–92.

Bellah, Robert N., Richard Madsen, William M. Sullivan, Ann Swidler, and Steven M. Tipton. 1985. *Habits of the Heart: Individualism and Commitment in American Life*. Berkeley: University of California Press.

Benedict, Ruth. 1934. *Patterns of Culture*. Boston: Houghton Mifflin.

Berg, Lauren. 2013. "Paying Tribute to the Past." November 10, 2013, modified November 15, 2019. *Daily Progress* [Charlottesville] (website). https://dailyprogress.com/archives/paying-tribute-to-the-past/article_66099e5e-49b0-11e3-a205-001a4bcf6878.html.

Blair, William. 2004. *Contesting the Memory of the Civil War in the South, 1865–1914*. Chapel Hill: University of North Carolina Press.

Blakey, Michael L., Teresa E. Leslie, and Joseph P. Reidy. 1994. "Frequency and Chronological Distribution of Dental Enamel Hypoplasia in Enslaved African Americans: A Test of the Weaning Hypothesis." *American Journal of Physical Anthropology* 95:371–83.

Bloch, Maurice, and Jonathan Parry. 1982. "Introduction." In *Death and the Regeneration of Life*, edited by Maurice Bloch and Jonathan Parry, 1–44. Cambridge: Cambridge University Press.

Bodie, Charles A. 2011. *Remarkable Rockbridge: The Story of Rockbridge County, Virginia*. Lexington, VA: Rockbridge Historical Society.

Bourdieu, Pierre. 1984. *Distinction: A Social Critique of the Judgement of Taste*. Translated by Richard Nice. Cambridge: Harvard University Press.

Bourgois, Philippe, and Jeff Schonberg. 2009. *Righteous Dopefiend*. Berkeley: University of California Press.

Brown, Molly McCully. 2017. *The Virginia State Colony for Epileptics and Feebleminded: Poems*. New York: Persea Books.

Buffalo Soldiers Association of West Point. n.d. "Buffalo Soldiers of West Point." Accessed October 4, 2020. Buffalo Soldiers Association of West Point (website). https://www.buffalosoldiersofwestpoint.org/buffalo-soldiers-at-westpoint.

Buffett, Jimmy. 1981. "Growing Older But Not Up." *Coconut Telegraph*. (studio album). Muscle Shoals Sound Studio.

Calello, Monique. 2022. "Efforts to preserve African American cemeteries in Augusta County build momentum." April 21, 2022. *Staunton News-Leader* (website). https://www.newsleader.com/story/news/2022/04/18/legacy-racism-african-american-cemeteries-augusta-county-black-history-virginia/7331600001/.

Cavallaro, Gabe. 2017. "Revolutionary War Soldier and Early Augusta Resident Honored at Swoope Cemetery." September 30, 2017. *Staunton News-Leader* (website). https://

www.newsleader.com/story/news/local/2017/09/30/swoope-va-cemetery-glebe
-revolutionary-war-soldier-augusta-john-mccain-descendants/719648001/.

Chan, Melissa. 2016. "Slain TV Reporter's Father on Shooting's 1-Year Anniversary: It's a 'Void in Our Souls.'" August 26, 2016. *Time* (website). https://time.com /4468770/virginia-tv-reporter-shooting-anniversary/.

Church, Eric. 2006. "Sinners Like Me." *Sinners Like Me* (studio album). Capitol Nashville.

Clapton, Eric. 1992. "Tears in Heaven." Unplugged (live album). Reprise, Duck, MTV.

Coates, Ta-Nehisi. 2015. *Between the World and Me*. New York: Spiegel & Grau.

Coffey, David W. 1985. National Register of Historic Places Inventory—Nomination Form, Maple Hall. Virginia Department of Historic Resources (website). https:// www.dhr.virginia.gov/VLR_to_transfer/PDFNoms/081-0041_Maple_Hall_1987 _Final_Nomination.pdf.

Conroy, K., and V. Malik. 2018. "Hearing Loss in the Trenches: A Hidden Morbidity of World War I." *Journal of Laryngology and Otology* 132 (11):952–55.

Crocker, J. Christopher. 1977. "The Social Functions of Rhetorical Forms." In *The Social Use of Metaphor*, edited by J. David Sapir and J. Christopher Crocker, 33–66. Philadelphia: University of Pennsylvania Press.

Crossland, Zoe. 2014. *Ancestral Encounters in Highland Madagascar: Material Signs and Traces of the Dead*. New York: Cambridge University Press.

Culbertson, Charles. 2014. "Old Western State Cemetery Hides in Plain Sight." October 3, 2014. *Staunton News-Leader* (website). https://www.newsleader.com/story/news /local/2014/10/03/old-western-state-cemetery-hides-plain-sight/16645645/.

Cullen, Lisa Takeuchi. 2006. *Remember Me: A Lively Tour of the New American Way of Death*. New York: Harper Collins.

Davenport, David and Gordon Lloyd. 2016. *Rugged Individualism: Dead or Alive?* Stanford, California: Hoover Institution Press.

Davis, Chester W. 1919. *The Story of the First Pioneer Infantry, U. S. A.* Utica, NY: Kirkland Press. Internet Archive. https://archive.org/stream/storyoffirstpionoodavirich /storyoffirstpionoodavirich_djvu.txt.

Dawdy, Shannon Lee. 2013. "Archaeology of Modern American Death: Grave Goods and Blithe Mementoes." In *The Oxford Handbook of the Archaeology of the Contemporary World*, edited by Paul Graves-Brown, Rodney Harrison, and Angela Piccini, 451–65. Oxford: Oxford University Press. https://doi.org/10.1093/oxfordhb /9780199602001.013.009.

———. 2016. *Patina: A Profane Archaeology*. Chicago: University of Chicago Press.

———. 2021. *American Afterlives: Reinventing Death in the Twenty First Century*. Princeton, NJ: Princeton University Press.

Deetz, James. (1977) 1996. *In Small Things Forgotten: An Archaeology of Early American Life*. New York: Doubleday.

Deetz, James, and Patricia Scott Deetz. 2000. *The Times of Their Lives: Life, Love, and Death in Plymouth Colony*. New York: Anchor.

Deetz, James, and Edwin S. Dethlefsen. 1967. "Death's Head, Cherub, Urn and Willow." *Natural History* 76 (3):29–37.

Deetz, Kelley Fanto. 2017. *Bound to the Fire: How Virginia's Enslaved Cooks Helped Invent American Cuisine*. Lexington: University Press of Kentucky.

De León, Jason. 2015. *The Land of Open Graves: Living and Dying on the Migrant Trail*. Oakland: University of California Press.

Dew, Charles B. 1994. *Bond of Iron: Master and Slave at Buffalo Forge*. New York: W. W. Norton.

Dobres, Marcia-Anne, and John E. Robb. 2000. "Agency in Archaeology: Paradigm or Platitude?" In *Agency in Archaeology*, edited by Marcia-Anne Dobres and John E. Robb, 3–17. London: Routledge.

Dorr, Gregory Michael. 2008. *Segregation's Science: Eugenics and Society in Virginia*. Charlottesville: University of Virginia Press.

———. 2015. "Joseph S. DeJarnette (1866–1957)." *Dictionary of Virginia Biography*. Virginia Humanities. Published July 8, 2013. Last modified November 2, 2015. Encyclopedia Virginia (website). https://www.encyclopediavirginia.org /DeJarnette_Joseph_Spencer_1866-1957.

Doss, Erika. 2010. *Memorial Mania: Public Feeling in America*. Chicago: University of Chicago Press.

Douglas, Mary. 1990. "No Free Gifts." foreword to *The Gift: The Form and Reason for Exchange in Archaic Societies*, by Marcel Mauss, ix–xxiii. New York: W. W. Norton.

Dumont, Louis. 1986. *Essays on Individualism: Modern Ideology in Anthropological Perspective*. Chicago: University of Chicago Press.

Eggener, Keith. 2010. *Cemeteries*. New York: W. W. Norton.

Engelke, Matthew. 2019. "The Anthropology of Death Revisited." *Annual Review of Anthropology* 48:29–44.

Evening Leader. 1953. "Body of Slain Soldier Is On Way Home." *The Evening Leader*, Staunton, Va. July 6, 1953. Newspapers.com (website). https://www.newspapers .com/image/316002517/?article=baa13bf2-8bf2-4b2e-9f50-3e1d16ac4bdc&focus =0.16403574,0.20658246,0.2848703,0.42109638&xid=3355.

Ferguson, Frances. 1974. "Randall Jarrell and the Flotations of Voice." Fall 1974. *The Georgia Review* (website). https://thegeorgiareview.com/posts/randall-jarrell-and -the-flotations-of-voice/.

Field, Eugene. 1947. "Wynken, Blynken, and Nod." The Poetry Foundation (website). https://www.poetryfoundation.org/poems/42920/wynken-blynken-and-nod.

Fletcher, Kami. 2020. "Founding Baltimore's Mount Auburn Cemetery and Its Importance to Understanding African American Burial Rights." In *Till Death Do Us Part: American Ethnic Cemeteries as Borders Uncrossed*, edited by Allan Amanik and Kami Fletcher, 129–56. Jackson: University Press of Mississippi.

Flood, Brian. 2016. "Here's Every Major Poll That Got Donald Trump's Election Win Wrong." November 9, 2016. *The Wrap* (website). https://www.thewrap.com/every -poll-that-got-election-wrong-donald-trump/.

Foster, Brian A. n.d. "About Together We Served." Accessed January 14, 2021. U.S. Air Force, Together We Served (website). https://airforce.togetherweserved.com/usaf /singlepage/landing/body/landing_about.jsp.

Foucault, Michel. (1961) 1999. *Madness and Civilization: A History of Insanity in the Age of Reason*. New York: Vintage Books.

Fowler, Chris. 2002. "Body Parts: Personhood and Materiality in the Earlier Manx Neolithic." In *Thinking through the Body: Archaeologies of Corporeality*, edited by Yannis Hamilakis, Mark Pluciennik, and Sarah Tarlow, 47–69. New York: Kluwer Academic/Plenum.

———. 2004. *The Archaeology of Personhood: An Anthropological Approach*. London: Routledge.

Fox, Annette Z. 1999. "Golf Tourney Played to Benefit 6-year-old with Cerebral Palsy." October 15, 1999. *Register Herald* [Beckley, WV]. Newspaper Archive (web site). https://newspaperarchive.com/beckley-register-herald-oct-15-1999-p-3/.

Frohne, Andrea E. 2015. *The African Burial Ground in New York City: Memory, Spirituality, and Space*. Syracuse: Syracuse University Press.

Garner, Dwight. 2017. "Beautiful Poems About a House of Horrors." Review of *The Virginia State Colony for Epileptics and Feebleminded: Poems,* by Molly McCully Brown (2017). March 14, 2017. *New York Times* (website). https://www.nytimes.com/2017/03/14/books/review-virginia-state-colony-for-epileptics-and-feebleminded-molly-mccully-brown.html.

Geertz, Clifford. 1973. *The Interpretation of Cultures.* New York: Basic Books.

Getting Word. n.d. a. "Brown Colbert." Accessed January 13, 2021. Monticello, Getting Word: African American Oral History Project (website). https://www.monticello.org/getting-word/people/brown-colbert.

———. n.d. b. "Colbert (Hemings) Family." Accessed January 13, 2021. Monticello, Getting Word: African American Oral History Project (website). https://www.monticello.org/getting-word/families/colbert-hemings-family.

———. n.d. c. "Elizabeth Hemings." Accessed January 13, 2021. Monticello, Getting Word: African American Oral History Project (website). https://www.monticello.org/getting-word/people/elizabeth-hemings.

———. n.d. d. "Elizabeth Hemings Family." Accessed January 13, 2021. Monticello, Getting Word: African American Oral History Project (website). https://www.monticello.org/getting-word/families/elizabeth-hemings-family.

Gill, Vince. 2009. "Go Rest High on that Mountain." October 7, 2009. Official music video with lyrics (video online). https://www.youtube.com/watch?v=6jXrmAKBBTU.

Glassie, Henry. 1975. *Folk Housing in Middle Virginia: A Structural Analysis of Historic Artifacts.* Knoxville: University of Tennessee Press.

———. 1982. *Passing the Time in Ballymenone.* Bloomington: Indiana University Press.

———. 1994. "The Practice and Purpose of History." *The Journal of American History* 81 (3):961–68.

———. 1999. *Material Culture.* Bloomington: Indiana University Press.

Gleach, Frederic. 2013. "Humanistic Anthropology." Oxford University Press. July 24, 2013. Oxford Bibliographies (website). https://doi.org/10.1093/OBO/9780199766567-0101.

Gordon-Reed, Annette. 2009. *The Hemingses of Monticello: An American Family.* New York: W. W. Norton.

Gould, Stephen Jay. 1980. *The Panda's Thumb: More Reflections in Natural History.* London: W W Norton.

Grand Order of Odd Fellows in America and Jurisdiction. n.d. "About the Oddfellows." Accessed January 8, 2021. Grand Order of Odd Fellows in America and Jurisdiction (website). https://guoofamerica.com/oddfellows_natl/Home.html.

Grant, Richard. 2016. "Deep in the Swamps, Archaeologists Are Finding How Fugitive Slaves Kept Their Freedom." September 2016. *Smithsonian Magazine* (website). https://www.smithsonianmag.com/history/deep-swamps-archaeologists-fugitive-slaves-kept-freedom-180960122/.

Grateful Dead. 1970. "Brokedown Palace." *American Beauty.* Warner Bros. Records.

———. 1970. "Sugar Magnolia." *American Beauty.* Warner Bros. Records.

Green, Bryan Clark and Susan Reed. 2012. *Architectural Evaluation of the Knights of Pythias Building, 319–321 North Main Street, Lexington, Virginia.* Prepared by Commonwealth Architects, Richmond, Virginia, for Virginia Military Institute, Lexington, Virginia. Virginia Department of Historic Resources File No. 117-0027-0166.

Hall, Donald. 2006. "The Painted Bed." Accessed January 24, 2021. Poets.org (website). https://poets.org/poem/painted-bed.

Hamilakis, Yannis, Mark Pluciennik, and Sarah Tarlow. 2002. "Introduction: Thinking through the Body." In *Thinking through the Body: Archaeologies of Corporeality*, edited by Yannis Hamilakis, Mark Pluciennik, and Sarah Tarlow, 1–21. New York: Kluwer Academic/Plenum.

Hanes, Leigh Buckner. 1930. "Trees in a Winter Storm." Accessed January 8, 2021. Poetry Foundation (website). https://www.poetryfoundation.org/poetrymagazine/browse?contentId=18803.

Harris, C. Leon. n.d. "Pension Application of Peter Haught S6981." Accessed October 4, 2020. Southern Campaigns Revolutionary War Pension Statements and Rosters (website). http://revwarapps.org/s6981.pdf.

Harrisonburg Daily News Record. "Bernice Kiser Drowns in River at B'Way." September 2, 1926. Newspaperarchive (website), https://newspaperarchive.com.

Hass, Robert. 1997. "Poet's Choice." November 16, 1997. *Washington Post* (website). https://www.washingtonpost.com/archive/entertainment/books/1997/11/16/poets-choice/86e3f4b7-9d5d-4ffa-8d9c-ac8a3af104ff/.

Hegazy, Amira. 2020. "Ruins for Those We Lost." The Future of Our Plans: SAIC Graduate Class of 2020. Accessed October 4, 2020. School of the Art Institute of Chicago (website). https://sites.saic.edu/gradshow2020/artists/amira-hegazy/.

Hertz, Robert. (1907) 1960. *Death and the Right Hand.* Translated by Rodney and Claudia Needham. Aberdeen: The University Press.

Heyse, Amy Lynn. 2008. "The Rhetoric of Memory-Making: Lessons from the UDC's Catechisms for Children." *Rhetoric Society Quarterly* 38 (4):408–432.

Hicks, Dan, and Mary C. Beaudry. 2018. *The Oxford Handbook of Material Culture Studies.* Oxford: Oxford University Press.

Hirshfield, Jane. 2006. *After: Poems.* New York: Harper.

Historic St. Mary's City. n.d. "Garrett Van Sweringen." Accessed October 4, 2020. Historic St. Mary's City: A Museum of History & Archaeology at Maryland's First Capital (website). https://www.hsmcdigshistory.org/pdf/Van-Sweringen.pdf.

Hofstra, Warren R. 2004. *The Planting of New Virginia: Settlement and Landscape in the Shenandoah Valley.* Baltimore: Johns Hopkins Press.

Hofstra, Warren R., and Clarence R. Geier. 2000. "Farm to Mill to Market: Historical Archaeology of an Emerging Grain Economy in the Shenandoah Valley." In *After the Backcountry: Rural Life in the Great Valley of Virginia 1800–1900*, edited by Kenneth E. Koons and Warren R. Hofstra, 48–61. Knoxville: University of Tennessee Press.

Horn, Marcia. 2006. Oral history interview with Jacob Trompeter, transcribed by Marcia Horn. December 3, 2006. United States Holocaust Memorial Museum (website). https://collections.ushmm.org/search/catalog/irn607954.

Horton, Tonia Woods. 2000. "Hidden Gardens: The Town Gardens of T.J. 'Stonewall' Jackson and His Lexington Contemporaries." In *After the Backcountry: Rural Life in the Great Valley of Virginia 1800–1900*, edited by Kenneth E. Koons and Warren R. Hofstra, 111–134. Knoxville: University of Tennessee Press.

Isaac, Rhys. 1982. *The Transformation of Virginia, 1740–1790.* Chapel Hill: Omohundro Institute and University of North Carolina Press.

Jackson, Nancy A. and Linda Brake Meyers. 2011. "Descendants of Edward Jackson." Jackson Brigade, Inc. (website). http://www.eg.bucknell.edu/~hyde/jackson/DescendantsEdwardJackson2011.html.

Jarrell, Randall. 1980. "The Death of the Ball Turret Gunner." Accessed January 14, 2021. Poetry Foundation (website). https://www.poetryfoundation.org/poems/57860/the-death-of-the-ball-turret-gunner.

Johnson, Matthew. 2000. "Self-Made Men and the Staging of Agency." In *Agency in Archaeology*, edited by Marcia-Anne Dobres and John E. Robb, 213–31. London: Routledge.

Jordan, Ervin L., Jr. 1995. *Black Confederates and Afro-Yankees in Civil War Virginia*. Charlottesville: University Press of Virginia.

Keller, Kenneth W. 1997. "The Outlook of Rhinelanders on the Virginia Frontier." In *Diversity and Accommodation: Essays on the Cultural Composition of the Virginia Frontier*, edited by Michael J. Puglisi, 99–126. Knoxville: University of Tennessee Press.

Kennedy, Stetson. 1990. *The Klan Unmasked*. Boca Raton: Florida Atlantic University Press.

Kercheval, Samuel. (1961) 1902. *A History of the Valley of Virginia*, Third Edition. Woodstock, Virginia: W.N. Grabill, Power Press.

Kiser's Cross. n.d. "Buffalo Soldiers in the Woevre Plain Operation." Accessed January 8, 2021. The Kaiser's Cross (website). http://www.kaiserscross.com/41815/239601.html.

Klein, Bob. n.d. "Obituaries/ Breeden." Accessed January 24, 2021. *Shiflett Family Genealogy* (website). http://www.klein-shiflett.com/Obit_Section/Obit_Related_Names/breeden.htm.

Koons, Kenneth E. 2000. "'The Staple of Our Country': Wheat in the Regional Farm Economy of the Nineteenth-Century Valley of Virginia." In *After the Backcountry: Rural Life in the Great Valley of Virginia 1800–1900*, edited by Kenneth E. Koons and Warren R. Hofstra, 3–20. Knoxville: University of Tennessee Press.

Koons, Kenneth E., and Warren R. Hofstra. 2000. "Introduction: The World Wheat Made." In *After the Backcountry: Rural Life in the Great Valley of Virginia 1800–1900*, edited by Kenneth E. Koons and Warren R. Hofstra, xvii–xxix. Knoxville: University of Tennessee Press.

Korda, Michael. 2014. *Clouds of Glory: The Life and the Legend of Robert E. Lee*. New York: Harper.

Larkin, Jack. 1988. *The Reshaping of Everyday Life in America, 1790–1840*. New York: Harper Perennial.

Latour, Bruno. 1993. *We Have Never Been Modern*, translated by Catherine Porter. Cambridge, MA: Harvard University Press.

Laurant, Darrell. 2012. "Lifelong CVTC Resident Died at 94." March 7, 2012. *News & Advance* [Lynchburg] (website). https://newsadvance.com/news/local/darrell-laurant-lifelong-cvtc-resident-died-at-94/article_e168f53d-ae59-55fa-a602-4a0a676881f2.html.

Ledbetter, Jeremy, and Kristin Sharman. 2015. Transcripts of Interviews with Widows on Choices of Grave Commemoration. Manuscript in author's files.

Lefferts, Peter M. 2012. "Black US Army Bands and Their Bandmasters in World War I." August 21, 2012. Faculty Publications: School of Music. University of Nebraska–Lincoln Digital Commons. http://digitalcommons.unl.edu/musicfacpub/25.

Leila Janah Foundation. 2021. "Leila Janah, October 9, 1982–January 24, 2020." The Leila Janah Foundation (website). https://www.leilajanahfoundation.org/rememberingleila.

Lexico. 2021. "Posse." Lexcio. Accessed January 29, 2021. Powered by Oxford (website). https://www.lexico.com/en/definition/posse.

Little, M. Ruth. 1998. *Sticks and Stones: Three Centuries of North Carolina Markers.* Chapel Hill: University of North Carolina Press.

Lombardo, Paul A. 2008. *Three Generations, No Imbeciles: Eugenics, the Supreme Court, and Buck v. Bell.* Baltimore: Johns Hopkins University Press.

Longenecker, Stephen L. 2000. "The Narrow Path: Antislavery, Plainness, and the Mainstream." In *After the Backcountry: Rural Life in the Great Valley of Virginia 1800–1900,* edited by Kenneth E. Koons and Warren R. Hofstra, 185–93. Knoxville: University of Tennessee Press.

Louis Berger Group, Inc. 2009. "Data Recovery at the Lackey Cemetery (Site 44RB0509 and NDHR No. 081-7093) Interstate-81 NB Truck Climbing Lanes Rockbridge County, Virginia." Prepared for the Virginia Department of Transportation. Richmond: The Louis Berger Group, Inc.

Lynyrd Skynyrd. 1973. "Simple Man." *Pronounced 'Lĕh-'nérd 'Skin-'nérd* (studio album). Sounds of the South.

———. 1974. "Free Bird." (Single). MCA.

MacMaster, Richard K. 1997. "Religion, Migration, and Pluralism: A Shenandoah Valley Community, 1740–1790." In *Diversity and Accommodation: Essays on the Cultural Composition of the Virginia Frontier,* edited by Michael J. Puglisi, 82–98. Knoxville: University of Tennessee Press.

Mann, Chris Zithulele. 1979. "Cookhouse Station." Accessed January 8, 2021. Chris Mann (website). http://chrismann.co.za/poems/Cookhouse%20Station.pdf.

Márquez, Gabriel García. 1988. *Love in the Time of Cholera.* New York: Alfred A. Knopf.

Massanutten Amateur Radio Association (MARA). 1997. "ARES Supports Search for Lost Biker." *MARA-VARA Monitor,* February 1997, vol. 97:02. MARA (website). http://mara.ws/wp-content/uploads/2020/03/Monitor-9702.pdf.

———. 1998. "Our Sympathy." *MARA-VARA Monitor,* September 1998, vol. 98:09. MARA (website). http://mara.ws/wp-content/uploads/2020/03/Monitor-9809.pdf.

Mauss, Marcel. 1950. *The Gift: The Form and Reason for Exchange in Archaic Societies.* New York: W. W. Norton.

McCleary, Ann E. 2000. "Forging a Regional Identity: Development of Rural Vernacular Architecture in the Central Shenandoah Valley, 1790–1850." In *After the Backcountry: Rural Life in the Great Valley of Virginia 1800–1900,* edited by Kenneth E. Koons and Warren R. Hofstra, 92–110. Knoxville: University of Tennessee Press.

McCleskey, Turk (1997). "The Price of Conformity: Class, Ethnicity, and Local Authority on the Colonial Virginia Frontier." *Diversity and Accommodation: Essays on the Cultural Composition of the Virginia Frontier,* edited by Michael J. Puglisi, 213–226. Knoxville: University of Tennessee Press.

———. 2014. *The Road to Black Ned's Forge: A Story of Race, Sex, and Trade on the Colonial American Frontier.* Charlottesville: University of Virginia Press.

McClung, Anne. 2012. "Emily Jane Borgus Adamson." Black History Month 2016 in Lexington, Virginia. Accessed January 13, 2021. Historic Lexington Foundation (website). http://www.historiclexington.org/assets/adamson_emily_final.pdf.

McNair, David. 2006. "Historic Treatment: Staunton Commits to Western State." February 2, 2006. *The Hook* [Charlottesville] (website). http://www.readthehook.com/98359/architecture-historic-treatment-staunton-commits-western-state.

Mennonite Central Committee. n.d. "CPS Unit Number 052-01." Accessed January 14, 2021. The Civilian Public Service Story (website). http://civilianpublicservice.org/camps/52/1.

Mercer, Eric. 1975. *English Vernacular Houses: A Study of Traditional Farmhouses and Cottages.* London: Royal Commission on Historical Monuments England. HM Stationery Office.

Metcalfe, Gayden, and Charlotte Hays. 2005. *Being Dead is No Excuse: The Official Southern Ladies Guide to Hosting the Perfect Funeral.* New York: Hachette Books.

Metcalf, Peter, and Richard Huntington. 1991. *Celebrations of Death: The Anthropology of Mortuary Ritual,* Second Edition. Cambridge: Cambridge University Press.

Meyer, Richard E. 2003. "Pardon Me for Not Standing: Modern American Graveyard Humor." In *Of Corpse: Death and Humor in Folklore and Popular Culture,* edited by Peter Narváez, 140–68. Logan: Utah State University Press.

Miller, Daniel. 2010. *Stuff.* Cambridge, UK: Polity Press.

Miller, Lulu. 2020. *Why Fish Don't Exist: A Story of Loss, Love, and the Hidden Order of Life.* New York: Simon and Schuster.

Milne, A. A. 2009. *The House at Pooh Corner.* New York: Dutton's Children's Books.

Misztal, Barbara. 2000. *Informality: Social Theory and Contemporary Practice.* London: Routledge.

Mitchell, Robert D. 1997. "'From the Ground Up': Space, Place, and Diversity in Frontier Studies." In *Diversity and Accommodation: Essays on the Cultural Composition of the Virginia Frontier,* edited by Michael J. Puglisi, 23–52. Knoxville: University of Tennessee Press.

———. 2000. "The Settlement Fabric of the Shenandoah Valley, 1790–1860: Pattern, Process, and Structure." In *After the Backcountry: Rural Life in the Great Valley of Virginia 1800–1900,* edited by Kenneth E. Koons and Warren R. Hofstra, 34–47. Knoxville: University of Tennessee Press.

Mitford, Jessica. 1998. *The American Way of Death Revisited.* New York: Vintage Books.

Moore, Michael. 2016. "Five Reasons Why Trump Will Win." Accessed September 25, 2020. Michael Moore (website). https://michaelmoore.com/trumpwillwin/.

Morgan, Edmund S. 1975. *American Slavery, American Freedom: The Ordeal of Colonial Virginia.* New York: W. W. Norton.

Morten, Oren. 1920. *A History of Rockbridge County, Virginia.* Staunton, VA: McClure.

Mudde, Cas, and Cristobal Rovira Kaltwasser. 2017. *Populism: A Very Short Introduction.* Oxford: Oxford University Press.

Musselwhite, Paul. 2019. *Urban Dreams, Rural Commonwealth: The Rise of Plantation Society in the Chesapeake.* Chicago: University of Chicago Press.

Mytum, Harold. 2004. *Mortuary Monuments and Burial Grounds of the Historic Period.* New York: Kluwer Academic/Plenum.

National Cemetery Administration. 2019. "Staunton National Cemetery." U.S. Department of Veterans Affairs. March 1, 2019. National Cemetery Administration (website). https://www.cem.va.gov/cems/nchp/staunton.asp.

National Park Service. n.d. "Kirkpatrick's Company, Virginia Light Artillery." Accessed February 5, 2021. The Civil War, Battle Unit Details, Confederate Virginia Troops (website). https://www.nps.gov/civilwar/search-battle-units-detail.htm?battleUnitCode=CVAKIRKCAL.

National Personnel Records Center. 2019. "The 1973 Fire, National Personnel Records Center." Accessed January 4, 2019. National Archives (website). https://www.archives.gov/personnel-records-center/fire-1973.

Newport, Frank. 2017. "More U.S. Protestants Have No Specific Denominational Identity." July 18, 2017. *Gallup* (website). https://news.gallup.com/poll/214208/protestants-no-specific-denominational-identity.aspx.

Nora, Pierre. 2011. "From 'Reasons for the Current Upsurge in Memory.'" In *The Collective Memory Reader,* edited by Jeffrey K. Olick, Vered Vinitzky-Seroussi, and Daniel Levy, 437–41. Oxford: Oxford University Press.

O'Hara, Theodore. 1847. "The Bivouac of the Dead." U.S. Department of Veterans Affairs. April 17, 2015. National Cemetery Administration (website). https://www.cem.va.gov/history/BODpoem.asp.

O'Neal, Lonnae. 2020. "George Floyd's Mother Was Not There, but He Used Her as a Sacred Invocation." May 30, 2020. *National Geographic* (website). https://www.nationalgeographic.com/history/2020/05/george-floyds-mother-not-there-he-used-her-as-sacred-invocation/.

Oxford English Dictionary. 2020. OED Online. Accessed January 24, 2021. Oxford University Press (website). https://www.oed.com/.

Parker Pearson, Mike. 1999. *The Archaeology of Death and Burial.* Stroud: Sutton Publishing.

Pastor, Iris Ruth. 2017. "Big Deal—My Dad Was a Ball Turret Gunner in World War II." Posted November 11, 2015. Modified December 6, 2017. *Huffington Post, The Blog* (website). https://www.huffpost.com/entry/my-dad-was-a-ball-turret-gunner_b_8342420.

Pegram, Cynthia T. n.d. (a). "Home Has Always Been 'The Colony.'" Copy of manuscript from Central Virginia Training Center museum. In author's files.

———. n.d. (b). "Fight to Reclaim Spirit Ends in Book: Training Center Resident Emerges as Storyteller." Copy of manuscript from Central Virginia Training Center museum. In author's files.

Perzel, Edward S. 1993. "WWI: Boot Camp in Charlotte." State Library of North Carolina. NCpedia (website). https://www.ncpedia.org/wwi-boot-camp-charlotte.

Pesti, József. 1966. *On the Edge of the Volcano.* Translated by Lee Wray. Charlottesville, VA: Jarman Press.

Pezzoni, J. Daniel. 2001. National Register of Historic Places Registration Form, Cedar Hill Church and Cemeteries. Virginia Department of Historic Resources (website). https://www.dhr.virginia.gov/VLR_to_transfer/PDFNoms/081-5466_Cedar_Hill_Church_and_Cemeteries_2002_Final_Nomination.pdf.

Piston, William. 2021. "Jackson, Thomas J. 'Stonewall' (1824–1863)." *Encyclopedia Virginia.* Virginia Humanities (website). https://encyclopediavirginia.org/entries/jackson-thomas-j-stonewall-1824-1863/.

Price, Cynthia R. 1979. Review of *In Small Things Forgotten: An Archaeology of Early American Life* by James Deetz (1977). *American Anthropologist* New Series 81 (2):391–92. https://anthrosource.onlinelibrary.wiley.com/doi/epdf/10.1525/aa.1979.81.2.02a00430.

Putnam, Robert D. 2000. *Bowling Alone: The Collapse and Revival of American Community.* New York: Simon and Schuster.

Pynn, Calvin. 2014. "A Dedication to Someone I Only Knew for Thirty Minutes." May 7, 2014. *The Southwest Times* [VA] (website). https://www.southwesttimes.com/2014/05/a-dedication-to-someone-i-only-knew-for-30-minutes/.

Rafuse, Ethan S. 2011. "Stonewall Brigade." Virginia Humanities. Published November 6, 2008. Modified April 5, 2011. Encyclopedia Virginia (website). https://www.encyclopediavirginia.org/Stonewall_Brigade.

Rainville, Lynn. 2014. *Hidden History: African American Cemeteries in Central Virginia.* Charlottesville: University of Virginia Press.

————. 2018. *Virginia and the Great War: Mobilization, Supply and Combat, 1914–1919.* Jefferson, NC: McFarland.

Richmond Dispatch. 1879. "Death of Colonel John [T.] Anderson." September 18, 1879. *Richmond [VA] Dispatch.* Newspapers.com (website). https://www.newspapers.com/image/466370407/?article=c570629a-c842-44ac-9a96-fa8da28418c4&focus=0.16441941,0.6946756,0.30307767,0.96185344&xid=3355.

Rolling Stone. 2013. "Readers' Poll: The 10 Saddest Songs of All Time." October 2, 2013. *Rolling Stone* (website). https://www.rollingstone.com/music/music-lists/readers-poll-the-10-saddest-songs-of-all-time-10875/1-eric-clapton-tears-in-heaven-208829/.

Rosaldo, Renato. 2014. *The Day of Shelly's Death: The Poetry and Ethnography of Grief.* Durham: Duke University Press.

————. 2018. "Grief and a Headhunter's Rage." In *Death, Mourning, and Burial: A Cross-Cultural Reader*, edited by Antonius C. G. M. Robben, 156–66. Hoboken, NJ: John Wiley and Sons.

Rosaldo, Renato, Smadar Lavie, and Kirin Narayan. 1993. "Introduction: Creativity in Anthropology." In *Creativity/Anthropology*, edited by Smadar Lavie, Kirin Narayan, and Renato Rosaldo, 1–8. Ithaca, NY: Cornell University Press.

Rumi, Mawlana Jalal al-Din. 2011. "Someone Digging in the Ground." Translated by Coleman Barks. Accessed January 8, 2021. Rumi Days (website). http://rumidays.blogspot.com/2011/02/someone-digging-in-ground.html.

Sanborn Map Company. 1886. Sanborn Fire Insurance Map from Lexington, Independent Cities, Virginia, Sanborn Map Company, February 1886, (Washington, D.C.: Library of Congress Geography and Map Division), Library of Congress (website). http://hdl.loc.gov/loc.gmd/g3884lm.g3884lm_g090371886.

Sanders, Stuart W. 2003. "Poet Pens Monument with 'Bivouac of Dead.'" March 29, 2003. Arlington National Cemetery (website). http://www.arlingtoncemetery.net/bivouac.htm.

Santos, Carlos. 2008. "Mental Patients' Bare Tombstones Call Out." July 27, 2008. *Richmond Times-Dispatch* (website). https://richmond.com/news/mental-patients-bare-tombstones-call-out/article_60146ff7-0a74-56b1-8714-e26d6bbc14dc.html.

Sapir, J. David. 1977. "The Anatomy of Metaphor." In *The Social Use of Metaphor*, edited by J. David Sapir and J. Christopher Crocker, 3–32. Philadelphia: University of Pennsylvania Press.

Sapir, J. David and J. Christopher Crocker, eds. 1977. *The Social Use of Metaphor: Essays on the Anthropology of Rhetoric.* Philadelphia: University of Pennsylvania Press.

Schechner, Richard. 1993. "Ritual, Violence, and Creativity." In *Creativity/Anthropology*, edited by Smadar Lavie, Kirin Narayan, and Renato Rosaldo, 296–320. Ithaca, NY: Cornell University Press.

Scott, Emmett J. 1919. *Scott's Official History of the American Negro in the World War.* https://net.lib.byu.edu/estu/wwi/comment/scott/ScottTC.htm.

Seelinger, Matthew J. n.d. "Nightmare at the Chosin Reservoir." Accessed October 4, 2020. The Army Historical Foundation National Museum of the United States Army (website). https://armyhistory.org/nightmare-at-the-chosin-reservoir/.

Service, Robert W. 1912. "The Lost Master." In *Rhymes of a Rolling Stone.* Updated January 15, 2013. Project Gutenberg (website). https://www.gutenberg.org/files/309/309-h/309-h.htm.

Shepherdstown Register. 1918. "Notes of Our Soldiers." December 12, 1918. *Shepherdstown Register* [Shepherdstown, West Virginia]. Newspapers.com (website). https://www.newspapers.com/.

Shinedown. 2008. "What a Shame." *The Sound of Madness.* (studio album). Atlantic.

Shultz, Jason. 2020. "Suspect Arrested in Fatal Shooting outside Popeye's." July 14, 2020. *The Palm Beach Post* [Florida] (website). https://www.palmbeachpost.com/story/news/2020/07/14/suspect-arrested-in-fatal-shooting-outside-popeyersquos/112237844/.

Silver, Nate. 2008. "FAQ and Statement of Methodology." August 7, 2008. FiveThirtyEight (website). https://fivethirtyeight.com/features/frequently-asked-questions-last-revised/.

Simmons, J. Susanne Schramm. 1997. "Augusta County's Other Pioneers: The African American Presence in Frontier Augusta County." In *Diversity and Accommodation: Essays on the Cultural Composition of the Virginia Frontier,* edited by Michael J. Puglisi, 159–71. Knoxville: University of Tennessee Press.

Simmons, J. Susanne, and Nancy T. Sorrells. 2000. "Slave Hire and the Development of Slavery in Augusta County, Virginia." In *After the Backcountry: Rural Life in the Great Valley of Virginia 1800–1900,* edited by Kenneth E. Koons and Warren R. Hofstra, 169–84. Knoxville: University of Tennessee Press.

Sloane, David Charles. 1991. *The Last Great Necessity: Cemeteries in American History.* Baltimore: Johns Hopkins University Press.

Smith, Jeffrey E. 2020. "Till Death Keeps Us Apart: Segregated Cemeteries and Social Values in St. Louis, Missouri." In *Till Death Do Us Part: American Ethnic Cemeteries as Borders Uncrossed,* edited by Allan Amanik and Kami Fletcher, 157–81. Jackson: University Press of Mississippi.

Society for Humanistic Anthropology. n.d. "Welcome!" September 25, 2020. Society for Humanistic Anthropology (website). http://sha.americananthro.org/.

Sofka, Carla J., Kathleen R. Gilbert, and Illene Noppe Cupit, eds. 2012. *Death, Dying, and Grief in an Online Universe.* New York: Springer.

Sons of Confederate Veterans. 2019. Sons of Confederate Veterans (website). https://scv.org/.

Southern Poverty Law Center. n.d. "Ku Klux Klan." Accessed October 4, 2020. Southern Poverty Law Center (website). https://www.splcenter.org/fighting-hate/extremist-files/ideology/ku-klux-klan.

Spencer, Hawes. 2018. *Summer of Hate: Charlottesville, USA.* Charlottesville: University of Virginia Press.

Springate, Megan E. 2015. *Coffin Hardware in Nineteenth-Century America.* Walnut Creek, CA: Left Coast Press.

Staunton News-Leader. 1951. "Cpl. Charles Dameron." *Staunton News-Leader.* September 29, 1951. Newspapers.com (website), https://www.newspapers.com.

Steenburgh, Nicole. 2016. "Century-Old Cemetery a Piece of CVTC's History." May 25, 2016. *News and Advance* [Lynchburg, VA] (website). https://newsadvance.com/new_era_progress/news/century-old-cemetery-a-piece-of-cvtc-s-history/article_0544a24c-4c65-5db2-a160-b4ca25dec599.html.

Stetzer, Ed. 2015. "The Rapid Rise of Nondenominational Christianity." June 12, 2015. *Christianity Today: The Exchange* (website). https://www.christianitytoday.com/edstetzer/2015/june/rapid-rise-of-non-denominational-christianity-my-most-recen.html.

Strathern, Marilyn. 1988. *The Gender of the Gift: Problems with Women and Problems with Society in Melanesia.* Berkeley: University of California Press.

Tarlow, Sarah. 1999. *Bereavement and Commemoration: An Archaeology of Mortality.* Oxford, UK: Blackwell Publishers.

———. 2002a. "The Aesthetic Corpse in Nineteenth-Century Britain." In *Thinking Through the Body*, edited by Yannis Hamilakis, Mark Pluciennik, and Sarah Tarlow, 85–97. New York: Kluwer Academic/Plenum.

———. 2011. *Ritual, Belief and the Dead in Early Modern Ireland*. Cambridge: Cambridge University Press.

Thomas, Julian. 2002. "Archaeology's Humanism and the Materiality of the Body." In *Thinking through the Body*, edited by Yannis Hamilakis, Mark Pluciennik, and Sarah Tarlow, 29–45. New York: Kluwer Academic/Plenum.

Thornton, Tim. 2008. "Heirs Preserve 1,600 acres of Farmland." April 9, 2008. *Roanoke Times* (website). https://roanoke.com/news/heirs-preserve-acres-of-farmland /article_0403aeda-c9c1-572f-86ca-c64168670d72.html.

Tilley, Christopher, Webb Keane, Susanne Küchler, Mike Rowlands, and Patricia Spyer, eds. 2013. *Handbook of Material Culture*. London: Sage.

Tocqueville, Alexis de. (1840) 2004. *Democracy in America*. Translated by Arthur Goldhammer. New York: The Library of America, Penguin Putnam.

Together We Served. n.d. "Fitzgerald, Lyle W., Sgt." Accessed January 14, 2021. U.S. Air Force. Together We Served (website). https://airforce.togetherweserved.com /usaf/servlet/tws.webapp.WebApp?cmd=ShadowBoxProfile&type=Person &ID=185566.

Traynor, Robert. 2014. "Hearing Loss in the Trenches of World War I." April 1, 2014. Hearing Health and Technology Matters (website). https://hearinghealthmatters .org/hearinginternational/2014/hearing-loss-trenches-wwi/.

Trist, Alan. 1989. *The Water of Life: A Tale of the Grateful Dead*. Eugene, OR: Hulogos'i Communications.

Turner, Victor. (1969) 1995. *The Ritual Process: Structure and Anti-Structure*. New York: Aldine de Gruyter.

———. 1974. *Dramas, Fields, and Metaphors: Symbolic Action in Human Society*. Ithaca, NY: Cornell University Press.

———. 1982. *From Ritual to Theatre: The Human Seriousness of Play*. New York: PAJ Publications.

Tyler, Lyon Gardiner. 1920. *A Confederate Catechism, The War of 1861–1865*. Accessed January 16, 2021. Digital Archive, College of William and Mary (website). https:// digitalarchive.wm.edu/bitstream/handle/10288/17891/A_Confederate _Catechism_1920.pdf?sequence=1.

Ulrich, Laurel Thatcher. 1994. *A Midwife's Tale: The Life of Martha Ballard, Based on Her Diary, 1785–1812*. New York: Vintage Books.

United Daughters of the Confederacy. n.d.a. "Catechisms." United Daughters of the Confederacy (website). Accessed January 16, 2021. https://hqudc.org/cofc-catechisms/.

———. n.d.b. "Reaffirmation of the Objectives of the United Daughters of the Confederacy." United Daughters of the Confederacy (website). Accessed January 16, 2021. https://hqudc.org/.

US Census Bureau. 2011. "Augusta County, Virginia." Accessed September 24, 2020. State and County QuickFacts (website). https://www.webcitation.org/5zyvLjJVV?url =http://quickfacts.census.gov/qfd/states/51/51015.html.

Vagnone, Franklin D., and Deborah E. Ryan. 2016. *Anarchist's Guide to Historic House Museums*. Walnut Creek, CA: Left Coast Press.

Valley Amateur Radio Association (VARA). n.d. "Welcome to VARA, Inc." Accessed October 4, 2020. Valley Amateur Radio Association (website). http://varava.club/.

Van Gennep, Arnold. 2018. Extract from "The Rites of Passage (1909)." In *Death, Mourning, and Burial: A Cross-Cultural Reader*, edited by Antonius C. G. M. Robben, 34–43. Hoboken, NJ: John Wiley and Sons. (First published in French 1909. Translated by Monika B. Vizedom and Gabrielle L. Caffee in 1960. Chicago: University of Chicago Press.)

Virginia Civil War Trails. n.d. "Mill Creek Church: War Strikes Peaceful Homes and Fields." Historic Marker at Mill Creek Church of the Brethren. Photographic record created by the author July 16, 2015. Port Republic, Virginia.

Virginia WWI and WWII Commemoration Commission. 2020. "WWI: Historical Overview for the US & Virginia: The Commonwealth's Involvement in the First World War." Accessed January 8, 2021. Virginia WWI and WWII Commemoration Commission (website). https://www.virginiawwiandwwii.org/wwioverview.

Vlach, J. 1978. Review of *Folk Housing in Middle Virginia: A Structural Analysis of Historic Artifacts* by Henry Glassie (1975). *Western Folklore* 37 (2): 134–37. https://doi .org/10.2307/1499320.

Walker, William H., and Lisa J. Lucero. 2000. "The Depositional History of Ritual and Power." In *Agency in Archaeology*, edited by Marcia-Anne Dobres and John E. Robb, 130–47. London: Routledge.

Wallenstein, Peter. 2007. *Cradle of America: Four Centuries of Virginia History*. Lawrence: University Press of Kansas.

Waynesboro Parks and Recreation. n.d. "Serenity Garden." Accessed January 4, 2021. Waynesboro Parks and Recreation (website). https://www.waynesboro.va.us/186 /Serenity-Garden.

Wells, Camille. 2018. *Material Witnesses: Domestic Architecture and Plantation Landscapes in Early Virginia*. Charlottesville: University of Virginia Press.

White, Alison, and Ina Hofland. 2004a. "Buck v. Bell: The Test Case for Virginia's Eugenical Sterilization Act." February 13, 2004. Eugenics: Three Generations, No Imbeciles: Virginia, Eugenics and Buck v. Bell (website). Historical Collections at the Claude Moore Health Sciences Library, University of Virginia. http://exhibits .hsl.virginia.edu/eugenics/3-buckvbell/.

———. 2004b. "Eugenics in Virginia: Buck v. Bell and Forced Sterilization." February 13, 2004. Eugenics: Three Generations, No Imbeciles: Virginia, Eugenics and Buck v. Bell (website). Historical Collections at the Claude Moore Health Sciences Library, University of Virginia. http://exhibits.hsl.virginia.edu/eugenics/.

Whitman, Walt. 1855. *Leaves of Grass*. New York: Library of America.

Williams, Hank, Jr. 1981. "All My Rowdy Friends Have Settled Down." Single from The Pressure Is On. Elektra/Curb.

Williams, Richard G., Jr. 2007. "Black Cemetery Doubt Remains." September 29, 2007. *Washington Times* (website). https://www.washingtontimes.com/news/2007/sep /29/black-cemetery-doubt-remains/.

———. 2013. *Lexington, Virginia and the Civil War*. Charleston, SC: History Press.

Wilson, Andrew and Christy Millweard. 2019. "'Children of the Confederacy Creed' plaque officially removed from Capitol wall." January 13, 2019. KVUE (website). https://www.kvue.com/article/news/politics/children-of-the-confederacy-creed -plaque-officially-removed-from-capitol-wall/269-297cff57-6701-4168-958b -be6ff7498cfa.

Wineman, Bradford A. 2010. "Fort Lee." November 23, 2010. Virginia Humanities. Encyclopedia Virginia (website). https://www.encyclopediavirginia.org/Fort_Lee.

Wise, Scott. 2017. "Losing Millions of Dollars, Colonial Williamsburg Makes 'Difficult Decisions.'" June 30, 2017. CBS 6 WTVR-TV [Richmond, Virginia] (website). https://www.wtvr.com/2017/06/29/colonial-williamsburg-cuts/.

Wobst, H. Martin. 2000. "Agency in (Spite of) Material Culture." In *Agency in Archaeology*, edited by Marcia-Anne Dobres and John E. Robb, 40–50. London: Routledge.

Wolf, Eric R. 1964. *Anthropology*. New York: W. W. Norton.

Wolfe, Thomas. 1940. *You Can't Go Home Again*. New York: Harper & Row.

Wood, Alice Davis. 2004. *Dr. Francis T. Stribling and Moral Medicine: Curing the Insane at Virginia's Western State Hospital, 1836–1874*. Bloomington, IN: Xlibris.

Woody, Joan. 1999. "Roy Williams Remembers the Early Days of CVTC." *Perspective*, Spring edition. Central Virginia Training Center. Copy of manuscript from Central Virginia Training Center museum. In author's files.

Woolridge, Kay Ellen. 2012. *Family Memories*. Copy of manuscript from the Central Virginia Training Center museum. In author's files.

Worsham, Gibson. 1988. National Register of Historic Places Registration Form, Barnett House, Montgomery County. Accessed October 4, 2020. Virginia Department of Historic Resources (website). https://www.dhr.virginia.gov/VLR_to_transfer /PDFNoms/060-0440_Barnett_House_1989_Final_Nomination.pdf.

Wythepedia: The George Wythe Encyclopedia. 2017. February 24, 2017. "William Cabel, Jr." William and Mary Law Library (website). https://lawlibrary.wm.edu/wythepedia /index.php/William_Cabell,_Jr.

Yalom, Marilyn. 2008. *The American Resting Place: 400 Years of History through Our Cemeteries and Burial Grounds*. New York: Houghton Mifflin Harcourt.

Yentsch, Anne Elizabeth and Mary C. Beaudry, eds. 1992. *The Art and Mystery of Historical Archaeology: Essays in Honor of James Deetz*. Cleveland: CRC Press.

Zeger, Jill. 1997. "Rachel's Special Gift." *Register Herald* [Beckley, WV]. July 3, 1997. Newspaper Archive (website), https://newspaperarchive.com.

Zox, Daniel, and Shannon Lee Dawdy. n.d. "My Star, My Dust." Accessed October 4, 2020. International Documentary Association (website). https://www.documentary.org /project/my-star-my-dust.

INDEX

Abbott, David L., Sr., 150

Accident, drowning, 45–46, 177

Accident, falling, 48, 183

Accident, vehicle, 37, 38, 45, 149, 156, 171, 202, 211

Act to Preserve Racial Integrity, 66

Adams, Alvie M., 117–18

Adamson, Emily Borgus, 119

Aesop, 207–8

Affinity, 169, 171–82, 193

Afghanistan, 26, 42, 158

African American cemeteries, 5, 13, 26, 45, 49, 85–86, 90–92, 153, 169

African American Woman, Unknown, 101, 103–7

African Americans (Black), 12–13, 26, 36, 78, 84–86, 89–96, 98–102, 106–7, 119–20, 137, 139, 202, 218, 220, 222

African Americans, enslaved. See Enslaved people

African Burial Ground, New York City, 101–2

African Diaspora, 18–19

Agency, 87–89, 102

Albemarle County, 24, 42, 46, 119, 158, 170, 211

Albert (enslaved person), 137

Albright, Grace Irene, 49

Alexander, Mary Catherine, 163

Alexander, Marylin Evans, 103, 106

Alexander, Robert R., 36

Alger, Horatio, 87

Alienation, 14, 16, 27, 144, 164–68, 193, 218–19

"All My Rowdy Friends" (song), 43

Alleghany County, 2, 11, 146, 209

Allegheny Mountains, 2, 5, 116, 179

Almarode, Oscar T., 118

Alone Community Cemetery, 31, 81

Amateur Radio (Ham), 179–80

"Amazing Grace" (song), 103

American Anthropological Association, 17, 81

American Revolutionary War, 26–27, 88, 110, 112–16, 135, 180, 204

American Sign Language, 173–74

Amherst County, 57, 93, 117

Amy (enslaved person), 137

Ancient Jane. See African American Woman, Unknown

Anderson, Francis T., 131

Anderson, John T., 131

Anderson, Joseph Washington, 131–32

Angel Island, 94

Angels Rest Memorial Gardens, 159

Angel-versary, 154

Anglicans, 9

Animals on grave markers, 4, 15–17, 27, 149, 168, 175–77, 188, 191–93, 197–98, 206, 208. See also Cats on grave markers;

Cows on grave markers; Dogs on grave markers; Emu on grave markers

Anthropology (book), 17

Anthropology (definition), 16–17

Anthropology of Death, 220–22

Antislavery, 11, 47–48, 136

Ants, 27–28, 207–8

Appleby, Joyce Oldham, 166

Appomattox Courthouse, 62, 93, 131, 171

Arbery, Ahmaud, 100, 107

Architecture, 10, 14, 60, 62, 142, 144

Architecture on grave markers, 4, 15, 176, 190–91, 195, 197, 208–10

Arehart, John Steven, 163, 174–75

Arey, O. A., 46

Argenbright, Elizabeth, 49

Argenbright, George, 49

Ariès, Philippe, 44

Arlington House, 88

Arlington National Cemetery, 109

Armstrong, June Gayle, 209

Arrington, Martha, 36

Art and Mystery of Historical Archaeology, 29

Ashes, human. See Cremains

Ashwell, Alyse Sisson, 150

Asylum (band), 157

Atlanta Braves, 4, 178–79

Augusta County, 12–13, 40–42, 45–46, 48, 50, 85–86, 90, 113, 118, 126–28, 132–33, 135, 148, 150, 153, 155, 161, 173–74, 189, 199, 204, 212
Augusta Memorial Gardens, 31, 46, 148, 155
Auschwitz, 122, 126, 218
Autism, 58

Baber, Andrew, 154
Baber, Colleen, 153–54
Baby Lands, 46
Bakhtin, Mikhail, 165, 168, 213
Balkanization, 150, 218
Baltimore, 59
Baltimore Orioles, 178
Banister, Alexander L., 94–95
Bannister, Nancy, 94
Bannister, Thornton, 94
Baptists, 9, 31–32, 48, 91, 96–97, 103, 134, 144, 177
Barr, Brayden "D," 37
Baseball, 4, 157, 159, 198
Bath County, 5–6, 75, 90
Battle-Baptiste, Whitney, 18–19
Beals, Peleg, 134
Beaudry, Mary, 29
Beckley, West Virginia, 15, 31, 38, 172–73, 186
Beer, 158
Behar, Ruth, 20–21
Belgium, 121–22
Bell, Charles William, 132
Bell, John, 69–70
Bellah, Robert, 167
Beloved, 19
Benches in cemeteries, 3, 34, 145–49, 173, 186, 188
Bequeath, Solomon, 134
Berkeley, California, 14, 52
Berkeley, Edmund, 72, 74
Berkeley, Henry, 73
Berkeley, John Hill, 72–74, 79
Berkeley, Louise, 73
Berkeley, Susan, 73
Berkeley, Thomas N., 72–74, 79
Bernard, H. Russell, 17

Berry, Lloyd Y., 78–79
Beth Israel Cemetery, 122
Bethea, William Dallas, Jr., 155
Bethlehem Lutheran Church Cemetery, 13
Beverley, William Bradshaw, 160
Bible, 9, 25, 46, 50–51, 71–72, 74, 149, 179, 185, 188, 209, 213
Bickey, Cynthia, 172–73
Bickey, Daniel, 172–73
Birdsong, Loraine, 150
Birdsong, Simon, 150
Bishop, Elizabeth, 78
Bishopriggs, Delaney Faithe Crowder, 156
Black Feminist Archaeology, 19
Black Lives Matter, 137, 213, 218
Blackburn, Thomas, 60
Blacksburg, 7, 178
Bland County, 42, 121, 138, 153, 176, 187, 189, 191
Blindness, 63, 72, 74, 185
Blue Grass Cemetery, 7, 116
Blue Ridge Mountains, 5, 9–12, 24, 34, 179
Bolen, Lewis, 98
Bonar, Horatius, 185
Booth, John Wilkes, 138
Borgus, Brown Colbert, 118–20
Borgus, Laura Holloway, 119
Bortell, Remington Colt, 177
Boston Red Sox, 4
Botetourt County, 48, 131, 150, 154, 191
Bound to the Fire, 18
Bourdieu, Pierre, 218
Bourgois, Philippe, 89
Bowles, Billy Junior, 188
Bowling, 4, 60, 152, 167–68, 177
Bowling Alone, 167
Boyd, Clifford, 101, 103
Boyd, Donna, 101
Boyd, Mae E., 145, 147
Bradford, William, 18
Bradley, Benjamin A., 132
Branche, Shannon Briscoe, 188–89
Breeden, Brenda Kay, 175–76
Breeden, Charles Lee, 175–76

Breeden, Cody R., 150
Brennan, Kyle, 149–50, 157–58
Brethren Church, 9, 31–32, 47–48
Brickey Cemetery, 48, 150
Bridgewater, 39, 41, 45–46
Britton, Victoria, 149–150, 157
"Brokedown Palace" (song), 51–52
Brooks, Dorothy Lorene Carr, 199–200
Brown, Benjamin S., 45
Brown, Betty, 119
Brown, John G., 45
Brown, Michael, 100
Brown, Molly McCully, 77–78
Brown, Scott, 46
Bryant, Michael, 71
Buchanan, 188
Buck, Adeline Emma Harlow, 74
Buck, Carrie, 74–75, 77
Buck, Davy, 89
Buck, Vivian, 74
Buck v. Bell, 74–75
Buena Vista, 13, 191, 198–99
Buffalo Creek, 96
Buffalo Soldiers, 94–95
Buffett, Jimmy, 43
Bunton, Gerald Paul, 41–42
Burch, Faye Coleman, 198
Burch, Kenneth E., 197–98
Burial mounds, 7–8, 11

Cabaret, 174
Cabell, William, 53
California, 14, 29, 94
Calvary United Methodist Church Cemetery, 118, 122, 127, 189
Camp Greene, 117
Camp Lee, 98, 119
Camp Meade, 98
Campbell, Howard Lovin, 126–27
Campbell, Lula P., 127
Campbell, Talmage Lovin, 126–27
Cancer, 2, 37, 190, 220
Cancer Ward, 44
Carter, David Wayne, 76–77
Carter, Henry C., 134
Carter, Lucinda, 91
Carter, Peter, 91

Castile, Philando, 100
Catholics, 9, 31, 183
Cats on grave markers, 4, 168,
    175–76, 198, 206, 209
Catt, Michael, 114–15
Caul, Edward Yolanda, 45
Caul, Nancy Lee, 45
Cedar Hill Church Cemetery, 91, 96
Central Virginia Training Center. *See*
    State Colony for Epileptics and
    Feebleminded
Cerebral palsy, 38, 76, 78
Chancellorsville, Battle of, 84, 181
Characters, fictional on grave
    markers, 15–16, 157, 159, 195,
    200–201
Charleston, West Virginia, 95, 99
Charlottesville, 14, 24, 75, 183, 203,
    213–16
Chevrolet, 189
Children's burials, 46–49, 158–59
Chinese Army, 128
Chosin Reservoir, Battle of, 127–28
Christiansburg, 191
Church, Eric, 42
Civic Organizations, 177, 180, 190
Civil War, 2, 13, 26, 36, 47, 62, 83,
    86, 93, 94, 105, 109, 129–39,
    218
Civilian Conservation Corps, 125
Clapton, Conor, 48
Clapton, Eric, 48
Clark, James I., 156
Clark, William R., 93
Classic Horror Film Board, 200–201
Clatterbaugh, Dennis Lee, 195–96,
    200–201
Clatterbaugh, Doris, 200–201
Clatterbaugh, Jim, 200–201
Cleek, George W. Cemetery, 90
Cleek, Jane Gwin, 90
Cleek, John, 90
Cleek, Sallie Kime, 90
Clifton Forge, 45, 135
Cline, Patsy, 34
Clinton, Bill, 181–82
Clinton, Hillary, 21–22
Clowser, Hazel E., 210

Clowser, John T., 210
Coates, Ta-Nehisi, 106
Coffey, Martha Ann, 176–77
Coffey, Robert Lee, 176–77
Coiner, Joseph S., 132–33
Colbert, Brown, 119
Colbert, Mary, 119
Colbert, Robert, 119
Cold Harbor, Battle of, 72, 133
Cole, David, 76
Cole, Roy Albert, 138
College of William and Mary, 136
Collierstown Presbyterian Church
    Cemetery, 13, 45
Colored Grave Yard (Lexington), 85
Comer, Willis Jennings, 120
Communication between living
    and dead, 14, 17, 44, 141–43,
    145–47, 150–57, 159–62,
    192–93
Communitas, 206, 220
Community, immersion in, 5, 16,
    25, 27, 141–44, 159–62,
    166–68, 173, 193
Concentration camps, 120, 122–24
Confederate Army, 41, 62, 72–73,
    132, 171, 181
Confederate Catechisms, 136–37
Confederate Memorialization, 131,
    135–38, 218
Confederate States of America, 13,
    26–27, 83, 111 131, 135, 180
Confederate veterans' burials, 2,
    5, 27, 34, 73, 85–86, 129,
    131–35, 137–38, 169, 180–81,
    195
Consanguinity, 168–71, 193
Conscientious objectors, 124–26
Consumption, pulmonary. *See*
    Tuberculosis
"Convulsions Choir" (poem), 78
"Cookhouse Station" (poem), 29–30
Corbin, Michael Ray, 186–87
Corbin, Ray Borden, 186–87
COVID-19, 219–21
Cows on grave markers, 10, 185,
    191, 193, 209
Craig, Mary L., 79

Craig County, 48, 117, 150
Cremains, 34, 183, 192–93
Cross Keys, Battle of, 2, 47
Cullen, Lisa Takeuchi, 183
Cultural relativism, 79–80
Culture, definition, 16–17
Cummins, Beulah Jeanette Menefee,
    186
Cummins, Sam, 186
Custer, George Armstrong, 130
Cyrus (enslaved person), 137

Dafney ("Colored Servant"), 90
Dallas Cowboys, 16, 20, 164
Dameron, Charles W., 126
Dameron, Sarah, 126
Dameron, William, 126
Daniel, Jack, 36
Darwin, Charles, 68
Daughters of the American
    Revolution, 113–14
Davis, Dennis James, 197–98
Davis, John, 91
Davis, Phoebe Washington, 91
Davis-Vest, Bralyn Matthew, 156–57
Day, Douglas Turner, IV, 214
Dayton Cemetery, 32
De León, Jason, 20, 89
de Tocqueville, Alexis, 166–67
Dead End Kids, 157
Deafness, 63, 71, 95, 97, 99, 218
"Death of the Ball Turret Gunner"
    (poem), 121–22
Dedrick, Revonda H., 185
Dedrick, Virgil, 185
Deer on grave markers, 4, 7, 145,
    186, 191, 197–98, 206, 208–9
Deetz, James, 14, 16–18, 29, 40, 52,
    142–45, 162, 218
Deetz, Kelley Fanto, 18
Deetz, Patricia Scott, 18
Defective (eugenics), 66–68, 71, 74,
    81, 220
DeJarnette, Chertsey, 75
DeJarnette, Joseph, 65–68, 74–75,
    79
DeLaney, Theodore Carter, 103–5
Delirium, 64

Democracy in America, 166–67
Democrats, 22, 181–82
Depot Brigade, 98, 119
DePoy, Clint, 190–91
DePoy, James R., 190–91
DePoy, Mary Elizabeth, 190–91
Detamore, Carrie Buck. *See* Buck, Carrie
Detamore, Charles A., 75
DeWitt, Lew, 34
Diamond Hill, 96, 99
Dickerson, Alley, 163
Dickerson, Eugene, 163
Diener, Albert, 122
Diener, Sari, 122
Diphtheria, 47
Disability, 57, 63, 68, 72, 74, 76, 78, 81
Disappointed love, 62, 74
Dissipation, 64
Dogs on grave markers, 4, 159, 176–77, 188, 191–92, 197–98
Do-It-Yourself (DIY), 202, 205, 215–16, 218
Dold, James A., 133
Donne, John, 167
Douglas, James A., 78–79
Dove, William, 134
Draft, Military. *See* Selective Service
Drunkenness. *See* Intemperance
Dublin Cemetery, 145
DuBois, W. E. B., 19
Duck Run Natural Cemetery, 34
Dumont, Louis, 166
Dunkers, 9, 11
Dunovant, Adelia A., 136–37
DuPont Plant, 40, 126

Earhart, Brad, 188
Earhart, Jeffrey, 177
Early, Jubal, 72, 130
Early, Reginald, 103
East End Cemetery, 34, 197
Eaton, Emmanuel, 46
Ebenezer Methodist Church Cemetery, 86
Echols, John, 169
Echols, John Percy, 169

Education and eugenics, 67, 69–70
808 Pioneer Infantry, 98
Einstein, Albert, 89
Elizabeth, Queen I, 36
Elk Run Cemetery, 31, 135, 148, 175–76
Elkton, 31, 135, 148, 150, 175–76, 188–89
Ellinger, Garland, 212
Ellinger, Shirley, 212
Emma (enslaved person), 137
Emotion, 20–21
Emu on grave markers, 15, 17, 175–76, 206
England, 9–12, 112
Enslaved people (African Americans), 11–12, 18–19, 26, 36, 47–48, 53, 64, 85, 88–94, 96, 101, 105, 119, 136–37, 139
Entsminger, Jimmy, 39
Epilepsy, 54, 63, 66–67, 78
Episcopalian, 32, 42, 46
Essays on Individualism, 166
Eugenics, 13, 25, 65–72, 74–75, 79, 196, 218
Europe, 44, 111, 112, 116–17, 131, 141–43, 160, 164–66, 171
Evans, David Gray, 99
Evans, Della, 99
Evans, Thelma Pettigrew, 99
Evergreen Cemetery (Lexington), 30, 36, 84–85, 93

Fairfield, 8, 49, 132
Fallen Timber, Battle of, 170
Falling Spring Presbyterian Church Cemetery, 86–87, 112–13, 131
Feeblemindedness, 25, 64, 67–69, 74, 218–19
Ferguson, Frances, 122
Field, Eugene, 46–47
Fielding, Eppa, 86
Fielding, Judy H. Cowardin, 179–80
Fielding, Wilson L., 179–80
Fincastle, 135
Fincastle Presbyterian Church Cemetery, 131
Find a Grave, 58, 75, 157, 159–60

Finley, George W., 134
Finley, William W., 133
Fire, cause of death, 45, 217
First Baptist Church, Lexington, 91, 96–97, 103
Fisher, Ulysses Grant, 93
Fishersville, 85–86, 128, 130, 133
Fishersville United Methodist Church, 85
Fishing. *See* Hunting and fishing on grave markers
Fitzgerald, Carolyn Hite, 174–75
Fitzgerald, Hansford, 121
Fitzgerald, Lyle W., 121–22
Fitzgerald, Mary Julia, 121
Fitzgerald, Mrs. Matthew (Inez C.), 41
FiveThirtyEight, 21–22
Fix, Joe M., II, 178
Fix, Melinda, 209
Fix, Thomas, 209
Flag, American, 35, 86, 134–35, 138, 145, 154
Flag, Confederate, 26–27, 131, 135, 137–38, 180, 213
Flag, welcome, 145–47, 172–73
Fletcher, Kami, 101
Flipping, John, 86
Florida, 20, 42
Flournoy, Ann Carrington Cabell, 53–57, 79
Flournoy, John James, 53
Flournoy, Mitchell Wayne, 138
Flournoy, Russell "Cliff" Clifton, 138
Flournoy, Thomas Stanhope, 53
Flournoy, William C., 53
"Flowers on the Wall" (song), 34
Floyd, George, 100–101
Folk Housing in Middle Virginia, 144
Forbes, Sarah Anne, 49
Ford, James, 134
Ford, James A., 45
Fort Delaware, 181
Fort Duncan, 114
Fort Laurens, 114
Fort McDowell, 94
Fort McIntosh, 114
Fort Riley, 94

Fort Sumpter, 138
Foucault, Michel, 63
Fowler, Chris, 165
France, 9, 11, 63–64, 71, 98, 114,
    117–18, 120–21, 128
Franklin, Smiley, 96
Frederick County, 5
"Free Bird" (song), 208
Freedman's Cemetery, Dallas, 92
French and Indian War, 9, 26, 110,
    170
Friedens Church Cemetery, 31
Front Royal, 145, 147, 154
Frost, Consider, 35
Frozen Chosin, 127–28
Futch, Mark Richard, 209

Gaines Mill, Battle of, 134
Gainsback, Carl Michael, 182–83
Galton, Francis, 68
Gangrene, 59
Gangwer, Robert Leroy, 120
Garner, Eric, 100
Garner, Margaret, 19
General Assembly, Virginia, 41, 53,
    75, 131
Genizah, 31
George (enslaved person), 137
George, Jeremiah Ifiok, 46
George Mason University, 182
Germany, 9–11, 31, 42, 63, 66–67,
    70, 75
Gettysburg, Battle of, 72, 171, 181
Gibson, John Alexander, 91–92
Gibson, John Beard, 91–92
Gibson-Lackey Cemetery, 91–92
Gift exchange between living and
    dead, 141, 150–51, 159–62
Gifts on graves, 17, 25, 145–49,
    152–55, 157–59, 215
Giles County, 138, 159, 188, 198
Gill, Vince, 42
Gilmore, A. K., 134
Glasgow, 86
Glassie, Henry, 14, 16–18, 21–22,
    89, 111–12, 142, 144, 218
Glebe Burying Ground, 50, 161, 204
Godwin Cemetery, 135

Golf, 37, 157
Gooch, Mitchell Douglas, 117
Gooch, Richard, 117
Gooch, Signora, 117
Gooch, William, 9, 114
Good, Wanda F., 186
Gordon, Clarence Henry, 186
Gordon, Mary Lou Little, 186
Goshen, 192–93
Gough, Hiram, 54, 59
Gould, Stephen Jay, 89
Graber, Shari Lynn, 171
Grady, Robert B., 43
Grand United Order of Oddfellows,
    94, 96
Grant, Ulysses S., 93, 130
Grasshopper, 27–28, 207–8
Grateful Dead (band), 15, 51–52
"Grateful Dead" (folktale), 110–11
Grave shafts, 142–43
Great War. See World War I
Green, Brian, 60
Green cemeteries. See Natural
    cemeteries
Green Hill Cemetery, 13, 198–99
Greenville, 48, 128
Greenwood Ames Cemetery, 39
Gregory, Charles A., 127
Grigsby, Elizabeth, 112
Grigsby, John, 112–13
"Growing Older but Not Up"
    (song), 43

Haight, Gardiner M., 178
Hall, Donald, 173
Hall, Samuel, 42
Hamilton, James W., 133
Hamlet, 143
Hancock, Andrew G., 120–21
Hanes, Leigh Buckner, 34–35
Hanna, Matthew, 89
Hanover County, 72, 74
Hard study, 26, 61–62
Hardin, Ernest Allen, 145
Harley Davidson, 149, 163, 168,
    183, 188, 196
Harrisonburg, 7, 24, 45, 48, 79,
    124–25, 179

Harry Potter and the Sorcerer's Stone, 159
Hart, Teresa Downey, 188–89
Hartman, Alfred D., 45
Hartman, Christian, 47–48
Hartman, Elizabeth Diehl, 47–48
Hartman, Isaac, 47
Hartman, John, 47
Hartman, Mary, 47
Hartman, Peter, 47
Hartman, Samuel, 47
Haught, Peter, 114–16
Haught, Sarah Jones, 114–15
Heard, Coye, 137
Heart failure, 69
Heaven, 2, 11, 33, 38, 42–43, 46,
    48–49, 124, 150, 156–57, 159,
    161, 165, 173, 185, 211
Hebrew cemeteries, 31, 50, 122–24
Hegazy, Amira, 220–23
Hell, 165
Hemings, Elizabeth, 119
Henley, Joseph Eugene "Jody," 37
Henry, John C., 207–8
Hensley, Gladys, 185
Hensley, Stuart B., Jr., 185
Herman, Harold, 173–74
Herman, Linde Hayen, 173–74
Herrald, Lional August, 37–39
Herring, Ella, 39
Herring, Florence, 39
Herring, Margaret Back, 39
Herring, Philander, 39–41
Hetty (enslaved person), 137
Hewett, T. Wayne, 174
Heyer, Heather, 215
Highland County, 5–7, 116, 190–91
Hines, Fannie C., 54–56, 73, 79
Hines, John, 54
Hines, Mary, 54
Hinkle, Margaret Jane, 59
Hinkle, Peter, 59
Hinson, Kaitlyn J., 46
Hinton, Preston, 98
Hinton, William Henry, 98
Hiroshima, 120, 126, 218
Hirshfield, Jane, 36
Hite, Becky, 186
Hite, Benny, 186

Hite, George R., 181–82
Hitler, Adolf, 66–67
Holidays, dead involved in, 147, 152–54, 156
Holmes, Jane E., 93
Holmes, Oliver Wendell, 75
Holmes, W. H., 93
Holocaust, 21, 26, 120, 122–24
Home, gravesites as, 145–50, 192–93
Homer, 184–85
Horace, 134
Horses, 62, 84, 149, 193, 198
Horseshoes, 15, 197–98
Hostetter, Garlet E., 198
Hostetter, Phyllis L., 198
Hour of Our Death, 44
Humanistic Anthropology, 17–20
Humble, Charles, 93
Humor, 18, 25, 27, 162, 196–97, 212–13, 217
Humphries, Aubrey Russell, Jr., 212
Humphries, Beverly Ann, 212
Humphries, Eunice Henson, 189, 199
Humphries, James Lewis, 189, 199
Hunter, David, 130
Hunting and fishing on grave markers, 150, 197, 208–9, 212

Identity. *See* Personhood
Idiocy, 67, 69
Igbo Language, 31
Iliad, 184–85
Imbecility, 64, 66, 68, 74–75
In Small Things Forgotten, 14, 144
Indian Wars. *See* French and Indian War
Individualism, 14, 16, 27, 142–45, 164–67
Indoor Air Quality Network, 163–64
Influenza, 117, 217
Informality, 25, 27, 196, 210–12
Insanity, 26, 54, 57, 59, 61, 63–65, 67–68, 71
Intemperance, 64–66, 71
Iraq, 26, 110, 158
Ireland, 9, 63, 150, 157–58, 165

Iroquois Confederacy, 8
"It Was Like This" (poem), 36
Italy, 120, 124, 128

Jackson, Andrew, 19
Jackson, James, 93
Jackson, John, 93
Jackson, Kizzie Anna, 93
Jackson, Lucy, 93
Jackson, Thomas J., 93
Jackson, Thomas J. Stonewall, 34, 84, 88, 99, 106, 131, 137–38, 181, 203, 218
James Madison University, 178
James River Valley, 5
Jamestown, 12
Janah, Leila, 89
Jarrell, Randall, 121–22
Jeep, 168, 187–89, 198
Jefferson, Thomas, 60, 106, 119
Jenkins, Donald C., 187
Jenkins, Ernest N., 79
Jenkins, Shelvy M., 187
Jerry ("colored servant"), 90
Jesus, 15, 31, 36, 42, 46, 49, 51, 74, 112, 133, 149–50, 179, 185, 197–98
Jewish people, 26, 31, 122–24, 202, 213
Jim Crow, 105, 139
Jonnhaty, 8
Jonontore, 8
Jordan, Harvey, 66
Julius Caesar, 36

Kansas, 94
Keister, Joseph E., 45
Kellogg, John Harvey, 71–72
Kelly, Gigi, 195
Kelly, Joe, 195
Kenney, Brian K., 51–52
Kercheval, Samuel, 8
Kibler, Billy, 185
Kibler, Harry E., Jr., 138
King, Joyce Harman, 189
King, Thomas M., 189
Kinship, 169–71, 198–201. *See also* Affinity; Consanguinity

Kirkpatrick, Andrew, 31
Kiser, Carrie Bernice, 45–46
Klinger, Valentine, 35
Knick Cemetery, 31, 39
Knick, Hugh T., 39
Knick, Rachel Lula, 39
Knights of Phythias, 94
Knox, John, 169
Korean War, 26, 37, 110, 126–28, 149, 160, 179, 207
Kroeber, Alfred L., 17
Ku Klux Klan, 106, 170–71, 202, 213–14
Kudro, Hayley Elizabeth, 2–3

Lackey, Georgeanna, 91
Lackey, Phebe, 91
Lackey, William, 91
Land, personhood and, 190–93
Land of Open Graves, 20, 89
Landscape scenes on grave markers, 149, 168, 188, 191, 208–9
Lanzmann, Claude, 21
Last words, 36–37, 43, 138
Latin, 26, 31, 169, 205
Laughlin, Harry, 66
Laughter, 27, 162, 212–13
Leaves of Grass, 217
Lee, Anne Hill Carter, 88
Lee, Henry III, 88
Lee, Mary Anna Randolph Custis, 88
Lee, Robert E., 34, 83–84, 88, 93, 106, 130–31, 137, 203
Lee Chapel. *See* University Chapel, Washington and Lee
Lee Family Mausoleum, 83
Lee Highway, 130
Legislature of Virginia. *See* General Assembly, Virginia
Lemon, Larry, 186
Lemon, Linda, 186
Lescalleet, Mary Margaret, 176
Levi-Strauss, Claude, 112, 126
Lewis, James, 85
Lexington, 10, 12, 31, 33–34, 36, 41, 49, 76, 83–85, 89, 91, 93–106, 117, 119, 130, 137–38, 218, 221

Lexington, City of, Government, 31, 85, 103
Lexington Police Department, 103
Liberia, 119
Liberty Hall Volunteers, 131
Library of Virginia, 57–58
Life Gem, 183
Lights, solar-powered, 2, 32–33, 145, 147, 154, 159
Liminal, 205–6, 212
Liminoid, 206–8, 212
Lincoln, Abraham, 138
Lindamood, Lewis Allen, 160–61
Lindamood, Wingini Ferraba Dean, 160–61
Linkhous, William J., 178
Little Sorrel, 84
Loan, Clinton Dale, 150
Lockridge, G. W. Billy, 161
Lockridge, Goldie L. Snyder, 161–62
Lone Star Cemetery, 209
Longenecker, Stephen, 9
Lorencki, Nancy Ann, 179
Lorre, Chuck, 161
Los Angeles Dodgers, 178
Lost Cause, 27, 135–38
"Lost Master" (poem), 41–42
Lucas, Ronald Lee, 185
Lunsford, Thomas Preston, II, 211–12
Luray, 8
Lutherans, 13, 31, 32, 48, 135, 154
Lylburn Downing School, 106
Lyle, Dale, 192–93
Lyle, Henry Mason, 192–93
Lynchburg, 26, 68, 93
Lynyrd Skynyrd, 208

Mack, Louise, 93
Mack, Warner, 93
Madison, Elizabeth, 91
Madison, Henry, 91
Madness and Civilization, 63
Magary, George, 35
Malnutrition, 54, 62–63, 69. See also Marasmus; Pellagra
Manassas, First Battle of, 45, 132, 181

Manassas, Second Battle of, 133, 171
Mania, 54, 65, 67–68, 71
Mann, Chris, 29–30, 36–37
Marasmus, 54, 62–63
Márquez, Gabriel García, 42
Marshall, Linda J., 176
Marshall, Plesant, 169
Marshall, Roberta Clark, 169
Marshall, Thomas W., 176
Martin, Jane, 212
Martin, Ralph T., 150, 152
Martin, Trayvon, 100
Mary (enslaved person), 11
Mary Baldwin College, 179
Maryland, 10, 98, 125, 141–42, 162, 170
Mason, Russell Leroy "Rusty," 34
Massachusetts, 29
Masturbation, 26, 72
Material culture, 14, 16, 78, 142–44, 165, 175, 183–85, 193, 218
Materiality, 16, 184, 189
Matsuo Bashō, 42
McComb, William Luther, 133
McCown, Samuel, 208
McDowell, John, 8–9, 11
McDowell Cemetery, 8, 49, 132
McGee, Elizabeth, 222
McGhee, Margaret, 59–60
McGraw, Rachel Elaine, 37–39
McGuffin, John Bolar, 132
Meadow Natural Burial Ground, 33–34
Meadows, Kevin, 189
Meadows, Laura, 189
Melancholia, 62, 64, 68
Memento mori, 14, 16, 27, 31, 141–43, 160–62
Memorials, spontaneous, 202–3
"Mende's Law" (poem), 65–66
Mennonites, 9, 31–32, 46, 49
Merchant, Eliza, 93
Merica, Millar V., Jr., 186
Metaphors for death, 44–45, 49–52
Methodists, 9, 31–32, 37, 48, 49, 85–86, 103–4, 118, 122, 126–27, 150, 160, 176, 179, 182, 188–89, 209–10

Metonymy, 169, 184–93
Mexican-American War, 109
Mill Creek Church of the Brethren, 47
Millboro, 6
Miller, Fern, 94
Miller, Rufus, 94
Miller, Ruth Hall, 176
Milne, A. A., 38
Miss Jane. See African American Woman, Unknown
Mississippi, 131–32
Mitral regurgitation, 71
Modernity, 164–67, 193
Monacan, 7
Monongalia County, West Virginia, 114
Monsters from the Vault, 195–96, 200–201
Montgomery County, 185
Monticello, 119
Monticello Memorial Park, 158, 170
Moore, Cindy J., 188
Moore, John Poague, 131
Moore, Michael, 22
Moose Lodge, 177
Moral medicine, 60, 62, 64–65, 79
Morning Star Temple Hill Cemetery, 121, 153, 187
Morrison, Toni, 19
"Mortality" (poem), 169
Mosser, Rhonda Joann, 178
Mount Hebron Cemetery, 48, 51, 129, 184
Mount Lydia Church Cemetery, 86
Mounted Service School Division, 94
Moyer, Chanel, 176
Moyer, Linda, 176
Mt. Carmel Presbyterian Church Cemetery, 42, 132, 150, 199
Mt. Hermon Cemetery, 173–74
Murat, 91
Murder, 42, 45, 202
Museums, 18, 83–84, 203
Musical instruments on grave markers, 149–50, 168, 179
Muslims, 31, 202

NASCAR, 15, 178–79, 188, 198
National Cathedral, 34
National Geographic, 14
Native Americans, 7–9, 11–12, 114–16, 171, 220
Natural cemeteries, 34
Nazis, 13, 26, 66, 75
Neighbours, Kathleen O., 155
Neil, Bonnie S., 4
Netherlands, 9, 170
New England, 14, 143–45
New Jersey, 35
New Market, Battle of, 130
New River Valley, 5
New York (State), 8
New York City, 48, 101–2, 134, 183–84
New York Times, 181–82
New York Yankees, 178
Newsome, Bree, 213
Nicely, Peter M, 135
Nicholas, William Roy, 116
Nichols, India, 104
Nicknames, 27, 211–12
Nida, Bettie Jane, 209–10
Nida, Leonard Ray, Jr., 211
Nida, Leonard Ray, Sr., 209–10
Niece, Marie Letty, 184–85
Nike, 16
92nd Division, 98
Nininger, Mayo Scott, 179
Nolan, Hugh, 112
Nondenominational churches, 203
Nora, Pierre, 202
North Carolina, 11, 117, 171
North Korea, 127–28
Northern Ireland, 9, 21, 35, 112
Nostradamus, 36

Oak Grove Cemetery, 41, 84, 89
Oakland, California, 94
Oakwood Cemetery, 75
Obama, Barack, 22
Oberlin College, 35
O'Hara, Theodore, 109
Ohio, 22, 35, 114, 134
On the Edge of the Volcano, 185
Onanism. *See* Masturbation

O'Neal, Lonnae, 100–101
Oneida, 8
Onondaga, 8
Orientation of graves, 49–50, 89

Pacifism, 47–48
Page County, 36, 176, 185
Paint Bank, 117
"Painted Bed, The" (poem), 173
Palatinate, 9
Parker, Alison, 203
Parker, Deborah Ann, 163
Parker Pearson, Mike, 12, 131
Patrie, Hannah R., 171
Patrie, J. M., 171
Patterson, Anthony W., 209
Pauley, Earl G., 120
Pauley, Harry Edward, Sr., 187
Paxton, John, 113
Paxton, Phoebe Alexander, 113
Pellagra, 54, 68
Pence, Allie Beverley, 134
Pence, David, 134
Pence, Helen L., 177
Pence, Martin R., 177
Pennsylvania, 8–11, 22, 35, 114
Perdue, Jeffery Wade, 138
Periwinkle, 87, 101
Personhood, 13, 164–65, 168–69, 187, 191–93, 196, 218
Pesti, Jóseph, 185
Pesti, Lee Elizabeth, 185
Petersburg, 98, 119, 132, 171
Peterson, Albert Stanley, 212
Petrie, Samuel I., 171
Petry, Samuel, 171
Petry, Susannah, 171
Pets on grave markers, 175–77. *See also* Animals on grave markers; Cats on grave markers; Cows on grave markers; Dogs on grave markers; Emu on grave markers
Pettigrew, Alfred W., 95–96
Pettigrew, Frances Louisa, 95–96
Pettigrew, James (Wonderful), 99
Pettigrew, Johnson, Jr., 99
Pettigrew, Johnson A., Sr., 96–97, 99

Pettigrew, Johnston. *See* Pettigrew, Johnson A., Sr.
Pettigrew, Virginia C. Franklin, 96
Pettigrew, Wonderful Price, 95–101, 106–7, 218
Phillips, James M., 179
Photographs on gravesites, 126–27, 138, 145, 147, 152–53, 156, 176–78, 189, 209, 211
Pickup trucks, 2, 15, 149, 189, 192, 195, 197–98
Piedmont, 2, 5, 12, 144
Pilgrims, 154, 164, 171
Pines Chapel Presbyterian Church Cemetery, 128
Pioneer Infantry Regiment, 98, 117
Pittsburg Steelers, 168, 178
Plants, 52, 87, 101, 145, 221–23
Pleasants, Alfred W., 93
Pleasants, Christopher Columbus, 171
Pleurisy, 69
Pneumonia, 69, 73
Poague, James Wilson, 131
Pokomoke River, 125
Poland, 124
Polio, 70
Populism, 28, 201–4, 206–16, 212, 218
Porches, 37, 130, 145–48, 184, 190, 192, 196, 219
Port Republic, Battle of, 2, 35
Porter, John Warren, 171
Potomac River, 5
Poverty, 67, 89, 105, 136
Presbyterians, 9–10, 13, 31–32, 41–42, 49–50, 86–87, 89–90, 112–13, 128, 131–34, 150, 152, 161–62, 176, 193, 198–99, 209, 212
Presidential election of 2016, 5, 21–22, 207
Price, Glen Allen, 160
Price Edward County, 53
Priddy, Albert, 68
Promiscuity, 74, 76
Prospect Hill Cemetery, 145, 147, 154

Protestants, 9, 11, 32, 49, 114, 143, 165, 203
Pseudonyms, use of, 58
Pulaski County, 49, 122–23, 127, 160, 207
Purgatory, 165–66
Putnam, Robert D., 167–68, 201–2

Quakers, 9, 11
Qualitative research, 21–22, 24–25
Quillin, Maria, 103–4

Radford University, 101, 103
Rainville, Lynn, 116
Randolph, Margaret C., 41
Randolph, William H., 134
Randolph Street United Methodist Church, 103–4
Rauch, Jay Edwin, 171
Reagan, Ronald, 22
Reciprocity, 157, 159, 168, 201. See also Gift exchange between living and dead
Redd, Pricilla Kern, 209–10
Religious excitement, 26, 61–62
Renaissance, 142, 165
Republicans, 181
"Rest High on the Mountain" (song), 42
Resurrection, 49–50, 166
Rice, Tamir, 100
Richardson Park, 106
Richmond, 24, 58, 134
Rites of Passage (book), 205
Rites of passage, 205–6, 219–20
Ritter, David Charles, 179
Riverheads, 121–22
Riverview Cemetery, 32, 151, 155–56, 176, 208
Roanoke, 7, 24, 35, 122–24, 182, 192, 203
Roanoke River Valley, 5
Robinson, Emily, 96
Robinson, Mary E., 93
Rock Creek Cemetery, 181–82
Rockbridge County, 8, 10–13, 31, 34, 39, 41–42, 45, 49–50, 81, 86–87, 91, 94, 96, 103, 112–13, 117, 130–32, 152, 158, 191–92, 197–99
Rockbridge County Courthouse, 101–3
Rockbridge County government, 103
Rockingham County, 31–32, 34, 40, 47, 112–113, 124, 146, 176, 180, 190, 198, 203
Rodriquez-Loya, Jose Martin, 46
Rogers, Michelle Yvonne, 146
Romney, Mitt, 22
Ronald Reagan, 134
Roosters, 163, 174–75

Salem, 192
Salisbury, Hubert William, 86
Sambrook, Larry, 163–164
Sanborn Map Company, 102
Sanders, Bernie, 22
Sanders, Bobby G., 198
Sanger, Joel, 171
Sanger, Sarah, 171
Saponi, 7
Sarver, Ronald L., 48
Schonberg, Jeff, 89
Schroers, Chloe Marie, 48
Schroers, Krystle Lynn, 48
Schroers, Lindsey Jean, 48
Schuler, Ken, 163
Schwartz, Erin, 104
Scotland, 9, 204
Scots Irish, 10–11, 41, 112
Secularization, 197–201
Seekford, John David, 46–47
Segregation, 13, 85, 89, 98, 105
Selective Service, 89, 97–98, 116–21, 124
Seminole War, 170
Seneca, 3
Senger, Elizabeth, 171
Senger, Jacob, 171
September 11, 2001, 183–84
Serenity Garden, 37
Service, Robert, 41
Services of Supplies Units, 98
Settlement, European, 7–12, 113–14, 171, 204

Sexual Derangement, 71–72
Sharon Union Baptist Church Cemetery, 135, 146
Sheffer, Ricky Lee, 138
Shelton, Billy, 185
Shemariah Presbyterian Church Cemetery, 41
Shenandoah County, 46–47, 130, 138
Shenandoah River, 5
Shenandoah Valley, 5, 8, 10, 130, 180
Sheridan, Philip, 130
Shifflett, Jason Lee, 211–12
Shifflett, Robert Lee, 211
Shinedown, 42
Shirley Plantation, 88
Shoah, 21
Shooting, cause of death, 40, 42, 84, 95, 99, 128, 138, 218
Showalter, Mary E. Witmer, 124–25
Showalter, Nathan E., 124–25
Simmerman, James Landon, 198
"Simple Man" (song), 208
Simpson, James, 35
Sin, 42, 71–72, 74, 77
Singleton, W. G., 115
"Sinners Like Me" (song), 42
Slavery. See Enslaved people
Smith, Barbara Gray Armistead, 138
Smith, Julia, 93
Smith, Luly Walker, 90
Smith, Michael L., Sr., 178
Smith, Milton, 93
Smith, Todd Aaron, 15
Smith, William Harrington, Jr., 138
Smith, Winfred Lee, 128
Snell, Ann Houston, 179
Snowmen, 163, 174–75
Snyder, Andrew Hale, 138
Social capital, 168, 201–2, 210, 218
Society for Humanistic Anthropology, 17
Softball, 4
Soil Conservation Service, 125
Solzhenitsyn, Aleksandr, 44
Sons of Confederate Veterans, 135–37, 180

Sons of the American Revolution, 112–14, 116, 204

South Africa, 29

South Korea, 128

South River, 130

Southern Cross of Honor, 27, 86, 131, 135, 137, 180

Southwest Virginia Veterans Cemetery, 127, 160, 179, 207–8

Spanish American War, 110

Speck, William R., 41

Spelling of names, 171

Spencer, Titus Croston, 46

Sports on grave markers, 15, 168, 177–79

Spotsylvania County, 131

Spotsylvania Courthouse, Battle of, 132–33, 181

St. James Lutheran Church, 135

St. Mary's City, 170

Stanford University, 78

Star of David, 122–23, 198

Star Trek, 4

Starship (USS) Enterprise, 4

Starvation, 20, 59, 64, 67, 75, 105, 124, 128. *See also* Marasmus; Pellagra

State Colony for Epileptics and Feebleminded (Central Virginia Training Center), 26, 57–58, 68–71, 74–78, 80, 218

State Colony for Epileptics and Feebleminded Cemetery, 58, 76

Statler Brothers, 34

Staunton, 1–4, 7, 13, 26, 31, 35, 45, 48–49, 53–57, 59, 73, 75, 79, 114, 134, 138, 157, 164, 169, 179, 195–96, 200

Staunton National Cemetery, 35, 134

Steele, Wanda, 76–77

Stephenson, Roy T., 173–74

Stephenson, Wanda N., 173–74

Sterilization, 65–66, 69–70, 74–75. *See also* Eugenics

Stewart, Joseph Clay, Sr., 185, 191–92

Stillborn infants, 46, 199–200

Stoddard, Helen Mar, 171

Stone, Buck, 156

Stonewall Brigade, 134, 181

Stonewall Jackson Memorial Cemetery. *See* Oak Grove Cemetery

Straub, Marie, 200

Straub, Scott, 200

Stribling, Francis T., 59–60, 62–65, 67, 79

Structure, 87–89, 102

Stuarts Draft, 127

Stullenburg, Kyle D., 150–51

"Sugar Magnolia" (song), 51

Suicide, 40, 62, 65, 67–68, 128, 150–51, 220

Sunset Cemetery, 191

Sunset Memorial Park, 15, 31, 38, 172–73, 186

Sunset View Memorial Gardens, 47

Superman, 15–16

Supreme Court, US, 75

Supreme Court, Virginia, 131

Susquehanna River, 8

Sutphin, Eric Evine, 160

Swaringen, Wilber Fisk, II, 171

Swaringen, Wilber Fisk, III, 171

"Sweet Dreams" (song), 34

Sword, James W., 178

Synecdoche, 169, 182–84

Talbott, Jerry W., 182

Tame death, 44, 52

Tarlow, Sarah, 150, 165–66

Taylor, Breonna, 100, 106

"Tears in Heaven" (song), 48

Technology, grave marker production, 196–97, 200–201

Temple Emanuel Cemetery, 122–23

Tennant, Joseph, 115

Tennessee, 5, 19

Thomas, Billy S., 120

Thomas, Jabe, 179

Thomas, Wiley Eugene, 210–11

Thompson, Donna R., 188

Thompson, Irene, 103

Thompson, James L., 188

Thompson, John B., 94

Thompson, Lillian Elizabeth, 94

Thompson, Mary, 94

Thompson, Nannie A., 94

Thornrose Cemetery, 1–4, 13, 31, 114, 138, 157, 164, 169, 179, 195–96

Thornton, Eddie Preston, 173

Thornton, Sandra Ann, 173

"Three Deaths" (short story), 44

367th Infantry, 98

Timber Ridge Presbyterian Church, 49

Times of Their Lives, 18

Tinkling Spring Presbyterian Church Cemetery, 113, 132–34, 161–62

Todd's Tavern, Battle of, 131

Together We Served, 122

Tokyo, 120, 218

Tolstoy, Leo, 44

Tools on grave markers, 185, 190–91, 212

Trailways Bus, 164, 186

Traveller, 84

Trayman, Teri, 155

Trevey, Andrew, 40

Trimble, Mary, 161

Trissel, Alice Blosser, 198–99

Trissel, David Lloyd, 198–99

Trompeter, Abraham, 124

Trompeter, Geraldine, 122

Trompeter, Jacob A., 122–23

Trompeter, Max, 122–24

Trompeter, Mordechai, 124

Trompeter, Moshe, 123–24

Trompeter, Netta, 124

Trompeter, Rivkah, 124

Trompeter, Rosa, 124

Trompeter, Samuel, 124

Trompeter, Sholom, 124

Trompeter, Simchah, 124

Troutville, 188

Trump, Donald, 22, 207, 220

Tuberculosis , 60, 69, 117
Tully, Paul Raymond, 181–82
Tunkers, 9
Turkeys, 7, 76, 154
Turner, Victor, 205–6, 212
Tuscarawas River, 114
Tutelo, 7
Twain, Mark, 3
25th Infantry Regiment, 94
Tyler, John, 136
Tyler, Lyon Gardiner, 136

Union Army (Civil War), 130–31
Union veterans' burials, 35, 133–34,
    180. *See also* US Army
Unite the Right Rally, 213–15
United Daughters of the
    Confederacy, 136–37, 180
University Chapel, Washington and
    Lee, 83
University of California at Berkeley,
    14
University of Delaware, 146
University of Mississippi, 78
University of Virginia, 14, 60, 66,
    178, 183
Unknown soldiers' burials, 133–34
US Air Force, 37, 122, 128
US Army, 94, 97–99, 120, 124, 126,
    128, 149, 174, 207
US Marine Corps, 127–28
US Military Academy at West Point,
    88, 94–95
US Navy, 7, 120, 138, 178–79, 182

Valley Amateur Radio Association,
    179–80
Valley Forge, 113
Van Gennep, Arnold, 205
Van Sweringen, Garrett, 170
Van Sweringen, Nora Spotswood,
    170
Van Sweringen, Wilden Fisk, IV,
    170–71
Vaughan, Jason Matthew, 188
Vehicles on grave markers, 4, 15,
    138, 149–50, 168, 176, 179,

185–90, 195, 198, 206, 209–10.
    See also Jeeps; Pickup trucks
Venery, 71
Vicksburg, Battle of, 132
Vietnam War, 26, 128–29, 160, 174,
    178, 185
Virginia Colony for Epileptics
    and Feebleminded. *See* State
    Colony for Epileptics and
    Feebleminded
Virginia Military Institute, 84, 88,
    94, 97, 99, 103, 119–20, 130,
    137–38, 178
*Virginia State Colony for Epileptics and
    Feebleminded: Poems*, 77–78
Virginia Tech, 145, 157, 178
Volkswagen, 161, 188–89, 195

Waggy, Randy Wayne, 32
Walker, J. Frank, 197
Wallace, Samuel, 132
War of 1812, 59, 180
War on Terror, 26
Ward, Adam, 203
Washington, Ann, 91
Washington, Charlie, 91
Washington, DC, 5, 34, 181–82
Washington, George, 88, 106
Washington, Hy, 91
Washington, Martha, 88
Washington and Lee University,
    83–84, 88, 93, 98, 103, 130,
    188–89, 220–23
Washington College. *See* Washington
    and Lee University
Washington County, 5
Washington Nationals, 157
Washington Redskins, 4, 178–79
Wayles, John, 119
Waynesboro, 32, 34, 37, 40, 43,
    45–46, 49, 51, 126, 130, 151,
    155–56, 176, 208
Waynesboro Veterans Burial Team,
    126
Weaver, William, 11
Weavers Mennonite Church
    Cemetery, 45, 124–25

Weeks, Cesear, 91
Weeks, Hannah, 91
Wells, Michael, 20, 89
Wesley, John, 160
West, Cornel, 214–15
West Point. *See* US Military Academy
    at West Point
West Virginia, 15, 24, 31, 37–38,
    97, 99, 114, 119, 134, 172–73,
    177, 180, 186, 218
Western State Hospital (Lunatic
    Asylum), 13, 26, 53–68, 71–75,
    78–81, 114, 218
Western State Hospital (Lunatic
    Asylum) Cemeteries, 53–57,
    67–68, 72–74, 78–79, 114
Westview Cemetery, 178
"What a Shame" (song), 42
Wheatland Lutheran Church
    Cemetery, 154
Whitman, Walt, 217
Wilderness, Battle of, 181
Will, Maynard L., 189
Williams, Hank, Jr., 43
Williams, Roy, 70–71
Williamsburg, 17
Willson, Eliza, 91
Willson, William, 91
Wilson, Edith Bolling, 34
Wilson, John, 50
Wilson, Martha, 50
Wilson, Woodrow, 34
Wilson Memorial High School, 128
Wilt, Amanda Leigh, 169–70
Wilt, Edward Lee, 169–70
Winchester, 7, 10, 24, 34, 43, 48, 51,
    129, 132, 134, 138, 147, 173,
    176, 182, 184, 191
Winchester National Cemetery,
    109–10, 133–34
Winkelspecht, Richard Allen
    "Buddy," 157, 159–60
Winnie-the-Pooh, 38
Winslett, Jamie, 222
Wisconsin, 22
Wolf, Eric , 17
Wolfe, Thomas, 223

Wonder Woman, 213
Wood, Ann, 53
Wood, Henry, 53–54
Woodbine Cemetery, 48
Woodland Union Church
     Cemetery, 6
Woodstock, Virginia, 138
Wooldridge, Ramona Moonbeam, 93
Wooldridge, Sam, 93
Woolfrey, Donald Lee, 188

Work and Personhood, 185–87,
     193, 208
World War I, 26–27, 86, 89, 93,
     97–99, 116–20, 139, 218
World War I veterans' burials, 86,
     95–97, 100, 116–20
World War II, 26, 40, 89, 120–26
World War II veterans' burials, 86,
     94, 110, 120–22
Wright, Kim Yoshiko, 120

Wright, Randolph William, 120
"Wynken, Blynken, and Nod"
     (poem), 46–47
Wythe County, 198
Wytheville, 24, 34, 154, 185, 197

Yentsch, Anne Elizabeth, 29
Yorick, 143
You Can't Go Home Again, 223
Young, John, 204